Cambridge Studies in American Literature and Culture

Fictions of capital

Cambridge Studies in American Literature and Culture

Editor
Albert Gelpi, Stanford University

Advisory Board
Nina Baym, University of Illinois, Champaign-Urbana
Sacvan Bercovitch, Harvard University
Richard Bridgman, University of California, Berkeley
David Levin, University of Virginia
Joel Porte, Cornell University
Mike Weaver, Oxford University

Fictions of capital

The American novel from James to Mailer

RICHARD GODDEN
University of Keele

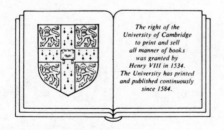

The right of the
University of Cambridge
to print and sell
all manner of books
was granted by
Henry VIII in 1534.
The University has printed
and published continuously
since 1584.

CAMBRIDGE UNIVERSITY PRESS

CAMBRIDGE
NEW YORK   PORT CHESTER
MELBOURNE   SYDNEY

Published by the Press Syndicate of the University of Cambridge
The Pitt Building, Trumpington Street, Cambridge CB2 1RP
40 West 20th Street, New York, NY 10011, USA
10 Stamford Road, Oakleigh, Melbourne 3166, Australia

First published 1990

Printed in Great Britain at the University Press, Cambridge

British Library cataloguing in publication data

Godden, Richard
Fictions of capital: the American novel
from James to Mailer – (Cambridge studies in
American literature and culture)
1.   Fiction in English. American writers, 1830–1977 –
Critical studies
1.   Title
813'.009

Library of Congress cataloguing in publication data

Godden, Richard, 1946–
Fictions of capital: the American novel from James to
Mailer / Richard Godden.
       p.   cm. – (Cambridge studies in American literature and culture)
Includes bibliographies.
ISBN 0-521-38131-2
1.   American fiction – 20th century – History and criticism.
2.   Capitalism and literature – United States.   3.   Social classes in
literature.   1.   Title.   11.   Series.
PS374.C36G64   1990
813'.509358 – dc20   89-9923 CIP

ISBN 0 521 38131 2

SE

To Rhian Hughes

Contents

Acknowledgements

I once heard it said that if, as Marx argues, 'language *is* practical consciousness', it follows that most of us are practically unconscious. Many voices worked on my lack of consciousness over several years; while there is a chronology to the ensuing list there is no hierarchy, save to say that the first group have been at it longest, and without them this book would not have been written. I thank Lorraine Hewitt, who first told me about Marx and Adorno and who still insists on 'the standpoint of redemption'; Charles Swann, whose scepticism came armed with revelatory reading lists; Rhian Hughes, whose generosity of perception persuades me that everyone merits 'reading against the grain'; and Colin Richmond for his conversation. These four in their different ways have changed the way I think. Others have helped enormously and variously: Ian Bell, at dark times, evinced more belief in the project than I did; whenever I needed historical advice or information, Martin Crawford bore with my eccentricities; two graduate students, Pamela Rhodes and Geoff Cox, always argued and pointed out that it was no good writing in a foreign language; Karen Harrison typed, re-typed and bullied the chapters towards deadlines; Keith Carabine taught me to value the question, 'But what does it mean?' Particular sections were closely read by Robert Clark, Peter Nicholls and Mark Jancovich, whose editorial intelligence not only saw opacity where I had seen clarity, but pointed out how I might reduce the murk. All these people are in varying degrees responsible for what follows: I hope that these essays will not shame their responsibility.

Portions and versions of some of the chapters have appeared elsewhere; grateful acknowledgement is made to the following journals and editors for permission to reprint those materials here. Chapter 1 first appeared in *Henry James: Fiction As History*, edited by Ian Bell (London:

Vision Press, 1984); chapter 2 is loosely based on an essay printed in *Essays in Poetics* (vol. 8, no. 1, 1983); chapter 3 was published in the *Journal of American Studies* (vol. 16, no. 3, 1983); chapter 4 appeared in shorter form in *Literature and History* (vol. 12, no. 1, 1986). Lothar Hönnighausen has agreed that the Faulkner section of chapter 5 may be reprinted from *Faulkner's Discourse: An International Symposium* (Tübingen: Niemeyer, 1989), and Bill Riches has given permission for chapter 7 to be taken from *The Turbulent Decade: The United States in the 1960s* (Jordanstown: The University of Ulster Press, 1987).

Introduction

It must relate to property; because nothing else survives in this world. Love grows cold and dies; hatred is pacified by annihilation. (Nathaniel Hawthorne, *The American Claimant*).[1]

I

Frederick Olmsted laid out Central Park (1858–60) and planned a park in Boston (1870) in the hope that 'a man of any class' might say to his wife before departing for business:

> My dear, when the children come home from school, put some bread and
> butter and salad in a basket, and go to the spring under the chestnut tree ... I
> will join you there as soon as I can get away from the office. We will walk to
> the dairy-man's cottage and get some tea, and some fresh milk for the children,
> and take our supper by the brook-side.[2]

Presumably, businessmen had less need of picnics in 'bath[s] of sunny air'[3] than those from among the great unwashed. Addressing a meeting of the American Social Science Association in Boston (1870), Olmsted nominated 'courtesy, self control and temperance'[4] as qualities resulting from exposure to 'air disinfected by sunlight and foliage';[5] a park, it seems, might metamorphose 'the most lawless classes of the city'[6] into honorary members of the bourgeoisie. Symptomatically, as James's Basil Ransom and Verena Tarrant quit Central Park they witness 'groups of the unemployed' at its boundaries. These loitering 'children of disappointment from beyond the seas'[7] complement Olmsted's 'young men in lounging attitudes rudely obstructing the sidewalks'. The architect is convinced that men with 'their feet in the gutter', though tending 'to drink and eat all manner of vile things', are 'under the influence of the same impulse which some satisfy about the tea-table with neighbours and wives and mothers and children'.[8] The immigrants in *The Bostonians* seem undisposed to take tea with the middle classes,

1

though their posture, 'propped against the low sunny wall of the park', suggests that they are not averse to disinfectant.

Disappointed immigrants at the margins catch the eye during the 1870s, a decade of considerable labour unrest: Olmsted counters their rudeness by offering drawing-rooms for the masses – a piece of horticulture designed to engineer pliancy among workers. Viewed aslant through Olmsted's own writing, Central Park is a school of etiquette opened to the reserve army of labour during periods of reduced production; its design is political and its purpose economic. Lessons in the park will be by example and may be given by a lady with a little dog. It is to be hoped that those with enforced leisure will watch the habits of 'conspicuous'[9] ease that they may be 'harmonized' and 'refined'.[10] Veblen interprets what the immigrant is to envy. First, the corset (between 1870 and 1900 waists tended to the 'hazardously slender'):[11]

> The corset is, in economic theory, substantially a mutilation undergone for the purpose of lowering the subject's vitality and rendering her permanently and obviously unfit for work . . . but the loss suffered on that score is offset by the gain in reputability which comes of her visibly increased expensiveness and infirmity.[12]

Nor is the dog any less deformed: bred for a lap and treasured littleness, it may virtually have 'disowned its own feet'.[13] Like its mistress, it has a double function, to display 'expense' and manifest 'inutility':

> dog[s] which have been bred into grotesque deformity by the dog-fancier are in good faith accounted beautiful by many. These varieties of dogs . . . are rated and graded in aesthetic value somewhat in proportion to the degree of grotesqueness and instability of the particular fashion which the deformity takes in the given case.[14]

High-grade 'grotesqueness' evidences 'greater scarcity and consequent expense'.[15]

Veblen could be wrong about the nuanced nastiness of dogs: some urban 'rockwork grottoes'[16] may fall short of political intention – yet it remains the case that manners and their preferred places of display are best read as part of an extended social economy. Since the wealth of any wealth class is ultimately derived from a labouring class, manifestations of that wealth are 'conspicuous' insofar as they are double-directed, to the co-members of the class and to the immigrants at the margin (be they the nouveaux riches or the labouring poor). Manners, then, are a defensive demonstration of economic standing: they have to be practised and take considerable muscle from their practitioners' sense of the inevitability of their infringement. Each year, on or around any November 15, Edith Wharton notes that Mrs Archer (one of the first hundred families), 'always said that New York was very much changed'.[17] Her 'punctual' 'enumeration' of 'the minute signs of disintegration'[18] paradoxically strengthens her sense of the stability of the social order — lacking transgression, the mannered mores of her world would lack visibility (indeed, without anxiety, Mrs Archer would be unable to see *her* New York). The defining co-presence of manner and offence remains true for those who live in Fitzgerald's West Egg during the early 1920s. Veblen has it that 'the leisure class live by the industrial community rather than in it';[19] it is therefore apt that to visit New York by rail, Tom Buchanan and his kind must skirt the 'valley of ashes' (with Veblenite propriety the railroad 'shrink[s] away from' this 'desolate area of land').[20] However, Buchanan tacitly acknowledges the class conflict imminent in his leisured existence when, in order to preserve his marriage, he uses labour (the 'ashen' Wilson) to murder the *nouveau riche* intruder (Gatsby) whose adultery threatens to deprive him of Daisy (in Veblen's terms, 'the badge' or 'token' of the Buchanan accumu-lations[21]). Veblen's 'live by' in this instance means simultaneously 'in proximity to' and 'by means of', exemplifying how far the behaviour of any leisure class is founded on the desire to control, and ideally to forget, the behaviour of the labouring class. James O'Connor makes the point in broader terms: 'Economic recoveries and expansions occur when capital successfully restores its domination of labour by restructuring the directly producing class itself.'[22]

If so, to talk about economic facts is necessarily to talk about the social conflicts from which the economic facts take on substance. The essays in this collection seek to establish that the changing processes through which wealth is stolen and shown are neither impersonal nor narrowly economic: they are always made by historical subjects. Moreover, in the competitive environment of capital, those subjects are liable to take class names and to be variously contentious. Stated aphoristically: I have assumed throughout that the economy of leisured life grows from and contains its own relation to wage labour. The clarity with which the relation is witnessed varies historically. In James's Boston (1877–9), Olive Chancellor's drawing-room looks across the Back Bay towards 'the chimneys of dirty "works"',[23] its owner tends to turn the 'sordid tubes of . . . engine-shops'[24] into a study by Whistler, but nonetheless she *sees* the evidence of production as a prelude to misquotation. On Fitzgerald's Riviera it might be thought that blue skies are less easily translated into 'cryptograms for factory chimneys',[25] if only because the USA's levels of production during the industrial revolution of the 1920s required a broadening consumption basket, and as a result producers were taught to double as consumers. Where, in the 1870s, the 'marble palaces' pandered only to the bourgeoisie, by the 1920s department stores were open to an enlarged middle class and their windows invited all. The term 'Fordism' has been widely applied to that regime of capital where centralized and hierarchic structures are developed to manage the processes not only of production but also of purchase. During the 1920s the social imperatives emerging from intensified accumulation were a new problem, a matter for market leaders ('partial Fordism'). By the 1940s, and more particularly after the war, issues of labour rationalization, management hierarchy, broadening sales and the control of desire affected the market as a whole ('full Fordism'). Those who would increase production must necessarily generalize consumption, erasing the memory of labour through the gratification of leisure. Advertisers recognized that in order to service corporate wealth they had to 'restructure' the memory of the producing class, a task involving the suppression of rather more intimate experiences of 'dirty "works"' than those available to Olive Chancellor. Amnesia has always been one of the staples of a successful commodity culture; however, as the sales pitch broadens, first in the twenties and again in the fifties and sixties, forgetting becomes imperative. The advertisers' journal, *Printer's Ink*, noted retrospectively in 1938:

> The first advertising sold the name of the product. In the second stage, the specifications of the product were outlined. Then came emphasis upon the uses of the product. With each step the advertisement moved farther away from the factory viewpoint and edged itself closer to the mental processes of the consumer.[26]

Nonetheless, only from the advertiser's angle does the moment of purchase and its attendant 'mental process' become a cultural absolute. Consumer capitalism sought to limit the images and identities through which consumers might represent themselves precisely because it was in difficulties – difficulties which exacerbated class tensions. I do not wish to summarize accounts and arguments that I have attempted elsewhere: I simply want to stress (in opposition to several recent readings of commodity aesthetics[27]) that the commodity and the commodified self are events that should be read within the class history that produces them.

Jean Baudrillard has outlined a paradigm in which indifference to class is *de rigueur* in questions of commodity. He argues that persons are persons and things are things only by virtue of their passage through an environment of sale, 'a system of exchange value that is now almost total'.[28] Granted that totality, the production and use of an object are subordinate to its status as a locus of signifiers geared to the act of exchange; ergo, the consumers of such objects are no longer "subjects" (having "needs"),[29] they are, rather, the momentary realization of the signifying cluster that is the commodity. As Walter Michaels puts it:

> one must . . . say that the logic of capitalism produces objects of desire only insofar as it produces subjects, since what makes the objects desirable is only the constitutive trace of subjectivity those objects bear – what Dreiser calls 'the voice of the so-called inanimate'.[30]

In a recent study, Rachel Bowlby pursues that voice, via Baudrillard's logic, back through the palaces of consumption which sprang up in Paris, London and New York during the second half of the nineteenth century. In the structure of the window shoppers' gaze she discovers truths with consequences for naturalist fiction and for the women fetishized both within the fiction and in the bourgeois home. But the problem with *Just Looking* is that it is too ready to generalize from the moment of anticipated purchase to all moments. Bowlby assumes 'a radical shift in the concerns of industry: from production to selling and from the satisfaction of stable needs to the invention of new desires'[31] that translates commodities into a total "reality" – or "illusion". Neither term will do since, as Baudrillard has it, 'illusion is no longer possible because the real is no longer possible'.[32] Bowlby is not to be outdone in de-materialization: 'The window [from Bon Marché to Macy's] smashes the illusion that there is a meaningful distinction in modern society between illusion and reality, fact and fantasy, false and genuine images of the self.'[33] Such an assertion complies with the amnesia which it seeks to analyse.

Goods behind plate glass may proclaim that they have no past and that their future is both eternal and ideal, but their purchasers, whether as employers, employees or wives, can have no such confidence. The history of consumption (and of some naturalist novels as a chapter of that history) should be set within the history of the riotous unrest which the logic of its development provoked; as the White City of the World's Fair in Chicago opened its gates in May 1893, so banks and factories closed theirs in the worst financial panic of US history. McKinley beat populism, but *because* the desires of window shoppers in 1894 were the active focus of centralizing capital, their gaze took place in a perspective of crisis.

Those who collapse "use" too easily into "exchange", view commodity as a theoretical abstraction and therefore avoid the historical complications of consumption. It is doubtful whether even store owners or managers saw with such idealistic purity: Alfred Chandler's work on the managerial revolution in American business indicates that the unprecedented levels of selling which fuelled the ideology of consumerism depended upon methods of mass retailing involving a co-ordinated flow from supplier to consumer along a complex distribution network. The engineers of flow – from mail clerk to sales manager – knew the processes that went into the window. (It was not Adam Smith who was fined 50 cents per item on any delayed element of a mass order that had to be sent pre-paid express.[34]) The invisible market forces were by the 1880s thoroughly visible, and their impetus derived from the threat of excess capacity. Workers, managers, owners and purchasers might have been persuaded to forget some of this some of the time, but the satisfaction of "just looking" cannot have been lasting.

My point is a simple one, but worth reiterating: consumption cannot be divorced from production. Just to look from the viewpoint of exchange compounds cultural commodification, turning 'the social relation between men . . . [into] the fantastic form of a relation between things'.[35] Marx corrects the myopia of fetishism with the observation that those who are objectified within a system of production and exchange achieve self-knowledge as a class via the recognition that the damage done to them is shared by some and inflicted by others. Of course, the system of production changes, deterring sociability among producers; indeed, part of my intention is to pursue shifts within the history of production as they affect the forms of "self" privileged by the shifting logic of exchange and available to writers caught up in that logic. Nonetheless, even as the blue collars whitened, with the onset of full Fordism during the 1950s, class subjects did not simply vanish into the consumer as a universal subject; distinctions continued to form around issues of race, gender, non-union and part-time labour, thereby providing an evaluative "outside" from which the dominant culture might be resisted. To speak of 'the logic of capital' is not to speak of one thing. Capitalist logic changes as the owning class struggles to overcome the tendency of the rate of profit to fall. Technological revolutions and innovations in sales methods reconstitute both those who own and those who labour: such revision leaves shards of redundant logic and traditions of resistance littered across the marketplace. It is through the logics of this illogical market that I attempt to read the work of Fitzgerald and Mailer.

II

As the essays in this book proliferated, and began to centre more obviously on the economic and the literary, I became increasingly preoccupied with metaphor. At first this seemed happenstance – perhaps a throwback to a New Critical literary training – and to suggest now that attention to metaphor is part of a sustained method would be opportunistic. I confess that allusions to theory, here and later, are offered very much in the spirit of Heath Robinson's design to raise a wine glass five floors up the outside of a block of flats – all pin, string, plank and 'any port in a storm', nor do I suppose that a careful reading of the essays that follow could result in a return to the introduction in a spirit of 'QED'. Nonetheless, I suspect that the centrality of metaphor to these studies grows trepidatiously from the work of Vološinov and Ricoeur, for whom (though in very different ways) language is a social intention acting on, and through, that to which it refers. If so, it follows that linguistic objects, whether they are vocal inflexions or literary texts, are constructed from social conflict: as Vološinov puts it:

> Social psychology is first and foremost an atmosphere made up of multifarious *speech performances* that engulf and wash over persistent forms and kinds of ideological creativity: unofficial discussions, exchanges of opinion at the theater or a concert or at various types of social gathering, purely chance exchanges of words, one's manner of verbal reaction to happenings in one's life and daily existence, one's inner-world manners of identifying oneself and identifying one's position in society, and so on. Social psychology exists primarily in a wide variety of forms of 'utterance,' of little *speech-genres* of internal and external kinds . . . Were we to apply a more detailed analysis we would see that enormous significance belongs to *the hierarchical factor* in the process of verbal interchange and what a powerful influence is exerted on forms of utterance by the hierarchical organization of communication. Language etiquette, speech tact, and other forms of adjusting an utterance to the hierarchical organization of society have tremendous importance in the process of devising the basic behaviour genres.
>
> Every sign, as we know, is constructed between socially organized persons in the process of their interaction. Therefore, *the forms of signs are conditioned above all by the social organization of the participants involved and also by the immediate conditions of their interaction.* When these forms change so does the sign.[36]

Any study attempting to trace 'the problem of the relationship between sign and existence',[37] within a group of novels, must be preoccupied with exactly how existence gets into the sign. Vološinov's idea of meaning as the sedimentation of diverse and hierarchic vocal mannerisms pushes the question towards typicalities of exchange, as in the linguistics of M.A.K. Halliday, for whom 'semantic style is a function of social relationships and situation types generated by social structure'.[38] Yet, despite my working conviction that a homology between the history of capital and the meaning of novels should be fruitful, I was left feeling like a trickster because unsure of how language and that to which it refers interact. The structuralist (pure and post-) and semiological disciplines were of little help, since they tended to displace the whole question of reference by means of the claim that the sign system refers to other systems in an intertextual spiral that stops either at an epochal episteme or some notion of the "subject" as a code amalgam. Vološinov's insight is that language is indexical, not of things, but of the complex social relations through which things materialize. The Saussurean tradition could only weaken or dispense with the economic causality that I wished to see as 'in the last instance' linking the sign to what it signifies.

Ricoeur's work on metaphor illuminated my impasse by substituting one question for another: 'How does existence get into the sign?' became, 'How and why was the sign ever divorced from existence?' For Ricoeur, all language 'aims beyond itself',[39] being thrown forward into the world by means of the speaker's intention: since intentions produce actions, and actions alter what is extant, the literal was never so, being rather a form of metaphoric act in which meaning materializes from a collision of intentions (note, intentions not signs). The literal is the locus of words, intentions and actions so imposingly typical as to have been naturalized. We walk on and among dead metaphors, themselves the sediment of 'speech genres' and 'social organization[s]', whose meanings in Fordist USA are largely engineered by capital.

Arguably, the commodity is simply a very American metaphor, in which a vehicle, 'use', and a tenor, 'exchange', meet to produce a third term, 'capitalist realism'[40] – which in the narrowed context of consumerism becomes the new literalism, and within which citizens and authors are invited to live 'real lives' constituted from promise and wish. (Hemingway can be read as the laureate of 'capitalist realism' once his efforts to perfect literalism are recognized as one strand in a wider metaphoric act.) However, Ricoeur notes that the terms elided in metaphor cannot forget their path, because the resemblance from which the new metaphoric meaning emerges contains within it the "likes" and "unlikes" out of which the metaphor was first made:

> All new rapprochement runs against a previous categorization which resists, or rather which yields while resisting . . . This is what the idea of semantic impertinence or incongruence preserves. In order that a metaphor obtains, one must continue to identify the previous incompatibility through the new compatibility. The predicative assimilation involves, in that way, a specific kind of tension which is not so much between a subject and a predicate as between semantic incongruence and congruence. The insight into likeness is the perception of the conflict between the previous incompatibility and the new compatibility . . . To see the like is to see the same in spite of, and through, the different. This tension between sameness and difference characterizes the logical structure of likeness.[41]

Since metaphor is an 'assimilation' retaining 'sameness' and 'difference' in its unsignalled "likeness", it produces, at least potentially, a 'split referent':[42] that is to say, a referent in which the old and putatively mistaken category of meaning (and social intention) haunts the new congruence. Nor is the residual ambiguity of metaphor merely a function of poetic language, rather it stems back to what Vološinov calls 'the hierarchical organization of communication'. Alice's question to Humpty Dumpty seems pertinent:

> Alice: The question is whether you can make words mean so many things.
> Humpty Dumpty: The question is who is to be master.

Mastery, although a temporary historical fact, is in the long run a semantic delusion, since, as Ricoeur (by way of I.A. Richards) points out, meanings are never mastered. No word can have a "proper" or literal sense, because what that word means is delegated to it by its context, which in turn is abridged by that word:

> Words are not at all the names of ideas present to the mind; they are not constituted by any fixed association with data, whatever that data might be. All they do is refer back to the missing parts of the context. Consequently, constancy of meaning is never anything but constancy of contexts. And this constancy is not a self-evident phenomenon: stability is itself something to be explained . . .
>
> Consequently, nothing prevents a word from signifying more than one thing. Since it refers back to 'contextually missing parts,' these parts can belong to opposed contexts. By their 'over-determination,' therefore, words express the 'large scale rivalries between contexts.'[43]

On these grounds it would seem that metaphors do what most words do, only more so; they mean by means of suppressed contexts, conflicts of social intention, 'split referents' and, by extension, 'split referees'. All of which is particularly revealing in a culture where the dominant system of production is geared to the manufacture of an extended and often unacknowledged metaphor, 'capitalist realism'. The novels of Fitzgerald and Mailer counter the market's broad metaphoricity through a sustained exploration of the 'missing parts' latent in consumerism's favoured tropes – a habit born of a fascinated mistrust for the "reality" to which the respective historical moments of their class have apprenticed them.

My introduction is in danger of simultaneously losing the wine glass at the second floor, and of turning into an anthology of essay trailers. However, one thing remains to do: I should offer some account of why these novelists were chosen, and of how I settled on a chronology for the essays. As I wrote the book I began to realize that it was premised on two assumptions: that economic relations are finally a guise assumed by social relations, and that social relations are the source of what stories can and can't be told. The changing economy of consumption is the historical base for my attempt to describe certain narrative and vocal options inherent in an economy based on growth. I needed some way to detail first the emergence of consumer capitalism in the 1880s, and then the two calculated expansions in the consumer market taking place during the 1920s and 1950s. The economic writings of Ernst Mandel and Alfred

Chandler allowed me loosely to periodize this history, and Mandel's distinction between the spheres of Accumulation and Reproduction proved particularly suggestive, identifying what might be termed two of capital's deeper narratives: the plot to accumulate and expand resource, with a particular eye to finance capital (1880 to the First World War); and the plot to ensure the reproduction of the expanded resource (preoccupying what Mandel calls 'late capitalism', but already an issue for market leaders in the 1920s).[44] Any attempt to situate the overlapping issues of manners and consumerism within the context of capital required some account of the whole context, from the onset of the sales culture to its climacteric in the 1960s. Consequently, I juxtapose James and Fitzgerald to cover the move from accumulation to reproduction, while the Fitzgerald/Mailer relation is explored as a way into a new tension in the growth imperative (resolved through the linking of the permanent-arms economy (destruction) to the ubiquitous shop window (desire) as a capital motor). Fitzgerald and Mailer stand respectively at the beginning and end of the Fordist form of consumption: I chose them to be inclusive, and in order to discuss the changing anthology of selves (and of politically disputatious sub-texts) that a culture of consumption makes available to consumers and writers alike.

The novels that feature most substantially in these essays do so because, in varied ways, they represent responses to key moments in the USA's growth economy. To cover the earlier period I worked with *The Bostonians* because the novel's concern with the immediate aftermath of the Civil War allowed me to focus on how "modern" capitalist society grew from forces brought to maturity by that war, and by its consolidation of the internal continental market. James focusses on the re-unification of the nation through a marriage plot, in which the male suitor is a Southerner with distinctly economic ambitions. The regional question allows James to approach the problem of a unified capitalist class, even as the reform plot (turning on the education of Verena Tarrant as a public speaker) pushes him towards 'Publicity' in its relation to the invention of the bourgeoisie as a class of consumers. The jump from the Boston of James to Hemingway's Paris is large, but I hoped that by the early introduction of a reading of Hemingway as an exponent of 'capitalist realism' – that is to say, of a style of writing unknowingly saturated in the logic of consumerism – I might be able to identify some of the aesthetic premises and historical determinants of that logic, in uncluttered form. With the ways in which the 'voice' of commodity seeks to restructure the self outlined, the ensuing discussion of Fitzgerald's more complex response to that commodification, and to the crisis of 1929, should be clearer. I allow myself one other interruption of the chronologically developed James/Fitzgerald/Mailer axis on which the book turns. The introduction of an essay on Southern writing during the Depression, into a study concerned with the novel and consumer capitalism, may seem wilful, yet up to the end of the 1930s the South, as a low-wage economy, resisted the shop window; if there is a case to be made for the influence of commodity aesthetics on the narrative options of certain kinds of writing, there is surely a parallel case to be made for the preferred poetics of regional writers who perceive themselves as standing against consumerism and its attendant forms of labour. I hope that the essay on Ransom, Faulkner and Tate outlines a shared aesthetic of anti-development.

The Fordist imperative reached its climacteric in the mid-1960s, fuelled by the increased production associated with the Vietnam War. Given a concern with fictions of growth, it seemed necessary to consider the writer who responded most immediately to that war-related expansion, and to its political effects on the wealth class. Consequently, the last quarter of the book is taken up with close readings of *Why Are We in Vietnam?* (1967) and *Armies of the Night* (1968). The Mailer material is introduced by a short essay surveying the liberal critique of post-war capitalism, as exemplified by the writings of Daniel Bell. This may seem an alienating approach to Mailer. However, one of the problems of the book as a whole is the integration of history and literary analysis. I wrote the 'historical interlude' (as I wrote the opening sections of chapters 1, 2 and 5) to ease the grounding of the textual in the historical. Mailer's struggle to locate a voice of resistance to the corporatist state is prefaced by a brief history of the emergence of that state out of a crisis in Fordism; the preface is intended to stand as a stencil through which the reader may focus Mailer's vocal dispersion.

Having reached the end of the index, some post-hoc summary statement seems both necessary and impossible, primarily because the work that follows is not organized by a thesis; it would be fairer to say that it has emerged from a preoccupation, perhaps even an obsession, and one that is far from resolved. What follows are several loosely organized efforts to understand how different fictions take their forms from the economic history that is their finally determining context. Even as I say this, I am reminded of Linus's attempt at a close-reading of 'Hey Diddle Diddle': 'The way I see it, "The cow jumped over the moon" indicates a rise in farm prices . . . The part about the dish running away with the spoon must refer to the consumer.' Asked to comment, Charlie Brown demurs, observing, 'I don't pretend to be a student of prophetic literature.' Perhaps the wine glass has reached the seventh floor.

1

Some slight shifts in the manner of the novel of manners

I

The foundation of manners is economic; and as economic structures change, so manners change. But what does it mean to argue for an economy of manners? An elaborate place setting, involving careful discrimination as to the position of the fish knives, bears witness to an accumulation of knowledge made manifest. That knowledge depends upon leisure time, which in turn derives from a secure property base. As Veblen put it in 1899, 'the pervading principle and abiding test of good breeding is the requirement of a substantial and patent waste of time'.[1] *The Theory of the Leisure Class* introduces the phrases 'conspicuous leisure' and 'conspicuous consumption', as it makes the case that leisure is not indolence but a state of high competition, in which the weaponry may range from a classical education to pedigree dogs, but where the prize is constant – the prize being the right to social 'emulation'. When Mr Sillerton Jackson notes that the Archers' butler has not been told 'never to slice cucumbers with a steel knife',[2] the reader of *The Age of Innocence* is aware that marginal repositioning has occurred among the first hundred families of New York. For Veblen that gentleman's saliva would be a highly cultivated artifact, an 'immaterial' object offering 'serviceable evidence of an unproductive expenditure of time'.[3] Such items protest their naturalness even as they enact a symbolic pantomime of mastery – "If you lack the etiquette don't sit at the tables". Each makes plain in its 'quasi' artistic, 'quasi' honorific[4] status, its distance from the marketplace upon which its very development depends; as Veblen puts it, 'the leisure class live by the industrial community rather than in it'.[5]

A silver palate and a keen grip on the fish knives are as valued by the late nineteenth-century leisure class as are the Kula objects that circulate among high-ranking male Trobriand Islanders:

> the most precious are the oldest, which have been transferred the most carefully and hardly ever displayed. Their names are known, and it is an honour to have one's own name associated with the name of a famous valuable. Indeed what is being transacted in the top sphere is really shared knowledge about a network of mutual confidence. The actual goods are the visible tip of the iceberg. The rest is a submerged classified catalogue of names of persons, places, objects, and dates. The main activity is a continuous attempt to standardize their values as precisely as possible.[6]

The meaning, indeed the very materiality, of such objects is separate from any immediate utility or function: it consists in their capacity to bear names and to carry distinctions. Leisure-class objects are good to think rather than to use, for in thinking them those in the know take confidence as to their hold on an information network that adds up to cultural power. The prestige attendant upon an object intensifies in exact proportion to the number of discriminations sedimented within it. For example, Veblen's leisure class expends great energy breeding pedigree dogs, while the van der Luydens, first among Wharton's New York families, tend orchids: the acme of each form is an exemplar that perishes almost as it is conceived – the perfect pug has a face so flat that an operation is required at birth to free its nasal passages, the finest orchid is but a brief flower. Rarefication attends privileged surfaces from the Trobriand Islands to the novels of James: whether or not Gilbert Osmond (*The Portrait of a Lady*) or Adam Verver (*The Golden Bowl*) stands ethically judged, their tendency to turn person and thing into 'a rarity, an object of beauty, an object of price . . . a *morceau de musée*'[7] typifies a habit of perception wider than their own. In his preface to *The Spoils of Poynton* James observes:

> Life being all inclusion and confusion, and art being all discrimination and selection, the latter, in search of the hard latent *value* with which alone it is concerned, sniffs around the mass as instinctively and unerringly as a dog suspicious of some buried bone. The difference here, however, is that, while the dog desires his bone but to destroy it, the artist finds in *his* tiny nugget, washed free of awkward accretions and hammered into a sacred hardness, the very stuff for a clear affirmation, the happiest chance for the indestructible.[8]

For James, 'surfaces' are less elements in an historical context than they are crystallizations of aesthetic information. The most casual object or perspective inclines, via the labour of informed perception, towards a collector's item. Indeed, a capacity for 'discrimination and selection' seems, in *The Bostonians*, to condition physique. Those who possess the social graces, most manifestly Mrs Farrinder and Mrs Burrage, are given to 'angularity',[9] while poverty of manner results in poor shape. To exist in 'the social dusk of that mysterious democracy' (p. 79) is to suffer a 'vagueness of boundary' (p. 37): Miss Birdseye is pursued by synonyms for 'formless' (p. 38), among which 'muffled in laxity' (p. 51) is mighty; and Mr Tarrant transcends the 'weary-looking overcoats' (p. 40) of his peers, in a waterproof that rarely leaves his person and obscures it. Where social discretion aids muscular tone (it is to be remembered that Madam Merle, that most socially equipped female, is 'too complete'[10]), mental tone is necessarily structured around a recognition of distinctions. Jamesian 'appreciation' is quite literally mannered, in that, like items gracing a bourgeois drawing-room, his observations never exhaust themselves in the function they serve – be that denotation or advancing action – rather they take on the significance of prestige. They no longer designate 'the world', but the being and social acumen of the observer – they are accumulative.[11] At the risk of straining the analogy between perceptual habit and drawing-room, both are solid with and through cumulative nicety; where the term 'solid' applies equally to observation, furnishing and business enterprise.

'Interior', too, for the 'solid' Victorian, was a term involving the person and her rooms. For Hobsbawm 'the home' is 'the quintessential bourgeois world',[12] in which objects may modify owners. Furnishings 'had value in themselves as expressions of personality, as both the programme and the reality of bourgeois life, even as transformers of man. In the home all these were expressed and concentrated. Hence its internal accumulation.'[13] The pressure of furniture on selfhood is well caught by Wharton in a description of an 1870s interior:

> There was something about the luxury of the Welland house and the density of the Welland atmosphere, so charged with minute observances and exactions, that always stole into his system like a narcotic. The heavy carpets, the watchful servants, the perpetually reminding tick of disciplined clocks, the perpetually renewed stack of cards and invitations on the hall table, the whole chain of tyrannical trifles binding one hour to the next, and each member of the household to all the others, made any less systematized and affluent existence seem unreal and precarious.[14]

Time and the air are created by the latent law of manners made plain through decoration. Time is retrospective where a clock 'remind(s)' the present that the past is its measure and corrective. Each social season in Wharton's New York repeats the events of the previous season. Received manners give form and protect that form from change. Not surprisingly, the carpet is 'heavy', the atmosphere 'narcotic' and the stack of cards, through its changes, remains the same. Taste in the 1870s must encourage inertia, in order to proclaim the stability of the accumulated wealth from which it arises. Not all the decade's 'interiors' are simply 'solid': Olive Chancellor's 'parlor', viewed by her Southern cousin, manages to ally habitual taste with curiosity:

> it seemed to him he had never seen an interior that was so much an interior as this queer corridor-shaped drawing-room of his new-found cousin; he had never felt himself in the presence of so much organized privacy or of so many objects that spoke of habits and tastes . . . he had never before seen so many accessories. The general character of the place struck him as Bostonian: this was, in fact, very much what he had supposed Boston to be. He had always heard Boston was a city of culture, and now there was culture in Miss Chancellor's tables and sofas, in the books that were everywhere, on little shelves like brackets (as if a book were a statuette), in the photographs and water-colours that covered the walls, in the curtains that were festooned rather stiffly in the doorways.   (p. 27)

Everything is protected and surrounded – the doors by the curtains, the books by the shelves – while the word 'interior' encircles itself in tautology. At one level, the framing serves purposes of display; however, its very redundancy teeters on the edge of sequestration. A drawing-room that is 'corridor-shaped' begs a question as to where it leads – inwards or outwards? The reader might risk an answer, in that she already knows that the proprietor suffers 'fits' of shyness, during which she is 'unable to meet even her own eyes in the mirror' (p. 22). Olive's elusive self-image is the key to her room's instability: 'the Chancellors belonged to the *bourgeoisie* – the oldest and best' (p. 42). One of their daughters, Mrs Luna, fulfils the 'conspicuous' duties of her leisure, the other longs 'to put off invidious differences and mingle in the common life' (p. 33). Since 'invidious difference' is a structural principle of bourgeois accessories, Olive is at odds with her own room. The Wellands' 'home' is a seamless network of information. Olive's objects 'speak' 'culture'; item by item each frame ennobles its object and so, as an ensemble, the room is a show. James's hint of the catalogue implies more than the perceiver's Southernness – a little 'stiff', it catches the uncertainty of Olive's 'queer' social trajectory.

Whatever the distinction drawn between these rooms as economic messages, they would both have been read by their contemporaries as feminized spaces. By the mid-nineteenth century, increasing industrial production consolidated a clear distinction between 'home' and 'market', 'leisure' and 'labour'. The latter, in each case, was a male sphere associated with competition, aggression and self-seeking. Deprived of her earlier role as a producer within the domestic economy, the mid-nineteenth-century woman learned to consume. What man earned, at least in the middle class, woman displayed. The 'home' became a 'separate sphere' in which 'nurture', 'sensibility', 'influence' and 'consumption' might be practised as a compensatory labour, at once legitimizing economic dependency while granting a limited identity.[15] Veblen is sceptical as to whether this alternative role extends far beyond display among the leisured. He notes that the woman is a 'badge', 'prize' and 'trophy', and that any degree of exemption from labour marks only her husband's accumulations – insofar as 'she is useless and expensive . . . she is consequently valuable evidence of pecuniary strength'.[16] In a culture where labour and property are the means to 'authoritative selfhood',[17] a woman's individuality is threatened by the demise of domestic industry,[18] and is only marginally redeemed by 'motherhood' and 'marble palaces' (the department stores that proliferated during the 1870s).

In her double role as display case and womb, or womb-to-be, the bourgeois woman had also to constitute herself as the antithesis of the male: her passivity must soften his activity; his aggression should elicit her sensitivity so that female unselfishness might modify his necessary selfishness. Deformity, invisibility and amnesia stalk such a selfhood. The woman, at the centre of her drawing-room, becomes the medium through which the man forgets labour and transforms consumption into sentimental privacy and into art.[19] Consequently, the novel of manners is preoccupied with the transfer of such cultural shaman; that is to say, with marriage as a dicey exchange of accumulations in their double form as economic fact and cultural artifact (or veil). Consider Wharton's description of the young and recently married May Welland:

> Perhaps that faculty of unawareness was what gave her eyes that transparency and her face the look of representing a type rather than a person; as if she might have been chosen to pose for a Civic Virtue or a Greek goddess. The blood that ran so close to her fair skin might have been a preserving fluid rather than a ravaging element; yet her look of indestructible youthfulness made her seem neither hard nor dull, but only primitive and pure.   (p. 167)

The woman, viewed by her husband, becomes statuesque; her blood, through which his property will be transferred, is 'preserving fluid', and her eye, at least to his eye, is 'transparent'. There is nothing behind it to resist his purposes; she is pure to the point of becoming a *tabula rasa* upon which he may write.

Such properties belong, not to one character, but to a 'type' that elicits male desire among the leisured. "Artifact", "innocence", "preservative", are standard features that can be variously permutated. In *The Bostonians* Verena Tarrant is to Ransom a 'moving statue' (p. 62) and a 'picture' (p. 63), while Mr Burrage 'liked her for the same reason that he liked old enamels and old embroideries' (p. 136). The 'brightness of her nature' (p. 61) strains the lexicon of virginity; the more Verena 'shines', the more she inclines to that ultimate male bolt-hole, the white page on which may be written a sentimental novel and a balance sheet. Even her voice, her singular contribution to feminism, is 'pure and rich' (p. 230), a fashion to be 'tasted' (p. 234), found 'sweet' (p. 65), and absorbed. Since James gives us little of what she says, and much of how she says it, it is to be presumed that he trusts Ransom's ear.

Pansy Osmond is simply the essence of the model: her stepmother learns that to be a lady is to be a portrait, and consents to the frame in part to protect a ward 'so formed and finished' as to be 'a sheet of blank paper'.[20] *The Portrait of a Lady* was published in 1881, but as late as 1925 leisure-class functions continued to disembody the leisured females of fiction. Daisy Buchanan, named for the flower of innocence, first appears in *The Great Gatsby* in 'white', 'ballooned' and seemingly weightless among billowing curtains. Formed to display, she has repressed her body and cashed in her voice, which is described as 'full of money'.[21] In contradistinction, the body of the working-class woman, Myrtle Wilson, uncommitted to the production of manners, is described most frequently in terms of 'blood', 'flesh' and 'vitality'.

From Isabel Archer to Daisy Buchanan, the wealthy female in her feminized space (that most immaterial of 'immaterial objects') protects and distributes the accumulations of her class. She is the guardian of what Lionel Trilling calls 'culture's hum and buzz of implication':

> What I understand by manners . . . is culture's hum and buzz of implication. I mean the whole evanescent context in which its explicit statements are made. It is that part of a culture which is made up of half-uttered or unuttered or unutterable expressions of value. They are hinted at by small actions, sometimes by the arts of dress or decoration, sometimes by tone, gesture, emphasis or rhythm, sometimes by the words that are used with a special frequency or a special meaning. They are the things that for good or bad draw the people of a culture together and that separate them from the people of another culture. They make the part of a culture which is not art, or religion, or morals, or politics, and yet it relates to all these highly formulated departments of culture. It is modified by them; it modifies them; it is generated by them; it generates them. In this part of culture assumption rules, which is often stronger than reason.[22]

Trilling's claims are questionable in that they suppress conflicts of class and gender. The degree to which the notion of 'culture' as an 'evanescent' and 'unuttered' 'context' obscures the presence of uttered contradictions is exactly the measure of the definition's usefulness as an account of what well-mannered people thought manners to be towards the close of the nineteenth century. To speak the fact that the cards that mount on the Wellands' hall table are an act of class control (whereby the bourgeoisie monitor the meetings of their sons and daughters who, with the development of the department store and the park, were mingling in new ways[23]) is to insist that as economic patterns shift so manners shift. Frederick Olmsted designed parks explicitly to offer, to the rising proletariat, a horticultural version of the 'softening and refining' 'tea table' of the middle class.[24] 'The marble palaces' were built to guarantee the viability of that tea table: as temples to advertising they sought sufficient sales to cover the drastically increased production that resulted from the consolidated investment of the eighties and nineties. To read Central Park or a corset as economic facts is to blow Trilling's cover and to submit manners to the shifting history of capital and its accumulations.

II

If that history is, from 1850 to 1900, largely a story of expansion and accumulation of resources, it is clear that during the opening three decades of the new century the very form of capital was seen to change – and with it the form of manners. But first some facts and figures. While a worker's income increased by an average of 14 per cent between 1923 and 1929, corporate profit rose in the same period by 62 per cent, and corporate dividends by 65 per cent. The reason for this may be glossed in two terms, 'centralization' and 'standardization'. Mergers were endemic: from 1919 to 1930, 8,000 businesses disappeared. Among the most significant fields of take-over were electricity and banking: the electric generator, primary machine of what has been called the second industrial revolution, was incorporated.[25] Even as the energy that drove industrial capital centralized, so the credit that financed expansion passed into fewer and fewer hands; large banks swallowed small banks or established branches that took their business, so that by 1929 1 per cent of the banking facilities of the country controlled over 46 per cent of the nation's banking resources.[26] Well financed, mergers fell into two waves, reaching peaks between 1897 and 1905 and during the second half of the 1920s. Their form was also twofold: the horizontal merger involved the absorption of a number of competitors in a given field by one producer; the vertical merger (more popular in the twenties) saw one corporation buy out its suppliers or its customers. Both forms relieved the capitalist of his fear of the glutted market since the new corporation could limit competition by setting price and production levels. The net effect of centralization was an increasing rationalization of resources, and with it fresh fears of an excess capacity. To ensure continuous and full use of their accumulations, firms had to move into new markets and to develop new lines. Each expansion put greater strain on the running of production, and a managerial revolution, coupled with the multiplication of national distribution systems, simply fuelled the cause of standardized and efficient administration.

By the 1920s, 'administration' was gargantuan in ambition: as scientific management and technological innovation guaranteed that expanding and incorporating capital could produce cheaply, advertising sought to monitor and create market needs:

> Advertising has to deal with the greatest principles underlying the relation of man to man . . . It is the medium of communication between the world's greatest forces – demand and supply. It is a more powerful element in human progress than steam or electricity . . . That this state of things [the neglect of advertising] will continue, cannot be possible, and men may look forward to a day when advertising will be what it has long deserved to be, one of the world's great sciences.[27]

The copywriter failed to note that his copy would become 'an aggressive device of corporate survival'.[28] By 1920 it was plain that only by controlling desire could corporate capital reproduce itself. The 'captain of industry' had to become the 'captain of consciousness' if his accumulations were to survive; not surprisingly, between 1900 and 1930 national advertising revenues increased thirteenfold.

Statistics can indicate the quantity of change but miss the qualitative shift. What one witnesses between 1900 and 1930 is a shift in economic emphasis from 'accumulation' to 'reproduction'. A monopoly is inherently less responsive to market fluctuation than other systems of manufacture; its profitability is geared to a large number of invariable overheads that have to be maintained through slump or boom. The corporation can lay off men or reduce wages, it cannot so easily forgo interest payments on loans or insurance, nor can it cease to maintain its research programmes, its plant or rent. Therefore, in order to preserve its own huge accumulation, it must look to the future (and to the distant future), that is, to the problem of 'reproduction'. Put crudely: by 1900 the accumulated capital existed; the real issue was how to produce sufficient profit to support that accumulation. Neither Taylor's time and motion studies, nor Ford's flow production, in and of themselves, offers adequate protection, because high productivity can yield the necessary profit only if the markets are primed to consume what has been produced.

Arguably, consumers are the most important product of late capitalism: they are the primary machine without which 'the very play time of the people' could not be 'run . . . into certain moulds':[29]

> Consumption is the name given to the new doctrine; and it is admitted today to be the greatest idea that America has given to the world; the idea that the workmen and masses be looked upon not simply as workers and producers,

but as *consumers* . . . Pay them more, sell them more, prosper more is the equation.[30]

In the words of Paula Fass, analysing collegiate youth in the twenties, 'the big sell had become synonymous with America's contribution to Western Civilization'.[31] High schools and colleges prepared students for corporate employment via peer-group instruction in conformity and competition; their graduates were the new intellectual proletariat who would service the managerial revolution, while consuming the high output to which that revolution contributed:

> Competition within conformity and conformity in the service of competition were the structuring facts of campus life in the twenties . . . values that in a specific American social context were made to read like a twentieth century text on business success and consumer habits.[32]

Note 'consumer habits'; the employee as worker *and* consumer contributes to the reproduction of surplus value – accumulation is frowned upon while indulgence is blessed. At both domestic and national levels the American economy was running on high credit, in that the institution of credit allows speedier production and speedier consumption. Consequently, 'to be wholly part of the economic life of the new society, the young had to be *not* accumulating entrepreneurs but at once workers and consumers'.[33]

All this may seem a disturbing distance from fish knives and the true taste of cucumber; the gap marks a considerable transition in manners. Though the Jamesian interior may well manifest conspicuous leisure and conspicuous consumption, it cannot guarantee a high turnover in consumption, and it positively mitigates against a truly mass market for the items that it contains. Those items are 'solid', even as the manners that surround them are 'solid' (so scrupulously learned as to appear innate). What capital increasingly needs after 1900 is a highly mobile, highly reproducible and highly controllable system of manners. That is to say, fashion must supplant manners: where taste once stood, style must stand. Manners and taste are cumulative and integrative, indeed the selfhood that they realize is its own ultimate possession. Fashions and styles are equally an extension of capital, but of capital focussed on the sphere of reproduction. Fashion penetrates the mannered self and opens it for the market. The new 'science' of advertising invested heavily in social insecurity. Consumers of the twenties were taught to denigrate their own bodies: in 1920 Listerene was just another general antiseptic – with the help of 'halitosis' (exhumed from an old medical dictionary) and a story line ('He never knew why') the copywriters Feasley and Seagrove invented a new habit and with it a new anxiety. Between 1921 and 1929 Listerene's 'virtues' spread panic through pore and orifice: the public learned of its capacities as a dandruff, cold and sore-throat cure, astringent, deodorant and douche. 'Bromodosis' (sweaty feet), 'office hips', 'accelerator toe', 'vacation knees', 'ashtray breath' and 'spoon-fed face' may be dated diseases, but the sustained economic assault on the consumer's 'integrity' is far from over, and its direction is ever inwards – witness vaginal deodorants and suppository selling. The problem lies in the finances of the corporate body, and not in the sweetness of the bodies on the street. Likewise, the solution is corporate: the consumer, anxious and amnesiac, must forget his or her deficient 'self', and purchase the selves made available by the business community. Fashion is always *dis*integrative; it aims to give us several selves, thereby providing capital with a diversification of markets.[34]

One way of focussing the interconnected histories of self and of capital is to present their liaison in schematic form:

Sphere of accumulation	Sphere of reproduction
Inertia of capital ('emulation')	High turnover of capital (mass market)
Leisure class	Culture industry
Manners	Fashion
Integrative selfhood	Disintegrative selfhood
(A drawing-room)	(Hollywood)

Or as Mandel puts it, almost as schematically:

> The real consequence of the reduced turnover-time of fixed capital . . . is a shift in the emphasis of the activity of the major owners of capital. In the age of freely competitive capitalism, this emphasis lay principally in the immediate sphere of production, and in the age of classical imperialism in the sphere of accumulation (the dominance of financial capital); today, in the age of late capitalism, it lies in the sphere of reproduction.[35]

Fitzgerald's writing straddles the transition from 'classical imperialism' to 'late capitalism', and is an extremely sensitive register of it. Daisy Buchanan is a display case for leisure-class wealth, yet she is drawn to Gatsby. Where Tom Buchanan's money is inherited and his body solid ('cruel', 'capable of leverage'[36]), Gatsby's assets are quite literally liquid: he heads a bootlegging empire, and his voice sounds like a quick flick 'through a dozen magazines'.[37] Daisy assures him, '"You resemble the advertisement of the man," she went on innocently, "You know, the advertisement of the man – ".'[38] Her sentence remains unfinished because Gatsby embodies every conceivable selling line. His selfhood, at least to Daisy's eye, is as liquid as his assets. The structure of Daisy's desire is economic, her adultery is hot for the new activities of the new owners of the new capital, and therefore its location shifts from the drawing-room of East Egg to Gatsby's lawns, where parties epitomize mobility, and "romance" enters the sphere of reproduction:

> Almost the last thing I remember was standing with Daisy and watching the moving-picture director and his Star. They were still under the white-plum tree and their faces were touching except for a pale, thin ray of moonlight between. It occurred to me that he had been very slowly bending toward her all evening to attain this proximity, and even while I watched I saw him stoop one ultimate degree and kiss her cheek.
> 'I like her,' said Daisy, 'I think she's lovely.'
> But the rest offended her – and inarguably, because it wasn't a gesture but an emotion.[39]

'Emotion' and 'gesture' are carefully distinguished: 'emotion' implies an integral self that feels; 'gesture' locates that self outside in a repeatable event. As the director kisses his star, he constructs a movie-still that might be used to advertise a film or to promote a style. Daisy is excited because she can see herself, and consume herself, in the mirror of that highly marketable gesture.

The two novels that follow *The Great Gatsby* chart Fitzgerald's sense of the changing structures of capital. *Tender is the Night* (1934) centres on the career of a psychiatrist, Dick Diver, who treats and eventually marries the incestuously spoiled daughter of the Warrens, a noted Chicago family. Incest could be read as an economic crime: the father, rather than exchange his daughter, penetrates her as he might penetrate a market, and accumulates her sexuality to his own. Incest is integrative in its denial of the mixing of different bloods and classes. Dick's marriage, therefore, ties him to an absolute 'token' of the leisure class. However, Nicole cannot be exchanged fully since, at a subconscious level, she has been locked up among her father's assets. Dick's attention duly wanders to Rosemary Hoyt, a film star whose first success was *Daddy's Girl*. Rosemary, too, is the child of capital, but her image belongs to the culture industry and so is liable to endless reproduction. In taking Rosemary, Dick escapes from the sphere of accumulation – in whose traumatic bed he must replay the acquisitiveness of the greedy father – only to enter the sphere of reproduction, where, although he turns down a screen test, he comes apart, sensing in his every move a gesture without substance.

Fitzgerald's final novel, *The Last Tycoon* (1941), does not veer between economic spheres; it is almost hermetically set in a Hollywood studio, where its hero is a producer responsible for the reproduction of reality in a consumable form. When Munroe Stahr falls in love, he does so with a woman who reminds him of the screen image of his dead wife – an image that he helped to conceive. Stahr is the perfect capitalist: if all men were Stahr, the fixed overheads on corporate investment would

constitute no risk to profitability, since there could be no overproduction or underconsumption. Stahr consumes what he produces, and
his products (Minna Davis, his first wife) standardize and predicate his
needs (Kathleen, his mistress).

III

If the framework that I have outlined may be used to map shifts within
one literary career, it ought to facilitate close readings of particular
novels. *The Bostonians* (1886) is a useful example because it deals with the
relationship between advertising and manners, and does so at a
problematic moment within the history of capital. Despite its publication date it would be wrong to fix *The Bostonians* in what Mandel calls
'the sphere of accumulation', in part because of the difficulty of
specifying dates for economic phases; for example, there is the
suggestion that by the 1840s Lowell's textile production was 'a miniature
of the corporate industrial society of the twentieth century'.[40] More
sensibly, Alfred Chandler has risked a periodization of large US
enterprise; he divides its expansion into four fairly distinct states:

1 initial expansion and accumulation of resources (1880–1914);
2 rationalization in the use of resources (1900–20);
3 expansion into new markets and lines to help assure continuing and
   full use of resources (for some firms, 1920s; most, 1930s);
4 development of new 'structure' to make possible continuing and
   effective mobilization – this involves an increasingly long-term and
   global view of market activity (pioneered during 1920s; most firms,
   1940s and 1950s).[41]

Certain industries and locations will act as innovators, so that decisive
dating is difficult. The real problem is to decide when a system of
economic organization is sufficiently widespread to produce social
patterns that may be said to be typical.

By the 1870s, the decade in which the novel is set, the post-Civil War
boom had glutted the market, inducing slump and necessitating forced
'combinations' to control price and production. In 1882 the Standard Oil
Company formed the first trust, and by 1889 New Jersey, sensing the
drift to consolidation, amended its incorporation law to allow one trust
to purchase the stocks of another. Provision for the general incorporation of holding companies was rapidly instigated by other states. Verena
and Ransom court in a ruined shipyard; Ransom's business in New
York is sparse. The 1870s were, indeed, a decade of depression; however,
by 1886 the first great corporate enterprises had appeared, carrying with
them the structural problem of reproduction. 'The need to keep the

consolidated production activities working steadily called for close co-ordination with customer demand through the creation of marketing organization.'[42] Boston appears to have been good ground in which to grow advertising agents:[43] Rowell and Dodd opened there in 1865 and, via the *Advertiser's Gazette*, pioneered and taught the skills of purchasing newspaper space and retailing to advertisers. The 'new science' was Bostonian in origin, and between 1870 and 1900 it prospered, increasing tenfold in national volume.

Mrs Luna likens Verena to 'a walking advertisement' (p. 226), and on the day of her great address, 'all the walls and fences of Boston flam[ed] ... with her name' (p. 358). For James, Verena is a spectacle before she is a feminist, and it is with his uncertain response to publicity that I am most concerned. David Howard argues, persuasively, that the novel may be read as an attempt by various persons to gain a managerial influence over Verena.[44] At her debut Verena is the medium whereby Selah Tarrant publicizes his own occult powers: from the first this spiritualist was *in* publicity; he started as a door to door vendor of lead pencils. Olive Chancellor, quite literally, buys off the father's interest in order to train Verena as an outlet for her ideas on the rights of women (it is envisaged that she will rival Mrs Farrinder on the lecture circuit). Meanwhile, Verena is variously courted, most symptomatically by Matthias Pardon. James calls Pardon a 'son of his age' because of his 'state of intimacy with the newspapers' and his 'cultivation of the great arts of publicity' (p. 115). Pardon is an early gossip-columnist:

> He regarded the mission of mankind upon the earth as a perpetual evolution of telegrams; everything to him was very much the same, he had no sense of proportion or quality; but the newest thing was what came nearest exciting in his mind the sentiment of respect. (p. 116)

Newness excites him because, in a commercial age – an age of 'receding concreteness' – to be new is to appear authentic. The phrase 'receding concreteness' is Adorno's: he argues that, given mass production, the surfaces of the world seem predictable, even as our experience of those surfaces is pre-conditioned:

> The never-changing quality of machine-produced goods, the lattice of socialization that enmeshes and assimilates equally objects and [our] view of them, converts everything encountered into ... a fortuitous specimen of a species, the *doppel-gänger* of a model. The layer of unpremeditatedness, freedom from intentions ... seems consumed. Of it the idea of newness dreams. Itself unattainable, newness installs itself ... amidst the first consciousness of the decay of experience.[45]

Adorno's point is twofold: that hope for the new is an assault on commercial surfaces; and that that hope is false, since newness itself is a consumer device. Newness is the shock that sells. For Pardon, Verena is just such a 'sensation' (p. 305). She is an anthology of telegrams to editors; as he tells Mrs Luna on the eve of the Boston launch:

> We want to know how she feels about tonight; what report she makes of her nerves, her anticipations; how she looks, what she had on, up to six o'clock . . . But can't you tell me any little personal items – the sort of thing the people like? What is she going to have for supper? or is she going to speak–a–without previous nourishment?   (p. 362)

Adorno consigns the recession of concreteness to 'decay'; it should be remembered, however, that sensation and the sensory object also have a history. 'Decay' is historically imprecise. For Veblen the materials of the leisure-class are *made*; their structure may be a network of false distinctions, but their manufacture takes time. Consequently, Olive Chancellor's 'interior' is a regulative space in which a whole history of leisured labour overtly and silently declares itself. In constradistinction, the kinds of item that appear for sale in newspaper columns and whose brand names are 'inlaid' in the letter-writing tables of hotel vestibules (p. 100), suppress their past. The concreteness of their production must be denied lest it impede the rapidity of their exchange and consumption. Mr Tarrant is prophetic in his recognition that 'human existence . . . was a huge publicity' (p. 97). He 'haunts' 'editorial elbows' and 'compositors' (p. 100) because he knows that 'newspapers [are] the richest expression . . . of human life' – a sentiment whose validity James was bitterly to confess only in 1903, when he acknowledged that newspapers 'were all the furniture of . . . consciousness'.[46] Furniture matters to James: the confession must have troubled him. Yet Verena is more her father's protégée than she is Olive's; indeed, as a proto-star she is entirely at odds with the objects that surround her in the Chancellor drawing-room. They, albeit ambivalently, 'spoke of habits and tastes'. Verena's voice is an assault on all that they might say, since, as organized publicity, Verena is indiscriminately consumable: her interior, from nerve ends to stomach contents, exists to furnish a newspaper column. Her social range is capacious; from the South End of Boston to the salons of New York, from the 'garb of toil' pervaded by 'an odour of India-rubber' (p. 40) to 'the best society' (p. 218), few remain unsold. What she sells matters less than how she sells it. This is her voice to Ransom's ear:

> Her speech, in itself, had about the value of a pretty essay, committed to memory and delivered by a bright girl at an 'academy'; it was vague, thin, rambling, a tissue of generalities that glittered agreeably enough in Mrs. Burrage's veiled lamplight . . . He asked himself what either he or any one else would think of it if Miss Chancellor – or even Mrs. Luna – had been on the

platform instead of the actual declaimer. Nevertheless, its importance was high, and consisted precisely, in part, of the fact that the voice was not the voice of Olive or of Adeline. Its importance was that Verena was unspeakably attractive, and this was all the greater for him in the light of the fact, which quietly dawned upon him as he stood there, that he was falling in love with her. It had tapped at his heart for recognition, and before he could hesitate or challenge, the door had sprung open and the mansion was illuminated. He gave no outward sign; he stood gazing as at a picture; but the room wavered before his eyes, even Verena's figure danced a little. This did not make the sequel of her discourse more clear to him; her meaning faded again into the agreeable vague, and he simply felt her presence, tasted her voice.

(p. 234)

Despite Olive's political concerns, the voice has an oddly similar effect upon her:

The habit of public speaking, the training, the practice, in which she had been immersed, enabled Verena to unroll a coil of propositions dedicated even to a private interest with the most touching, most cumulative effect. Olive was completely aware of this, and she stilled herself, while the girl uttered one soft, pleading sentence after another, into the same rapt attention she was in the habit of sending up from the benches of an auditorium. She looked at Verena fixedly, felt that she was stirred to her depths, that she was exquisitely passionate and sincere, that she was a quivering spotless, consecrated maiden, that she really had renounced [Ransom], that they were both safe . . . She came to her slowly, took her in her arms and held her long – giving her a silent kiss. From which Verena knew that she believed her.   (p. 261)

Verena converts her listeners into an audience and recasts each vocal context as a venue. Her delivery elides the political and the personal to a single promise, singly given – an offer of "desire" set within a private interior. In a voice, evocative of a 'mansion' behind a door, she displays that icon designed for the bourgeois dream of domestic space, the 'spotless . . . maiden'. Listening, both believe that Verena proposes 'privacy'. To Ransom, 'she was meant . . . for privacy, for him, for love' (p. 234); to Olive, even the Music Hall must be approached obliquely via a series of secret hiding places. Verena promotes 'love' in a form that has more to do with the mid-century vogue for sentimental fictions than with early feminist advocacy of 'rational love' or 'free unions' (p. 114).[47] Her 'publicity' is all for 'privacy', that is for the 1870s palliative to the increasing coherence of the market; her voice conjures the sentimental within the domestic, and is therefore essential to capital as it gears itself to the dream life of a consumer culture.

As early as 1868, in his *Hints to Advertizers*, David Frohman insists, 'a man can't do business without advertizing';[48] Pardon is of Frohman's persuasion. The columnist appreciates that Verena's manner can absorb any matter; as he insinuates to Olive, she has 'charm' for which there is 'a great demand . . . nowadays in connection with new ideas' (p. 118), 'ideas' in the plural refers to more than the plurality of women's rights. For Pardon, Verena could 'take a new line' (p. 118), presumably on almost anything – she has as many selves as there are available markets. I am reminded of the ubiquity of Orson Welles, or at least of his speech rhythms in television commercials. Welles himself may have been under contract to a sherry manufacturer, but his phrasing introduced Victor Borge to Danish lager and is responsible for many a liaison between utterance and commodity. Verena is Welles at a higher pitch. The economics of such voices are 'spectacular', where 'the spectacle is *capital* to such a degree of accumulation that it becomes an image'.[49] Guy Debord's assertion is merely as gnomic as the history that it compresses: to unpack – 'degree of accumulation' refers to corporate capital's growing difficulty over the quick realization of surplus value. Only if a product can be promoted can it be sold with seemly haste, therefore its 'image' is of its essence. Labour and price are secondary considerations; like money before it, the capacity to be 'image[d]' (advertised) has become a form of equivalence essential to sociability and so to economic calm.

Though Verena eventually becomes a centre piece in one domestic sphere (the Ransom household), her lexicon of light is for most of the novel capable of double articulation: 'radiant', 'shining', 'brightness', 'living in the gaslight', 'divine spark', 'dazzling' . . . each term or phrase could be read as part of the almost statutory network that submits the woman to the wife and the blank page to the property contract (integrative). However, as Verena perfects 'her brightness . . . her air of being a public character' (p. 198), moving towards 'her real beginning' (p. 305) at the Music Hall, so her illumination inclines to the promotional (disintegrative). James will not face his own split reference because it links the spheres of accumulation and reproduction, a developmental line that ties Verena to Fitzgerald's Rosemary Hoyt and leads eventually to Mailer's Marilyn Monroe. To avoid emergent economic plots, James marries his problem to a Southern conservative, one of the 'landless' 'landed gentry' (p. 172) who knowingly strikes her 'dumb' (p. 277) and is last seen 'cloak[ing]' and 'conceal[ing]' her face (p. 384), copies of which will subsequently not be worth the paper they are printed on to the select stores of Boston (p. 180).

James appreciates his own dilemma because, as John Goode has argued, 'he is saturated in the values of capitalism; in its metaphysical notions of a substantial self'.[50] Goode's judgement is striking but imprecise – the capital that soaks James is capital in its second phase of 'classical imperialism'; the 'metaphysics of the substantial self' does not belong to late capitalism. A 'substantial' selfhood is the property of a possessive individual who guarantees his own intrinsicality by possessing others and resisting his own possession. Olive and Ransom are nominally of this stamp, yet *The Bostonians*, in terms of its materials, is awkwardly positioned on the edge of very different kinds of social relation, and therefore of an alternative selfhood. If 'self' may be said to accord with the pulse of accumulation, as accumulation changes so too does the pulse of the self. Consequently, Olive's 'pure ego',[51] for all its possessiveness, is deeply divided. She is self-declaredly of 'the *bourgeoisie*' (p. 47) and yet, almost literally, tears herself apart. Masochism is her leitmotif. Since, for Olive, men are 'organized atrociousness' (p. 249), it is only apt that they should also be a 'brutal, blood-stained ravaging race' (p. 44) capable of all manner of torture and crucifixion. Nonetheless, Olive's suffering crosses gender lines – she is a Joan of Arc (p. 132) who burns as readily under Verena's hand as Ransom's. Indeed, Ransom and Verena are so allied in Olive's imagination that they constitute the structure of her masochism. Olive assures Verena that she had 'a definite prevision' of Verena's first visit to the Chancellor house; during the same conversation she explains that such 'forebodings' are 'a peculiarity of her organization' (p. 77), and offers as further evidence 'the sudden dread that had come to her . . . after proposing to Mr Ransom to go with her to Miss Birdseye's' (p. 78). According to Verena, her friend's capacity to prophesy depends upon 'force of will' (p. 78) – if so, that will is radically split, projecting simultaneously a love object and the block to that object. Ransom is as much Olive's creation as is Verena; indeed, it is my point that she created both of them simultaneously. Her 'intuition' and 'foreboding' (p. 254) transforms an obscure cousin into a haunting fear (p. 262), a 'sudden horror' (p. 311) and 'the trap of fate' (p. 248). His unwanted manifestations strike her as 'fantastic' (p. 86) to the point of being spectral: he afflicts her as 'dread', 'palpitation' (p. 248) and 'a kind of concussion' (p. 312). It is important to recognize that her 'wound[s]' (p. 128) are not only self-inflicted and self-delighting, but are out of all proportion to their cause – unless one considers that impact to be more than sexual.

René Girard argues that desire cannot come into being without the mediating presence of a third party. By insisting that an Other attends any loving couple he offers access to Olive's tripartite heart:

> Jealousy and envy imply a third presence: object, subject, and a third person toward whom the jealousy or envy is directed. These two 'vices' are therefore triangular; however we never recognize a model in the person who arouses jealousy because we always take the jealous person's attitude toward the problem of jealousy. Like all victims of internal mediation, the jealous person easily convinces *herself* that *her* desire is spontaneous, in other words, that it is

deeply rooted in the object and in this object alone. As a result *she* always maintains that *her* desire preceded the intervention of the mediator. *She* would have us to see him as an intruder, a bore, a *terzo incomodo* who interrupts a delightful tête-à-tête. Jealousy is thus reduced to the irritation we all experience when one of our desires is accidently thwarted. But true jealousy is infinitely more profound and complex; it always contains an element of fascination with the insolent rival.[52]

Olive's desire, for all its seeming spontaneity, is mediated by a third who walks always beside her. The simultaneous arrival of intruder and lover indicates the uncertainty of Olive's social position. 'The miseries and mysteries of the People' (p. 104) fascinate but elude her until she discovers feminism, at which point paths to 'the inexpressibly low' (p. 104) seem to open, and she is able to 'mingle' more easily with 'the common life' (p. 33). However, the poor come quarantined in oratory: neither 'the social dusk of that mysterious democracy' (p. 79) nor 'the romance of the people, (p. 42) can be stretched to cover the plight of labour in the depression of the seventies:

> The divergence between the interests of employer and worker and the increasing loss of personal contact between the two sides of industry as the scale of manufacturing increased were helping to develop class feeling in the United States; but the great strikes of 1877 acted as a catalyst in making people consciously aware of social distinctions.[53]

'The people', in their negative aspect, are, for Olive, 'Charlie' – a figure in 'a white overcoat and paper collar', a perpetually 'obtrusive swain' ever able to distract 'poor girl[s]' from the ballot (p. 42). If labour is Charlie then labour knows nothing of unions, of the Greenback party, of the 'Molly Maguires' or of twenty-six rioters dead in Pittsburgh – such Charlies can be kept out.

The door to Olive's pet project, a hypothetical 'evening club' for female workers, is doubly barred against incursions from the under-class. Seen first as poorly paid women and second as a suitor, the proletarian, already shrouded in 'dusk', is vitally obscured. Ransom is Charlie writ large but different, the disquieting face of a threatening class is replaced by the troubling smile of the dispossessed gentry. Re-cast as a proprietor without property who, despite defeat, embodies national unity (does he not visit a war memorial to his enemy?), Charlie vanishes under his masks. And yet no displacement entirely forgets its path: the archaeology of Ransom's quasi-spectral effect goes some way to explain his energies in Olive's mind. Olive needs Ransom as much as she needs Verena. His Southernness defers the proletariat even as his passion re-casts a problematic liaison between capital and labour (Verena and 'Charlie') as an essentially bourgeois love-match (Verena and Ransom).

The displacements make labour possible for Olive and allows her to approach 'the dusk' (while not seeing it), and, via Verena, to re-negotiate a workable relationship with 'the People'.

The Verena affair distances Olive from her class, or at least marks an emphatic shift in how she uses her family monies. As one who previously wished to work among 'pale shop-maidens' (p. 42), her interest in 'the common life' was deeply conservative. The provisions of an 'evening club for her fatigued, underpaid sisters' (p. 43), though benefiting the staff of the 'marble palaces', would increase their daytime efficiency and relieve pressure on employers to provide adequate facilities *in situ*.[54] Such a project, albeit a feminist concern, protects the owners of capital, and more particularly the owners of consumer capital. By working with Verena, Olive does more than protect, she joins those owners. The philanthropist becomes an entrepreneur, handling a new voice. Personal management gives way to business management as Filer is hired to realize Pardon's promotional hint over the suitability of the Music Hall as venue. Olive's commitment to her protégée is both emotional and financial – the extent to which that investment modifies the typical forms of bourgeois accumulation is, however, the measure of her need for the ubiquity of Ransom.

Olive's jealousy is at once formally imaginative and socially repressive; taking shape as 'a sort of mystical foreboding' (p. 240), it contains in miniature a double narrative resolution. Having masked the proletariat, Ransom protects Olive from the unpalatable logic of the development of the bourgeoisie. If Olive is ever to return to 'the oldest and best' drawing-rooms of her class, she must lose Verena to Ransom. The final scene in the antechambers of the Music Hall, with Filer pricing every quarter of a second at \$500, and the police at the door to protect the new form of wealth, is not just one of emotional re-alliance. Ransom takes Verena, and in so doing either halts Olive's economic drift or forces her to become a 'spectacle' in her own right. Whether Olive becomes the new 'voice' is a mute point; James shows her 'rush' towards the platform, and notes 'the quick, complete and tremendous silence' (p. 384) which greets her arrival. By maintaining that silence, he effectively deserts Olive at the most interesting point of her career – the moment of 'publicity' – the moment when the self-possession of the bourgeoisie must change if it is to ensure both the continuing profitability of its properties and the lasting comforts of a self-image that is more than an archaism. However, having granted intrinsic selfhood to Verena, by force of matrimony, it is unlikely that he will disintegrate her manager.

The notion of the disintegral self has no lasting appeal to James; as he wrote to Grace Norton in 1883:

You are right in your consciousness that we are all echoes and reverberations of the *same*, and you are noble when your interests and pity as to everything that surrounds you, appears to have a sustaining and harmonizing power. Only don't, I beseech you, *generalize* too much as to these sympathies and tendernesses – remember that every life is a special problem which is not yours but another's, and content yourself with the terrible algebra of your own. Don't melt too much into the universe, be as solid and dense as you can.[55]

Verena is a melter, and only the Jamesian commitment to the possessive ego – to the right of everyone to accumulate property in themselves (where property provides intrinsicality) – means that she may melt just so far. Late in *The Bostonians* James steps awkwardly back from Verena's approach to the disintegral sphere of reproduction:

> No stranger situation can be imagined than that of these extraordinary young women . . . it was so singular on Verena's part, in particular, that I despair of presenting it to the reader with the air of reality. To understand it, one must bear in mind her peculiar frankness, natural and acquired, her habit of discussing questions, sentiments, moralities, her education, in the atmosphere of lecture rooms, of *séances*, her familiarity with the vocabulary of emotion, the mysteries of 'the spiritual life'. She had learned to breathe and move in a rarefied air, as she would have learned to speak Chinese if her success in life had depended upon it; but this dazzling trick, and all her artlessly artful facilities, were not part of her essence, an expression of her innermost preferences. What *was* a part of her essence was the extraordinary generosity with which she would expose herself, give herself away, turn herself inside out, for the satisfaction of a person who made demands of her. Olive, as we know, had made the reflection that no one was naturally less preoccupied with the idea of her dignity, and . . . it must be admitted that in reality she was very deficient in the desire to be consistent with herself.   (pp. 325–6; italics in source)

Despite her metamorphic proclivities, and by dint of emphasis rather than argument, Verena retains an 'essence', a structure formed, like the fish knives, from discrimination – 'an expression of her innermost *preferences*' (italics mine). Where that property might lodge in a being capable of 'turn[ing] herself inside out' is debatable. Nonetheless, James will have it so. His contradictory defence of the 'solid' and the 'dense' is a form of self-defence, indicating how narrow is his affiliation to one moment of capital, and to the uses made of that moment and of that capital by a particular leisure class.

The narrowness of James's economic commitment is borne out by Ransom's career. Earlier, I argued that Ransom releases James from an emergent economic plot: nominally the Southerner wins Verena for his archaic conservatism. Olive, without Verena, will probably return to her 'queer corridor-shaped drawing-room' (p. 27), authorially rescued from an incipient shift within her class. However, Ransom's political epithet, 'conservative', is as janus-faced as Verena's 'brightness': both qualities constitute split referents which, read one way, point firmly towards a future that James sees, but must not see. To make my case, I need to challenge the prevalent reading of Ransom's Southernness, which stems from a double failure: firstly, to date the novel correctly, and then to recognize the very particular significance of that dating. James notes that Verena moves in with Olive, 'during the winter of 187–' (p. 144); early in the following spring she takes Ransom to Harvard's Memorial Hall, 'consecrated to the sons of the university who fell in the long Civil War' (p. 212). The visit decodes the dash. Until 1877 Union troops occupied the South: consequently, prior to that date Ransom's readiness to forgive and forget (p. 212) is unthinkable. With troop withdrawal, an ex-Confederate officer's prayer for the Union dead is not only possible but fashionable.[56] On Memorial Day 1877, President Hayes went to Tennessee to assist in the decoration of war graves. The novel spans two years; it follows that any such period, post 1876 but starting in the decade, will do. I favour 1877–9, since I take the events of 1877 to be crucial.[57]

Prayers could be offered by Northerners in the South, and Southerners in the North, because of the success of what has become known as 'the Compromise of 1877'[58] which marked a political revision of sectional relations; revision is too polite, reversal would be more apt. Prior to the Compromise, during the last year of Grant's unhappy second administration, the Republican party was bound in a misalliance: 'The party of wealth and property and privilege in the North . . . appealed in the South to a propertyless, oppressed, Negro labouring class.'[59] The Republican Reconstruction of the South (1865–77), engineered by the party's Radical wing (the Carpetbaggers), was founded on an attempt to disenfranchise Southern conservatives, and where possible to confiscate their land-holdings in order to achieve votes, offices, civil rights and perhaps forty acres apiece for blacks. As Barrington Moore argues, an alliance between Northern men of substance and Southern ex-slaves is a temporary aberration awaiting correction in the form of 'the characteristic reactionary coalition between urban and landed elites'.[60] 1877 saw the re-alliance of Northern industrialists and Southern planters. The agents of the change were known as Redeemers – Southern conservatives (both Republican and Democrat) whose economic interests were Whiggish, and whose rallying-cry was 'internal improvements', to be financed by Northern capital (whether federal or private). To contemporary observers, it sometimes seemed that the road to reunion was a railroad. Effectively, what the Redeemers wanted was the re-financing of the Southern ruling class, its inherited wealth all but wiped out by the Civil War, re-erased by the Panic of '73 and further flattened by the Depression of '77. In return for a promise to back Hayes (the Republican presidential candidate) in his electoral dispute with Tilden (the Democrat), the South's governing class got "home rule" and a considerable influx of monies.

It should be remembered that Ransom goes North for capital. On the opening page of the novel it is first remarked that he is a Southerner, and then that he is 'a long sum in addition', tall enough to resemble 'a column of figures' (p. 18). Mrs Luna does not need to ask in which column the figures stand: he 'looked poor' (p. 18). Where the Redeemer's projected source of funds is federal, his is marital. We first encounter him taking an inventory of his second-cousin's drawing-room. Having replied to Olive's invitation with the assurance that 'he would come to see her . . . the first time his business should taken him to Boston': 'He had now come in redemption to his grateful vow, and even this did not make Miss Chancellor feel that she had courted danger' (p. 26). A Southern "redeemer" in Boston on 'business' is 'courted' by a Northern bourgeois cousin. On learning that the courtship would involve a political mismatch on a Reconstruction scale – she being 'a roaring radical' and 'a female Jacobin' (p. 19) – Ransom allows himself a single expletive ('Oh, murder!') before turning to her sister, of whom he notes that her very open arms are leg-like: 'Mrs Luna was drawing on her gloves; Ransom had never seen any that were so long; they reminded him of stockings and he wondered how she managed without garters above the elbow' (p. 19). He will later confess that 'he once had a vision of spending his life in [Mrs Luna's] society' (p. 224).

One source for the Southerner suggests the contextual relevance of the Compromise: writing to John Hay, in 1885, James indicates that Senator Lucius Q.C. Lamar of Mississippi may have shaped his conception of the character:

> I am immensely touched and gratified by your friendly note anent the *Bostonians* and the noble Lamar. It was a kind thought in you that led you to repeat to me his appreciative judgement of my rather reckless attempts to represent a youthful Southron. It makes me believe for a moment that that attempt is less futile than it has seemed to me on seeing the story in print; and I am delighted, at any rate, that the benevolent Senator should have recognized in it some intelligence of intention, some happy divination. He himself, for that matter is in it a little, for I met him once or twice in Washington and he is one of the few very [sic] Mississippians with whom I have had the pleasure of conversing.[61]

James met Lamar in 1882; by then the Senator had a national reputation on two accounts, as "reconciler" and as "corrupter". His eulogy on the death of Charles Sumner (1874) made him, almost overnight, a leading spokesman for sectional conciliation: his chairing of the sub-committee on the Texas Pacific Railroad Bill (December 1876/January 1877) earned him other names. The *Nation* warned that by 'fathering' Tom Scott's bill he risked 'rascality', adding that his alliance with Scott, a railroad empire-builder, and their joint attempt at a 'wholesale raid upon the Treasury', threatened 'to open up the abyss of corruption in national politics'. The *Nation* feared that Lamar, 'representative, *par excellence*, of the South in the new order of things', was rewriting the 'needs' of his region and 'the wisdom of conciliation' as a charter for 'speculators', 'jobbers' and 'promoters'.[62] I work with the pages of the *Nation*, though those of the *New York Times* or the *Chicago Tribune* would have been more fruitfully vituperative, because that journal supplied James with much of his political commentary; indeed, Leon Edel speaks of James as the *Nation*'s 'informal correspondent-at-large in England', and adds that during the 1870s his writings for the *Nation* were a source of constant, if marginal, income.[63] For James the significant encounter with Lamar took place in 1877, via journalism. By 1882, Lamar's political career was effectively over – one biographer describes him as 'a member in name only' of the forty-seventh Congress.[64] Nonetheless, his joint reputation as "reconciler" and "appropriator" affirms that for Redeemers any reunion between the ruling classes of North and South could be achieved only by means of capital transfer.

If Lamar lies behind Ransom, and Ransom moves North circa 1877/8, then Ransom cannot be read as he is generally read, that is as 'an unreconstructed Southerner'[65] and all-round throw-back to antebellum days. Having discerned an 'aristocrat', critics most typically point him temporally, economically and politically backwards, and tag him 'conservative'. The term is frequently applied by James; however, Southern conservatives in the late 1870s were not nostalgic for 'Scott and images of medieval chivalry'.[66] Rather, the title referred to Whigs, who were sometimes planters, but who were always affiliated to capitalistic interests:

> Old Southern commonwealths that had once been the bailiwicks of planter statesmen, with a peculiar institution to serve, were now found to be organized in the service of a new set of interests. Virginia had been redeemed by a combination of old-line Whigs, conservative Republicans, and Confederate Democrats, who took the official name of Conservative party.[67]

What was true of Virginia was true of Ransom's home state, Mississippi, under Lamar (who called himself a 'conservative' Democrat).

I am aware that my argument for Ransom as a Redeemer rests heavily

on veiled political signals and extra-textual evidence; it is therefore open
to the charge that had James meant as much, he would have said so.
Indeed, it could be argued that he says the opposite. Ransom *is* a ruined
planter (many of whom were economic Whigs), much given to
'chivalry' (though well capable of declaring it 'moonshine' (p. 335)). At
first glance, he has 'a superior head' on 'sedentary shoulders' (p. 18),
features that might suit him to out-ennui the best Southron (were it not
that 'few Northerners were . . . so energetic as he' (p. 27)). He 'liked his
pedigree [and] revered his forefathers' (p. 169) (by the 1880s designer-
genealogy would become something of a cult among the new Southern
bourgeoisie[68]). He regards Mississippi as a lady, for whom he has a
'passionate tenderness'; he will not therefore 'prate in the market place'
about her 'wounds' (p. 54) ('internal improvements' appear to be ruled
out, except that Ransom has senatorial ambitions (p. 285) and, in this
instance, is merely refusing Mrs Farrinder's request that he speak to a
roomful of radicals whose historical moment has, in any case, passed). He
affects fatalism in the best-blood manner, indicating that 'slow process'
and 'the sensible beneficence of time' (p. 55) alone will heal his state (yet
he knows that 'the old ideas in the South are played out' (p. 30), and
recognizes that 'a moderate capital' would sustain his 'immense desire for
success' (p. 28)). He reads Carlyle, has doubts about popular education
and is 'very suspicious of modern democracy' (p. 169); indeed, faced
with a democratic gathering in Boston's Music Hall, he re-casts a
collection of reformers and their sympathizers as 'a mob' (p. 268) that
'grin[s] and babble[s]' (p. 377). (Aristocrats hold no patent on
'reactionary' views (p. 169); moreover, the end of Radical Reconstruction permits every Mississippian of ruined property and spoiled standing
to bad-mouth the masses, confident that their new Northern allies will
have similar suspicions about labour and radicalism.)

In building a list of parenthetical antitheses poised on the question, "Is
Ransom aristocrat or Redeemer?", I hope to establish two things: first,
that the generic terms in question need not be mutually exclusive, and
second, that Ransom's character is composite. He has too many and
opposed characteristics to be consistent. Alfred Habegger has recently
argued that James is deeply confused about Ransom – a Southerner who
wears a Western hat (p. 19) and fails to recognize chewing-tobacco when
he sees it (p. 369); a linguist who masters German in a single summer, but
cannot talk to the German regulars in his bar because 'their colloquial
tongue' was unknown to him (p. 169). Having just over-indulged one
list, I will not ghost Habegger's persuasive tracery of contradiction, save
to say that it need not add up to Habegger's conclusion, that 'James's
basic invention of Basil's career . . . is threadbare' and sustains 'no decent

representational illusion'.[69] To recognize Ransom as an anthology of antitheses may simply be to locate him as a member of the Southern ruling class circa 1877–9.

Dating, however, cannot disperse all the contradictions. Furthermore, it generates its own awkward question, "If Ransom comes North after the money why does he marry Verena?" Even allowing that Verena, purchased and primed by Olive, is more Chancellor than Tarrant, it remains the case that she lacks funds. "Love" appears to have carried all before it, including economic logic – and "love" is such an unspecific term. Yet that is exactly the point: as with Olive so with Ransom, the vagaries of "love" express, and at the same time impede, a class transition. Ransom proposes to Verena only when his writing is a success; the editor of the *Rational Review* accepts an essay and pays in advance of publication. The size of the pre-payment and Ransom's reaction to it marks the event as climactic and anticipatory.[70] In effect, James signals that Ransom's public career is off and running, and simultaneously cripples him with a union that can only return him to a struggling legal practice.

Separation from Verena restores Olive to the bourgeoisie, 'the oldest and the best'. Marriage to Verena breaks Basil's 'conservative'/ Redeemer trajectory (whereas, with Mrs Luna's funds behind him, his energies might have found expression in the Senate). In both instances James will not pursue a narrative logic that carries him towards unions which substantiate capital's newer forms. Olive, married to Verena, would be committed to Pardon and to publicity. Ransom, married to almost anyone with a creditable drawing-room, might have lived up to Pardon's misrecognition, by becoming, if not a reporter, then one of the reported on (p. 363). Mooted marriages unmade imply that James will not countenance those potential uses to which an emergent bourgeoisie must put its capital if it is to remain viable.

By the early 1880s, thanks to the consolidation of the continental internal market by the Compromise of '77, the capitalist class of all sections was united in the experience of accumulation and its difficulties. From the viewpoint of the Northern urban elite the Civil War had worked: 'What was at stake in the Northern war effort was . . . simultaneously the direct penetration of capitalism to the entire territory of the Union . . . and the political and ideological unification of the nation under the industrial and financial bourgeoisie.'[71] Which is not to say that gilding the age was easy. During the last third of the nineteenth century, the USA built up the most powerful heavy industry in the world, but the same period saw the long phase of a depression (1873–97). The bourgeoisie faced two fundamental problems: it had both to remake labour and to remake itself. In many ways, given a seemingly bottomless reservoir of Central and Southern European immigrants, the first task was the easier. A largely immigrant proletariat, speaking various languages and having diverse ethnic and religious affiliations, did struggle bitterly against exploitation and degraded living conditions, without finally losing a deep longing for cultural assimilation. Labour unrest reached revolutionary levels: in 1877 a national railroad strike attracted such support among other workers and small farmers that fear of a new civil war flared, comparisons with the Paris Commune of 1871 were prevalent, and the events became known as 'The Great Rebellion'. The strike failed, in part because employers had more than company police and local militia to hand; the norms of "individualism", "stable family life", and "monetary gain" were a powerful spur to labour discipline. The symbolic offer of assimilation into the consumption norms of the petty-bourgeoisie paid off, and as they learned to manipulate the promise (with armed venality), businessmen became more obviously a ruling class. However, they too experienced contradictions, whose nature is well caught by Alan Trachtenberg: 'Within the age of robber barons, another age and another form took shape, that of the giant corporate body. The age of celebrated individualism harboured the decisive decline of proprietors, family businesses, simple partnerships: the familiar forms of capital.'[72]

To accumulate, beyond a certain point, is inevitably to experience the problems of reproduction: problems that change capital's shape, even as capital changes in its relations with the financier, the worker, the machine, the commodity and the consumer. If economic relations may be understood as a guise assumed by social relations, then incorporation must express a revolution in the social body of the bourgeoisie. I have been reading *The Bostonians* within this problematic, since I can best explain James's narrative decisions as expressions of an historically based class anxiety. I would stress that James invites his reader to approach the novel as 'a very *American* tale . . . as local, as American, as possible'.[73] Consequently, its unions should be seen as a reflection on the sectional and social alliances underpinning the Union itself. To summarize: labour's threat is displaced, first as Charlie, then as Verena; Olive seeks 'the people' only to find a union that innoculates the working class; the liaison remains dangerous insofar as it draws Olive out of bourgeois solidity; Basil takes Verena, thereby relieving Olive of the need to transform herself, but in so doing is himself deprived of the funds that would remake a portion of the Southern ruling class in the image of incorporating Northern capital.

The plot of *The Bostonians*, at the simplest level of who does what to whom (but not for why), is a tissue of displacements. Character relations assume one form rather than another in order to keep out two feared forces: the scarcely seen but ever-present threat of labour; and the all too pervasive threat of publicity. Just as anxious economic preference informs Jamesian plotting, so his favoured settings feature a decor that crystallizes from discrimination; since discrimination involves the discriminating in comparative judgement and select information, taste acts as a form of exclusion. 'Beauty' like plot design keeps Charlie and Pardon from the door, thereby guaranteeing a secure substance to the contents of the drawing-room. If my analogy is true, *The Bostonians*, in detail and in structure, derives its shape from a singular shift in the history of accumulation, singularly negotiated.

2

'You've got to see it, feel it, smell it, hear it', buy it: Hemingway's commercial forms

Writing in 1931 for the *Saturday Evening Post*, in nostalgic vein, Fitzgerald observed that 'the Jazz Age . . . raced along under its own power, served by great filling stations full of money'.[1] Dos Passos wrote of 'the billiondollar speedup',[2] while abroad Americans were asked, '"Everybody's rich in your country . . . ?" and steam shovels suddenly bit into the hills, gold washed itself from the rivers, skyscrapers rose, heiresses were kidnaped – we saw the America they wished us to see and admired it.'[3]

Whether treating of the opulent, the merely respectable or the poor, the fiction of the 1920s seems well aware of 'The Big Money'. It may be Gatsby's enormous liquid assets or Clyde Griffiths's 'downpour of small change',[4] but its influence is felt across the board. On the evidence of a rise in disposable income and an increase in consumer credit, it would be fair to assume that, if not on your street, then on someone else's, 'a whole race [was] going hedonistic, deciding on pleasure'.[5] The Lynds note drily of Middletown – their 'mid-channel sort of American community' – that 'more and more of the activities of living are coming to be strained through the bars of the dollar sign'.[6]

The twenties were *par excellence* a commercial age. Monopoly capitalism flourished, as corporations, employing criteria of efficiency, standardized production in the pursuit of steadily rising sales – and were successful. 'Ten years after the war conspicuous consumption had become a national mania.'[7] Accordingly, chain stores, car lots, service industries, cinemas and advertising agencies proliferated. The shop window was necessarily and nervously everywhere.

Nervously, because much of the spending was financed by consumer credit. After the slump in demand (1920–2) and the labour unrest of the immediate post-war years (1919–21), American capital persuaded its workforce to buy it out of trouble. By learning the equation, 'Pay them more, sell them more, prosper more',[8] with an emphasis on the last two terms, capital nominally avoided the overproduction latent in its war-prompted technological revolution. 'The consumer dollar' also inhibited workforce resistance to massive workplace innovation: 'time and motion', 'job segmentation', 'speed up', 'flow' and the increasingly visible hand of management, silk-gloved in 'science', effectively obliterated a class – the craft worker. Iron moulders, rollers and heaters, glass blowers, bricklayers, machinists, jigger-men in potteries, lasters in shoe factories, mule-spinners . . . the roll is as long as the replacement list is short: for the most part by the mid-twenties 'machine minders' were supervised by 'managers'. Systematic management grew from systematic de-skilling; someone had to put together what labour subdivision had taken apart. The net gain was a 50 per cent increase in manufacturing production between 1922 and 1929, accompanied by a revision in class relations. The middle managers (a new salariat) who integrated the fast-flow, high-innovation, fast-distribution systems were founded on a violent theft of class knowledge. Taylor, primary theorist of the revolution, is plain; as early as 1911 he insists that, 'the great mass of traditional knowledge, which in the past has been in the head of the workman', must be transferred to management. Force will be necessary if worker autonomy and codes of ethical work behaviour are to be abolished: 'It is only through *enforced* standardization of methods, *enforced* adoption of the best implements and working conditions, *enforced* cooperation that this faster work can be assured.'[9]

Not for Taylor the panacea that technological 'progress' is 'natural' or 'inevitable': it is rather a clash of class wills. Ford's modernizations were untypical only in their earliness: by 1911 Ford had adopted Taylor's principles, but a line which by 1925 could produce a car every ten seconds was a line that lost men almost as fast. In 1913 Ford required 13,000 workers to run his plant; in that year 5,000 quit. The fact that when, in January 1914, Ford announced the $5 day, 10,000 men rioted and fought for jobs outside his gates, does not make him a benefactor. The $5 would enlarge the worker's consumption basket – enabling him perhaps to buy a Ford – but only if he was over twenty-one, had six months unbroken employment and consumed neither tobacco nor alcohol. The enlarged wage packet, like the fast line, was a form of labour control. As parts of a history of technological change they, like the history of most things, are elements in a 'story of who rides whom and how'.[10]

What is disarming about the labour history of the twenties after 1922 is the ease with which the riders and the ridden appeared to enjoy their 'progress'. Strikes were rare, union membership fell away steeply from its 5 million high, and the entire tone of labour's struggle changed. Between 1910 and 1922 it was characterized by a direct, mass-involved challenge to managerial authority, and was explicitly dedicated to 'workers' control'. The primary demand for the eight-hour day should be read as a demand for the management of 'time'. Increasingly, post-1922, with the eight-hour day grudgingly won, and an average 14 per cent increase in wages, the employed manufacturing worker was ready to see labour protest less as class antagonism than as a means to the right to be a better consumer.

Contemplating the shop window, with his 14 per cent, the worker could not know, but might have suspected, that the financial growth of corporations, between 1922 and 1929, averaged 286 per cent. A boom in consumer credit was his placebo and their mainstay. Nonetheless, a reorganization of capital on the scale of the teens and the twenties must involve crisis. It is to be remembered that even as the war stimulated the centralization of capital, so, during each year of the USA's participation, over 1 million workers struck (more than in any single year prior to 1915). Furthermore, between 1915 and 1922, the ratio of striking to employed workers in all industrial and service industries remained constantly on a par with levels reached between 1934 and 1937. The economic historian James O'Connor argues: 'Economic recoveries and expansions occur when capital successfully restores its domination of labour by restructuring the directly producing class itself.'[11] Put crudely, post-war capital offered its workforce full Taylorism for a fuller consumption basket, and the offer was accepted. Production and sales soared. But the solution, higher wages, high credit and more shop windows, was a large part of the crisis that it sought to obviate. By raising consumer expectation and pricing as many needs as possible, capital caused consumer credit to overtake investment credit and so risked pricing itself out of profitability. To make a surplus when labour costs rise and credit time shortens is increasingly difficult: 'Crises progressively result in more proletarianization, increased commodification of needs, expanded markets, increased capital concentration/centralization, hence increased chances of more frequent and more severe crises.'[12] In other words, US manufacturers had to produce more and different products, in diversified markets, at greater speed and with diminished turn-over time, since only by affording to run faster could they manage to stand still. Innovation, whether in production or sales, is costly; consequently, capital needs the very credit that it is forcing elsewhere. The profits of the 1920s rested simultaneously on antithetical consumer and investment credits, that is on self-contradicting debts.

Arguably, in backing consumerism, capital contributed to the crash: the manufacture of 'the consumer', and worker defence of gains constituted a barrier to capitalist accumulation. 1929 was therefore built into the shop window of 1922.

If the shop window is less than transparent, the experience of the window gazer during the decade is opacity itself. The price of entry is the wage packet and credit, but the capacity to put 'just a little bit down' depends on a contract with 'the iron man'.[13] The worker works harder and faster for a machine that de-skills him; he may resent credit on such terms. The manager or the businessman will appreciate that in a consumer economy money is definitive: a leading citizen of Middletown observes, 'It's perfectly natural. You see, they know money, and they don't know you.'[14] But money is not easily known: in a single year Middletown's leading paper bases 'property' on production ('The first duty of a citizen is to produce'), on consumption ('consumption is a new necessity'), and on saving ('Better start saving late than never'), while simultaneously locating economic progress in 'natural reasons', 'the spirit of hopefulness' and the home-spent dollar. The Lynds are modest in 'wonder[ing] if the business men, too, are not somewhat bewildered'.[15]

One source of confusion shared by consumers of all classes was their own seemingly natural 'individualism'. In order to maximize profit, capital must privatize need; there is more money to be made from the gratifications of the *isolato* than from the shared satisfactions of a group. For example, if the home can be privatized and the family individualized, then potential points of sale are multiplied. During the twenties 'professionalized motherhood' and 'scientific housework' were heavily marketed. By subdividing a previously unified activity like housework into various distinct tasks, each of which requires a machine, capital produces a range of separate industries and of separate opportunities for surplus. Throughout the decade new kitchens shrank, since the segmentation and capitalization of home production meant that space was no longer required for canning, sewing, bread baking, cleaning. At the same time the sociability latent in those activities diminished. With fast foods and clothing brands readily purchasable, satisfaction increasingly became a matter between the individual and his dollar. The 'individual' is therefore a market target: social 'indivisibility' must give way to 'individualism', as selfhood is persuaded to reside in the isolated and full gratification of needs through commodities.

This, of course, is an abstract fantasy: need is never purely a form of capital. To read *Middletown* is to recognize that needs construed as commodities, and often satisfied as such, were experienced as social needs frustrated. Time and again the new means to leisure elicit reference to older pleasures. A voice will celebrate the private home ('I do very little visiting – mostly keep in touch with my friends by telephone') while another recalls the neighbourhood ('Neighbours used to be in each other's houses much more than they are now').[16] 'Radio' recalls 'chorus choir', 'washing machine' recalls 'laundry'[17] and repeated allusions to car and movie rarely occur without recognition of their de-centralizing effects on the family. The associations are not nostalgic: they are resentful – based on an active experience of the slippage of 'use' into 'exchange' which attends the historical extension of abstract labour and of the abstracted individual. The Lynds imply that even at the decade's height consumerism was a troubled comforter.

As the segmentation of markets proliferated and the hard sell hardened, the consumer was more likely to experience the tensions latent within 'individualism': free, but at liberty to buy; autonomous, but market-dependent; internally atomized, while addressed as the single focus of knowledge, sensation and decision; intensely active (whether as a worker or a manager) and yet passively receptive of goods which satisfied while dissatisfying. The contradictions concentrate into a cultural type for whom the shop window induces anxiety and resentment as a muted underpinning to the pleasures on display.

II

For Hemingway, at least, the great good place did not lie in the shop window. Indeed his shop windows sell the escape from shop windows:

> We were standing in front of the leather goods shop. There were riding boots, a rucksack and ski boots in the window. Each article was set apart as an exhibit; the rucksack in the centre, the riding boots on one side and the ski boots on the other. The leather was dark and oiled smooth as a used saddle. The electric light made high lights on the dull oiled leather.[18]

He offers open spaces, trout streams, mountain slopes and bullrings as venues where man may experience 'the real thing' directly.

Tony Tanner typifies a dominant reading when he assures us that for Hemingway 'only concrete things, perceptible manifestations of nature, have certain value', and that 'the prose makes permanent the attentive wonder of the senses: it mimes out the whole process, impression by impression'.[19] He adds that the liaison between nature's objects and man's senses is most pure when undertaken by one man alone in the natural world. Little seems more innocent of the big-sell than an uncaught trout far from any town:

> He watched them holding themselves with their noses into the current, many trout in deep, fast moving water, slightly distorted as he watched far down

through the glassy convex surface of the pool, its surface pushing and swelling smooth against the resistance of the log-driven piles of the bridge. At the bottom of the pool were the big trout. Nick did not see them at first. Then he saw them at the bottom of the pool, big trout looking to hold themselves on the gravel bottom in a varying mist of gravel and sand, raised in spurts by the current.

Nick looked down into the pool from the bridge. It was a hot day. A kingfisher flew up the stream. It was a long time since Nick had looked into a stream and seen trout. They were very satisfactory. As the shadow of the kingfisher moved up the stream, a big trout shot upstream in a long angle, only his shadow marking the angle, then lost his shadow as he came through the surface of the water, caught the sun, and then, as he went back into the stream under the surface, his shadow seemed to float down the stream with the current, unresisting, to his post under the bridge where he tightened facing up into the current.

Nick's heart tightened as the trout moved. He felt all the old feeling.

(1924)[20]

If I may ventriloquize . . . for Tanner the passage could embody Hemingway's 'radical honesty of . . . eye': an 'unprejudiced eye' is 'accurate [to] the parts' of what it sees, which are 'delicately and carefully separated out' so that attention is maximized and preconception minimized. Priority is given to the 'itemizing senses over the classifying mind' because, in Hemingway, 'a proper reverence for the world preceded intellectual understanding'. Tanner takes Hemingway on Hemingway's terms, and elucidates those terms fully. What he ignores is that the appeal to simple things and immediate sensations is made at the very moment when things and sensations are neither direct nor simple (if indeed they ever were). Hemingway celebrates 'actual things' and 'the emotion which they produce'[21] just when those actualities are being transformed by the second industrial revolution.

In the era of the Model T Ford, of federal highway expansion and a growing national park system, it must have been increasingly difficult to find a trout stream which, at least conceptually, was not an extension of the workplace. To be amused, in a decade noted for the production of amusement goods, is to prolong production; and '"leisure time" . . . quite characteristically in a pecuniary society is "spent"'.[22] Nick Adams seeks to forget the larger context, emphatically reassuring himself that, 'The river was there' (p. 186). Hemingway is compliant, emphatically burning the township of Seney to establish Nature in contrast to Society – and yet what Nick watches are effectively cryptograms for the intrusion of industrial production into Nature and into the nature of perception. My phrasing derives from Adorno. Commenting on the ears of corn blowing in the wind at the close of Chaplin's *The Great Dictator* (1940), Adorno notes, 'Nature is viewed . . . as a healthy contrast to society, and is therefore denatured. Pictures showing green trees, a blue sky, and moving clouds make these aspects of nature into so many cryptograms for factory chimneys and service stations.'[23]

To make a case for re-reading Hemingway's blue skies from within the system of commodity production that was his historical environment, I shall try to relocate his central preoccupation with perception and the perceived object in what for me is its true context – the context of consumption. My main concern is to establish the hegemony of price in Hemingway's fiction, so that the poverty of critical terms like "real", "matter of fact", "objective", "immediate", "concrete" and "experiential" may at least be considered. Of necessity, I find myself paraphrasing and echoing various accounts of commodity and exchange theory. By drawing analogies between things behind shop windows and Hemingway's "real things", and between the uniquely seeing, feeling, smelling, hearing Hemingway hero and the individualized consumer, I hope to lay grounds for a distinctly different way of reading Hemingway.

To return to Nick Adams's trout – there is something abstracted about the phenomenological innocence through which the fish is viewed: 'the real thing, the sequence of motion and fact', arrives in the prose attended by a commercial after-image. The trout would not look out of place behind glass; it would complement the rucksacks and riding boots in the display case that tempts Frederick Henry and Catherine Barkley. An object in a shop window is a strange kind of object. If it could speak, and were honestly inclined, it might confess to a double life, both real and abstract. Existing here and now and in immediate fullness, it prompts passers-by to consider not its uses, but the advertising copy-writer's promise of its uses. For George F. Babbitt a khaki blanket 'bought . . . for a camping trip which had never come off' symbolizes 'gorgeous loafing, gorgeous cursing, virile flannel shirts'.[24] Babbitt mentally fingers copy, not cloth. Nick Adams succeeds in getting away from it all; however, as he watches the 'slightly distorted' trout 'far down through the glassy convex surface of the pool', he too sees with an eye conditioned by consumption. He is like any window shopper. Gradually, the onlooker distils an image of the object: but with touch and use denied by the glassy surface, the image may misrepresent. Behind their windows the equivocal promise of objects is most manifest:

> There, in the market place, things stand still. They are under the spell of one activity only; to change owners. They stand there waiting to be sold. While they are there for exchange they are not there for use. A commodity marked out at a definite price, for instance, is looked upon as being frozen to absolute immutability throughout the time during which its price remains unaltered. And the spell does not only bind the doings of man. Even nature herself is

supposed to abstain from any ravages in the body of this commodity and to
hold her breath, as it were, for the sake of the social business of man.[25]

Those with an eye to Nature would challenge my intrusion of the
marketplace into Nick's perceptual habits. Tanner emphasizes immediacy and transience: his reading of the story casts Nick as a meticulous
observer whose refusal to be distracted from the present pays off –
intense moments of experience are achieved, and through them a
'rapport', albeit 'fading', 'with nature'. The reading is partial. The gleam
of light on the side of the leaping trout is anything but momentary, since
it can never re-enter the stream: it is forever a snapshot of immediacy.
The trout is timeless, but not with the recurrent and cyclical eternity of
the so-called "natural-world": it has a history because its 'now' contains
the 'now and forever' promised by the window display. More correctly,
the trout's promise is multiple, each stage of its leap being recorded and
fixed in immutability. Much of the effect results from the repetition of
the possessive 'his' in 'his shadow': initially the phrase could refer to the
kingfisher or to the fish – a trout rising to strike at a bird's shadow as at a
fly – the third usage undoes the elision, defining the shadow as the
trout's. The pronoun does not shift in pursuit of the exact 'facts of the
matter' or to recover 'the textures and contours of the objective world'
(Tanner): 'his' is precisely *in*accurate in order to prejudice our eye in
favour of a radical segmentation of objects. Delayed, and eventually
sorted out, the trout yields several trout, rising, jumping, turning,
returning – a photographic sequence worthy of the *National Geographic*.

Nick sees like a good consumer, 'successively' (Tanner) in private, and
without much thought. To think too much might be to waken
numerous anxieties. Consumerism sticks with surface and sensation, the
better to ignore 'the iron man' and all the complexities of labour, capital
and credit, from which the surfaces take their shine. As Nick fishes the
Black River, corporate capital subdivides the senses in order to sell to
each and every manufactured modality. Nick's eye is culturally
responsive; his sight increases gratification by granting autonomy to
each of the trout's several parts.

Nature, Nick and the reader hold their breath as, via the immutability
of time and place that the image guarantees, the trout passes through
reverence towards price. Such transitions are delicate: the trout remains a
trout, but everything is changed. The objective structures of the animal
are no longer simply 'natural', rather they express the cultural moment
of the perceiver's life.

As objects increasingly exist for their price, so their physicality is
translated. Instead of money being the temporary realization of the price
of commodities, the commodities become temporary realizations of

their price. The manner of the trout's abstracted physicality embodies a particular moment in the history of exchange abstraction. Although immersed in its primary animal-nature, the fish is a socially synthetic shadow – a formulation of Nick's commercially formed perception. Haug draws a persuasive distinction between 'use' and 'impression of use': he argues that in a culture oriented around exchange the uses pertaining to any object are increasingly viewed from the seller's perspective, that is as lures with which to attract a buyer. Consequently, 'use' gives way to 'promise . . . appearance . . . impression of use'. When the shift is endemic 'use impression' will turn into the object's 'second skin'; 'sensuality in this context becomes the vehicle of an economic function'.[26] Nick may act like a user but in a culture of sellers his perception, too, will modify; where the 'perfect' second skin of the commodity prevails, its illusion is the socially proper form of the sensual.

Hemingway's prose – near to its best in Nick's story – does not treat real things and their perception directly, nor, given its history, can it be expected to do so. It may be objected that although Nick fishes in the USA, where even burning cannot quite erase Seney, Hemingway's heroes more typically fish or hunt at a greater distance from the cycles of production and consumption. On the face of it, there would seem to be a clear cultural and economic contrast between the USA and the chosen European places: Hemingway set no major novel in his country of origin, the preferred ground being Spain, France, Italy . . . but preferably Spain. It should, however, be remembered that the heroes are most typically tourists, for whom alternative cultures come 'thinned out'.[27] A trout stream in the Basque country may be stocked with immediacies for the expatriate eye because it does what consumer items do, only better; where the shop window deracinates its contents from the history of their production, the European tour proffers a panorama of clean objects, deprived of social and linguistic density, and existing to please (at a price). Yet, if Hemingway is a tourist, he nonetheless stays. He lived in Paris from 1921 to 1926 and constantly returned to Spain as a literary source – Jake Barnes's therapeutic trips to Pamplona is simply one of several extended memories of underdevelopment. The case for Hemingway's conscious rejection of his own production-oriented culture is superficially affirmed by his affection for Cuba. But it remains the case that, whether in Europe or the Caribbean, Hemingway's literary and actual residency is one facet of a much larger act of appropriation.

During the twenties the United States turned itself into a 'promotional state';[28] the second industrial revolution required secured raw materials and enlarged markets: as a result, the USA's shop window positively had to go global. Herbert Feis speaks of 'the diplomacy of the dollar' while Emily Rosenberg notes: 'The United States flooded the world with products, branch plants and investment capital in the 1920s, making the decade one of the most economically expansive periods in the nation's history.'[29] Complete operations or assembly plants were moved overseas, allowing US investors to avoid foreign tariffs and to take advantage of cheap labour and locations closer to emerging markets and raw materials. Direct investment abroad ran at $3.8 million in 1919 and rose to $7.9 billion by 1929.[30] Much of it was supply oriented as the United States began to operate what was, in effect, a global policy of resource provision. Zinc carried the dollar into Silesia; sugar drew it to Cuba; oil to Mesopotamia; timber requirements induced the dollar purchase of huge tracts of Canadian forest, and by the mid–twenties Armour and Swift were slaughtering two-thirds of Argentinian cattle. One upshot was a growing divergence between the industrialized and the non–industrialized world, but this should not be read as a way of repositing a "natural" world for Hemingway to fish: 'Under utilized land and untapped resources came into production in the 20s and provided less developed countries with new exports to finance a growing volume of purchases, particularly manufactured goods from the united states.'[31]

Neither Cuba nor Spain was exempt from 'colonialism by contract';[32] indeed Cuba was an early "beneficiary" of the all-suffusing dollar. Although the defeat of Spain led to a period of military rule (1899–1902), the island was "developed" so that the gun-boat might vanish into the small print of private investment and loan agreements. In 1918 the head of the Latin American Division of the State Department concluded:

> During the decade following the termination of our war with Spain the island of Cuba, guided by American influence, increased her trade with us over four hundred and thirty million dollars. This unprecedented development of Cuba may serve as an illustration of what probably would take place in the central American countries provided this government extended to them aid of a practical character as it did in Cuba.[33]

Hemingway lived where Coca-Cola and Hershey had gone frequently and thoroughly before:[34] investment in Cuban sugar production and refinement soared during the twenties, with an attendant orientation of Cuban political processes towards US corporate demands. Spain too was increasingly drawn to 'the universal balm' (Feis's phrase for the dollar as it engaged in 'exuberant tours of the world [looking] for something to do'[35]). 1918 to 1920 saw a sharp increase in American investment, and, despite internal unrest, tourists visited in increasing numbers (passing the 40,000 a year figure at one point).[36] Hemingway was one among many, and as such part of an economic dynamic whereby one culture imposes itself on another. He goes on extended holidays to "primitive" places where his countrymen are already engaged in production: in 1925, for example, American Telephone and Telegraph (ITT) won a contract to establish a national service in Spain. Like the railways of the nineteenth century, the communication networks of the twentieth exist to facilitate the free flow of goods and services, tourists and financiers. For Emily Rosenberg the extent of that flow during the twenties yielded 'a global expansion of American property holding'.[37] My contention is simply that Nick's eye can be seen to be culturally responsive and very American, as soon as his habits of perception are set within the historical context of that expansion.

Nonetheless, it remains comforting to pretend that sensation is constant, and that even if the world was buying American by means of American loans, primary objects seen, felt, smelled and heard, stayed the same and always will. Hemingway readers, by and large, comfort themselves with a faith in the five senses and the nature to which they apply. Their faith is misguided: the real thing in the twenties, as now, is exchange abstraction – an experience deep in the corporality of things and of persons, of production and consumption. As commercial forms, both the object and the perceiver are sensuous in large part through their value.[38] The terminology may be strange and the phrasing self-reflexive but the idea should discourage appeals to the belief that things and sensations are "natural", or that Hemingway's or anyone's senses can ever be objective. Hegel is plain-spoken: 'sense certainty is nothing else than the mere history of its process'. To put it another way: things and sensations should be understood as deriving from their own particular and fundamental economic relations, relations out of which they unfold. In a culture premised on consumption all objects are double-bodied, or capable of at least two forms of sensuality: that associated with our use of them; and that associated with the 'promise of use'. (Where promises become pervasive, uses are liable to disappoint or confuse.) As consumerism expands, so use, need and matter recede, leaving "capitalist reality",[39] at whose logical extreme objects will cease to be sensual because they have become vehicles for exchange value. The sensuality of matter will eventually take the form of money's sensuality, within which all objects are equatable. Léger saw as much while window shopping in Paris (1924): 'The display-window spectacle has become a major source of anxiety in the retailer's activity. Frantic competition reigns there: *to be looked at more than the neighbouring store is the violent desire* that animates our streets.'[40] Léger reprises Baudelaire, his sense of the 'endlessly varied spectacle'[41] having been available in Paris since the creation of the arcades during the 1840s and 1850s. In a city designed to expose for sale, where commercial promiscuity has been a cliché since the Second Empire, even the most innocent American abroad will know that each thing has its price, and may begin to suspect that prices modify the very materiality of the things that are their vehicles.

Pound's observation that Hemingway 'could never tell one person from another . . . and never much cared' may be apocryphal. Nonetheless, it ought to be true, since it bears a striking resemblance to Hemingway's view of objects; trout, bulls and white pebbles in a blue stream are equally, and almost interchangeably, opportunities for the creation of perfect and disembodied moments of isolate satisfaction. I run ahead of myself: at this stage it is necessary only to claim that Hemingway is a 'capitalist realist', laureate to a new kind of "thing" – an essentially American thing, but available to him from Paris to Pamplona.

III

All of which may seem to carry one trout rather too far into the market place. The bullring lends itself more readily to shop-window status, for although Hemingway underplays Romero's commercial status, in *The Sun Also Rises* (1926), the bullfighter *is* a commodity. At first he does not look like one:

> When he had finished his work with the muleta and was ready to kill, the crowd made him go on. They did not want the bull killed yet, they did not want it to be over. Romero went on. It was like a course in bull-fighting. All the passes he linked up, all completed, all slow, templed and smooth. There were no tricks and no mystifications. There was no brusqueness. And each pass as it reached the summit gave you a sudden ache inside. The crowd did not want it ever to be finished.[42]

This is the very stuff of immediacy: those with 'aficion' may recognize 'the quality of slowness, suavity, and rhythm in a bullfighter's work'.[43] Others may have to check the glossary to *Death in the Afternoon* before experiencing an epiphany in which the physical is ritualized to affirm man's potential oneness with his own body. Style – Romero's and Hemingway's – poses as a measured means to grace. Romero's cape work is like a course in the Hemingway sentence: it is as simple as primary nouns and operator verbs, resisting decoration as Hemingway resists the abstract term; its moves are as successive as plain syntax, with its links as apparent as a repeated conjunction or preposition, and above all it too exists to maximize intensity.[44] On the face of it, content and form comply to actualize a style of fighting and a style of writing. If this is fair, events in the ring at Pamplona are a metaphor for the event on the page. The very notion of metaphor is disconcerting in so literal a context, but 'templed' (outside the glossary) is a metaphor, and a strange one. 'To temple', in plain English, is to enshrine or to make into or like a temple. Are we to assume that Romero's cape is a religious icon? The blasphemy would be inaccurate; it is the motion of the cape that is worthy of a shrine. But to capture it needs a camera, and the result might, presumably, resemble the photographic essays on Belmonte, Villalta and others in *Death in the Afternoon*. However, such pictures tend to the postcard, as the narrator of 'Banal story' well knows, a form that reduces the icon to the saleable relic. 'Templed' is initially a religious metaphor drawing 'pass' and 'summit' into its framework, but the high place implied in Romero's motion is not without price. With the religiosity of the metaphor recognized, Romero is abstracted from himself, becoming almost a sacred embodiment of the commercial form. As a commodity Romero has a 'charm' capable of considerable 'sorcery'. His spell is the witchery exercised by the commodity that, 'realised as a price, can be exchanged for the desired object of every need'.[45] He offers a communion in which aficionados, tourists, Jake, Hemingway and readers may share: each brings a completely different set of words, meanings, incidents and desires; each takes a different set of gratifications. Romero is capable of this degree of 'metaphysical subtlety', approaching 'theological proportion', because, as the 'value' at the centre of *The Sun Also Rises*, and as a commodity, he embodies that essence which links all things and persons in a commercial world. What this means is that Romero, in his 'temple', stands waiting to be sold.

Whether in an arena or a shop window, money is the crucial agent, the veritable place of abstraction. Its reach is extensive. The assumption that everything has its price affects each thing: one way of comparing the expensive trout on your plate to a bullfight is through the common language of price. We might link both 'gratifications' to the number of hours worked earning the necessary funds – in so doing we instil abstraction into our heads and hands and into the length of our days. Moreover, objects suffer transformations. Any particularity loses much of its discreteness, and as it does so takes upon itself a 'mystical character'. For Hemingway critics, 'mystical' values have much to do with the ways of the flesh. The reader might be better served attending to the way of the dollar which did, after all, smooth the way of the expatriates:

> There sprang into being a new race of tourists . . . the parasites of exchange . . . Exchange! It happened that old Europe, the continent of immemorial standards had lost them all: it had only prices, which changed from country to country, from village to village, it seemed from hour to hour. Tuesday in Hamburg you might order a banquet for eight cents (or was it five?); Thursday in Paris you might buy twenty cigarettes for the price of a week's lodging in Vienna.[46]

It may seem a far cry from a bureau de change in Hamburg, Paris or Vienna to Romero's bullring: indeed, Jake and his entourage have quit

Paris to rediscover 'immemorial standards' and primary needs in Pamplona. What they find is the perfect commodity. Romero's work is capable of quasi-heavenly status because it expresses purely the forms of 'value'. He offers to his spectators as many 'perfect' moments as they may choose to take. To become the agent of such moments is to obey the dictates of the product rather than of the self, and to render one's personality unassertive. The sentence, 'All the passes he linked up, all completed, all slow, templed and smooth', would read more easily without the pronoun. Romero is an extension of his function, not only because Hemingway's syntax inclines to the impersonal (though it does: 'There were . . . There was') but because both fighter and syntactical inclination reflect the priority of the object over the producer within the market place.

Romero's brand-name might be 'the old thing' (p. 193), with which we are told he draws the crowds. The phrase is resonant with knowledge of the trade, introducing to the blood and the sand, the unlikely tones of auction room and wine cellar:

> The comparison with wine drinking is not so far-fetched as it might seem. Wine is one of the most civilised things in the world and one of the natural things of the world that has been brought to the greatest perfection, and it offers a greater range for enjoyment and appreciation than, possibly, any other purely sensory thing which may be purchased.[47]

The comparison addresses the nature of connoisseurship: a bullfight is like a glass of wine insofar as appreciating either involves comparative acts that imply or eventually lead to an absolute ('the old thing'). The connoisseur's mean is often gold-tinted, perhaps because it shares with money's archaic essence an aura of infinite capability. For Romero's 'purity' to become such a mean, his cape work must require the co-presence of Belmonte's impurities and of Montoya's photographic canon. Similarly, a good wine summons the memory of many wines into its palate. So the cape and the wine censor their own singularity by becoming the 'summit' of a scale of measurement. To appreciate such 'old thing[s]' the connoisseur must engage in acts of comparison with something that is not finally there. Just this kind of comparability attends much of Hemingway's writing. The famous favoured adjectives, 'good', 'fine' and 'nice', are comparative terms, depending upon the bad, not so fine and nasty that they imply. 'More' and 'less' shadow each usage with a readiness to compare that raises equivalence to a degree that has the quality of cardinal numbers. Within the opening four paragraphs of chapter 10 of *The Sun Also Rises* we are told that Bayonne is 'a nice town', with 'a nice cathedral, nice and dim'; 'nice' is not co-terminous with being 'a very good example of' – a phrase which, since it belongs to

Cohn, is presumably of a different status from the 'pretty good' applied to a rod, or the 'good look' given to 'some lovely gardens'. If one wished to compute the comparative goodness of 'good', one would have to take as a mean the untranslatable 'Buen hombre', a rare articulation from the largely silent speech of *aficion* (p. 152). Such adjectives are finally and conspicuously vacuous. With nothing to define, save a relationship of greater than or smaller than or equal to, Hemingway's comparatives give an impression of mathematical reasoning.

The effect of quantification is to colour the entire text. In *The Sun Also Rises* Romero's style is a standard of measurement: the messes made by Cohn and the manner of Jake's cleaning up, along with 'aficion', drinking, talking, the use of a menu, fighting, fishing and the words of the book itself, are valued in terms of the 'templed' peak of Romero's cape. Indeed, the novel could be read as an anthology of styles in transit towards a missing measure – a reading that is affirmed by Hemingway's own account of his writing methods during the twenties.

> But sometimes when I was starting a new story and could not get it going, I would sit in front of the fire and squeeze the peel of little oranges into the edge of the flame and watch the sputter of the blue that they made. I would stand and look out over the roofs of Paris and think, 'Do not worry. You have always written before and you will write now. All you have to do is write one true sentence. Write the truest sentence you know.' So finally I would write one true sentence, and then go on from there. It was easy then because there was always one true sentence that I knew or had seen or had heard someone say. If I started to write elaborately, or like someone introducing or presenting something, I found that I could cut the scroll-work or ornament out and throw it away and start with the first true simple declarative sentence I had written.[48]

Hemingway revives his imagination by setting it in competition with itself. Initially, he considers styles for artistic blockage: how to sit, where to stand, the translation of orange peelings into objects for an imagistic exercise are a prelude to the recovery of 'one true sentence', a notion that prompts the reader to compete with the writer in his method. Each sentence in each fiction is made potentially comparable to every other sentence. The reader is involved in considerable cancellation as she pares the text away. Chances that the sentence will be discovered are, however, thin, since Hemingway's emphasis on the writer as he who knows what to omit, places the perfect sentence somewhere in the fifth dimension:

> How far prose can be carried if anyone is serious enough and has luck. There is a fourth and fifth dimension that can be gotten . . . It is a prose that has never been written. But it can be written, without tricks and without cheating. With nothing that will go bad afterwards.[49]

Just as Romero has 'the old thing' against which to measure his work, so Hemingway has the missing 'fifth dimension': these are abstractions that are objectified through the activities of fighting or writing in a certain way, and yet abstractions that live in their actualizations as an immutable state that has yet to be achieved – the truest sentence, the oldest thing, the notion of Value itself. Again, I am reminded of Léger in Paris:

> A while ago, a drink cost three sous. Today it costs three francs. Every object has become valuable in itself. There is no more waste.
> A nail, a stub of candle, a shoelace can cost a man's life or a regiment's. In contemporary life, if one looks twice, and this is an admirable thing to do, *there is no longer anything of negligible value.* Everything counts, everything competes, and the scale of ordinary and conventional values is overturned . . . The valuable man, the valuable object, the valuable machine ruthlessly assume their natural hierarchy. Contemporary life is the state of war – that's why I profoundly admire my epoch. It is hard and sharp, but with its immense senses it sees clearly and always wants to see more clearly . . . Too bad for those with weak eyes.[50]

Léger alludes to the trenches as though to minor skirmishes prior to the major engagement in the arcades. For him the great war is a price war and it makes his epoch admirable. 'Every object has become valuable in itself' because, ironically, it discovers its value outside itself, in a series of comparisons with more competitively priced versions of what it has to offer. Nails defeat nails while shoelaces struggle among themselves. To look at such things is always and necessarily to look twice. Léger's 'senses' grow 'hard', 'sharp' and 'immense' in direct proportion to their education on the open market, savagely developed. Money is the implied optic that allows him to see for miles, since through money (at least within the logic of exchange) all things may be seen, compared and evaluated. That this should be deemed synonymous with "clarity" indicates a myopia characteristic of the imagist moment within modernism. What F.S. Flint's hygienist dictat – 'Direct treatment of the "thing", whether subjective or objective'[51] – misses is the state of acute competition which Léger and Hemingway find characteristic of these 'things' so seemingly bereft of 'ideas'.[52]

Haug provides a useful economic gloss on Léger's look, and on the mysterious measure latent in Hemingway's words and things:

> It is crucial for the exchange value standpoint's relation to its objects that, despite the sensual differentiation of an object, attention is constantly focused on the quantitative uniformity of each value. From this standpoint every object is potentially a substitute for another, or for the object of currency which stands for all others – money. Every sensual characteristic and all material independence has always already been annihilated.[53]

Pushed to its logical extreme, objects (as such) cease to be sensual because they have become excuses or opportunities for exchange value, while the essence of exchange (Value) takes on a dazzling sensuality (the money fetish):

> If the relationship between needs and objects is broken, the latter are rendered interchangeable and non sensual, being only disguises for exchange values; while on the other side the sensualization of the non sensual occurs, since exchange value has taken on its own individual shape, essentially independent and qualitatively different.[54]

Exchange value is the secret sharer that ghosts Hemingway's prose, rendering its sensualities mere shadows of their best, yet 'essentially independent', forms. Consequently, *The Sun Also Rises*, like the average Hemingway sentence, stands in for a 'qualitatively different' version of itself that is missing, and may be said to be in its entirety a metaphor. The idea is not as fanciful as it may sound; it is, after all, a common response among readers to protest that of course 'Big Two-Hearted River' is about trout fishing, and something else, even as 'Cat in the rain' means what it says, but implies more. Most typically, the literal in Hemingway is both unquestionably literal and uncomfortably metaphoric: the instability resembles that described by Marx in his account of the object's transition from use to exchange: 'Not an atom of matter enters into the objectivity of commodities as values; in this it is the direct opposite of the coarsely sensuous objectivity of commodities as physical objectives.'[55]

"Price" guarantees that the 'objectivity' of the commodity form differs from the coarse 'objectivity' of the object. An item entering the process of circulation for the purpose of exchange takes on the discrete quality of its tag. The idea is perhaps best approached through the Marxist alphabet for circulation. In a barter economy money is a mere facilitator (C–M–C). Under capital, however, money is alchemical; ceasing to be a temporary equivalent it takes on the power of transformation in and of itself ($M-C-M^1$), where M^1 is the greater return expected by the capitalist for the labour of investing. High–credit economies, such as that of the USA during the twenties, produce money that begets money. As Marx puts it:

> In simple circulation, C–M–C, the value of commodities attained at the most a form independent of their use-values, i.e., the form of money; but that same value now in the circulation [M–C–M, or the circulation] of capital, suddenly presents itself as an independent substance, endowed with a motion of its own, passing through a life-process of its own, in which money and commodities are mere forms which it assumes and casts off in turn. Nay, more: instead of simply representing the relations of commodities, it enters now, so to say, into private relations with itself.[56]

Under full capitalism all things are metaphoric: they are what they are used for but they are also what they cost. In an economy experiencing a massive expansion of abstract labour, with its attendant translation of social relations into wage relations, things and persons take on the form of their prevalent sociability – the price mechanism. "Price" subordinates "use", even as American capital employs consumer satisfaction to contain worker dissatisfaction.

If we have the price, then our "wish" is fulfilled through the materialization of our "desire". Price short-circuits labour, since thinking about having the price makes work a mere means to an end, where that end is "wish". Hemingway's things and persons are all, to greater or lesser degree, cast in the ideal form of 'value' – matter made mainly from wish and desire. Born of a culture oriented towards production, exchange and consumption, and of an economy preoccupied with countering overproduction through pitching the ideal product at the perfect price (reduced circulation time), Hemingway's objects quite literally stand for their better selves, which is to say that they stand (all unknowingly) for their own realization within the commercial form.

It must be stressed that exchange abstraction is not an idea, but 'a structure of feeling'.[57] It is comforting to present the price as just so much wrapping through which the taste of trout or the frisson at the bull's death remains unimpaired. However, as 'the big sell' becomes 'synonymous with American civilisation',[58] the particularities of life are turned into an opportunity for monetary exchange, and their content becomes its form. As the Lynds note of 'getting a living' in the twenties: 'This whole complex of doing day after day fortuitously assigned things, chiefly at the behest of other people, has in the main to be strained through a pecuniary sieve before it assumes vital meaning.'[59]

And yet Hemingway goes back to the trout streams and the bullrings, insisting that 'You've got to see it, feel it, smell it, hear it',[60] protesting the difficulties of putting down 'what really happened in action'.[61] But, even as he confidently asserts a programme for objectivity, he at times glimpses – tentatively – the history that has produced his urge to be objective. There is much talk in the criticism of a neutral style, of prose imagism and the 'objective correlative'. However, discussion is scant on why a language of concrete nouns, ambulatory verbs, prepositions and precious little else wherever possible should appeal in the first place.[62]

Writing in 1919, Eliot proposes that interior states can be externalized as formulaic objects. Eliot's objectivity is symptomatic of a more general problem:

> The only way of expressing emotion in the form of art is by finding an 'objective correlative'; in other words, a set of objects, a situation, a chain of

> events which shall be the formula of that *particular* emotion; such that when the
> external facts, which must terminate in sensory experience are given, the
> emotion is immediately evoked.[63]

The claim is preposterous, but partially convincing to a culture whose
members are increasingly encouraged to treat themselves as objects and
to pleasure themselves through objects. Take

> Arms that are braceleted and white and bare
> (But in the lamplight, downed with light brown hair!)[64]

Depending upon one's cosmetic-politics, the undepilated arm is more or
less attractive. Immaculately mimed, its expressive precision is nil. What
Eliot has produced is an overpowering object freighted with an aura of
umplumbable depths. Hemingway's icebergs are similarly engineered:

> Brett did not turn up, so about quarter to six I went down to the bar and had a
> Jack Rose with George the barman. Brett had not been in the bar either, and so
> I looked for her upstairs on my way out, and took a taxi to the Café Select.
> Crossing the Seine I saw a string of barges being towed empty down the
> current, riding high, the bargemen at the sweeps as they came towards the
> bridge. The river looked nice. It was always pleasant crossing bridges in Paris.
>
> (*The Sun Also Rises*, p. 50)

Troubled, Jake is liable to distract himself with things, which *can* be read
as correlative to his mood: the barges are his way of trying 'not to think
about it' (p. 39) – but not to think about what? Unpunctuality, Brett,
Brett's sexuality, the wound, the war, *nada* . . .? We are aware that Jake is
waving, he tells us as much, having his taxi round 'the statue of the
inventor of semaphore doing the same'. His code is, however,
unreadable because it consists of self-censoring objects, inflated by their
duty to reveal the pressure of that which they busily conceal. Whatever
troubles Jake, has been brought from below (from some interior) only
insofar as it implies a below to bring it from. At this point it is customary
to appeal to the subconscious or to the deep experience of war. Philip
Young has charted Hemingway's entire career in terms of the injury on
the night of 8 July 1918: the degree to which the different width of the
river at the site of wounding does or does not return is the degree to
which the text is charged with repressed pain.[65] However, the pattern of
expression through repression is at least as amenable to interpretation via
the more general cultural form of commodity production.

It is undeniable that Hemingway's body was a perambulating
museum of violence. Where and whenever possible he sought wars, and
converted anything from Parisian café tables to obstetrics into armed
struggle. It is also the case that the hunt for 'the maximum of exposure'
(p. 194) and its attendant 'purity' (or simplification) may be a response to

an intensely atomized and combative society. Capital production generates its own "depths" – "depths" sustained by the systematic self-deception of those who produce the goods. To work within the capitalist system is to wound oneself and to forget, not the wound, but how the wound was made. 'The iron man' separates the process of labour from the will of the producers, for whom that which they make seems 'other', something belonging to a system quite beyond them. Alienation is most obvious for the worker, but applies equally to the salariat. Those in Taylor's new planning departments, caught between labour and capital, recently promoted from the hand towards the head, yet firmly divorced from the owners, may well have experienced themselves as little more than a fragment within production – scheduling, coordinating and rewarded (as were the workers) with items of consumption that gratified individuals while disappointing their social needs.

I have schematized the separation of the process of production from the will of the producers to point a paradox: social damage on this scale (quasi-military) can be achieved only with the compliance of the damaged. In return for their loss of will the producers receive 'autonomous individualism', a phenomenal form which appears to 'free' them from structural domination, while trivializing that freedom except as a means to reproduce dependency through consumption. The phrase 'autonomous individualism' derives from the work of Richard Lichtman, who argues that such selfhood is necessarily damaged in that its desires 'are continually more standardized through commodities':

> Under capitalism, need is continually transformed into 'needness'. Since desire is more and more satisfied through commodities, we find ourselves required to barter and purchase the entities or techniques that are necessary to our gratification. On the one hand we become instruments of our own self manipulation. On the other, we become dependent upon 'skilled experts' for the provision of culture, 'commonsense', entertainment, pleasure in sport or sexual intimacy . . . And since the purpose of this commodity production is to exploit us for commerical gain, we quite reasonably become suspicious of the commodities we depend on and eventually, of commoditized needs themselves.[66]

Suspicion is inherent in the gratification that attends the surrender of one will (the will to sociability) and the taking up of another (the will to isolate satisfaction). Encouraged to exercise their wills in the market-place, consumers are likely to sense that what is on offer is a debased form of authority (a will-less will). Customers may always be right in the aphorism, but their wills seem divorced from participation in real choices. Faced with a shrinkage of social power, those who buy are driven anxiously back to private remedies. Arguably, the market insistence that selves be realized through isolated consumption narrows what it is to be human, leaving consumers in pursuit of an imperative that wounds as it pleases. My description is diagrammatic;[67] however, in order to approach the perceptual habits of Hemingway's expatriates, for whom avoidance of social complexity is a reflex, I feel justified in offering a sketch of structural determinations which reduces individuals, temporarily, to economic categories.

The characters themselves offer me my lead: Cohn refers to Jake as his 'tennis friend' (p. 11); the mode of designation could be generalized – with Bill as Jake's "drinking friend", Brett as the "sexual friend", Harris as a "fishing friend" – even as Brett takes Romero as "phallus" and Mike as "title". It is sometimes difficult to distinguish between these characters, because Hemingway equates them in his tendency to be interested in "character" as, "he/she who bears and would exchange a skill". As in the marketplace:

> insofar as the commodity of labour is conceived of only as exchange value, and the relation in which the various commodities are brought into connection with one another is conceived as the exchange of these exchange values with one another, as their equation, then the individuals, the subjects between whom this process goes on, are simply and only conceived of as exchangers. As far as the formal character is concerned, there is absolutely no distinction between them.[68]

The Paris of *The Sun Also Rises* is very much a market. Scott Donaldson points out that 'Hemingway reveals much more about his characters' financial conditions and spending habits than about their appearance.'[69] But critical responsibility goes beyond counting how often specific sums of money are mentioned, or proclaiming that, 'financial soundness mirrors moral strength'.[70] Hemingway's expatriates do live in a world dominated by price and credit: bankers' orders from home, inflated by a high dollar, make them for Cowley 'parasites of exchange'.[71] However, if one generalizes their context, they become both 'parasites' *and* ambassadors. To schematize my earlier account of 'dollar diplomacy' – the United States emerged from the war with a great capital surplus and owning much of the world's gold. To sell abroad it had to transfer wealth to potential buyers. From 1921 the government encouraged private overseas loans as a way of recycling cash for the purchase of US exports. As a result, between 1924 and 1929, 80 per cent of the capital borrowed by German credit institutions came from American banks. Arguably, central US finance houses tried to function as an international bank in order to engineer an integrated global economy: 'granting loans to countries that followed their stabilization procedures, selling and buying foreign exchange to influence gold movements and exchange rates, and trying to coordinate the domestic monetary strategies of other countries'.[72]

Like their nation, Hemingway's expatriates 'follow the dollar',[73] and therefore experience one cultural imperative in an intense and exclusive form. The strongest statement of this line would involve an analogy between the gold standard and the ubiquity of Hemingwayese. In New York, Cowley remembers:

> being taken to an unfamiliar saloon – it was the winter of 1925–26 – and finding that the back room was full of young writers and their wives just home from Paris. They were all telling stories about Hemingway, whose first book had just appeared, they were talking in what I afterward came to recognize as the Hemingway dialect – tough, matter-of-fact and confidential.[74]

Between 1925 and 1928 the United States persuaded most European countries back on to gold, so that US international investment might benefit from a single measure. Hemingway is golden-tongued; his tones are measured and standardized, he quantifies and objectifies. The heroes of the decade declare a 'separate peace' from virtually everything except a single style of speech. Their linguistic habit allows Nick Adams, Jake Barnes and Frederick Henry to amass less memory and fewer connections than Faulkner's Benjy Compson. Consequently their exposure to the overt and hidden forms of the decade's central experience – money as standard – is uncluttered by other determinants. Whether or not Hemingway knows it, their individuality is easily and aptly reduced to economic categories. Just as they reproduce their own interiors objectively, so the reader may perceive in that self-objectifica-tion the workings of exchange value. Self-composition as still-life involves suppressions on a par with those created by the extension of abstract labour. And it is here, in the cultural fact of forgotten but resurgent social complexity, that the true source of the famed 'disquiet'[75] or wound is to be found.

The wound is initially a war wound, but its repeated and sexual form derives conclusively from the market. Witness Frederick Henry during the final stages of the retreat from Caporetto. Apprehended at the river Tagliamento by his own Italian officers, who suspect his accent, he is accused of being a German spy. He escapes, swims the river, jumps a train and unsurprisingly declares a separate peace. The manner of the declaration is surprising: alone, under the tarpaulin of a gun transporter, he dismembers himself, casting away body parts that he deems to be not his:[76] one knee belongs to the surgeon, Valentini, who has 'done a fine job . . . It was his knee alright'; the other is Henry's, along with the head and 'the inside of the belly'. However, proprietorial claims are insecure, since the belly 'turn[s] over on itself' and the head, being 'not to think with', denies its bearer rights of use. Ownership is marked as altogether ambivalent by the shiftiness of the possessive pronoun: 'my' gives way to 'his' only to become 'your' in a progression that signals dismemberment as a general condition. The passage continues with an extended simile likening an officer's loss of troops in battle to stock depletion during a store fire. Henry explains his own circumstance through that of the hypothetical salesman:

> You had no more obligation. If they shot floorwalkers after a fire in the department store because they spoke with an accent they had always had, then certainly the floorwalkers would not be expected to return when the store opened again for business. They might seek other employment; if there was any other employment and the police did not get them.[77]

The simile is explicit, war is transferred from the Italian front to a department store. Hemingway's route to Léger's insight is intriguing; lying on the car-floor, Henry tries not to remember Catherine, but even as he distracts himself with objects (the speed and sound of the wagon, light on canvas, the floor itself), he finds himself married to the objects, 'and . . . lying with Catherine on the floor of the car. Hard as the floor of the car to lie not thinking only feeling . . .'[78] The movement of the rolling-stock simulates sexual motion and the floor of the car elicits tumescence – the phrase, 'hard as the floor of the car' censors what it states ('hard' can mean both 'difficult' and 'rigid'). Henry, effectively, takes the 'hard floor for a wife',[79] which turns floorwalking into a second instance of muted confession. Having given parts of his body away, he learns that objects re-embody him, or, to be more explicit, that he is re-membered by things. In which case the sudden appearance of a department store is explicable. A soldier resembles a floorwalker insofar as both take their function from external objects (be they guns or stock). Furthermore, damage to those objects puts their functionaries at risk. Henry challenges the elision between his body and things by making the salesman in his simile party to a bad contract; the management may insist that, since the floorwalker is an extension of his goods, their destruction should be his death – the floorwalker demurs, and seeks employment elsewhere. There is no suggestion that he goes to find a space beyond the market, all he can hope for is a better contract. Likewise, subjected to irrational decisions by military managers, Henry quits, and departs for Switzerland where he will find that life is conducted equably on a monetary basis.

The analogy between business and war is sustained, indeed its length may cause readers to forget the early 'as' which identifies the species of comparison. As simile strays towards metaphor, so the assertion 'A is like B' weakens, inclining to the entirely different assertion 'A is B'. Robbe-

Grillet's observation that 'metaphor is never an innocent figure of speech' is pertinent; he adds, 'Metaphor, which is supposed merely to express a straight-forward comparison, in fact introduces a subterranean communication, a sympathetic (or antipathetic) modification, which is its real *raison d'être*.'[80] By reading his physical situation through the stencil of a wage contract in the service industry, Henry sets up a 'subterranean communication' between two kinds of competition. For a moment I shall render the subterranean overt; by reducing the tension between the terms of the comparison and privileging business over war, one can make Henry's argument run as follows: he who enters an agreement to labour allocates his body parts to someone else; he recognizes that the contract shall transcend prior affiliations (in this instance, to nations); a contractor is at liberty to take his labour to the best market (Switzerland), and he may incidentally appreciate that by selling himself, in order to consume, he complies in his own reification (which is to say, in department stores, whether buying or selling, we wound ourselves). My reading works against the grain of the genre to trace the market rather than the military logic latent in a figure of speech with which I have openly tampered. I would defend myself by pointing out that the comparison belongs to Henry, and by noting its date. *A Farewell to Arms* appeared in September 1929, almost exactly a month before the Great Crash and over a decade after the Great War, time enough for Hemingway to recognize that wounds and their attendant disquiet may have several sources.

Whatever their origin the wounds cluster around the groin. Nick is hit in the spine, Jake is sexually but unspecifically damaged, Frederick Henry is wounded in the leg. Perhaps the extreme type for all three is the unnamed castrato in 'God rest you merry, gentlemen' (1933); the youth, refused medical assistance, operates on himself and misguidedly removes the member while leaving the means. Such phallic ambivalence arises from an absolute contradiction between what capitalist production does to the individual and what bourgeois ideology claims for the maimed and individualized self. Capital wounds what the ideology would heal with its notion of 'autonomous individualism'; as I have argued, the destruction of the social will is veiled by the offer of a private and restorative will. Acceptance authenticates the senses as the locus of all satisfaction, while at the same time modifying the body:

> in the commodity age, need as a purely physical and material impulse (as something 'natural') has given way to a structure of artificial stimuli, artificial longings, such that it is no longer possible to separate the true from the false, the primary from the luxury satisfaction in them.[81]

In a culture where the human activities of sociability and labour are alienated, the alternative satisfactions of eating, sleeping and procreating become compulsory. In Hemingway's terms, seeing, feeling, smelling and hearing for oneself grow obsessional. In the fiction, as in the culture, the refuge of the private body turns tyrannical. Put tersely, for Hemingway, as for his culture, primitivism replaces reciprocity, and animal functions (infinitely refined) are presented as humanity's last and only tango. The double slippage of the collective into the private and of the private into the physical, is well caught by an account of morality offered early in *Death in the Afternoon*: 'So far, about morals, I know only what is moral is what you feel good after and what is immoral is what you feel bad after.'[82] A third slippage is implied: Hemingway goes to the bullring to see death, exclusively male death, and potentially male death at a moment of perfection (note how closely Romero works to the bull). Again, for me, the roots of the pathology are economic: Paul Baran argues that 'people steeped in the culture of monopoly capitalism do not want what they need and do not need what they want';[83] his point being that, driven back to 'artificial longings', the consumers' only way out may be to want not to need. The slippages proceed apace, with death as the final and compensatory pleasure.

The logic of the progression is encapsulated in the story 'A pursuit race' (1927). William Campbell, 'advance man'[84] for a burlesque show, is finally 'caught' by the burlesque that he is paid to advertise. The story is set in a Kansas City hotel bedroom. Campbell is drunk in bed; Turner, his manager, attempts to persuade him to take 'a cure' and fails. He leaves, but Campbell is not left alone; alcohol and heroin have altered the advance man's perceptions, he is attended by a 'wolf' at the door, and a sheet that doubles as a mistress. The sheet elicits caresses from lips, tongue and eyelashes, so that when Turner sits on the bed, Campbell senses a rival and declares his love, 'I just started to love this sheet.'[85] Given that the lover declines to rise from his bed and be cured of his *amour fou*, it would seem that his sheet will eventually be his shroud: in which case, the line of 'small blue circles around tiny dark blue punctures',[86] from wrist to elbow, through which he ensures the sheet's constancy, may be seen as the making of a good death. At first glance the title, 'A pursuit race', sets the story in the context of a sport which Hemingway believed to be merely 'sportif',[87] (no more than a commercial exercise); however, by the end of the story, not only has Campbell's pursuit changed, but the roles have shifted. Initially he was the front rider, the burlesque pursued him: alone in bed, he pursues, and the front rider is his own death. Campbell's need for the sheet is, in the last instance, a need not to need, whose context is both unmistakably commercial and wholly male. The sheet is feminized, but only as a prop to lonely pleasure.

'Feel[ing] good' for Hemingway happens most often during the predominantly male activities of fishing, hunting, bullfighting and war: in each instance pain, or its possibility, attends pleasure, and pleasure is very much a matter of technical mastery (be it of rod, pen or gun). These are the commonplaces of Hemingway criticism; what is more often missed can be reached by slightly re-inflecting the basic premise, 'to feel good is to risk a wound', so that the statement reads 'pleasure involves self-mutilation'. Since the pleasurable places are so exclusively male, the focus of the happy wound is necessarily phallic. However, the phallus here is not a simple sign of male sexuality; rather, it is the endangered locus of a will to quasi-eroticized technical perfection. Where pleasure is at once intimately physical, risky and 'artificial', that maleness which results from "feeling good" is deeply ambivalent.

The male mark in Hemingway is often asserted even as it is erased, perhaps because in that sign is focussed the whole problem of cultural dismemberment as re-memberment. Once the path to quasi-phallic authority is recognized as the path to 'autonomous individualism', then a species of castration is to be expected, since the social will is to be cut away in favour of a narrowed physicality. Hemingway feels the wound, but only as an idea coming into existence, not as a more general critique. Nonetheless, his heroes of the twenties, like their culture, are destined simultaneously to have not and to have: the phallus removed or threatened produces a compensatory and unsettled phallus. It could be objected that in 'Fathers and sons' (1933) Nick Adams talks to a child that he has engendered, but the boy might as well be adopted for all that we are told about his conception and upbringing.[88] The capacity to inseminate blights Frederick Henry who, though happiest in bed, views parenthood as a biological trap.[89] His worst fears are endorsed by the manner of Catherine's death; the child that kills her is self-ensnared – its umbilicus ties an internal noose. Hemingway's deep logic of the scrotum wins through: male potency (or phallic individualism) is finally and for the most part a deathly and yet necessary delusion.

Jake Barnes has only to suffer the fact, he cannot inflict it on others. Yet the plot of *The Sun Also Rises* involves a second castration that is arguably self-inflicted. Incapable of sexual release, Jake has a compensatory 'passion' – 'aficion means passion' (p. 152). The site of that satisfaction is male and exclusive; its geographical location is in Montoya's hotel and its physical embodiment is Romero. Yet, knowing Brett's sexual proclivities and the carelessness of her entourage, Jake signs her in and introduces her to Romero. She achieves a good deal more than the bull's ears, but leaves those particular laurels among cigarette butts at the back of her hotel-room drawer. Montoya returns the ears to Jake who, given his wound, is incapable of wearing horns. Jake must have been aware that the trip to Pamplona would *de*vitalize. Brett and Mike can only treat the likes of Montoya and Romero as functionaries; Mike borrows money from the hotelier and Brett borrows the bullfighter's potency. Jake makes it happen and knows it, so that when Cohn accuses him of pimping, Jake takes the beating almost with relief. His passivity before Cohn's aggression signals his recognition that he is what Cohn implies, a commercial agent. In which case, Pamplona is a tourist trap and Romero one of the goods on offer. On the day after the beating, and in the same chapter, Jake will sympathize with a particular waiter for whom the accidental death of a peasant in the bull-run is 'No fun' (p. 227). The observation leads him to identify the dead man, to visit Pamplona's railway station for the departure of the coffin, and to pursue the pedigree of the offending bull. The bull's ears prove to be those 'shoved' by Brett 'far back in the drawer of the bed-table' in the Hotel Montoya (p. 228). The translation of an object – the ears – into a clue, involves Jake in entirely uncharacteristic detective work; instead of leaving out, he fills in, and does so because of a double affinity with a waiter and a peasant. Seen from below, the pleasures of the tourist, so intimately involved with his own identity, are merely dangerous litter. After such self-knowledge there is little left to forgive. Cohn's term 'pimp' (p. 219) refers to a male who profits from sexual exchange; Jake has monetarized much more than sexuality – the effect of his punishment is likewise more general:

> Walking across the square to the hotel everything looked new and changed. I had never seen the trees before. I had never seen the flagpoles before, nor the front of the theatre. It was all different. I felt as I felt once coming home from an out-of-town football game. I was carrying a suitcase with my football things in it, and I walked up the street from the station in the town I had lived in all my life and it was all new. They were raking the lawns and burning leaves in the road, and I stopped for a long time and watched. It was all strange. Then I went on, and my feet seemed to be a long way off, and everything seemed to come from a long way off, and I could hear my feet walking a great distance away. I had been kicked in the head early in the game. It was like that crossing the square. It was like that going up the stairs in the hotel. Going up the stairs took a long time, and I had the feeling that I was carrying my suitcase. (p. 160)

When Cohn beat Romero, the bullfighter kept standing up: Jake goes down and stays down. Having been knocked unconscious, he recovers only to experience temporary body-loss and perceptual incoherence on a scale tantamount to a failure of his world. Cohn has affected a double amputation: his charge exposes Romero as Jake's surrogate phallus, and his blows incapacitate Jake's senses. Without the facility to generate objective correlatives the victim faces the unrepressed contents of his unease. It is symptomatic that having curtailed Jake's perceptual and phallic means to 'individualism', Hemingway, the master of omission, cannot countenance inclusion. At the end of his tether, Jake has that tether celebrated. The pure but distorted surfaces and the secondary will through which he realizes his life have been priced; nonetheless they are restored with their distortions declared positive and natural. Jake's social estrangement induces a revaluing of exactly that which has been challenged: the impaired perception of the dismembered and atomized 'individual' is read as exceptional clarity ('It was all different') so that the wound itself becomes the means to singularity. Jake, at this point, is simultaneously most individualized (he is the "artist" who "makes strange" and therefore recovers the world[90]) *and* most damaged.

It is difficult to assess the extent to which Jake Barnes's self-dismemberment constitutes a critique of the will-less will (and therefore of 'autonomous individualism'). His recovery so mystifies the second wound that only archaeologists of the lower reaches of putative icebergs may hope for access to the unopened 'suitcase'. The contradiction remains uncontradictory for Hemingway because the very poverty of cultural determinants that enables him impeccably to enact commodification also impedes a more sustainedly complex relation of resistance to that commodification. His heroes suffer 'brilliantly',[91] but their clarity is finally as risky as their sexuality. The famed 'real thing' is a famous ideological effect: the 'things' are 'actual' only insofar as they materialize, and therefore enable a form of forgetting. By treating all reality as war, Hemingway creates real appearances[92] of intense and narrow sensuality which veil the conditions of their own generation. He can go this far because he recognizes the pervasiveness of 'objectivity' and 'indifference' in his culture, but he misrecognizes the source of that ubiquity. The ground rules of capital are militarized for Hemingway, who reads them as the militant facts of life – to be celebrated as means to a badge of courage. However, the war hangover is an excuse, releasing him from an exploration of the 'disquiet' that ghosts his own sense system. Nick Adams, Jake Barnes and Frederick Henry compulsively counter anxiety by revaluing objects 'objectively'. They seek to escape their own 'indifference' through a grace with things that is akin to art: by obeying the object they become the form of its life – a still life. To overstate the case: in order to remain satisfactorily human they become objects. Thus the dominant impulse of Hemingway's writing, while it celebrates a world of natural things, essentially reiterates the very market processes which eliminate that nature, thereby extending the system of production that it denies.

IV

There are moments when Hemingway's senses do not turn back from the contradictions that they veil and embody: instead, they become – briefly and haltingly – theoreticians of their own practice. The logic of

Jake's self-spoilure is thereby carried through and beyond a war-torn physicality.

'Hills like white elephants' (1927) is a story about a simile. A young woman likens the 'long . . . white' hills 'across the valley of the Ebro' to 'white elephants'.[93] In that its creator is pregnant and considering an abortion, the analogy cannot be read as a merely felicitous phrasing. Seated at a café table in the Ebro valley, and perhaps prompted by a fortuitous resemblance between the river's name and her own state (Ebro/embryo), she attempts comparisons. The hills are 'long' rather than rounded; in her terms they are not very pregnant and are therefore a metaphor for the early stages of pregnancy. Their beauty is consequently ambiguous; a white elephant is both a rare beast and an unwanted object up for sale, even as her embryo is a singular creation and a disposable item. The network of resemblance is complex, particularly as the woman is using 'hills' both as a metaphor and as the first term of a simile. The double form of this analogy dramatizes her confusion, since metaphor and simile constitute different forms of making sense of the world:

> I would argue that the distinction between simile and metaphor is fundamental. A simile is a mere rhetorical device. It likens something to something else. By establishing similarities, it does not create a new image but on the contrary, keeps the separate elements, no matter how much they are alike, firmly apart. If my love is *like* a red rose, then my love and the red rose are similar but separate. If, however, in genuine metaphor, my love is a red rose, the two images become fused and a new, third image is created by a process which is a mixture of invention and discovery.[94]

A metaphor which declares pregnancy to be the fertile slopes of a valley is traditionally pastoral; it assumes an organic link between human and non-human nature in order to assure us of our naturalness. However, the simile which likens that comforting image to the contradictory possibilities of 'white elephants' is disruptive, to say the least. It begs the question, 'Is bountiful nature a place of rare beauty, or can it be marketed?'

The potential father will have none of it. He neither unpacks the metaphor nor hears the confused anxiety of the simile:

> The girl was looking off at the line of hills. They were white in the sun and the country was brown and dry.
> 'They look like white elephants', she said.
> 'I've never seen one.' The man drank his beer. (p. 249)

His retreat to the literal is initially effective: brow-beaten, the woman presents her suggestive analogy as a picturesque trope worthy of paraphrase: 'They're lovely hills', she said. 'They don't really look like white elephants. I just meant the colouring of their skin through the trees' (p. 250). 'Their' refers to white elephants (since hills do not have 'skins'); however, having bowed to male literalism, the woman returns to her metaphor. Had she remarked, 'I just meant the colouring of their skin', paraphrase would have been achieved. By adding, 'through the trees', she grants syntactical leeway to the possessive pronoun, making 'their' refer simultaneously to elephants (colour) and to hills (seen through trees) – so valley forestation collapses back into animal pigmentation, and the metaphor is restored, albeit in diminutive disguise. Conversation returns to the projected abortion, only for the repressed figure of speech to recur a fourth time as the undeclared focus through which the woman perceives the entirety of her situation:

> The girl stood up and walked to the end of the station. Across, on the other side, were fields of grain and trees along the banks of the Ebro. Far away, beyond the river, were mountains. The shadow of a cloud moved across the field of grain and she saw the river through the trees.
> 'And we could have all this', she said. 'And we could have everything and every day we make it more impossible.'
> 'What did you say?'
> 'I said we could have everything.'
> 'We can have everything.'
> 'No, we can't.'
> 'We can have the whole world.'
> 'No, we can't.'
> 'We can go everywhere.'
> 'No, we can't. It isn't ours any more.'
> 'It's ours.'
> 'No, it isn't. And once they take it away, you never get it back.' (p. 252)

The Ebro valley bears fruit as, from its drier side, the woman links her fertility to that of the grain and the trees. The tone is elegiac, stressing distance; indeed, the pastoral recovery of the Ebro's banks is only possible because of the qualified assumptions latent within her first metaphor. '"And we could have all this", she said.' 'To have' at this point is metaphoric: its two meanings, 'to give birth' and 'to take possession', fuse in a new and redemptive image, balancing Arcadia, tourism and pre-history – the very image that the white elephant simile, in its rare-beast aspect, sought to realize. However, the repeated, disputed and conditional use of the metaphor reduces the verb to one meaning: by the time the man declares, 'We can have the whole world', 'to have' means simply to take possession of. At which point, the woman declares herself dispossessed of metaphor and child alike, 'It isn't ours any more.' The impersonal pronoun has a split referent, referring simultaneously to the embryo that will be aborted and to the world made available to American tourists by a healthy rate of exchange. The two references elide ('it' too is a metaphor) affirming that abortion is a monetary exchange. Fertility and price fuse in a new image, as the harsh impersonality of the woman's pronoun implies that, for her at least, the white elephant simile has come to stand solely for the cheapening of her own fertility and a demise of the natural world into the marketplace.

Both the simile's terms are now apparent and separate. The hills are like white elephants because, like everything else, they have a price. The emphasis within the figure of speech and the title has shifted, moving from metaphor, through simile, to the literal (where the literal is a metaphor for price). The progression is perfectly in accord with Hemingway's aesthetic criteria, and perfectly embarrasses those criteria. Directness, instead of revealing necessary and trustworthy sensations, discovers that matter (in and of itself) no longer exists, other than as a realization of exchange. It follows that when the man repeatedly insists 'You've got to realize' (p. 252) the verb 'to realize' is awkward, particularly in the context of Spanish coinage, where 'four reales' buys two drinks and ensures a pun in which the actual and the monetary exist in difficult parity. The woman may well insist, 'I feel fine', twice during the last line of the story, but her feelings are in no simple way "natural", because luxury has entered the very feel of things, and is part even of the feeling of hurt and loss.

I shy away from the description of her feelings as either genuine or artificial, in that the terms imply the possible existence and recovery of a primary realm of nature and experience outside culture. Such places do exist for Hemingway, but whether located in the Gulf Stream or among the green hills of the Serengeti, they constitute an Arcadian resource that his better writing ignores. Arguably, the choice of 'white elephants' is not unrelated to the author's own dream of an unspoiled African continent, but that longing is only one element in a figure whose development dramatizes the degree to which the natural surfaces of the world are a transparent construction, as are the sensations through which those constructions are approached. The girl's exasperated relation to nature and to her own body has a felt cause in the increasing abstractions of "value". "Artificial" would do scant justice to sensations so subtly historicized.

V

Generally, Hemingway is not so subtle. Even if my argument has established that the account of Hemingway as the champion of phenomenological accuracy is at best partial, I would not wish to substitute a claim for him as a historian of commodity. Rather, I would suggest that, because he trains his senses so finely and writes of them so precisely, he experiences the contradiction that to revel in the surface of things within nature is to revel in their reproduction within exchange. In its extreme form that contradiction becomes a confused revulsion from what is celebrated.

For one who supposedly delights in the feel of things, Hemingway writes frequently of feelings blocked and sensations overworked. Wounds and impaired parts are sufficiently common to suggest that many of Hemingway's characters take at least as much damage as delight from the physical world. Indeed, as has been argued, damage and delight are significantly linked in the careers of Nick Adams, Jake Barnes and Frederick Henry, the major heroes of his twenties fiction. Each has been wounded and yet each is capable of a directness of perception which surpasses that of those around him. The logic which systematically declares the perception of a wounded man acute rather than impaired is intriguing. The wound is extra-sensory for Hemingway because it marks the directness of its bearer's relation to things; a proximity so absolute that the external has broken the skin. The reasoning is well expressed by a caption beneath the photograph of Villalta 'spinning' a bull, 'and if there is no blood on his belly afterwards you ought to get your money back'. The bullfighter who works close can never work close enough; if the horn brushes the belly on the first pass, it must bruise on the second, and so on, to death. But the wounds that result are only superficially inflicted by bulls or wars; their logic is deeply commercial. Machine-produced goods have a never-changing quality: 'The lattice of socialization that enmeshes and assimilates equally objects and the view of them, converts everything encountered into what always was . . . the *doppel gänger* of a model.'[95] The bullfighter halts the receding concreteness of the market place. Like the soldier, his relation to things is necessarily spontaneous and unpremeditated. What he encounters is free of socialization; what he experiences is intensely new − or so the logic would have it. In fact, the newness of exposure-survived grows rapidly old and requires renewal through greater risk. Consequently, what Hemingway intends as a critique of the commercial form turns into a version of that form. What was to redeem the senses merely stimulates them. In the excitement of combat, the celebrant of immediacy becomes the promoter of sensationalism:

> *Maera lay still, his head on his arms, his face in the sand. He felt warm and sticky from the bleeding. Each time he felt the horn coming. Sometimes the bull only bumped him with his head. Once the horn went all the way through him and he felt it go into the sand. Someone had the bull by the tail. They were swearing at him and flopping the capes in his face. Then the bull was gone. Some men picked Maera up and started to run with him towards the barriers through the gate out the passageway around under the grandstand to the infirmary. They laid Maera down on a cot and one of the men*

went out for the doctor. The others stood around. The doctor came running from the corral where he had been sewing up picador horses. He had to stop and wash his hands. There was a great shouting going on in the grandstand overhead. Maera felt everything getting larger and larger and then smaller and smaller. Then it got larger and larger and then smaller and smaller. Then everything commenced to run faster and faster and faster as when they speed up on cinematograph film. Then he was dead.[96]

When Hemingway wrote this he had never seen a bullfight and Maera was alive. But if the vignette does not have the validity of reportage, how should the reader locate the reality of its immediacy? The question is made no easier by the shifting nature of that immediacy. 'Maera lay still', is an observation made from the barriers, while 'Each time he felt the horn coming' is delivered from sand level. Had the fifth sentence read 'Once the horn went through him and into the sand', it, and its paragraph, would have been much simpler: the phrase 'all the way' slows the wounding down, segmenting an act of penetration to heighten its sensation – the assertion that this is what Maera felt is earned. But what follows is light relief: by echoing the aphorism, 'to take the bull by the horns', the sentence 'Someone had the bull by the tail' combines the immediacy of Maera's confusion as to who hinders the bull, with the detachment of a vaudeville joke. The oscillation in tone and distance is sustained, as the men who run with Maera are required to run just too far and too fast and too precisely. The comedy latent in their movement is reiterated in their standing still: 'and one of the men went out for the doctor. The others stood around.' Does the preposition achieve exactly the tight circle of faces that form round Maera's cot, or is it part of the idiomatic phrase, 'to stand around'? A note casual enough to be nervously laughable when struck in the context of a room containing a dying man. The allusion to speeding film even as it accords with Maera's giddy perspective, nudges the entire incident towards a one-reel movie, with a punch-line terse as any caption from a silent black comedy.

My point is not that Hemingway has misjudged his tone, but that the reality of the incident and its parodic after-image are inextricable. Parody attends intensity to guarantee that the transition from physical immediacy to the social form of language shall not constitute its own veiling lattice. Self-parody is a constant presence in the writing because, *as* writing, it is assumed not to be reality, and can only sustain its reality by existing on the edge of self-correction. The double movement is difficult to maintain, and at times Hemingway's fear for the recession of concreteness leads him to parody the content of intensity, even before it is given. So that when he writes of the actual death of Maera, in 'Banal story' (1926), he can write only of failing to write:

So he ate an orange, slowing spitting out the seeds. Outside the snow was turning to rain. Inside, the electric stove seemed to give no heat and rising from his writing-table, he sat down upon the stove. How good it felt! Here, at last, was life.

He reached for another orange. Far away in Paris, Mascart had knocked Danny Frush cuckoo in the second round. Far off in Mesopotamia, twenty-one feet of snow had fallen. Across the world in distant Australia, the English cricketers were sharpening up their wickets. *There* was Romance.

Patrons of the arts and letters have discovered *The Forum* he read. It is the guide, philosopher, and friend of the thinking minority. Prize short stories – will their authors write our best sellers of tomorrow?[97]

'Here' and '*There*' are directional imperatives commanding an intensity that can be obeyed only through sexual innuendo, a form of which Hemingway (in this mood) is fond, since it grants penetrative edge or penetrated frisson to the most inert and inconsequential items. His surroundings lack all edge, and in order to recover oranges, stove, writing-table and rain, he accuses them of being literary and parodies their status as literary events. In Paris the oranges which he ate when unable to write turned into imagist poems; other oranges are banal by comparison, but obviously taste good. While an electric stove is dull, it can be made less so by being used as a prop in a low literary joke against writers who seek "the real" while sitting on it. Parody and self-parody proliferate, deepening the layers of verbal sedimentation. Finally, two pages on and in the last paragraph, Hemingway reaches for that experience with edge – the death of Maera – which originally prompted his desire to write:

And meanwhile, stretched flat on a bed in a darkened room in his house in Triana, Manual Garcia Maera lay with a tube in each lung, drowning with the pneumonia. All the papers in Andalucia devoted special supplements to his death, which had been expected for some days. Men and boys bought full-length coloured pictures of him to remember him by, and lost the picture they had of him in their memories by looking at the lithographs.   (p. 334)

The shift in tone suggests that we have reached 'one true sentence' set among the dross that it exposes. However, special supplements, lithographs and newspaper coverage jeopardize the integrity of that sentence: a medical detail may fulfil a reportorial need to top what has gone before. As shock value, the sentence grows from a literary and parodic impulse at the core of its own immediacy. In fact, the perfect sentence remains unwritten. The opening paragraph begins, 'So he ate an orange', implying that he ate because of something omitted. It would seem that news of the darkened room in Triana made the writer dissatisfied with his surroundings and his work, but as that news, like all news, comes couched in commercial forms, it yields no 'true sentence'.

Hemingway cannot write a straight elegy for Maera because of a contradiction within his experience of the world. The immediacy of the real thing is quite unavailable to him unless guaranteed by a parody of that immediacy. Symptomatically, many of Hemingway's privileged intensities involve sports, and particularly trophy sports. Heads, horns, skins and fish are a common consequence of his moments of 'maximum exposure'. Taxidermy is implicit in much of the fiction. The presence of stuffed beasts is awkward for a writer preoccupied with 'the real thing'. The taxidermist, like the realist, is engaged in intimate interferences productive of unnatural naturalism. He too reproduces the real from the real for gain. His product looks like itself, is tagged and very often stands mounted behind glass. Hemingway is well aware of his secret-sharer. *The Sun Also Rises* contains a number of taxidermy jokes, and features the projected stuffing of several dogs, two race-horses and a horse-drawn cab, not to mention the more conventional bulls' heads and fish. The joke is not a simple one. Like the parodic impulse, it derives from a conviction that authenticity is at risk because concreteness is in laughable retreat from itself.

VI

So much of our popular fiction is little more than stuffed Hemingway. However, the insistence of the master is that the prose take the living creature alive. His heroes are all stylists, many of them writers. In 'The snows of Kilimanjaro' (1935) Harry, a writer, goes to Africa with his wealthy wife to work off the fat of a leisured existence. But Hemingway knows full well that money alters reality, particularly the reality of authors. In *Green Hills of Africa* (1935) he protests that the United States destroys its writers: 'We destroy them in many ways. First, economically. They make money . . . Then our writers when they have made some money increase their standard of living and they are caught . . . and they write slop' (p. 29). This predicament forms the nub of the story. Like Nick Adams before him, Harry focusses on nature through a 'glassy convex surface'. When it really matters, the camera eye fails – as attempts at objectivity always will. The water-buck bolt, Harry scratches himself on a thorn, contracts gangrene and, while waiting to die, contemplates the writing that he failed to write. Carlos Baker has no hesitation in linking this scenario to Hemingway's life:

> Ernest later explained how he had arrived at the conception which governed his story. It all began, said he, with the rich woman who had invited him to tea in New York in April, 1934, and offered to stake him to another safari. Back in Key West that summer he had done some daydreaming about how things would have turned out if he had accepted her offer. The dying writer in the story was an image of himself as he might have been. Might have been, that is, if the temptation to lead the aimless life of the very rich had overcome his integrity as an artist.[98]

It is my contention that Harry is an image of Hemingway as he *is*, and that the 'integrity' of both artists rests firmly in their unknowing adherence to the forms of wealth. Harry protests that he 'traded' his 'talent'[99] for financial security, or, more specifically, that he traded his 'pen' for his sexual prowess. As a lover, his penetrative capacity rose in direct relation to the wealth of the woman penetrated. But despite recognizing the commerciality of his own sexual power, he elects that other creativity – his writing – to authenticity, parodically preserving it well outside the market in the form of silently composed drafts left unwritten on a deathbed. His pen, though remiss, is finally privileged. While he quite literally "goes bad", it draws the "good" out of him as prose. The pieces italicized in the story constitute Harry's alternative biography – they are both his real work and his real life, and in each case they are beyond the reach of his wife and the luxurious existence for which she stands.

However, Harry is deluded; the market is as much in the 'true stuff'[100] as in the marriage: the extracts are as abstracted as Nick's trout or Romero's cape. Each is in competition with the others, for, although they are 'a prose that has never been written' (*Green Hills of Africa*, p. 27), Harry's conviction that 'you might put it all into one paragraph if you could get it right' (p. 74) requires some cancelling down. My own favourite may perhaps stand for the degree and kind of abstraction involved.

> There was a log house, chinked white with mortar, on a hill above the lake. There was a bell on a pole by the door to call people in to meals. Behind the house were fields and behind the fields was the timber. A line of lombardy poplars ran from the house to the dock. Other poplars ran along the point. A road went up to the hills along the edge of the timber and along that road he picked blackberries. Then that log house was burned down and all the guns that had been on deer foot racks above the open fire place were burned and after-wards their barrels, with the lead melted in the magazines, and the stocks burned away, lay out on the heap of ashes that were used to make lye for the big iron soap kettles, and you asked Grandfather if you could have them to play with, and he said, no.
> (p. 74; italics in source)

Numerous prepositions draw details into measurable lines and quantifiable angles, producing a geometrical figure which dispels the particularity of the repeated 'there'. So great is the concern for the relative position of the parts, that no scene emerges. The people in this place are likewise abstracted, becoming functions of syntactical distribution, so that the linear continuity of the road is spoiled by the presence of a blackberry picker: by repeating 'along' Hemingway encourages the extension of a line that he then interrupts ('A road went up to the hills along the edge of the timber and along/that road he picked blackberries'). The interruption is slight; the boy, obeying the logic of the piece, becomes a figure in a snapshot. Caught forever engaged in a task that would summarize "childhood", he is divorced from any specificity of place or time. To know that the house belongs to Grandpa Bacon; that it stands on Walloon Lake, and that the 'you' who speaks is Hemingway (Harry), simply submits these particularities to the more powerful process of abstraction. Biography, whether Hemingway's or Harry's, is another resource for conversion to a form that has all the marks of shop-window stillness.

> The pronouncement . . . that memories are the only possessions which no-one can take from us, belongs in the storehouse of impotently sentimental consolation that the subject, resignedly withdrawing into inwardness, would like to believe the very fulfilment that he has given up. In setting up his own archives, the subject seizes his own stock of experience as property so making it something wholly external to himself.[101]

In cheering himself up with such fragments Harry sells his past back to himself. Such nostalgia is a form of retreat most apparent in the marketplace, where commodities exist in an intimate relation with parody. As forms of money their substance expresses that value to which there is 'not an atom of matter': theirs is a dubious solidity. Further, as the diminished double, both of themselves when new and of the general model from which they stem, their authenticity is constantly devalued. Production works at such devaluation. Rapid changes in style, engineered to maintain purchasing levels, ensure that the commodities of yesterday are ridiculed and even destroyed by those who possess the commodities of today. The ridicule involves self-damage:

> It was strange, too, wasn't it, that when he fell in love with another woman, that woman should always have more money than the last one? But when he no longer was in love, when he was only lying, as to this woman, now, who had the most money of all, who had all the money that was, who had had a husband and children, who had taken lovers and been dissatisfied with them, and who loved him dearly as a writer, as a man, as a companion and as a proud possession; it was strange that when he did not love her at all and was lying, that he should be able to give her more for her money than when he had really loved. (pp. 66–7)

Harry is a consumer mocking the workings of the market even within his own sensations. Perhaps the closest equivalent to his fragments are old films and old songs: on seeing and hearing them we may feel old. If so, it is because the need for a profitable turn-over in styles has foreshortened our feeling of aging, so that we, who have bought a style and identified ourselves through it, experience a death as the style changes. The experience is ghosted by knowledge in self-parodic forms, since the purchasers who bought feel sold out and experience the play of the market in themselves. Various reactions are possible: a contempt for the old style (even for it as a part of ourselves); a rage at the market (which is in us, and which is self-loathing); or purchase of the old style made new and re-priced by nostalgia (which is to buy our own memory).[102] Whatever the response, the status of commodity, within the structure of feeling that it creates and is created by, indicates the precarious history of things and desires in a reified age.

Hemingway and Harry feel that precariousness without sensing its history, and as a result are intensely bewildered. The critical consensus would have it otherwise, taking the writing of the fragments to be a purgative prelude to the final ascent of Kilimanjaro's 'metaphysical' fastness. The flight is variously read, but it is generally agreed that the snows stand on the better side of a sequence of oppositions that divide the story. Mountain/plain; spirit/body; idealism/materialism; immortality/mortality; cleanliness/decay; permanence/transience; these are some of the dualities usually proffered.[103] But the very notion of opposition and of transition from one side to the other is misguided. Harry does ascend, but only to the ideal form of what he already had (in marriage *and* art). '*Close to the western summit . . .* [of] *the House of God*', clean in its well-lighted space, stands a perfect piece of taxidermy perpetrated by Value on Nature, to the greater glory of exchange abstraction. This may sound like a riddle still more intractable than the relation of the leopard in the epigraph to the story itself. The epigraph is the crucial clue:

> *Kilimanjaro is a snow covered mountain 19,710 feet high, and is said to be the highest mountain in Africa. Its western summit is called the Msai 'Ngàje Ngài,' the House of God. Close to the western summit there is the dried and frozen carcass of a leopard. No one has explained what the leopard was seeking at that altitude.*
>
> (p. 58; italics in source).

At the risk of labouring a point: the leopard is supreme among Hemingway's commercial forms. Set in a shop window 'wide as all the world' (p. 82), it displays a double life. The leopard is a dried carcass that rises statuesque in the imagination of the reader – imposing as a photograph from the *National Geographic*. Like Nick's trout, it is immutable, theological and amnesia inducing. Quite properly, a beast that is the summation of the writer's desire for a certain kind of object will be a perfect and corrective measure for those objects that appear in his prose. But like any ideal it cannot be realized. Harry rises towards the leopard but, as far as we can tell, does not see it. His failure is not surprising; the leopard is beyond the five senses. Indeed, its positioning so close to the House of God makes it less an expression of value than 'Value' itself. The epigraph, like the leopard, like the 'one true sentence', remains on the edge, rather than within, his purview.

The leopard is Hemingway's, not Harry's: it expresses, in perfection, the form of much of his writing. That a dead animal should embody an aesthetic founded on 'the real thing, the sequence of motion and fact', is a contradiction that Hemingway is unwilling to hear. Nor is this surprising. It is just as contradictory that we speak unequivocally of the reality of commodities, when the primary function of such items is to realize a 'value' in which there is 'not an atom of matter'.

3

The Great Gatsby, *glamour on the turn*

I

Theodore MacManus, luminary behind Cadillac advertising, observed that war-time propaganda accustomed Americans to the notion that 'any surface and every surface, and all approaches through the senses' were appropriate to the advertiser.[1] While Hemingway was stipulating truth to things seen, the agencies promoted colour coding; the non-white sheet or towel, inventions of the mid-twenties, translated basics into fashion goods, and taught the eye to recognize obsolescence while appreciating tone as part of an "ensemble" or "look".[2] To see in 1925 was to see through the stencil of commodity.

One upshot of capital's assault on perception is 'capitalist realism',[3] or what Haug calls the 'second skin' of the advertised image: 'perfect', 'disembodied' and drifting 'unencumbered like a multicoloured spirit into every household, preparing the way for the real distribution of commodity'.[4] Haug might be describing Gatsby, whose 'unencumbered' surfaces – car, voice, smile, shirts, suits and mansion – seem to drift directly from 'the nation's advertising showcase',[5] that is from the *Saturday Evening Post*. However, to assume that Gatsby, 'resemble[s] the advertisement of the man',[6] and that is all (in other words to cast him as Robert Redford), is to ignore the narrative structure of the novel. Hemingway's fictions take place in an 'enormous present', whereas *The Great Gatsby* (1925) is premised on an awkward act of recollection. Amnesia, the staple of consumerism, is countered by Nick Carraway's attempts to remember the summer of 1922 from the significant distance of two years. Memory turns a man whose voice sounds like a quick flick 'through a dozen magazines' into the son of a dirt-farmer. As Gatsby's antecedents emerge and are repressed, 'capitalist realism' – that real fantasy – gives way to a form of realism best summarized by Brecht:

> Realistic means: discovering the causal complexes of society/unmasking the prevailing view of things as the view of those who are in power/writing from the standpoint of the class which offers the broadest solutions for the pressing difficulties in which human society is caught up/emphasizing the element of development/making possible the concrete, and making possible abstraction from it.[7]

In order to explore how Fitzgerald unmasks 'the causal complexes' of a consumer society, it is necessary to detail how Nick Carraway remembers.

II

Nick's first encounter with his neighbour establishes a pattern for the narrator's habits of recall. Gatsby indulges in a theatrical autobiography, prefaced by the mimed taking of an oath, and ranging from American childhood to Oxford education. Nick is persuaded, but cannot shake the suspicion that he is being lied to: indeed, an enquiry as to place of birth should have undermined the whole performance:

> 'What part of the Middle West?' I inquired casually.
> 'San Francisco.'
> 'I see.'
> 'My family all died and I came into a good deal of money.'
> His voice was solemn, as if the memory of that sudden extinction of a clan still haunted him. For a moment I suspected that he was pulling my leg, but a glance at him convinced me otherwise. (pp. 65–6)

Does Gatsby *know* where San Francisco is? If he does, his response is an odd gesture. 'Epic theatre is gestural', wrote Walter Benjamin of Brecht. Gatsby, too, is gestural: as Nick Carraway would have it, 'if personality is an unbroken series of successful gestures, then there was something gorgeous about him' (p. 2). Except that Gatsby's gestures are broken, and by Gatsby himself. To 'tell . . . God's truth' he raises his right hand – isn't that taking the truth a little too seriously? When speaking of loss he pauses in the right place; indeed, in a place so right that the addendum 'all dead now' might just be bad acting, not lying. The creator of a criminal network operating bond fraud on a national scale can surely manage better lies than the one about San Francisco?

If Gatsby is acting, to what end does he perform his *unsuccessful* gestures?

> He lifted up the words and nodded at them – with his smile. The smile comprehended Montenegro's troubled history and sympathized with the brave struggles of the Montenegrin people. It appreciated fully the chain of national circumstances which had elicited this tribute from Montenegro's warm little heart.   (pp. 66–7)

Gatsby's smile performs 'sympathetic understanding' in a style of which Brecht's Chinese actors would have approved:

> The [actor's] . . . object is to appear strange and even surprising to the audience. He achieves this by looking strangely at himself and his work. As a result everything put forward by him has a touch of the amazing . . . The coldness comes from the actor's holding himself remote from the character portrayed.[8]

Gatsby holds himself so remote from his character that he can lift up its words and nod at them with a smile that is portable – a facial expression that repeats one which might be found between glossy covers. 'My incredulity was submerged in fascination now', continues Nick, 'it was like skimming hastily through a dozen magazines'. Producing props, like rabbits from a hat, Gatsby displays the outward signs of the performance upon which he is engaged. And yet Nick Carraway, ignoring the self-interruptions, believes him:

> Then it was all true. I saw the skins of tigers flaming in his place on the Grand Canal; I saw him opening a chest of rubies to ease, with their crimson-lighted depths, the gnawings of his broken heart.   (p. 67)

But Nick protests too much. To assert belief Nick performs belief, and he half hears in his own voice the unstable tone of a man cheering himself up with empathy and broken hearts.

There are moments during the conversation when Carraway all but gives in to Gatsby's rhythm, when interruption becomes his own norm. Re-read, the exchange begins to look like a dialogue between Brechtian players in which 'nearly every sentence could be followed by a verdict of the audience, and practically every gesture is submitted to the public's approval'.[9] Writing from the Midwest, Carraway considers Gatsby's phrase 'educated at Oxford'; was it 'swallowed' or 'choked'? What of his own casual enquiry, could it have been casual even then? The narrator almost becomes he who observes himself, and in so doing can no longer completely lose himself in that character 'Nick Carraway'. The discovery that he too is strange, and that his own feelings need watching as they form, builds hesitation into Fitzgerald's narrative. Gatsby has *taught* this narrator not to trust himself. (This is not just Wayne Booth's point that readers should not trust first-person narrators.)

Individual words in Carraway's narrative are alienated from their setting, so that sentences tend to achieve unhappy montage rather than

linear growth. Edges are often and embarrassingly on show. Take 'clan':
'His voice was solemn, as if the memory of that sudden extinction of a
clan still haunted him' (pp. 65–6). The word is inappropriate, though
one can see why Carraway uses it; Gatsby has just spoken of 'ancestors'
and made a significantly aphoristic and endstopped appeal to 'a family
tradition'. 'Clan' is in keeping with the tenor of the dialogue – but was
that tenor ever right? Nick knows better; he too is a clan descendant:

> The Carraways are something of a clan, and we have a tradition that we're
> descended from the Dukes of Buccleuch, but the actual founder of my line was
> my grandfather's brother, who came here in fifty-one, sent a substitute to the
> Civil War, and started the wholesale hardware business that my father carries
> on today.   (pp. 2–3)

'Clan' then makes respectable the little murders from which family
fortunes rise. Nick is quite capable of interrupting Gatsby's usage, to
place it in the context of his own faked genealogy. Indeed, Gatsby's
'solemnity', so like a leg-pull, prompts him to do so. Perhaps Carraway
cannot respond because he has too much to defend. Living in the
Midwest, so far back in the bosom of his family that he tends to
'snobbishly repeat' what his father 'snobbishly suggest[s]' (p. 1), perhaps
now working in the wholesale hardware business, and married to the
woman whose upper lip sweats when she plays tennis (pp. 59–60), he
cannot afford to 'lift' the word 'clan' and 'nod at it with his smile'.
Instead, across the conspicuous interruption of two years[10] and half a
continent, he insists, 'Then it was all true.' Nick can no more sacrifice his
need to believe than he can forget that Gatsby comes from a Midwestern
San Francisco, though the memory is an awkward one for a would-be
biographer.

Before considering why Carraway writes 'a life' that Gatsby does not
deserve, however, the 'San Francisco' remark must be established as
typical, and its 'style' as entirely appropriate to the historical situation in
which Gatsby finds himself. The calculatedly unsuccessful gesture is
difficult to discern when those for whom it is performed wish to see
glamour and to prefix Gatsby with 'Great'. Consequently, readers have
alleged the 'eternally human' in Gatsby's life and have called up a
vocabulary of timeless verities, 'love', 'dream', 'tragedy'.[11] In Gatsby
and Daisy Buchanan a 'universal situation' is discovered, if the
'American Dream' can be spoken of so generically. As Brecht said of
'bourgeois theatre':

> Its story is arranged in such a way that Man with a capital M express[es]
> himself: a man of every period and every colour. All its incidents are just one
> enormous cue and this cue is followed by the eternal response: the inevitable,
> usual, natural, purely human response.[12]

The cues that emanate from Gatsby are, however, cues from a different theatre:

> 'Her voice is full of money', he said suddenly.
>   That was it. I'd never understood before. It was full of money – that was the inexhaustible charm that rose and fell in it, the jingle of it, the cymbals' song of it . . . High in a white palace the king's daughter, the golden girl. . . (p. 120)

Nick has heard and chosen not to listen: his rhythm is melodious, his phrasing assonant, his reference literary – an orchestration of the cash nexus. As a commentary on Gatsby's observation, the whole statement is liable to fall to pieces, with fault lines developing along the ellipses: in the gaps, love meets money and adultery speaks to class – a dialogue in which Nick would rather not participate.

The failure is doubly disappointing in that it is a dialogue that Gatsby wants heard and that Nick is elsewhere capable of hearing. Reporting later on the early courtship he notes:

> She had caught a cold, and it made her voice huskier and more charming than ever, and Gatsby was overwhelmingly aware of the youth and mystery that wealth imprisons and preserves, of the freshness of many clothes, and of Daisy, gleaming like silver, safe and proud above the hot struggles of the poor.
>
>   (pp. 149–50)

The passage is not without its evasions. To whom does the pun belong and is its economic force muted by alliteration? 'Safe' may be rendered so, as Veblen's assertion that 'the leisure class live by the industrial community rather than in it'[13] is deflected into an aesthetic niceness that matches 'cold' with 'hot'. Nonetheless, Nick hears 'silver' as a synonym for coinage. Like 'safe', the word is 'double voiced',[14] uncomfortably aware of another voice alongside, attempting an alternative social inflexion. Nick's lyricism gives way to its own inner polemic and releases Gatsby's resistant voice, reporting directly the surprise of one from the lower orders on being invited into the 'white palace' by 'the golden girl' – 'She thought I knew a lot because I knew different things from her' (p. 150).

By 1922 Gatsby is less shockable: in asking Nick to set up a meeting that will preface the affair, and in requesting the use of Nick's bungalow for his purpose, Gatsby is hiring a pimp to make a 'gonnection'. There is a pay off: Nick is offered 'confidential' information about bonds in a conversation which he sees as 'one of the crises of my life' (p. 83). However, 'because the offer was obviously and tactlessly for a service to be rendered' (p. 84), Nick changes the subject. By implication, a tactfully phrased offer would have proved acceptable. Why then does Gatsby abjure subtlety? With Cody, Daisy, Wolfsheim, he has his subtleties; with Nick he is obvious, risking 'crisis' in order to juxtapose crime and

adultery: to what end? Jimmy Gatz plays and is the lover: we remember
the cut grass, the white flowers, the dripping lilac trees; do we remember
that just before the liaison he reads 'a copy of Clay's *Economics*' (p. 85)?
The choice is apt in that Gatsby is engaged in economic subversion. He is
a thief who steals the 'badge', 'prize', or 'trophy' of a group – in the
language of Veblen's *The Theory of the Leisure Class*. As the leisure-class
female, Daisy's task is to display manifest consumption and manifest
leisure. She does it rather well, and her capacity for display attracted
Gatsby from the first: visiting her house with other officers from Camp
Taylor, and then alone, he senses 'a ripe mystery' in the length of
corridors and the sheer number of bedrooms. He is excited by knowing
that 'many men had already loved Daisy', a fact that 'increased her value
in his eyes' (p. 148).

Gatsby responds to the vibrancy of market emotions: the frisson that
he undoubtedly feels exists somewhere between mystery and inventory,
between emotional and monetary 'value', between sensuous and
economic 'appreciation'. Daisy's quality has a tendency to become a
quantity: how many bedrooms, how many men, what make of car?
Even as the object of Gatsby's desire is translated into 'commodity', so
Gatsby's desire is commodified. This does not deny Gatsby his 'romance'
– it would be inappropriate to deny the very quality that sells the novel;
it sets his 'romance' within a social context, and argues that Gatsby is
aware of the contradictions inherent in his adultery. For him Daisy's
glamour is glamour on the turn, and he would have Nick know it; but
Nick will not be distracted from his simple identifications with 'love': he
tells us that Gatsby reads Clay's *Economics* with suitably 'vacant eyes'.
Rather, Gatsby loves Daisy because she is his point of access to a
dominant class. Marriage would allow him to harden his liquid assets,
but would separate him from his origins and more importantly from
those among whom he works – the Wolfsheim milieu. Further, his love
ties him to a woman formed to display merchandise, who consequently
has repressed her body and cashed in her voice.

The contradictions are many, and yet there is evidence that Gatsby
faces them. Having achieved the 'token' that he loves, he stops the
parties. The lights are put out and the staff is changed in a conspicuous
interruption of his life style. Fearing that his neighbour is sick, Nick
visits, but is intimidated by 'an unfamiliar butler with a villainous face'
(p. 113). 'Squinted at', he retreats and solicits information from his
housekeeper, who informs him that the servants have been dismissed and
replaced by a set who do not bribe tradesmen, order moderately by
phone and leave the kitchen looking 'like a pigsty' (according to the
grocery boy). Unsurprisingly, the village is of the opinion that 'the new
people weren't servants at all' (p. 113). Gatsby staffs his house with

criminals and sets a villain at the door to play butler. His thin rationale is that it will prevent gossip over Daisy's afternoon visits. He can hardly hope to protect Daisy's good name by making the house of liaison conspicuous and by advertising its owner as one who consorts with rogues. Domestics, local tradesmen, particularly when aggrieved or fired, are gossip's very medium. He is not then protecting Daisy: rather, he is interrupting his smooth passage from purchaser through adulterer to husband. The ploy allows him to witness contradictions within himself. He who consents to steal the 'token' of the ruling class (perhaps because, as Marx has it, 'the ideas of the ruling class in every age, are the ruling ideas'), recognizes that his chosen course is neither obligatory nor apt.

Daisy is his 'prize', rather than another and perhaps unmarried leisure-class woman, because through her he can reclaim a particular stage in his own social transformation. With Daisy in 1919 he was economically naive, a sexual pirate plundering a class but impressed by the plunder. In 1922, and probably on the brink of financial incorporation, the very 'token' that will establish him socially will also allow him to remain in his own eyes something of a Dan Cody, an outlaw among financiers. The image has long appealed to him. As a boy, Jimmy Gatz instructed himself on the fly-leaf of a copy of *Hopalong Cassidy* to 'study electricity, etc.' (p. 174). His schedule was composed in 1906, when the extent and criminality of corporate empires in electricity was first becoming apparent.[15] It would seem that Jimmy Gatz knew from the first that Western heroes and corporate capitalists could be combined to produce an heroic self compounding the cowboy, the criminal and the entrepreneur.

Daisy is difficult, but only Daisy enables him to preserve his innocence while investing in his experience. Primarily though, divorced and remarried, she will grant him a degree of working respectability; by implication, her price is separation from Wolfsheim and his like. Gatsby, at the very moment of his success, takes the 'token' and sets it within the criminal milieu that made the theft possible. His self-division is apparent: dramatizing his opposed allegiances, he stands as a parable of the relationship between leisure-class capital and the industrial base that it criminally exploits and ignores.

Of course, Gatsby is a less than orthodox capitalist and a criminal rather than one of the 'ash gray' men. His liquid assets are doubtless plundered from all classes. But as the son of Henry C. Gatz, a poor Minnesota farmer, who eats 'like a hog' (p. 175) and wears 'a cheap ulster' (p. 167), he is by origin tied to the exploited class from among whom he has risen. The pattern of his rise evidences the control of the master class over the aspirations of the entire society. His interruption of that rise expresses his need for alternative forms of aspiration, forms that will acknowledge rather than repress the totality of his history. The gesture has the opposite consequence, removing him from all sociability: he is no longer lord of the revel, adulterer, criminal, social climber; he becomes he who interrupts. Within this style there is an embryonic conception of the world, or at least a revulsion from the lives that his culture permits him to lead. Arguably, that revulsion is intensified by the incomprehension that greets his gestures; they compel no audience, much less a group capable of finding in his style means to a practical transformation of reality. He dies almost unmourned, at his grave the father to whom he is a hero out of Horatio Alger, the biographer who scarcely understands him, and an owl-eyed party guest whom he did not invite and most probably never met. Conspicuous in her absence is the mistress he loved through commodity, but could not carry beyond commodity. There is, however, evidence that he tried to break the patterns of her desire – in Fredric Jameson's terms, to redeem her 'primary needs' from her 'luxury satisfactions'.

Where Brecht's Chinese actor *represents* anger 'by taking a lock of hair between his lips and chewing it', Gatsby represents love among the leisured by taking its outward signs and displaying them, with at times a curious remoteness. He guides us through lavish inventories that culminate in his own superabundant shirts (pp. 92–4). The elaborate process whereby Gatsby introduces Daisy into his house is at once formal and comic, as though the relationship between love and merchandise were being performed by a clown constrained to play straight-man. The short-cut to the house is abjured in favour of the perspective allowed by 'the big postern'. The rooms are named by period, 'Marie Antoinette music rooms', 'Restoration Salons', 'an Adam's [*sic*] study', 'the Merton College Library' – as the list edges antiquity towards brand name, history passes into the forgetfulness of commodity. But the reader may not forget: like a Brechtian audience, we are engaged 'in a complex rhythm whereby we relax during the stage action and concentrate during the breaks'.[16] Here, the action consists largely of perambulating inventories, while the pauses belong to Gatsby.

There is the moment when, gazing at Daisy, he manages almost to fall down stairs, and another when, shielding his eyes, he speaks with hilarity: it is as if he undertakes double-takes, shifting from auctioneer to lover to comic and back again at will. Later, Nick rightly compares him to Trimalchio, a name Fitzgerald toyed with, considering, *Trimalchio* and *Trimalchio in West Egg* as possible titles for the novel.[17] Admittedly, he was always free with his titles, but the name catches the precise nature of Gatsby's humour. Trimalchio gives a comic feast in the *Satyricon*, a Menippean satire whose roots are in carnival – a form that celebrates vicissitude and displays change through scandal, eccentricity, contrast and profanation. Gatsby, at this moment, might be the very spirit of carnival.[18] Reality is laughable because it is changeable. Gatsby was Jimmy Gatz, and look at him now. Daisy loves him through his property – perhaps she too may be changed. The case is a hard one. As Daisy takes up, with delight, the brush of pure dull gold, so she perceives Gatsby mirrored in Wealth, and forgets him. The shirts are a Trimalchian and necessary overplaying of that wealth in a final effort to interrupt her forgetfulness. The rhythm of the gesture is significant. 'One by one' the shirts are thrown: this is ritual not eruption. As the heap mounts higher, Nick, absorbed by the spectacle, commits himself to catalogue. But 'suddenly, with a strained sound, Daisy bent her head into the shirts and began to cry stormily'. Nick's assonantal infatuation requires 'stormily', and may even deprive us of the quality of that 'strained sound', but nothing can obscure the formal and unemphatic quality of the verb – 'to bend' is not 'to bury' or 'to sink'. The action that it describes is more considered. Daisy is on the edge of recovering Gatsby as he was, minus the merchandise and rendered classless by the anonymity of military uniform. In the event, all that she achieves is a sense that something has been lost; she hesitates and returns to Gatsby's possessions.

Once again, Brecht:

> The performer's self-observation, an artful and artistic act of self-alienation, stopped the spectator from losing himself in the character completely . . . Yet the spectator's empathy was not entirely rejected. The audience identifies itself with the actor as being an observer, and accordingly develops his attitude of observing or looking on.[19]

But in this case the audience (Daisy, Nick) fails to modify its empathy and to make the epic transition from spectator to observer. Unless the reader can make that transition, she is left with only the tired vocabulary of 'dream', 'tragedy', and 'romance'. These terms are resilient, and yet there is much about Gatsby that should qualify them. Take that somewhat notorious smile:

> He smiled understandingly – much more than understandingly. It was one of those rare smiles with a quality of eternal reassurance in it, that you may come across four or five times in life. It faced – or seemed to face – the whole external world for an instant, and then concentrated on *you* with an irresistible prejudice in your favor. It understood you just as far as you wanted to be understood, believed in you as you would like to believe in yourself, and assured you that it had precisely the impression of you that, at your best, you hoped to convey. Precisely at that point it vanished – and I was looking at an elegant young roughneck, a year or two over thirty, whose elaborate formality of speech just missed being absurd. Some time before he introduced himself I'd got a strong impression that he was picking his words with care.
>
> (p. 48)

The smile is essence of empathy; infinitely renewable and endlessly pleasing. It mirrors the recipients' ideal profiles, beliefs and hopes. Gatsby markets his face as though he stood in an exclusive window. Like any item of great price, his smile obliterates the actual relations and contexts that produce it, presenting itself as a unique facet of the onlooker's need. The gesture seals an exchange, granting the beneficiary access to the house, the car, the romance, the class, as perfect environments for her own best self-image. When the smiling stops, Gatsby displays his own past.

In Brecht's terms, the scenery shows. Gatsby is always 'mak[ing] visible the sources of light'. His gestures are in the spirit of Brecht's exercises in back projection: texts and pictorial documents were projected onto a canvas screen at the back of the stage, 'not . . . to help the spectator but to block him; they prevent his complete empathy, interrupt his being automatically carried away'.[20]

Few of Gatsby's means to this end are as theatrical as his clothes. On the hot day of revelations, Daisy compliments his sartorial coolness: '"You resemble the advertisement of the man", she went on innocently. "You know the advertisement of the man"' (p. 119). Matthew J. Bruccoli crassly prompts Daisy, substituting 'the classically handsome young man' of the Arrow Collar ads[21] for her silence. Gatsby embodies every conceivable logos; he can look like all the ads – and consequently he invents himself as a shining and empty space. His name matches his facility: 'Gat', the root shared by Gatz and Gatsby, in German means 'hole' and in Dutch 'hole, gap, break'.[22] The name announces its bearer's purpose, which is to interrupt the assumptions of others. Interrupted and unable to name her love for him, Daisy experiences what his smile gave to Nick, a glimpse of the inherent contradictions of the world of commodity.

As Gatsby dons the materiality of the commercial world, he displays its repression of his own materiality. The pink suit is a master stroke. Having assured Nick that his confession of adultery will be 'harrowing', he selects just the wrong colour for the 'scene' (p. 114). That the garment should meet a complementary carpet is a fortuity engineered by Fitzgerald to underline his character's creative independence: 'Gatsby stood in the centre of the crimson carpet and gazed around with fascinated eyes. Daisy watched him and laughed, her sweet, exciting laugh; a tiny gust of powder rose from her bosom into the air' (pp. 115–16). At this point it is as difficult to place Gatsby as it is to identify the quality of Daisy's laughter. Is he the victim or the victimizer of the commercial values in which he appears? The colour clash is a social collision that casts the garish light of carnival on the surfaces of a leisure-class drawing-room. While Tom Buchanan telephones a working-class mistress, his wife – the very skin of her bourgeois bosom powdering – is beguiled by an ex-proletarian capitalist of uncertain station.

To Georg Lukács:

> it even appears as if the decisive crisis period of capitalism may be characterised by the tendency to intensify reification, to bring it to a head . . . [O]n the one hand there is an increasing undermining of the forms of reification – one might describe it as a cracking of the crust because of the inner emptiness – their growing inability to do justice to the phenomena, even as isolated phenomena, even as the objects of reflection and calculation. On the other hand, we find the quantitative increase of the forms of reification, their empty extension to cover the whole surface of manifest phenomena. And the fact that these two aspects together are in conflict provides the key signature to the decline of bourgeois society.[23]

Gatsby's smile and his suit, his house and his car, extend 'the forms of reification'; but in his hands these properties are theatrical props with which he displays the repressive 'inner emptiness' of reified forms.

Of course Gatsby is no revolutionary class-hero, and his Brechtian gifts sometimes lapse, but even those failures should be read in a social context. Again Lukács is helpful; immediately after the passage quoted he notes:

> As the antagonism becomes more acute, two possibilities open up for the proletariat. It is given the opportunity to substitute its own positive contents for the emptied and bursting husks. But also it is exposed to the danger that for a time at least it might adapt itself ideologically to conform to these, the emptiest and most decadent forms of bourgeois culture.[24]

During his confession of adultery, Gatsby fails in ways which suggest that his self-alienation, though incapable of full adaptation to Daisy's culture, offers no alternative and 'positive' content beyond its own practice. Most conspicuously, he cannot persuade Daisy to deny all love for Tom; she will not say with conviction, 'I never loved him.' That Gatsby should ask for such an admission is generally read as a sign of adolescent infatuation, certainly 'romantic', perhaps naive. And yet, during his rehearsal of the 'scene' the night before, with Nick, Gatsby reacts tellingly to just this criticism:

> 'I wouldn't ask too much of her', I ventured. 'You can't repeat the past.'
> 'Can't repeat the past?' he cried incredulously. 'Why of course you can!'
> He looked around him wildly, as if the past were lurking here in the shadow of his house, just out of reach of his hand.
> 'I'm going to fix everything just the way it was before', he said, nodding determinedly. 'She'll see.'   (p. 111)

Gatsby is deluded, but his delusion is not a universal failing of adolescence, rather it is a flaw in a particular cultural outlook. Henry

Ford would have understood: by 1922 he had collected, at Dearborn, five acres of antiques. As the Reverend William Stidger observed:

> Mr. Ford has a passion for preserving his old home just as it was sixty years ago. He had them plough the ground up to a depth of six feet in order to unearth every knife, spoon, fork, wheel or anything else that his mother and father used and that he remembered as a boy. The home is exactly as it was sixty years ago in every detail.[25]

Right down to the sleigh-bells, of which Ford amassed a great number, because 'I wanted to find the exact note that I used to hear from bells on my father's horses in winter time.'[26] When Gatsby looks around (as though to turn his hand on the spot to physical reconstructions on a Dearborn scale), he demonstrates how commodity production has modified his perceptual world, and more particularly his sense of time.[27]

The marketplace, when it works well, compresses our sense of history. During the twenties Coca-Cola assured its addicts that it had been available to them 'through all the years since 1886'. Today a Coke affirms that multinationals are happy families, but in 1922 its point seems to have been that for significant items time does not pass. On paying, drinking and recovering our memory we (circa 1922) comfort ourselves with the idea that nothing changes since, in the marketplace, time is reversible. Henry Ford was simply obeying corporate policy on 'History' when he collected sleigh-bells. Unlike Ford, Gatsby at least sees the subjective consequences of living in such a 'time'. After the breakdown of the affair, and released from his single purpose, he acknowledges to Nick:

> 'Of course she might have loved him [Tom] just for a minute, when they were first married – and loved me more even then, do you see?'
> Suddenly he came out with a curious remark.
> 'In any case', he said, 'it was just personal.' What could you make of that, except to suspect some intensity in his conception of the affair that couldn't be measured? (p. 152)

Nick cannot see; after a moment's doubt, Gatsby's love is translated into an ideal passion, and his historical honesty betrayed.

Gatsby always knew that only a house full of money could hold a voice 'full of money', and that in order to love and be loved by Daisy he would have to bid for her in the open market. The house was his shop window. Across the bay, Daisy gazed from hers, the centrepiece in a presentation of her husband's wealth. The life in shop windows does exacting things to time and space. It is perhaps worth returning to the shop window according to Alfred Sohn-Rethel:

> There, in the market place and in shop windows, things stand still. They are under the spell of one activity only; to change owners. They stand there

waiting to be sold. While they are there for exchange they are not there for use. A commodity marked at a definite price, for instance, is looked upon as being frozen to absolute immutability throughout the time during which its price remains unaltered. And the spell does not only bind the doings of man. Even nature herself is supposed to abstain from any ravages in the body of this commodity and to hold her breath, as it were, for the sake of this social business of man.[28]

As a wife Daisy is officially unavailable for exchange. Nevertheless her life is circumscribed by commercial purposes. White, weightless and seemingly 'immutable', she is an object of consumption. Her time is an endless repetition, since it involves conspicuously repeating the unchanging substance of Tom Buchanan's property. Over on West Egg Jimmy Gatz labours to construct an adequate display case for what he has designed – 'Jay Gatsby'. As both producer and product he is potentially aware (as Daisy is not) of what he has done and why.

How much of this does Gatsby understand? My guess, based on his Brechtian skills, is that he feels himself to be a commodity. When he remarks to Nick that any marital affection felt by Daisy was 'just personal', he is not simply asserting romantically that it existed on a lower, sensual level; rather, he implies that, at its best, feeling is itself impersonal. The confession is considerable and debilitating, since it submits the heart to history – more specifically, to the historically prevalent mode of production. Gatsby's dismissal of the 'personal' complements Sohn-Rethel's judgement upon items in shop windows (since commodities are their price, they are not themselves). To exchange is to equalize and to abstract: various kinds of labour, ranges of need and qualities of material are declared comparable by the setting of a price:

> The effect of the world of commodities on real men . . . has factually separated or *abstracted* from man his 'subjectivity', i.e. his 'physical and mental energies', his capacity for work, and has transformed it into a separate essence. It has fixed human energy *as such* in the 'crystal' or 'congelation' of labour which is *value*, turning it into a distinct entity which is not only independent of man, but which also dominates him.[29]

The entrepreneur is an idealist, quasi-platonic in his insistence that there exists in 'value' a system of measurement whereby the real worth of all things may be declared. Gatsby's conviction that his own 'love' is the impersonal measure of all true love pursues entrepreneurial logic to its abstract and abstracting extreme. Nick is mistaken: in that Gatsby can take the measure of his affair, he is forced to recognize that his espousal of certain social means has formed him, and that his 'romance', in its emptiness and its fullness, is crucially impersonal. His failing is that he carries neither his mistress nor, for the most part, himself beyond the commercial forms that are their hearts' permitted medium.

If, as Lukács argues, 'the nature of history is precisely that every definition degenerates into an illusion' and that history is therefore *'the history of the unceasing overthrow of the objective forms that shape the life of man'*,[30] and if Gatsby's imagination *is* historical, then Gatsby has cast down the objective forms that shape his life and, lost for allegiances, can anticipate no future.

Two days after events at the Plaza he is murdered in circumstances that underline his isolation. George Wilson, a genuine proletarian, in effect kills one of his own at the behest of the powers that be, and then, obligingly, kills himself. The disposition of the corpse is suggestive:

> There was a faint, barely perceptible movement of the water as the fresh flow from one end urged its way toward the drain at the other. With little ripples that were hardly the shadows of waves, the laden mattress moved irregularly down the pool. A small gust of wind that scarcely corrugated the surface was enough to disturb its accidental course with its accidental burden.   (p. 162)

Liquidity and mobility are ironic constituents of the scene: neither has proved a sufficient force for change in a culture whose 'objective forms' neutralize social distinctions and impede the realization of contradiction. The reiteration of 'accidental', in circumstances of such manifest social collusion, is less than casual. After much talk of careless driving and a car accident that looks like homicide, the word is a loophole through which a reader may hear an unromantic story.

It must be stressed that the repetition of 'accidental' belongs to Nick, as, at least potentially, does the presentation of Gatsby's death as a minor skirmish in a continuing class-war. In such a reading, Tom Buchanan, having disembodied his own wife for purposes of display, can achieve satisfaction only through the body of the working-class female. A déclassé but upwardly mobile Gatsby seeks status via the release and theft of the feminine leisure-class body. In response, Tom extends the hegemony of his class to the abused industrial male. (One can only speculate on how it was done, but it would seem likely that appeals to sexual ownership prompt a man with minimal property to murder Gatsby and destroy himself.) The double death secures Buchanan's grip on the leisure-class 'token' and releases him from the growing threat of his own uneasy liaison with the industrial class. Along the way, vengeance is enacted by the leisure-class female on the offending body of her working-class counterpart – one of Myrtle's breasts is left flapping, the blood drains away and her vitality is conspicuously evacuated.

Nick cannot afford to write this kind of murder story. Social speculation, leading to a fuller sense of class relations, might induce in him 'an artistic act of self-alienation', from which perspective his own social position within the Carraway fortune, itself founded on the sending of a substitute to kill or be killed, might grow uncomfortable. Consequently, whenever the contradictions within his subject become too disquieting, he turns social aspiration into 'dream', sexual politics into 'romance', and translates class conflict as 'tragedy'.

III

To Nick must go some of the blame for the resilience of critics' slack and obscuring language. With such a biographer even the best Brechtian subject might be the recipient of uncomprehending appeals to empathy. But why does Nick romanticize? And why, as the presenter of Gatsby's self-interruption is Nick prepared to live within the contradictions that his subject exposes? The issue can best be appreciated through a fuller account of the friendship and of its limits. Much common ground is shared: neighbours, Midwesterners, brothers in the same corps with a mutual interest in bonds and social mobility. Indeed the affinity is so strong that Nick is prepared to play Gatsby's confessor, saying of the Cody–Wolfsheim information, 'He told me all this very much later' (p. 108). He checks the facts of the final day with the butler and the chauffeur, as though from the first projecting an act of biography. Moreover, he is briefly the executor of Gatsby's estate. It is Nick who arranges the funeral, supports the sad father and cleans the dirty words from the vacant walls. His reasons for doing so much for a man 'who represented everything for which I have an unaffected scorn' (p. 2) stem from a suppressed ambivalence towards his own class.

When Nick comes back from the Great War, he returns to a 'prominent, well-to-do' family boasting a civic history stretching back for three generations (p. 2). 'Aunts', 'uncles' and 'father[s]' surround him. Just as relatives advised on his prep school and most probably approved his following of his father to Yale, so the family 'grave[ly]' comply with the move East, while a paternal gift guarantees his first year in the bond business (p. 3). Nick colludes with his class, and one senses that he fell early and far into respectability. However, there remains some hesitancy about his complicity. A heritage founded on wholesale hardware, despite genealogical flirtations with the Dukes of Buccleuch, might well strike a 'restless' son with European experience as incurably provincial: in which case its privileges, its networks and its assumptions would approach self-parody even as they insisted upon their substance. Nick returns home only to leave it, finding in Gatsby an alternative self-image. The discovery is mutual. Gatsby's 'criminal' mobility complements Nick's move East; Nick's 'respectable' mobility complements Gatsby's marital ambitions. Hardware needs liquidity as liquidity needs hardware. However, the need of each man for the other involves a differing degree of self-consciousness. Gatsby's life has made him dramatically aware of his own social position and of his capacity to change it. In 1907 a smile raised him from casual labour into the service of speculative capital (Dan Cody made himself in silver and copper during the 1870s and is an exemplary gilded robber baron). In 1917 a military uniform carried him across the threshold of accumulated wealth, while the purchase of a mansion during the early twenties commits him to the problem of how to transform speculative monies into stable inheritance. To call Gatsby rich is to simplify; rather, he is the tool of capital (or capitals) – an object lesson to himself in the making and re-making of reality.

The Carraways have provided Nick with no such education. Instead, he has learned to resign himself to the family councils of the bourgeoisie, and to resent the resignation. His duplicity is exactly caught by his attitude to his father: paternal advice structures the first paragraph of the narrative, and the 'snobbish' tones of the father are 'snobbishly repeat[ed]' by the son (p. 1) – to repeat a father's favoured phrases even as one declares them 'snobbish' is to display hostility secreted within respect. But parody, even self-parody, is a two-edged weapon, since it reinstates the very laws that it transgresses. Nick, effectively, goes on holiday to the East and to Gatsby's Trimalchian energies, only to return articulate, chastened and less wise than he might be, because he cannot accommodate the range of social experience focussed by Gatsby's disruptive power. Gatsby demonstrates that even as distinct social groups live together, they do so in a manner that ought to make their lives unbearable. Nick can bear it because he replaces such intimate glimpses as Gatsby affords into class division and social totality with more manageable forms of division and totality: that is, with self-parody, and with those universal comforters 'romance', 'dream' and 'tragedy'.

An extensive and subtle failure of nerve inheres in Nick's writing of his book. That failure is at once particular and general; in Lukács's terms Nick's lies exemplify the necessary lies of his class:

> the veil drawn over the nature of bourgeois society is indispensable to the bourgeoisie itself. For the insoluble internal contradictions of the system become revealed with increasing starkness and so confront its supporters with a choice. Either they must consciously ignore insights which become increasingly urgent or else they must suppress their own moral instincts in order to be able to support with a good conscience an economic system that serves only their own interests.[31]

The attempt to explain why Nick romanticizes raises the larger issue of why Nick writes at all, particularly when his account of Gatsby must demonstrate the collapse of his own attempt to create an alternative life for himself. That attempt is disastrous, lasting less than a year. In the autumn of 1922 Nick returns West to settle in that 'warm center of the universe' (p. 3). For two years he sits at the family table, almost at the feet of his father, pondering paternal aphorisms – 'In my younger and more vulnerable years my father gave me some advice' (p. 1). The pleasure of 'reserved' communication within a small, known and financially secure group may go some way to soften any sense of failure: the move East had been intended, after all, to be permanent (p. 3), involving a broken engagement and much talk among aunts and uncles. Nick needs a surer salve than the pleasures of provincial snobbery: he needs a secret book. Consequently, he begins a romantic memoir, the outlines of which are precisely determined by his own disappointments and evasions: its hero must represent and extend the Nick who went East in 1922, while not troubling the Carraway who came back and is still writing in 1924. A tragic Alger-hero is formulated, to rise less through pluck (labour) and luck than through will. Nick, with a year's paternal finance, required little luck; he worked, but one senses that his 'conscientious hour[s]' in the Yale Club Library were very few (p. 57). Instead he willed 'permanent' change and lasted a year – so he makes the will of his hero as strong as his own was weak.

Hugh Kenner describes Gatsby as a hero of the 'will'[32] who, unlike Alger figures, does not need a long-lost and wealthy grandfather, or a rich kid to save from drowning, because he is prepared to 'Study electricity', 'Study needed inventions', and in so doing to master mysterious forces. Kenner does not go far enough: having studied and mastered specific mysteries – the mysteries of how Edison and Insull transformed electrical energy into the power of stocks[33] – Gatsby not only forgoes luck, he is prepared to market it. A 'gonnection' with the gambler Myer Wolfsheim adds technique to capital. In 1919 Wolfsheim's control over chance was sufficient to 'fix' a World Series. The gambler's company is called 'The Swastika Holding Company': prior to the Nazis, the swastika was an emblem of good luck. Given Wolfsheim's abilities and Gatsby's liquidity, the notion of cornering the market in luck, and stock-piling the commodity for subsequent sale in token form, seems less than far-fetched. We are not told whether Gatsby carried Wolfsheim's stock – but given mutual interests in Chicago, familiarity and favours (the second set of servants are sent on loan from Wolfsheim), a business liaison seems likely. In which case the company's name is in the Gatsby style.

Predictably, one has to work for such a reading: the man who might contemplate a market price for chance has outgrown Alger (though he merely anticipates those companies and magazines who sell 'chance' as part of a thoroughly costed package, promising prizes to a number of 'lucky' winners). However, Nick needs an Alger over-reacher, as much as he needs that hero to fall. Alger's heroes are two-edged: their climb encourages others to aspire; their success may embitter aspirants who fail. Moreover, not only does Carraway, by 1924, need a balm for failure, he needs a private labour that will preserve his faith in glamour from the rigours of the wholesale hardware trade. So for him Gatsby dies as a tragic victim of love rather than as the perpetrator of economic offences.

The tragic note is useful in Nick's systematic revision of Gatsby's career, allowing him the pity that pities all mankind and not a particular individual. As Tom drives Nick and Jordan back from the 'harrowing scene' in the Plaza towards a still more harrowing scene in the Valley of Ashes, Nick remembers that it is his birthday and assumes a quasi-tragic air:

> Thirty – the promise of a decade of loneliness, a thinning list of single men to know, a thinning brief-case of enthusiasm, thinning hair. But there was Jordan beside me, who, unlike Daisy, was too wise ever to carry well-forgotten dreams from age to age. As we passed over the dark bridge her wan face fell lazily against my coat's shoulder and the formidable stroke of thirty died away with the reassuring pressure of her hand.
> So we drove on toward death through the cooling twilight.   (pp. 136–7)

The 'death' that they approach is multiple – Myrtle, Gatsby and Wilson are soon to cool, as is Nick's relationship with Jordan – but the tone is elegiac. Nick notes the passing of all flesh through a twilight that chills the globe, rather than the very different ways in which he knows full well these singular lives have gone. Nostalgia, with an inclination to tragic infection, spreads empathy where analysis should be. The tone is self-defeating since it is not Gatsby's career that is 'tragic', but Nick's.

Gatsby aspires to re-form his social connections and experiences contradiction and self-betrayal when he does so. Nick can see this, but prefers the easier liberal conviction, that the self is so essentially isolated that it can admit of no final connections. In Gatsby, Nick finds one kind of hero (the double of his social desires) and creates another (the double of his liberal pain). It is to the latter that he most often turns. Nick's favoured Gatsby is free, self-willed, and self-fulfilled. It is to Nick, within earshot of his father's 'snobbish' words, that *this* Gatsby owes his 'platonic' absence of antecedents (p. 99). It is because Nick's eye will unerringly find a hair-line of sweat on a lover's upper lip, that *this* Gatsby, when he kisses at all, kisses the stars (p. 112) – not flesh. For Nick every move towards relationship ends in guilt; therefore, Nick's preferred hero is guiltless, since his moves are 'tragically' blocked.

Gatsby's 'romance' is born of Nick's romanticism, whose thinly disguised dark side is a distaste for the human and for himself.

These are large indictments. However, partial extraction of Nick's autobiography from Gatsby's biography yields a pattern of sexual aversion and social isolation which, thanks to Raymond Williams, may be called a 'liberal tragedy'. Williams allows that this is a catch-phrase for various forms of tragic writing stretching from romanticism's 'impulse to revolution, a new and absolute image of man',[34] to the despairing 'platitude' that converts 'all but one individual to an illusion' (p. 141). The genre is an anthology of selves in transit towards liberal dissolution: the 'romantic self' passes through the 'liberal self' into the 'self divided'. The entire range is applicable to Nick, in that each is not necessarily a chronological stage in the growth of the liberal-tragic hero, but may appear as a facet of a single character's changing mood: I shall paraphrase Williams in order to highlight that applicability. In Romantic literature man makes himself, but in so doing encounters the social world as an obstacle; the degree to which the socially extant is hostile to the hero's humanity is the degree to which the social criticism of the romantic 'tends to pass into nihilism' (p. 22). In 'liberal tragedy' the hero, if not the impulse to liberation, is generally broken: the self who stood against society internalizes his guilt, grows isolated and becomes 'his own victim' (p. 100). As Arthur Miller declares, at the end of *A View from the Bridge*, in order to live 'one must settle for half':

> And if this is so, in a false society which the individual alone cannot change, then the original liberal impulse to complete self-fulfilment becomes inevitably tragic . . . The self that wills and desires destroys the self that lives, yet the rejection of will and desire is also tragedy: a corroding insignificance, as the self is cut down. (p. 105)

Nick achieves 'will' and 'desire' in surrogate form on the pages of a secret book, while his life in the hardware trade 'corrodes' him. Nick's book is deadlocked in that it enables him only to divide himself and to victimize both halves. He who aspires dies, and he who remains dies. The fact that Gatsby is no kind of tragic hero, 'romantic' or 'liberal', is not the point. Of course, there is yet another book to be written, though not, finally, by Nick. The biographer Fitzgerald gives us is unable to make Gatsby's social recognitions cohere. He cannot, therefore, recover him as a Brechtian figure. Instead Nick leaves the smile, the suit, the jokes as problematic gaps in his text and tries to write over the top of them a biography that is a liberal tragedy in the 'heroic phase', a book about 'the individual destroyed in his attempt to climb out of his partial world' (p. 97). The book is broken-backed and further complicated by Nick's desire to compose an autobiography that 'settles for half', after the manner of stymied liberal art. The third and autobiographical outline is perhaps the most successful of the three skeletal volumes, but even the resigned tones of a 'self cut down' cannot entirely suppress their own history: Nick has created a figure from a romantic tragedy in order to make his own liberal tragedy bearable, and in so doing has not entirely missed the Brechtian point.

Herein lies the complexity both of Nick's insight and of his blindness. The autobiography commits him to averting his eyes from Gatsby's dramatization of contradiction: a book in the liberal-tragic vein could not survive the recognition that, since 'different social classes have different kinds of clarity',[35] every event is a collision of several worlds, or the repression of such diversity, or both. Ultimately, Nick heals his own divided consciousness by retreating from social dissonance to the stable 'half world' of the Carraway 'clan'. Surrounded only by the most predictable ties, self-enclosed and self-isolated, he writes in order to discover explanation within the private world of his own pathology. Although he can neither forgive nor forget Tom Buchanan (recognizing as he does the 'vast carelessness' (p. 180) of leisure-class money), he will shake hands with him. Social form requires it – almost as much as Nick needs the continuing illusion of a small and safe world in which all men are polite to one another. Besides which, that world has granted him other and more persuasive moral villains, all of them female.

By 1924 Carraway has either married his unsatisfactory home-town tennis partner or forgone sexual exchange; either way he is liable to blame women. "Woman as male nemesis" joins "tragedy" and "romance" in the biographer's lexicon of evasion. Daisy's 'carelessness', Jordan's 'lies' and Myrtle's body are at least partially generated by Nick's distaste for women – a distaste that displaces social division into sexual division, and surfaces most conspicuously when the death of Myrtle Wilson is recorded in a tone of suppressed celebration:

> The 'death car' as the newspapers called it, didn't stop . . . The other car, the one going toward New York, came to rest a hundred yards beyond, and its driver hurried back to where Myrtle Wilson, her life violently extinguished, knelt in the road and mingled her thick dark blood with the dust.
>
> Michaelis and this man reached her first, but when they had torn open her shirtwaist, still damp with perspiration, they saw that her left breast was swinging loose like a flap, and there was no need to listen for the heart beneath. The mouth was wide open and ripped at the corners, as though she had choked a little in giving up the tremendous vitality she had stored so long.
>
> (p. 138; my ellipsis)

The posture of submission is total: Myrtle kneels to be adroitly dispossessed of each of her vital signs (blood, flesh, voice). Any pleasure that Nick may feel cannot be explained simply in terms of one man's sexual disappointment. In a novel so thoroughly social, desire and fantasy have their social antecedents.

Married or unmarried, Nick seems to have withdrawn into a wider celibacy. His use of his writing to castigate the female body is part of a more general retraction from human exchange. In New York he had played Prufrock, picking out 'romantic women' on Fifth Avenue, following them to 'their apartments' 'in my mind', only to watch them 'fade through a door into the warm darkness'. The fantasy moves purposefully through an encounter's various stages, in order to release, with the closing of a door, 'a haunting loneliness' (p. 57). The plot is typical of Nick's endemic isolation, and of his satisfactions within it. He is inside a clan, but not quite of it: engaged but disengaged; writing a biography that is autobiographical. At all points he abstains from full exchange, thereby guaranteeing himself a kind of safety from the history that he has witnessed.

The witness that he bears is partially false because, paradoxically, his readiness to blame women allows him to sexualize 'history'. The body of the female is most acceptable to him in mammary form:

> Out of the corner of his eye Gatsby saw that the blocks of the sidewalks really formed a ladder and mounted to a secret place above the trees – he could climb to it, if he climbed alone, and once there he could suck on the pap of life, gulp down the incomparable milk of wonder.
>
> His heart beat faster and faster as Daisy's white face came up to his own. He knew that when he kissed this girl, and forever wed his unutterable visions to her perishable breath, his mind would never romp again like the mind of God. So he waited, listening for a moment longer to the tuning-fork that had been struck upon a star. Then he kissed her. At his lips' touch she blossomed for him like a flower and the incarnation was complete. (p. 112)

The 'secret place' of the mother's breast is replaced by a lover's mouth, and what is 'unutterable' (the milk) perishes. For just a moment the kiss is less than fatal, as male lips mouth metaphors to displace the female mouth. The metaphoric use of 'blossom' releases a floriate pun from 'incarnation': an investiture in flesh gives way to an embodiment in flowers. Daisy's name – a synonym for 'innocence' in the language of flowers – remains horticultural and her mouth sweet, complementing the lost arboreal space of the acceptable breast. 'Wed', 'blossomed' and 'incarnation' are the secondary terms of metaphors, which, in each case, over-write their primary term, in a deviation so powerful that the normal event – boy meets girl and, despite differing backgrounds, they kiss – is almost obliterated. The oedipal nuzzle erases the social embrace.

At just this point Nick substitutes his mouth for Gatsby's and continues the kiss:

Through all he said, even through his appalling sentimentality, I was reminded of something – an elusive rhythm, a fragment of lost words, that I had heard somewhere a long time ago. For a moment a phrase tried to take shape in my mouth and my lips parted like a dumb man's, as though there was more struggling upon them than a wisp of startled air. But they made no sound, and what I had almost remembered was uncommunicable forever.   (p. 112)

It is to be doubted whether Gatsby discussed his intimate sexual experiences with anyone: the 'appalling sentimentality' consequently belongs to Nick, as does the pathology. The 'pap', the 'milk', the floriate mouth, and the 'lost words' of a speech that is not speech (and must in this context be infantile) are the features of an incestuous desire, experienced as loss. No adequate objects can be found for needs whose gratification so obviously wanes with every post-natal day. The temporal logic of such oedipal desire is well described by Clement Rosset: whenever, in order to define incestuous longing, emphasis is put upon the absent cause of that longing:

> the world acquires as its double some other sort of world, in accordance with the following line of argument: there is an object that desire feels the lack of; hence the world does not contain each and every object that exists; there is at least one object that is missing, the one that desire feels the lack of; hence there is some other place that contains the key to desire [missing in this world].[36]

That 'place' for Nick is one in which differentiation collapses, language folds back into breath, humanity grows autochthonous and the child re-enters the mother. Nick's Midwestern homecoming is perhaps part of a more ambitious regression to a mythically 'warm center of the universe' (p. 3). From within such a place mere social distinctions may seem irrelevant.

The ahistorical impulse of Nick's sexuality extends to Gatsby's history. Nick concludes the autobiography with a beginning, or, more accurately, with one source for all beginnings; the mammary, the foliate, the floriate and the pre-linguistic recur in an incestuous image of continental proportion. Although the last page of the novel is much quoted, I shall risk quoting it again as preface to a detailed revision of its meaning:

> Most of the big shore places were closed now and there were hardly any lights except the shadowy, moving glow of a ferryboat across the Sound. And as the moon rose higher the inessential houses began to melt away until gradually I became aware of the old island here that flowered once for Dutch sailors' eyes – a fresh, green breast of the new world. Its vanished trees, the trees that had made way for Gatsby's house, had once pandered in whispers to the last and greatest of all human dreams; for a transitory enchanted moment man must

have held his breath in the presence of this continent, compelled into an aesthetic contemplation he neither understood nor desired, face to face for the last time in history with something commensurate to his capacity for wonder.

And as I sat there brooding on the old, unknown world, I thought of Gatsby's wonder when he first picked out the green light at the end of Daisy's dock. He had come a long way to this blue lawn, and his dream must have seemed so close that he could hardly fail to grasp it. He did not know that it was already behind him, somewhere back in that vast obscurity beyond the city where the dark fields of the republic rolled on under the night.

Gatsby believed in the green light, the orgastic future that year by year recedes before us. It eluded us then, but that's no matter – tomorrow we will run faster, stretch out our arms further . . . And one fine morning –

So we beat on, boats against the current, borne back ceaselessly into the past.

(p. 182)

The 'green breast' has little to do with Gatsby's biography and much to do with Carraway's needs. As Nick holds his breath, history flows backwards. The strands are many but the destination is singular. The 'old' becomes the 'new', the city gives way to the forest, and the observer turns into the earliest settler, in preparation for the recovery of the maternal body of the nation. Gatsby's 'green light' has indeed come a long way to re-appear as the image of national desire for an 'orgastic future'. The phrase is odd: 'orgastic' means 'pertaining to or characterized by orgasm'. By merely 'pertaining to', it displaces the intensity of orgasm; displaced gratification is doubly gratifying to Nick – it protects him from the fleshiness of sex (as 'orgasmic'[37] could not), while confirming the temporal structure of his desire in its regressive search for a missing gratification. The 'future' that is both 'green' and 'orgastic' is none other than the past beating its boats back into pre-history. Nick employs a traditional Romantic analogy in order to reverse the analogy. His river of life, had he sufficient will, would flow backwards; its coastal shelf, more breast than outcrop, instead of marking maturity, would offer sustenance ('the milk of wonder') for a journey inwards. He who ascends the stream will presumably watch as flesh fades to grass and the maternal earth opens for the child.

Carraway is a prose herbalist for whom autochthony is a favoured cure-all. Having earlier translated the problematic Daisy into a flower, he prepares the ground to receive his own awkward seed. The seeds of the caraway are traditionally thought 'to ease the pains of the wind collic', and have long been used in confectionery, cookery and perfumery to ease digestion and evacuate noxious gases.[38] True to his name, Carraway is a great deodorizer – all manner of unpalatable materials are expelled from his final and famous prose purgation. Indeed, very little of Gatsby is left, as particular social aspirations are translated into a national reverie which thinly disguises autobiographical pleading.

Carraway's erotic writing is just one of his isolate satisfactions: granted the 'romance', the 'tragedy', the pleasure of his text, he can endure the platitudes of home; and with his public and fantasy lives secure, there is every reason to believe that the memory of Jimmy Gatz from San Francisco, Minnesota, will grow increasingly vague and increasingly glamorous.

In describing the elements that constitute Nick's writing – biographical, autobiographical, historical – and in suggesting a poetic plot at work through suppression and over-writing, I have emphasized Nick's evasions and done scant justice to his insight. Although his sense of an ending seeks an intellectual deep-shelter in the single and self-enclosed world of his own sexuality, much of his text hesitates before evading, producing a form of 'double writing'. For Bakhtin:

> Directed at its object, the word collides within the object itself with [an] other person's word. The other person's word is not reproduced, it is merely implied, but the entire structure of speech would be entirely different if this reaction to the implied word were not present.[39]

By his own intent, Nick's writing 'lives a tense life on the border . . . of another consciousness'.[40] All too often, however, tension is sacrificed as the biographer tries to silence his subject. Symptomatically one of his last labours concerns an alternative form of writing:

> On the white steps an obscene word, scrawled by some boy with a piece of brick, stood out clearly in the moonlight, and I erased it, drawing my shoe raspingly along the stone. Then I wandered down to the beach and sprawled out on the sand.   (p. 181)

– to dream of the 'fresh, green breast of the new world'. Arguably, Nick rubs out Gatsby's word to inscribe his own. Gatsby, as Trimalchio, might have preferred profanity for an epitaph, given that the alternative is Nick's concluding paragraphs. However, the very proximity of an erased obscenity to Nick's over-writing constitutes a form of double articulation, albeit muted. As his florid speech looks sideways at the dirty inscription, Nick so far forgets himself as to recall that the trees of pre-history 'pander': the word hints that 'green breast[s]' are less than fresh, and that even 'the milk of wonder' has its price. For a moment Gatsby's voice resists erasure, before Nick's eulogy rolls on to its unshakable conclusion.

Elsewhere interruptions prove more lasting. Time and time again hesitation, reservation, repetition and ellipsis imply that the narrator may be hearing his own words in the mouth of another, at which points the surface of the text grows irregular and erratic. Of Daisy's last and unmade phonecall, Nick notes that during his last hours alive, and without his 'single dream', Gatsby must have 'lost the old warm world'; in its place stand leaves that frighten, 'grotesque' roses and 'raw' light falling from an 'unfamiliar sky': 'A new world, material without being real, where poor ghosts, breathing dreams like air, drifted fortuitously about . . . like that ashen, fantastic figure gliding toward him through the amorphous trees' (p. 162). Nick sees with unerring clarity the nature and extent of Gatsby's disappointment: he has lost Daisy and in so doing affirmed the poverty of the culture that constituted the very pattern of his desire. In the light of this discovery *the objective forms that shape the life of man'* (Lukács) crumble and the 'new world' grows 'material without being real' – reality being in the gift of the 'vast, vulgar and meretricious' (p. 99) system of production. The moment is one of 'self-alienation' for Gatsby and for his biographer. Nick perceives historically and feels his own biographical and autobiographical stances challenged. When he writes that Gatsby finds a rose 'grotesque', he criticizes himself. Earlier Daisy insisted to him, 'you remind me of a – of a rose, an absolute rose' (p. 15). He denied it then, he recalls it now. Neither the rose, nor the 'scarcely created grass', nor 'leaves' can carry him out of time. In contradistinction to his final eulogy, he recognizes that nothing is 'absolute', that worlds – from skies to swimming pools to Nick Carraway – are constructed, and that behind them lie dreams which are themselves dependent upon material conditions. Even here Nick would deny it. His ellipsis is striking. There is nothing 'fortuitous' about Mr Wilson's destination – he did not 'drift', he was sent, and his deepest purposes were determined by class antagonisms. Nick's hesitation is a response to another and resilient voice. Dialogue can almost be heard in the space of the pause; Nick's voice wins, but only just. The murderer emerges as an 'ashen and fantastic' figure; 'fantastic' because Nick refuses to conceive of Wilson's world and of the world of Gatsby's origins; 'ashen' because Nick cannot deny that he has seen the industrial heartland, witnessing in the valley of ashes the material production of his own existence and dreams.

The duplicity of 'ashen and fantastic', at once witnessing and bearing false witness, is typical of Carraway's style. *The Great Gatsby* is Nick Carraway's furtive text, and yet it is also the most finished and coherent of Fitzgerald's works. Fitzgerald's literary and moral stature lies in his choice of precisely the wrong biographer, and in his appreciation of the consequences of this choice for the reader. Effectively, the decision results in a novel within a novel. The surface is glamorous, empathetic and inappropriate; within it lie glimpses of a wasted hero. To find Carraway's subject we have to historicize Carraway. Reading instructs us in the unpicking of ellipsis, the pursuit of hesitation, the alienation of sentences from their sources and the scrutiny of gesture. If the reader learns, she will find herself within Gatsby's personal style – an apt member for that missing audience to whom the man in the pink suit is constantly telling 'the one about San Francisco'. To receive the joke is to appreciate the materiality of the joker. With Gatsby's "concreteness" made possible, it should be necessary to abstract from it by considering exactly how the 'second skin' of the advertisement may be shed.

4

Money makes manners make man make woman: Tender is the Night, *a familiar romance?*

I

Fitzgerald published *Tender is the Night* in 1934, but the novel deals with the period from 1925 to 1929. By the mid-thirties accumulation is a business fact, it is no longer a primary business principle. Nonetheless, its archaic plots constitute the foundation of the bourgeois self. Effectively, accumulation goes underground, shifting from the drawing-room to the unconscious. The claim sounds grand, but its premises are simple. If one accepts that beneath any set of economic facts lies a network of social relations which produce those facts, it should be possible to argue that repeated patterns of social activity, geared to making and sustaining particular kinds of property, will induce self-taught forms of forgetting. Put another way: a group that habitually removes something from its consciousness prepares grounds for a shared unconscious. For example, on the afternoon of Ransom's first visit to Olive Chancellor's drawing-room, a lamp arrives behind the visitor's back:

> He thought [the] prospect, from a city-house, almost romantic; and he turned from it back to the interior (illuminated now by a lamp which the parlour-maid had placed on a table while he stood at the window) as to something still more genial and interesting.[1]

So successful is the bracketing of the maid's hand that she scarcely interrupts the rhythm of the young man's perception or of James's syntax. In such 'interiors' certain preconditions (like a servant's labour) have become so much a matter of convention that they cease to be visible. In which case, the negotiation of the room elicits typical patterns of censorship deep enough to found a shared amnesia. Indeed, Freud, analyst to the children of these interiors, may be read as the historian of a high-spot of class amnesia from the 1890s to 1914. For Mandel these years fall within 'the monopoly stage of capital', a period during which corporations form, only to discover intimations of the instability inherent in their accumulations. Arguably, Freud's preoccupation with Oedipus reflects a business and professional clientele for whom artifacts, whether verbal or material, extend from the father's will, a will whose authority, as the century turned, was increasingly shaken. Obviously, "paternal power" and "maternal love" should join domestic labour in any full account of the constituents of Victorian privacy – constituents whose effectiveness depends upon suppressions that add up to a model of how and what to forget.[2]

Even without a detailed version of that account, it should be clear that the unconscious can be read as a space constructed from historically specific forms of forgetting: the elisions, displacements and lacunae that are its *modus vivendi* take their shape from what a ruling class needs to retain and to suppress. So, the Victorian bourgeoisie cannot forget the accumulating father, but must forget his worries; thrift over money and semen produces a solidity traduced with anxieties as to how to preserve what has been saved. A credit economy necessarily produces a different pattern of amnesia; the post-war American middle class, learning to spend, must remember that gratification should be a lonely business: their need is to forget the social and physical forms that might impede isolate satisfaction.

The history of what a class finds unthinkable is one measure of how that class maintains its integrity despite economic transition. *Tender is the Night*, balanced between residual and emergent economic forms, approaches the changing nature of the American bourgeoisie through the figure of the psychiatrist or professional guardian of the unthinkable. As with *The Bostonians*, selfhood resides in property, so that any talk of 'transference', 'condensation', or 'displacement' will have more to do with monetary than with psychic forces. Probably Fitzgerald read Freud; how much and when is difficult to gauge.[3] Nonetheless, the novel's psychiatric vocabulary operates primarily as a metaphor whose subject is the relocation of accumulations.

The word 'subconscious' occurs twice, first as a synonym for habitual memory:

> Intermittently she caught the gist of his sentences and supplied the rest from her subconscious, as one picks up the striking of a clock in the middle with only the rhythm of the first uncounted strokes lingering in the mind.[4]

The idea is developed by a second usage: as Rosemary brushes her hair in a Parisian hotel room she 'half notice[s]' her reflection in numerous 'refracting objects' – varnished wood, picture-frames, the facets of a pencil, ash-trays:

> the totality of this refraction – as appealing to equally subtle reflexes of the vision as well as to those associational fragments in the subconscious that we seem to hang on to, as a glass-fitter keeps the irregularly shaped pieces that may do some time – this fact might account for what Rosemary afterward mystically described as 'realizing' that there was someone in the room before she could determine it.   (p. 122)

The logic of the central simile is revealing: the 'subconscious' is a store of memories containing 'associational fragments', each of which is in turn a store of memories. By likening the fragments to a glazier's off-cuts, Fitzgerald flirts with Freudian notions of 'distortion' and 'condensation'; his flirtation is brief, because the glazier in question intends to re-use his spare pieces, in which case the 'fragment' becomes a window granting direct access to the interior.

I dawdle over two instances of one word in order to stress that the 'subconscious', as it appears in *Tender is the Night*, is no kind of Freudian mechanism: rather, it is a strategy that allows individuals to return to themselves, insofar as they may be said to possess a hidden place of permanent acquisition and accumulation. Arguably, such a place is simply an obscure chamber in the mansion of privacy, originally constructed as a necessary alternative to the workings of the market. Necessary because, even as capital required its subjects to define themselves as "free", "equal" and "autonomous" in their ability to contract their labour or to purchase in the market place, so the real workings of capital took those individual producers and consumers apart. Heads were divided from hands, as manual and intellectual labour were rigorously defined and split.[5] Public life was separated from private existence, as "leisure" was invented to allow for the necessary and hopefully full consumption of what was being produced. Gender was thoroughly polarized by the demarcation of the male sphere of production and wage from the female sphere of domestic and "unproductive" labour. While dismemberment proceeded, bourgeois society posited the individual personality as its central value. Something like the subconscious was needed to explain how the multiply subdivided person held together. Richard Lichtman argues:

> The more capitalism required the total fetishism of humanity, a necessity produced by the manner in which capitalism split the public and private realms and made the latter the arena of privatized selfhood and commoditized consumption, the more it required some apparatus to organize the internal realm and 'cure' its most obvious pathologies. Psychoanalytic theory provided the cornerstone for this construction.[6]

The history of two industrial revolutions is simultaneously a history of the discovery and elaboration of psychiatry. Like identical twins, separated at birth and re-united in slow motion ever since, reification and analysis deserve one another. The progressive alienation of labour from its own body, and of the bourgeoisie from the actuality of what produces its own status, is rightly described by Adorno as 'a form of forgetting',[7] whereas for Freud everything is recall, since 'in the unconscious nothing can be brought to an end, nothing is past or forgotten'.[8] The worker and the manager may have a limited sense of what determines their wages beyond circumstance and bitterness, but for the analyst 'no event is without a cause'.[9] The consumer durable, with its price obscuring its past,[10] is packaged to have no history; however, if removed from the shop window and re-located in slip or dream, the commodity will abound with causal schemes which fill the analysand with plots. Pivotal among the narratives is the family story: consequently, while incorporation progressively erased the names of founding business-fathers from company letter-headings, Freud recovered the patriarch. Redemption was more than cosmetic. The 'oedipal dragnet'[11] converts family members into 'global persons' as it re-writes desire in familial terms.[12] At a superficial level the appeal to the classical story may well have hinged on its capacity to place "father", "mother", "sister" and "brother" back on stage in a marketplace that was editing them out. In the mid-nineteenth century, home production gave way to social production and so progressively re-located authority in the centralizing corporate structure. Ernest Groves, a domestic historian writing during the twenties, noted that

> a family sense of enterprise was lost and the essential economic task of the family became the problem of distributing an income, usually inadequate, so as to meet the needs and if possible satisfy the desires of its different members.[13]

Moreover, the weighting of wages had changed; as mass production de-skilled, young hands rather than 'the learned skills of hand and eye'[14] were the order of the flow system. Where a nineteen-year-old produces more than his father, his wages and his pleasures will command the attention of the mass media and of advertising: 'Now the rapidly changing society which passes its judgement upon the old is represented not by the father, but by the child. The child, not the father, stands for reality.'[15] Not so for Freud, in the subconscious the 'reality' of the father remains central.

The intellectual appeal of psychiatry in the twenties, like the broader appeal of the domestic sphere in the seventies and eighties, rests on the belief that privacy (in this case the privacy of analysis) can return selfhood to the self. Stated generally, the subconscious is a strategy for preserving a ligature between a notion of identity and a faith in accumulated familial property. The logic runs – I am an individual because I have my own, singular subconscious: my consciousness of the world may be increasingly atomized, but beneath that consciousness lies that which guarantees me my identity, a "sub" or "un" consciousness founded on family membership.

II

Fitzgerald submits the appeal of psychiatry to his own analysis. To the psychiatrist falls joint guardianship of the subconscious and the bourgeoisie. Consequently, Professor Dohmler's head resembles 'some fine old house' (p. 155), and nods in the style of that arch-protector of all such properties, Sherlock Holmes (p. 142). The professor receives Devereux Warren's confession of incest from 'the focal armchair of the middle class' (p. 145) – a posture that casts some doubt upon his scientific detachment: ambivalence over the possessive 'of' raises the question, who possesses whom? Dohmler may clarify bourgeois desires but who owns his chair? Elsewhere ownership is less questionable. The clinic on the Zürichsee is a Warren investment, built on profits raised from land sales to railroad companies (p. 255). Its director, Dr Diver, is perceived primarily not as a scientist but as a hotelier – the preserver of the last and most exclusive resort of the *haute bourgeoisie*, the subconscious. He is a manager who takes on, nominally for life, a damaged child of 'feudal' monies (p. 142) and under a 'ducal' name (p. 175), in other words, the spoiled infant of accumulated capital. Nicole typifies his clients, who are for the most part the children or the entertainers of the leisured class (dancers, writers, painters, opera singers, etc.). For them he creates 'sureties' (p. 67), small, safe environments in which the broken may grow 'hard' again (p. 29). His integrative territories are not necessarily clinical: a beach umbrella, a café-table, a railway terminal, even the momentary radius of a voice can be made therapeutic. For a 'collapsed psychiatrist' at Zürichsee, Dick's speech is a last link with reality: 'The man tried to read his face for conviction, since he hung on the real world only through such reassurance as he could find in the resonance, or lack of it, in Doctor Diver's voice' (pp. 204–5).

Each space is resonant with Dick's manners, which are designed 'to give all the transitions their full value' and so 'to yield the utmost from the materials at hand' (p. 30). Gilbert Osmond would approve. Like a Jamesian collector or Trobriand islander, the psychiatrist creates a wealth of information where there was none before. Dick can transform any object or person into a set of signs, while convincing those around him that his signs are wonders belonging only to them. Symptomatically, he learned his manners from a master of drawing-rooms:

> Once in a strange town when I was first ordained, I went into a crowded room and was confused as to who was my hostess. Several people I knew came towards me, but I disregarded them because I had seen a grey-haired woman sitting by a window far across the room. I went over to her and introduced myself. After that, I made many friends in that town.   (p. 223)

The Reverend Diver is a clerical dandy more given to taste than to theology: his 'good heart' derives from 'good instincts' which are the creatures of his 'honour' and 'courtesy' and 'beautifully cut clerical clothes' (p. 223). Dick throughout his life 'referred judgements to what his father would probably have thought or done' (p. 222) in a consideration for the archaic, which is positively Veblenite, since for Veblen the leisured are characterized by 'arrested spiritual development' in so far as they resist change by indulging in 'spiritual survival and reversion' (p. 145). The arrest is striking. Fitzgerald calls Diver 'a spoiled priest':[16] as a psychiatrist Dr Diver ministers to the subconscious of a class, with the good manners of his good father. The therapy works because manners offer the comforts of amnesia. On the beach at Tarmes, Rosemary responds 'whole-heartedly' to 'the expensive simplicity' of the Diver manner:

> unaware that it was all a selection of quality rather than quantity from the run of the world's bazaar; and that the simplicity of behaviour . . . was part of a desperate bargain with the gods and had been attained through struggles she could not have guessed at. At that moment the Divers represented externally the exact furthermost evolution of a class, so that most people seemed awkward beside them – in reality a qualitative change had already set in that was not at all apparent to Rosemary.   (p. 30)

To attend to 'quality' is to forget 'quantity': when Nicole shops, she must not know of the chicle factories and the toothpaste vats (p. 65) – the processes and the profits which enable her to wander among luxuries. Dick's grace ensures her oblivion, in that he provides an alternative and distracting density: for the materiality of production he substitutes the materiality of manners – a space into which 'transitions' are so packed that each item and event materializes, and is materialized by, the system of discriminations that it affirms. Appreciation involves a 'complexity of training' allied to a 'simplicity of ideas' (p. 45). But the 'bargain' is 'desperate' because by 1925, particularly viewed from the perspective of 1934, economic emphasis has changed.[17] The world's 'bazaar' no longer promotes or runs on 'sureties'.

Dick's manners are anachronistic but they work up to a point: witness his achievement during an inauspicious party at the Villa Diana:

> Rosemary, as dewy with belief as a child from one of Mrs. Burnett's vicious tracts, had a conviction of home-coming, of a return from the derisive and salacious improvisations of the frontier . . . The table seemed to have risen a little toward the sky like a mechanical dancing platform, giving the people around it a sense of being alone with each other in the dark universe, nourished by its only good, warmed by its only lights. And . . . the two Divers began suddenly to warm and glow and expand, as if to make up to their guests, already so subtly assured of their importance, so flattered with politeness, for anything they might still miss from that country well left behind. Just for a moment they seemed to speak to every one at the table, singly and together, assuring them of their friendliness, their affection. And for a moment the faces turned up toward them were like the faces of poor children at a Christmas tree. Then abruptly the table broke up. (pp. 43–4)

The aura is one of return; expatriate Americans recover the USA as the essence of one leisure class. The period, for a moment, is 'the golden nineties' (p. 191) – Dick's phrase for a time of new 'landfall' (p. 191) and 'innocent expectation' (p. 192). Cap D'Antibes is not quite re-cast as 'the green breast of the new world', but the 'frontier' of 'the dark universe' is momentarily still out there, and Turner's thesis rings in every ear.[18] These people rest assured, their identities provided for by earlier appropriations – theirs is 'the only food', 'the only light'. Where selfhood resides in private property, privately improvised, mutuality takes form as mutual appreciation and 'emulation'; consequently, the guests feel at once 'alone' and 'with each other', even as their hosts speak to them 'singly' and 'together'. 'Flattery' and 'politeness' create a unifying 'sentiment', at once integrational and territorial. The Christmas-tree allusion marks it as a sentimentality, while 'the mechanical dancing platform' underscores contrivance. Nonetheless, Diver's manner has transformed a disintegrating group into an archaic leisure-class. The effect cannot long withstand the degree of its fabrication. The Villa Diana is as detached from the world of 1925 as Mrs Burnett's *Secret Garden* (1911), and it is only a matter of time before its proprietor's manners seem as mannered as those of her *Little Lord Fauntleroy* (1881). As capital develops, so the competitive struggles through which people define themselves change, changing what determines the individuality of individuals.

Dr Diver will not have it so. Symptomatically, 'the tensile strength' of Dick's social and psychiatric 'balance' (p. 76) is often ghosted by a language of toy making. He trains at Zurich, 'home of the toy . . . the funicular, the merry-go-round' (p. 132). Pregnant, Nicole believes herself 'a broken roly-poly that can't stand up straight' (p. 176); and later she suffers a relapse among fortune-tellers' tents and Punch-and-Judy shows (p. 207). Dick denies that 'he had stitched her together' (p. 153), although in Zurich he 'felt like a toy-maker . . . [and] did not underestimate the value of toy-making, of infinite precision, of infinite patience' (p. 133), credentials that achieve musical accompaniment as he tells his wife of her father's miracle cure to the tune of 'The wedding of the painted dolls' (p. 272). Toy making, in this instance, is not so far from taxidermy: Dick's social miniatures are frequently drawn by the metaphoric network towards the Victorian nursery. Dick is at home in that ambience, having an allusive fondness for the writings of Lewis Carroll and Jules Verne: among the remembered books stand sepia 'postcards of the Crown Prince and his fiancée' (p. 67) next to memorabilia of Victorian Christmases and grand tours. At the risk of stretching the allusive net – if memories were photographs, the shelves in the mind's eye of Dick's metaphor might feature a picture – circa 1895 – of a small boy in a 'starched duck sailor suit' attended by his equally stylish father (p. 222).[19]

Dick's skills as socialite and psychiatrist are synonymous, depending upon a capacity to reconstruct the mental interiors of others in the forms of the old bourgeoisie. In effect, Dick achieves a double displacement: the subconscious is represented as a drawing-room and made liable to the manners of that space; that interior is then transposed into a nursery. Displacement involves overdetermination, particularly of the bourgeois selfhood that is entrusted to his charge. As a result of a therapy that requires her to live in various well-run nurseries, Nicole's "interior" is locked into the attitudes of the 1900s.

I am aware that I have transposed to Dr Diver my reading of James's bad grace over the transition from 'classical imperialism' to 'late capitalism'. The difference is that Diver is not Fitzgerald. Incest is the key to Fitzgerald's understanding of the relationship between identity and economics. Where the doctor finds Oedipus, the author reaches through the oedipalized triangle to discover the broader (though partially familial) imperatives that materialize his character's world. However, before discussing the narrative implications of the trauma in the nursery, it is necessary to recognize its centrality. Devereux Warren's sexual pathology keeps cropping up. *Tender is the Night* is beset by ill-disguised fathers and under-aged girls. In Rome (city of Papal fathers), on his way to court to be tried for striking a plain-clothed policeman, Dick learns that a native of Frascati has been arrested for raping and killing a child: in court he cries out, 'I want to explain to these people how I raped a five-year-old girl. Maybe I did' (p. 256). Disturbed by the recent death of his own father, Dick perceives himself as a child molester because by 'transference'[20] he may be, in Nicole's eyes, the molesting father. In which case, Dick is two fathers: the good reverend father and the bad Devereux Warren. Paternity becomes him, but is always liable to become something else. He meets Rosemary on the eve of her eighteenth birthday; objects that he has no intention of marrying his daughter Topsy (p. 278), and threatens his son Lanier with divorce (p. 285). As though enough were enough, Fitzgerald cut from the last page of the manuscript the suggestion that Dr Diver of Lockport is 'entangled' not simply with 'a girl who worked in a grocery store', but with a sixteen-year-old.[21]

Not all the paternal duplicities relate directly to Dick. The Chilean aristocrat who begs treatment for his homosexual and alcoholic son is called Señor Pardo Y Cuidad Real – I offer in my own defence Dick's warning to Abe North, 'You can come if you want to play anagrams' (p. 121) – transposed, the Spanish might read, 'Senior, sorry, I see you Dad for real'. Once witnessed the indirect exposure of culpable fathers and consenting children proliferates and permutates. *Baby* Warren and *Daddy's* Girl are simply surface clues to an associative network capable of determining interpretation. Both casual and condensed usage contributes to an emergent, if occult, pattern which ghosts characters and modifies action. For example, Dick's cry as he assaults his policeman – 'first I'll fix this baby' (p. 246) – could be coincidence, while the inelegance of the carabinieri, 'grotesque in swaddling capes' (p. 247) may owe more to Hemingway's sartorial eye[22] than to a sub-plot pregnant with infantile desire. However, there is nothing casual about Dick's recalling Fatty Arbuckle as he relieves Rosemary of her stained Parisian bed linen – Arbuckle's career was cut short by charges of murderous attention to a child beneath the age of consent. Sexually poisonous adults achieve their nadir in the father of the American artist treated at Zürichsee for nervous eczema: she dies 'imprisoned' in an 'Iron Maiden' of scab (p. 202) as a result of neuro-syphilis, presumably contracted from her father at conception. Under-aged girls come no younger. The diagnosis is Dohmler's; Dick does not want to hear it, insisting, 'If she cared enough about her secret to take it away with her, let it go at that' (p. 263). Why is he so secretive? During the patient's decline, Dick 'went out to her, unreservedly, almost sexually. He wanted to gather her up in his arms as he so often had Nicole, and cherish even her mistakes, so deeply were they part of her' (p. 204). The doctor would 'cherish' the deep 'mistake' of incest, containing the 'secret' with the therapeutic advice, 'We must all try to be good' (p. 204). As an 'Iron Maiden' his patient is profanely pure and quite beyond sexual exchange; Dick's role as a surrogate good father is consequently eased. To conclude any account of what I would call the incest constellation with this particular extended example is to psychologize a sub-plot whose implications are far broader. The associative network should not be hidden within the psychology of one character, or indeed of the author, since Fitzgerald's preoccupation with the social and financial status of the father (good or bad), and with the subconscious as a place of accumulation, requires that incest be read economically.

III

I have already argued that Warren uses that which he is required to exchange. The father, according to the incest taboo, must release his daughter into marriage outside the family.[23] Warren's greed is such that he fails to exchange the one item that he is utterly obliged to exchange; he keeps his daughter for himself. The logic of accumulation transgresses the incest taboo, and Dick is hired to make good that transgression. The word "cure" would be inappropriate. Dick as the good father supplants the bad father, restoring Nicole to integrity: she is made 'complete' and 'hard', terms carrying a Jamesian freightage. However, restoration involves blocking the trauma. Nicole is denied access to her father's offence. Secret keys proliferate on Dick's person: plainly he is the key to the case, but during Dohmler's clinical report Dick remembers 'a scene in his childhood when everyone in the house was looking for the lost key to the silver closet', a key he had hidden in his mother's top drawer (p. 154). Janitorial duties started young. At some level Nicole recognizes him as her keeper: she bars Mrs McKisco from the troubled bathroom in the Villa Diana 'because the key was thrown down the well' (p. 185), and Nicole knows who did it. Her allusion, redolent of nursery rhyme, chimes in with her own earlier letter in which she described Dick as 'wise behind your face like a white cat' (p. 139). The wise "pussy" who joins the key at the bottom of the well presumably sees the solution as incarceration. When – with 'verbal inhumanity' seeping through the 'keyholes' – the reader finally enters 'the horror' in the bathroom, it is to witness Dick shutting doors:

> Nicole knelt beside the tub swaying sideways and sideways. 'It's you!' she cried, '– it's you come to intrude on the only privacy I have in the world – with your spread with red blood on it. I'll wear it for you – I'm not ashamed, though it was such a pity. On All Fools Day we had a party on the Zürichsee, and all the fools were there, and I wanted to come dressed in a spread but they wouldn't let me –'
> 'Control yourself!'
> '– so I sat in the bathroom and they brought me a domino and said wear that. I did. What else could I do?'
> 'Control yourself, Nicole!'
> 'I never expected you to love me – it was too late – only don't come in the

bathroom, the only place I can go for privacy, dragging spreads with red blood on them and asking me to fix them.'

'Control yourself. Get up –'

Rosemary, back in the salon, heard the bathroom door bang, and stood trembling: now she knew what Violet McKisco had seen in the bathroom at Villa Diana.   (pp. 125–6)

In a room designed for purgation Dick insists on repression. Nicole resists as she has resisted before. Her memory of procedures at the Zürichsee might be glossed, 'While at the clinic, among the foolish and the mad, I wished to wear a spread but was given a domino.' 'Spread' condenses a plot; prompted by stained bed-linen, the word recalls the sheet marked with the blood of Nicole's hymen. Despite 'spread['s]' declarative openness, the clinical staff gave her a 'domino' – an elaborate and often sequined mask. When Nicole tried to understand her trauma, her doctors sought to disguise it with the artifacts of mannered wealth. Dick is of their party. He holds the key to her subconscious accumulations and keeps the door locked. Nonetheless, the stain and the domino are complementary; if they were not, Dick's therapy could not work. The mask typifies the affluence of a particular class, even as its occasion and elaboration embody those discriminating principles which condense leisure objects into systems of 'invidious difference'. The stain too is a surface dense with comparative information: beneath it lies the father/phallus, but before he can be seen he is displaced by the hotel linen, the clinicians, the domino, Dick, Mcbeth . . .[24] Though the associative list can be extended, my point remains a simple one – items in both the bourgeois drawing-room and the unconscious solidify through cumulative nicety. The furnishing of each privacy depends upon an absent father; the Victorian interior expresses his solid aggression in the marketplace, while in the unconscious, according to Fitzgerald – oedipally organized – images solicit over interpretation and designate at the core of their wealth the missing and threatening father.

Dick's task, as psychiatrist and socialite, is to reduce the paternal threat while maintaining the father's good name. He is therefore an agent who extends the logic and imperatives of bourgeois privacy. In the feminized space of the bourgeois interior, daughters learned from mothers those immaterial arts which could represent first their father's and then their husband's accumulations. Nicole is Devereux Warren's continuity: his first daughter is 'wooden' and 'onanistic' (p. 232) and will possibly not marry; rebuilt by Dick, the damaged younger child will exchange with her proper mate, that is to say, with a male who can ensure the 'ducal' group's exclusivity and privilege. Warren's 'feudal' monies will be safe with Tommy Barban, mercenary in royal causes, opponent of socialism and trainee stock-speculator. Oddly, by preparing Nicole for the right marriage, Dick preserves the fount of his own gifts – the accumulations that foster and give purpose to his manners. As the Reverend Diver's child, nostalgic for 'religion and years of plenty and tremendous sureties and the exact relation that existed between the classes' (p. 67), he cannot afford to acknowledge that the monies of the *haute bourgeoisie* were corrupt, even at their head and point of distribution. He knows, better than most, how 'a century of middle-class love' finally 'spent' itself: he could doubtless map 'the last love battle' and measure to the inch the 'great gust of high explosive love' (p. 68); incest is very much his Western Front and the end of 'all [his] beautiful lovely safe world' (p. 68). He says as much on a visit to the trenches around Amiens; however, by globalizing incest Dick gnomically and unanalytically extends the power of the father. To find Beaumont-Hamil in the nursery and Thiepval among toys is to re-write the First World War in terms of the comforts and guilts of the bourgeois home. Rarely can Daddy and his girls have been so imperious, or so much have turned on the proper use of a daughter. The extent of Dick's amnesia is aptly stated by Deleuze and Guattari in their sustained attack on the oedipalization and familialization of the unconscious:

> we formulate the following rule, which we feel to be applicable in all cases: the father and the mother exist only as fragments, and are never organized into a figure . . . able . . . to represent the unconscious . . . The father, the mother, and the self are at grips with, and directly coupled to, the elements of the political and historical situation – the soldier, the cop, the occupier . . . – who constantly break all triangulations . . . The family does not engender its own ruptures. Families are filled with gaps and transected by breaks that are not familial: the Commune, the Dreyfus Affair, religion and atheism . . . – all these things form complexes of the unconscious, more effective than everlasting Oedipus . . . If in fact there are structures to the unconscious, they do not exist in the mind, in the shadow of the fantastic phallus distributing the lacunae, the passages and the articulations. Structures exist in the immediate impossible real.[25]

Dick did not have the benefit of such revisionists: the 'real' for him is heavily dependent upon the father, perceived as totality rather than 'fragment'. Reality is a mannered space expressive of paternal accumulation. The subconscious, oedipalized, strengthens the father's grip by re-casting the surface of immediacy as his theatre – albeit a theatre in which the lead has generally just slipped out. Dick is obliged to find paternity everywhere and to encourage the reader and Nicole to make and fear such revelations. At a late stage in their marriage Nicole objects, 'Am I going through the rest of my life flinching at the word "father"?' (p. 311). Her rebuke is a measure of her renewal: she ceases to be a child of two fathers and becomes instead her grandfather reincarnate – her voice and 'white crook's eyes' encourage her to believe that she has 'gone back to my true self' (p. 314). There is, however, nothing regressive about her return, since, in this instance, the double displacement of the father (Devereux and Dick) ensures the viability of the Warren monies. The whole point about crooked grandfathers is that they knew how to invest. Nicole as her grandfather's spirit circa 1929 would take his money to Hollywood:[26] symptomatically, she marries a man who likens himself to Ronald Colman and who, in her eyes, resembles 'all the adventurers in the movies' (p. 290).

Nicole is in no sense "cured"; she simply moves towards an alternative model of selfhood, negotiating the incest trauma by ignoring it. The 'cord' can be 'cut . . . forever' (p. 324) because she appreciates herself as a new species of consumer, one to whom accumulations are no longer of primary relevance. Consequently, the subconscious – cumulative, private, dense and supported by an etiquette equally weighted with 'interpretation or qualification' (p. 320) – can be forgotten. Indeed, amnesia is obligatory. The father–centred and integrative nursery must give way to brand name and movie-still if grandfather's capital (the capital of 'classical' imperialism, be it economic, psychic or mannered), is to adapt and counter the inertia of excess capacity. For Barban she crosses herself with Chanel Sixteen and hopes to resemble 'the moving pictures with their myriad faces of girl children' (p. 312); with Barban she stands 'black and white and metallic against the [Mediterranean] sky' (p. 326), an apt study for the movies; for Barban she dines 'at the new Beach Casino at Monte Carlo' and swims in only the most affluent postcards: 'in Beaulieu in a roofless cavern of white moonlight formed by a circle of pale boulders about a cup of phosphorescent water, facing Monaco and the blur of Mentone' (p. 319). Fitzgerald names brands to point a transition that was merely latent in Nicole's earlier patterns of consumption. The brand name and the tourist spot – no matter how exclusive – prompt rapid translation from word to material image, the better to speed consumption. Any associative pattern latent in the name has been pre-arrayed there by advertising. In contradistinction, the analysand's phrase or any item beneath the Diver's beach umbrella emanates density and stasis. For reasons having nothing to do with geography, Cap D'Antibes is not Beaulieu. Gausse's beach *is* a commodity, but it is a commodity manufactured by Dick, during the early twenties, which might have been modelled on a van der Luyden orchid. Veblen would have understood the doctor's tireless application of the rake (p. 302); like any rare hybrid, Gausse's sand denotes that key to 'good breeding', 'a substantial and patent waste of time'. However, by 1928 the leisured devotions due to 'a bright tan prayer rug of a beach' (p. 11) are no longer observed. The sand serves a different expenditure and signals an alternative form of wealth. When Dick and Nicole bought 'sailor trunks and sweaters' in Nice back-streets (p. 302), they did not intend to create fashion. Paris couturiers copied the style: Fitzgerald does not need to tell us that 'haute couture' pirated from *Vogue* or *Vanity Fair* became a market leader – the busy presence of an Associated Press photographer on the steps of Gausse's hotel indicates that the new users are more interested in 'image' and 'spectacle' than in etiquette. With 'beach umbrellas' and 'pneumatic rubber horse', 'new things . . . purchased from the first burst of luxury manufacturing after the War' (p. 37), the Divers make their version of a Victorian resort, and so manage temporarily to deny the very purpose of that wave of manufacture. They achieve 'absolute immobility' (p. 27) on the sand, where the future health of their capital stipulates absolute mobility. The adroit instillation of cumulative nuance into necessarily transitory luxury items is an archaic trait that the Warrens cannot afford. Equine inflatables are not and should not be Jamesian porcelains. At the novel's close, Dick quits a beach that is no longer his kind of artifact. Nicole, for all her recognition that it now serves 'the tastes of the tasteless' (p. 301), stays, presumably to be photographed by the Associated Press.

Each Diver accessory is for Fitzgerald a potential meeting-point between two forms of economic authority, which I have allegorized in short-hand as Accumulation and Reproduction. The meaning of the sweater or the umbrella depends upon who is economic master. Mastery involves a conflict whose history constitutes the texture of the object. Fitzgerald has an eye for the detail that retains the tracery of this struggle; he registers the economic latencies which divide objects as an archaeology lying at the very surface of things. At first glance Gausse's beach is easily consumable, but the image is fissured: as a 'prayer rug', it summons ceremonies whose form Veblen might have declared typical of leisure in the 1890s; as a tanning mat, it services "the body beautiful" – that curious site of narcissism and self-denigration which encourages tourists to replace their own bodies with "commodity selves" – shade and musculature, care of the socio-sexual market.

What passes on the beach (p. 30), like the beach itself, is a struggle between forms of power. One incident may be treated as typical: Dick emerges from the dressing tent in 'transparent lace drawers' *pour épater la nouvelle bourgeoisie*. His impulse is territorially effective; McKisco asserts his gender and insults the gender of his companions, while the knowing joke affirms the unity of the Diver entourage by releasing 'a nursery-like peace and goodwill'. In fairy stories frogs turn into princes at the drop of a kiss; Dick's transformation is only slightly less spectacular. Fitzgerald marks its importance by insisting, 'At that moment the Divers represented externally the exact furthermost evolution of a class.' As with incest, so with homosexuality: sexual preference in *Tender is the Night* should be read within an economic context. Dick, the keeper of Accumulation's daughter, appears to reveal his own phallus (the drawers *seem* transparent) by performing the absence of that member (the drawers *are* opaque). At one level the genital logic accords with Dick's phallic subordination to the bad father. The daughter approves the emasculation, since it is she who sews the trick costume. Her needlework – in all probability Dick's conception – is part of a treatment which enables her to assure Rosemary that she is 'a mean, hard woman'. As a bonus, this particularly 'invidious' piece of 'invidious comparison' captures the child of Reproduction. With a 'bubble' of 'delight' Rosemary is initiated into the group and into Dick's love. Accumulation rules. However, 'in reality a qualitative change had already set in that was not at all apparent to Rosemary'. It *is* apparent to Fitzgerald, for whom the 'pansy's trick' is capable of double articulation as two plots. Read from within the imperatives of reproduction, Dick transgresses the bounds of phallic sexuality through a stage-managed and 'spectacular' multiplication of his own gender. He woos and wins a very different Daddy's girl by establishing a disintegrative selfhood. Fitzgerald's point about the 'furthermost evolution of a class' refers to the moment at which a class becomes conscious of the need to assume alternative forms of behaviour, sexuality, spending and finance. Their 'bargain with the gods' is 'desperate' because transition is awkward. In this instance Nicole will make it, Dick won't. For Dr Diver 'gods' will always, in the last analysis, wear 'finely cut clerical clothes'. For Nicole the 'gods' will increasingly become the mass audience in the cheaper seats whose desires her fashions and her monies will seek to renew and control.

Though the demise of phallocentrism – with its attendant etiquette and economics – looks complete, it is neither easy nor radical. What Fitzgerald bears witness to via his semantic sub-plot or sub-articulation is a shift in the administration of power rather than the overthrow of that power. Dick's homosexual play leads, through the pun on 'gods' (theological and theatrical), to the world of the 'spectacle'. Unlike James, Fitzgerald is prepared to explore what is in effect a major economic transition. Since in market terms so much of that transition focusses on the re-distribution of the human body (particularly the body of the female), it is perhaps unsurprising that Fitzgerald should approach the economic through the sexual. His choice, like any argument by analogy, involves him in risky insights which may best be read as cultural intimations rather than as truths. Any culture that commodifies the erotic, by eliding money and the body, produces the option of resistance through a pursuit of that elision to disconcerting lengths. For example, and returning to the shocked beach, Dick's drawers render his phallus questionable; since he is named for that member, the trick disintegrates him diversely. It is predictable, within the constraints of the symptomatic body/money simile, that the disintegral self will find a matching sexuality. Fitzgerald's logic leads him to homo- or bi-sexuality as disintegral gender-forms, a discovery that disturbs him. Without adopting Hemingway's name-calling he continues anxious.

Autobiography, Leslie Fiedler to the contrary, doesn't explain.[27] A curious scene in a Parisian gallery offers clues to Fitzgerald's position within what he takes to be an awkward perception about his culture (ch.17, pp. 82–7). The architecture is particularly revealing in that 'the outer shell, the masonry seemed . . . to enclose the future'. The gallery is 'a long hall of blue steel' hung with 'oddly bevelled mirrors'; similes involving 'jagged broken glass' and 'a highly polished moving stairway' redouble its reflecting surfaces. This 'set' is built within a house 'hewn from the frame of Cardinal de Retz's palace'.Glass (the future) meets masonry (the past) in a street called 'Rue Monsieur'. Inside, 'thirty people, mostly women' challenge such confident nomination. Rosemary experiences an attempted lesbian pick-up by 'a poster of a girl', while three 'cobra women', their heads 'groomed like manikins', look on. It is intriguing that Fitzgerald should liaise homosexuality and fashion, implying that the disintegral environment of the future challenges gender as part of its programmatic multiplication of selves. The environment is negotiable, though at considerable risk:

> they [the people] functioned on this set as cautiously, as precisely, as does a human hand picking up jagged broken glass. Neither individually nor as a crowd could they be said to dominate the environment, as one comes to dominate a work of art he may possess, no matter how esoteric, no one knew what this room meant because it was evolving into something else, becoming everything a room was not; to exist in it was as difficult as walking on a highly polished moving stairway, and no one could succeed at all save with the aforementioned qualities of a hand moving among broken glass – which qualities limited and defined the majority of those present.   (p. 83)

An unconventional pronoun shift from 'one' to 'he' occurring over the issue of possession indicates Fitzgerald's trepidation. He shifts his shifter[28] back from the anonymous (double-gendered) to the male in order to orient himself within more than his own untypically over-extended syntax. 'He' hangs on to authority through ownership. It would be fun to argue that the linguistic impropriety of this victory enacts the collapse of phallocentrism even as it denies it. Such nuances are too nice. Fitzgerald, at this point, *needs* the reassurance of the male pronoun, although he knows exactly why the forms which sustain it are in transition.

IV

Nonetheless, it would be a mistake to associate Dick too exclusively with the values of the father and of a pre-war leisure-class. His 'sureties' *do* grant pervasive power and miraculous longevity to the father (after a brief interview with Dick, Warren takes up his bed and walks). Nonetheless, the incestuous father is Janus-faced. Earlier I argued that for Fitzgerald sexual pathology operates as an economic metaphor, transposing Devereux Warren's act, in all its irresponsibility, into a symptom of compulsive accumulation. Seen within a longer economic perspective, the metaphor is two-sided: it embodies accumulation, but simultaneously transgresses limits (sexual). By penetrating Nicole, Warren becomes father *and* lover, even as he makes his child into daughter *and* mistress. Incest creates *dis*integral selves through a multiplication of roles which, by analogy, I would liken to a shift in economic emphasis. An intersection between psychological and economic trauma registers precisely how a change in the history of capital changes the history of bourgeois selfhood.[29]

The incest metaphor lies at the narrative core of *Tender is the Night*: compressing a plot of considerable complexity, it predicates particular character groupings in order to realize the fullness of that complexity. Put schematically: Fitzgerald marries Dick to Nicole to explore accumulation, and supplies him with Rosemary as an entrée to the sphere of reproduction. Still more deductively: Dick's affections shift between Daddy's girls to externalize the contradictory nature of Warren's incest. At one level, the father refuses to exchange his child beyond the family; at another, and opposed level, he denies both the differentiation of social roles and the familial organization deriving from the incest prohibition – that is to say, Warren's sexual energy seeks unrealized relations and forms. The plot latent in the sexual/economic overlap thickens. Accumulation stores money, distributing its energy along regulated and increasingly centralized channels. Within the sphere of reproduction that same energy must, if it is to avoid the potential inertia of its own enormous overheads, create new needs and discover new markets. Consequently, late capitalism builds into each of us its own realm of desires lacking adequate objects, the better to pre-sell those objects.[30]

Rosemary markets desire. A product of the culture industry, she has too many fathers, too many selves and absolutely no trauma about it. By responding, Dr Diver shifts allegiance from the integrating subconscious (the last territory of the private, bourgeois self) to a disintegrative and global image (Rosemary films in Rome and Hollywood, and screenings of her work seem available almost anywhere). Rosemary is Publicity, and the changing pattern of desire which she instigates makes a comparison with Nicole obligatory. The two women, one 'hard' (dense) and the other transparent, stand at different moments in the history of desire. Veblen's terms still apply to Nicole, or at least to Mrs Diver, but Rosemary requires a new vocabulary. When Nicole's dress and manners provoke others to 'invidious comparison' or 'emulation,' she can afford to ignore it because her 'ducal' wealth, though 'regulative' of others, protects her from being regulated back. Rosemary, as Publicity, stimulates envy but is inextricably tied to the gaze of those who envy her. While Nicole's private social labour turns her accoutrements into declarations of a particular class history, Rosemary's history – professional and biographical – is erased. To create a star her managers must edit out her life even as their screen gives her an alternative identity:

> The agent of the spectacle . . . is the opposite of the individual; he is the enemy of the individual in himself as in others. Passing into the spectacle as a model for identification, the agent has renounced all autonomous qualities in order to identify himself with the general law of obedience to the course of things.[31]

'Obedience' refers to the "progress" of profitable consumerism which leaves the process of production and the lives of the producers necessarily undiscussed. Rosemary cannot be self-conscious, since she has no self to be conscious of; she is, however, audience-aware. Under Dick's tuition Nicole achieved self-possession, she grew 'hard', 'whole', 'complete' and anachronistic. Rosemary's self is a number of styles which exist to be alienated from her; like fashion, she is created to earn envy so that her style(s) may be purchased by others.

Walter Benjamin, in his essay 'The work of art in the age of mechanical reproduction',[32] clarifies my distinction between density and transparency, through the distinction he draws between 'person' and 'personality'. Benjamin suggests that actors in front of a camera are overcome by strangeness because they recognize that their image is 'transferable', they can never forget that the image is to appear before consumers who constitute a market, consumers with whom, unlike the stage actor, they lack rapport. While an actor in a theatre may regulate gesture in response to audience reaction, building a 'complete' performance over the span of the play, film actors are subjected to camera shifts and editorial decisions which fragment their role. The film industry responds to this shrivelling of the actor's 'person' with an artificial build up of the 'personality' outside the studio: 'The cult of the movie star, fostered by the money of the film industry, preserves not the unique aura of the person but the "spell of the personality", the phoney spell of a commodity.'[33] I have my doubts about 'unique aura[s]': the Jamesian possessive individual *is* denser than Benjamin's cinematic personality, but both should be set within that anthology of selves which constitutes a history of the identities that culture has recommended. Rosemary is a 'star' in Benjamin's terms. The disintegrative requirements of cinematic capital are as immediate to her as the solidities of accumulated wealth are natural to Mrs Diver.

Rosemary's greatest compliment to Dick is the offer of a screen test, even as 'the most sincere thing' she says to him is 'we're such *actors* – you and I' (p. 118; italics in source). Her 'love' is gestural and involves careful self-direction, a dance of camera angles culminating in the ultimate movie-still. Scene: Paris, a hotel. Enter two lovers, who are to walk up five flights of stairs. 'At the first landing they stopped and kissed.' Each landing is the site of variously careful kisses, until the final 'good-bye with their hands stretching to touch along the diagonal of the banister and then the fingers slipping apart' (p. 87). Freeze frame. The example is unfortunate insofar as it implies a degree of manipulation by Rosemary. What I am trying to suggest is rather different: that at "spontaneous", "intuitive", "instinctive" levels the system of production within which she works modifies her desire. Take her response to the director, Brady, in Monte Carlo: the director 'looked her over completely': he desires her, and 'in so far as her virginal emotions went', she 'contemplates surrender': 'It was a click . . . Yet she knew she would forget him half an hour after she left him – like an actor kissed in a picture' (p. 33). Brady desires the image of her that he might produce; she, in his looks as in a mirror, admires the image of herself remade: 'It was a click.' He has made her; she has bought it. Fitzgerald's terse noun is richly physiological *and* mechanical. Camera (lens) meets body (orifice) in a metaphor whose impertinence resides in the suggestion that desire is a machine. Fetishized and fetishistic, Rosemary is passive; she is pleasured by becoming an image in the directorial eye. Her frisson approaches that of Allen Berg's Lulu: 'When I looked at myself in the mirror I wished I were a man – a man married to me.'[34] Both images solicit male desire while remaining auto-erotic. In each the figure of the man is an intimate shadow who watches and is expelled. Jean Baudrillard generalizes the response as typical of desire elicited by the fetish:

> What fascinates us is that which always radically excludes us in the name of its internal logic or perfection: a mathematical formula, a concrete jungle, a useless object, or again, a smooth body, without orifices, doubled and redoubled by a mirror, devoted to perverse auto satisfaction.[35]

Rosemary, a screen virgin with a penchant for mirrors, is both penetrable and impenetrable, because to maximize profits she must, like the fetish, be available to all and possessed by none. Therefore, in Paris, when Collis Clay mentions her 'indiscretion' in a locked compartment of the Chicago train, Dick is agonized by 'the image of a third person' coming between himself and Rosemary. However, his obsessionally recurrent question, 'Do you mind if I pull down the curtain?' (p. 100) casts him in two roles: as the lover who pulls down the blind and as the intruder requesting blindness. His duplicity conforms to the structure of the fetish within which violation is inextricable from innocence:

> The vividly pictured hand on Rosemary's cheek, the quicker breath, the white excitement of the event viewed from outside, the inviolable secret warmth within.
> '– Do you mind if I pull down the curtain?'   (p. 100)

Repression succeeds only in generating phrases that censor as they sensualize: 'white excitement' and 'inviolable secret warmth' are split referents offering double-sensed messages which dramatize the mental musculature of the recipient of commodified sex. Since the viewer of pictures is stimulated by what he cannot have, innocence fuses with semen ('white'), while, like a hymen within a hymen, Rosemary's virginity (?), locked in a compartment, enfolds the mind's eye of the voyeur in its 'warmth'. Nathanael West was to present the contradiction with cartoon clarity in *The Day of the Locust* (1939); his would-be starlet, Faye Greenier, though a part-time prostitute, is most typically described as an egg, a cork, a tree and as having legs like scissors – all to underline her impenetrability. When we finally witness her penetration, two-thirds of the way through the novel, she raises a sheet in front of her face and vanishes. It is her last appearance because, possessed and thoroughly witnessed as possessed, she is no longer in the market.

At the broader economic level the star remains quasi-pristine because she must 'incarnate the *inaccessible* result of social labour by miming the sub-products of this labour which are magically transferred above it as a goal, power and vacations, decision and consumption, which are the beginning and end of an *undiscussed* process'.[36] A life dedicated to the fantasy of divorce from 'social labour' is liable at its most intimate levels to take the form of 'the seemingly lived' through which its earns its livelihood. Rosemary lives her body as a series of takes: in love she makes 'an exit that she had learned young, and on which no director had ever tried to improve' (p. 122), while 'a sort of ballet step' carries her clear of a dead black on her bed (p. 122). Neither move is artificial; hers is simply a physicality keyed to the emergent forms of economic reality. Dick, appearing at the onset of her stardom, offers a brief regression to an earlier though still active social form – an affair of nostalgia for the world of archaic fathers. Though technically the child of two fathers – military and medical – Rosemary is really the adopted daughter of the new fathers, anonymous, corporate figures who work to establish different modes of authority, protected and indeed naturalized by consumer desires, or rather by consumer frustrations. Possessed, Rosemary is no longer a star. During the final, protracted consummation of the affair in Rome, Dick wonders whether he is first or six hundred and forty-first; Rosemary's assurance that her previous sexual experience has been 'abortive' (p. 231) hardly reassures. Dick will never know, nor will he need to know, since consummation cancels his desire (at least for the fetish in this manifestation).

v

In many ways the damage has been done. Two events stand as symptoms of what is generally and mistakenly read as Diver's 'decline' – the death of the Reverend Diver and the beating in Rome. His father's death discontinues Dick's ties with the 'sureties' of the nineteenth century, more importantly the funeral allows him to recognize that severance. 'Good-by, my father – good-by, all my fathers' (p. 224) is rhetorically precise. Dick casts the Reverend Diver as a global figure in whose allegorical light he can see to cancel his debt to all manner of paternal economies. He challenges those patterns of causality and social activity which he has grouped within the name of the father. That the paternal term remains shaken is evidenced by the continuing resonance of Dick's allegorical outcry. The reader, rather more than the character, may find in the return to Europe several clues to fallen paternity. McKisco shares Dick's passage: Fitzgerald notes that he has made a literary name from 'pastiche', and adds, tellingly, the 'feat . . . [is] not to be disparaged' (p. 225). Misrepresentation of an original can, it seems, be the basis for 'new self respect'. As though seeking to underline the extent to which Dick moves through parable, Fitzgerald comments that McKisco's success 'was founded psychologically upon his duel with Tommy Barban' (p. 225): one has only to turn back to the duel on the golf course to see how thoroughly that foundation was itself a parody of a Turgenev story.[37] Even as pastiche ramifies, calling into question the authority of valid sources, Fitzgerald moves the reader forward through the assurance that 'fine dives have been made from flimsier spring-boards' (p. 225). The echo is both intended and prophetic – Diver will soon dive from a flimsy board to finalize his divorce from Nicole. The character's sense of an allegorical encounter is, however, necessarily more tentative and regressive: discovering 'a miserable family of two girls and their mother' at a loss for a father, Dick immediately stands in – his 'pleasure' at enabling them 'to regain their proper egotism' is brief and based, he now knows, on 'plot' and 'illusion' (p. 226). The "ego", as underwritten by the father, suffers further damage as Dick books into the hotel Quirinal in Rome and consummates his affair with Rosemary. Quirinus is a god of war identified with the deified Romulus. Fitzgerald's taste in hotels is less than casual: Dick beds the daughter of the new economic fathers in a room dedicated to a founding classical paternity. As if sacrilege against one deity were not enough, Dick finds the city of Papal fathers 'dirty', liable to 'Victorian dust' (p. 241) and to the 'sweat of exhausted cultures' (p. 244). A setting well-suited to disaffiliation and to the guilty self-dismemberment which succeeds it. The imbroglio with the taxi drivers results directly from Dick's disappointment at failing to contact a girl in a night club:

> She was a young English girl, with blonde hair and a healthy pretty English face and she smiled at him again with an invitation he understood, that denied the flesh even in the act of tendering it . . . 'She looks like somebody in the movies', he said.   (pp. 242–3)

The pick-up – a commercial extension of Rosemary – is not picked up; nonetheless, Dick gets himself beaten up as punishment for his desire: 'He felt his nose break like a shingle and his eyes jerk as if they had snapped back on a rubber band into his head. A rib splintered under a stamping heel' (p. 246). Dick asks for it, as though to prove to himself the evacuation of his own "integrity". In the shadow play of allegory he has cast down multiple fathers and has responded to the delights of the sphere of reproduction; he can, therefore, no longer experience selfhood as an entity. In court he has no option other than to insist that *he* raped the five-year-old girl because, 'Maybe I did' (p. 256). By straining to bury the bad father and to resurrect the good, so that Nicole may be made 'whole' again, Dick's entire professional and domestic life up to this seemingly ludicrous protestation may have served only to repeat the bad father's crime. Hasn't Rome, and Dick's commitment to a Daddy's girl whose very existence is wealth's new experiment with untraced channels of expenditure, *proved* that at one level *he* raped Nicole? My question is at once gnomic and dogmatic.

If I may be permitted the luxury of self-translation: read retrospectively, incest embodies accumulation; read as a projection having a different economic emphasis, Warren's act and Dick's complicity become expressions of accumulation's new problematic, the problematic of self-transgression – whereby energy (in this case sexual) needs to try untried combinations and to multiply selves as a multiplication of markets. Having acknowledged incest, Dick can only come apart multitudinously. The logic of reproduction has it that self-destruction, or rather a systematic revision of selfhood, is integral to the continuity of capital. The bourgeoisie of this phase are ever their own best barbarians, only by putting themselves to the sword, in the form of the advertising-copywriter's pen, can they ensure class longevity. Breakage becomes a structural principle of the bourgeoisie during the 1920s and therefore informs the latent plots and available personalities of that class.

The affair with Rosemary intensifies Dick's dawning sense of his own theatricality. In Rome he assures her 'gently' that his own social gifts are a 'trick' (p. 236); earlier, on the Riviera, he made a similar declaration to her mother, but then he cheered himself up with the phrase 'a trick of the heart' (p. 181). The integrative capacity of that iconic organ will not, however, withstand his later, careful distinction between 'manner' and 'morale'. Discussing his own transformation, he tells Rosemary at their final meeting, 'The change came a long way back – but at first it didn't show. The manner remains intact for some time after the morale cracks' (p. 307). His moral would seem to be: where manners are experienced as mannerisms, 'whole soul[s]' can no longer crystallize from their systematic application.[38]

The degree of Dick's self-knowledge belies the critical consensus which deprives him of an active place in his own fall. The very vocabulary of 'decline' charges an external force with responsibility: alcohol, money and authorial autobiography are prime suspects.[39] However, Dick's knowledge of his own position within a sexual and economic trauma makes the term 'failure' a critical whitewash. Consider a seemingly minor aspect of that so called 'failure' – loss of ear. In book III Dick's language coarsens and his vocal control diminishes. On a visit to the elevated Mary North, now Minghetti, he uses the term 'spic' in front of her Asian husband. Challenged on it by Nicole, he protests:

> 'Excuse me, I meant smoke. The tongue slipped.'
> 'Dick, this isn't faintly like you.'
> 'Excuse me again. I'm not much like myself anymore.'   (p. 280)

Slips proliferate. Prior to the Minghetti visit, Dr Gregovorius suggests, 'Why not try another leave of abstinence?' (p. 276); Dick's correction is 'automatic', but ignores the intent behind his partner's error. Franz has made the 'abstinence/absence' mistake once before (p. 213), and since his English is otherwise impeccable and we are led to believe that he is in all things efficient, Dick has obviously failed to hear disguised criticism. Once he ceases to practise psychiatry, mistakes multiply and are often characterized as phonological lapses. On board the aptly named *Margin* he misses the 'connotation of imminent peril' in Lady Caroline's 'terminal "what?"', and 'double-edged "Quite!"' (p. 282); his voice is untypically 'dogmatic', and he is snubbed. Even the servants talk back; the cook, Augustine, threatens Dick with a butcher knife until he 'master[s] a firmer tone' (p. 286). Fitzgerald's concern with vocal reception and exchange extends to Nicole, who senses from Dick's voice, 'throbbing with insincerity', that a transition is occurring: 'For months every word has seemed to have an overtone of some other meaning, soon to be resolved under circumstances that Dick would determine' (p. 301). Such 'overtones' no longer issue from the skilful negotiation of social context or from the paternal connotations of that ambience – tones with which Mrs Diver is presumably *au fait*; rather, phonological collapse produces uncontrolled innuendo as Dick fails to disguise his growing need to leave Nicole.

The vocal rot sets in most strikingly in Rome, where sexual slang makes a sudden and untypical appearance. Within the space of four pages a high-class prostitute is referred to as a 'frail', a 'tart' and a 'trick' (pp. 239–42). The incursion of a new vocabulary offers two opportunities. Either the slang is read as part of a wider removal of women towards commodity and fetish ('trick[s]', as Collis Clay rightly has it, are 'quick'; Fitzgerald's assonance speeds an already speedy epithet, and so generalizes Dick's Roman mood). Or, habituated to double articulation, with its attendant associative thickening, the reader hears 'frail' through its antonym 'hard' (as in 'I'm a mean hard woman' (p. 29)), thereby locating the term within the oppositional lexicons of accumulation and reproduction. Similarly, 'trick', given Dick's double insistence that his charm is trickery, transcribes to manners the coloration of purchase. In both cases a semantic collision between two worlds – the drawing-room and the sexual marketplace – produces a double-voiced word and therefore a split referent.[40] Preference for one world will result in a particular form of semantic stabilization, while inability to decide produces a clash which is eventually political insofar as the reader remains uncertain about her position within a crucial economic shift.

My polysemic exercise may sound like semantic taxidermy (stuffing an epithet with enough plot to fill a novel), but even if some version of reader hesitation occurs over these words, then, as Dick's ear fails him, the reader's ear grows in acuity. It might be objected that all successful novels sensitize their readers to the multiple significance of terms; it is, however, to be remembered that within the psychological framework of *this* novel, polysemy leads to the father (or, at least, simultaneously points to paternity even as it obscures paternal cupidity). The discovery that one has developed a good ear involves a vocal transference setting the reader in 'the focal armchair of the leisure class' which Dick has quit. As work on associative structures builds a particular and divided semantic density, so reading begins to resemble, at one level, the labour which makes manners meaningful – what Dick might call 'giv[ing] all the transitions their full value' (p. 30). If it can be said that the semantics of *Tender is the Night* are partially constituted after the cumulative forms of the *haute bourgeoisie*, then readers become, in Rosemary's phrase about Dick, 'curator[s] of a richly incrusted happiness' (p. 87), where readerly bliss derives from the creation of Byzantine semantic artifacts founded on the father's name. A word of warning: 'the father' is uncertain ground to build on, since the novel establishes that the image of the father is a divided image and that the accumulations made in his name – be they psychic, economic or mannered – are capable of two histories. It would be as well to remember that since a double sense of accumulation lies at the heart of polysemy, all associations are not equal, nor need more necessarily be better.

Appreciation of polysemy almost of necessity involves re-reading. At first encounter, the associative conflict latent in 'frail' and 'trick' is barely audible: re-reading instils plots into single terms by setting them within a central tension. So, reading again thickens what before was thin. For example:

> Across from the hotel two *carabinieri*, grotesque in swaddling capes and harlequin hats, swimming voluminously from this side and that, like mains'ls coming about, and watching them she [Baby] thought of the guards' officer who had stared at her so intensely at lunch. He had possessed the arrogance of a tall member of a short race, with no obligation save to be tall. Had he come up to her and said: 'Let's go along, you and I,' she would have answered, 'Why not?' – at least it seemed so now, for she was still disembodied by an unfamiliar background.
>
> Her thoughts drifted back slowly through the guardsman to the two *carabinieri*, to Dick – she got into bed and turned out the light.   (p, 247)

It is quite likely that the innuendo of 'tall member', activated by Baby's sexual reverie, might affect how 'Dick' was read first time round. But the fact that on the previous page Dick has been arrested for 'fix[ing]' a 'baby' who, it transpires, is a policeman in plain clothes, alerts us to an affinity between Authority, Infancy and Disguise, which is further enhanced by 'swaddling capes', and by Baby's effect on the American consul: '[her] clean-sweeping irrational temper that had broken the moral back of a race and made a nursery out of a continent, was too much for him' (p. 253). Linked networks emerge as meanings (or more properly as coherently split referents) only when the incest plot grows clear. Clarification may involve reading the novel several times. However, to read *Tender is the Night* more than once is to read in the full light of Dick's abdication; consequently, to read again is to build a semantic model mirroring the shifting disciplines of accumulation even as Dick deserts those disciplines.

VI

Before explaining the implications of the reader's bad timing, I had best establish briefly and I hope clearly that Dick neither declines nor falls – he jumps or, more specifically, takes a dive. His repeated failure to raise a man on his shoulders while riding an aquaplane can be taken as an expression of middle-aged vanity or as the nostalgia of a dissolute athlete; however, such readings ignore the pervasive vocabulary of theatre running through the incident. Arguably, Dick's manner of parting company with the Baby Gar is the last act in his release from and of Nicole. Immediately after the event, on the beach with Rosemary and Nicole, Dick discusses acting in what is effectively a gloss on his own recent performance. He promotes a style of 'burlesque' arising from the actor's compulsive need to retain audience attention, arguing that, since the audience can 'do the "responding" for themselves', the duty of the performer is 'to do something unexpected': 'If the audience thinks the character is hard she goes soft on them – if they think she's soft she goes hard. You go all *out* of character – you understand?' (pp. 309–10; italics in source). Dick outlines his own method on the board. He too went 'all *out* of character'. Where the audience thinks him adroit, he is inept. Where the audience hopes for direction, he mismanages. A performance of decline is undertaken at some distance from the facts of decline – almost in the style of one of Brecht's Chinese actors:

> The performer portrays incidents of utmost passion, but without his delivery becoming heated. At those points where the character portrayed is deeply excited the performer takes a lock of hair between his lips and chews it. But this is like a ritual, there is nothing eruptive about it. It is quite clearly somebody else's repetition of the incident: a representation.[41]

Dick's 'alienation effect' entails the representation of dissolution so that Nicole may be released to the new forms of money. Moreover, the workshop with Rosemary underlines the point for Nicole. She is told that her 'lover is dead' and that in order to retain her class position (perceived as a relationship with a mass audience) she must avoid 'response' (emotion) and pursue gesture. Significantly, in his theatrical masterclass Dick casts himself as the 'murdered Chinese', perhaps as an ironic reflection upon his status as disposable body-servant. The lesson (which might be entitled, 'Burlesque, and how to do it') is the culmination of Dick's language of fabrication, and reflects his conviction that the social arena has become a stage on which audience demand is paramount; consequently, 'charm' and 'grace' give way to mere lying, as the mass market requires of its market leaders only that they surprise and so, through provision of the 'new', continue to lead. Nicole obeys instructions: she turns directly to Barban and to brand name, going 'all *out* of character' in order to retain the characteristics of a changing class. She leaves the beach feeling 'new and happy' (p. 310). 'Knowing vaguely that Dick has planned for her to have it' (p. 311), she writes a letter propositioning her next husband.

If my reading stands, Dick is an active agent through his decision not to act. By book III he is no longer a spontaneous taker of initiatives; 'the fine glowing surface' onto which passers-by had tended to spring, 'like monkeys with cries of relief' (p. 94), is dulled. Effectively, Dick declares himself no longer effective, no longer a centre, an author or indeed a responsible agent of action. All is lethargy, parody and scorn: witness the sustained metaphors of vampirism, Dick's bouts of 'interior laughter' (p. 337), and his final act – 'with a papal cross he blessed the beach from the high terrace' (p. 337) – the gesture cuts both ways, "spoiling" his antecedents and his future, his father's and his own professions. Dick abdicates comprehensively from what has made him, from his familial and professional tasks, and, more disturbingly, from what he has been made – a 'whole-souled' (p. 67), integral being.

Fitzgerald's critics, for the most part addicted to the "romance" of Fitzgerald and to the "heroic" individuality of his heroes, can see the strain but will permit no abdication. Typically, Matthew Bruccoli's most recent work is titled '*The Last of the Novelists*': in his 'Preliminaries' Bruccoli strikes his general note:

> Fitzgerald believed in ordered social structures and in the role of the individual character in maintaining them. His concept of character was romanticized however, for he also believed in great men . . . Fitzgerald was a believer. He grew up believing in the promise of America. He believed in the possibilities of life. He believed in character. He believed in decency, honor, courage, responsibility.[42]

One can almost hear the cavalry chafing at the sunset. Though extreme, Bruccoli is representative. His last-ditch believer is easily transformed into the liberal suicide, without the slightest challenge to the idea of an integral subject, be he author or character. Read through 'The crack-up' (1935), Dick's withdrawal becomes preparatory writing for Fitzgerald's despair: by means of the author's 'there was not an "I" any more',[43] the character's 'I' is returned to him, albeit in misery.[44] A neat critical trick, locking integrity back into a character who is no longer there to receive it.

Dick cannot be put together again nor ought the reader comfortably to read his decline through integrative Jamesian spectacles. Poised above contrary movements within the capital which provides his foundation, the character experiences how 'I' becomes 'we', and how 'we' becomes 'us'. To adapt an Althusserian distinction: he loses interest in himself as an 'individual' because he recognizes himself as a 'subject', that is as something subjected and produced by and productive of forces that he learns to despise.[45] In response, he quits the crucial sites of 'interpolation',[46] those places at which we are bound over and into those lives which our culture would prefer. In no particular order, and virtually all at once, he deserts the psychiatric armchair, the surrogate drawing-rooms, the nursery, the phallus and even (projecting) the sound-stage. Dick's dive is complete and outdistances the critics. Perhaps 'the old interior laughter' (p. 337) prompted the selection of an aquaplane from which to parody his surname, thereby matching the doubling and splitting of his christian name achieved by his profession. To push the pun (maybe no further than Fitzgerald intended) Dick does not resurface: without fixed abode or declared destination, his movements after his return to America are quite literally mapped by Nicole, but they are not understood. Symptomatically, he rejects her offer of money and no longer 'ask[s] for the children to be sent' (p. 338), capital and the family being two of the mediations through which he made himself what he was and is no longer.

The problem remains: if Dick "decides" to quit, and money, alcohol, general dissolution or Fitzgerald's autobiography cannot in any emphatic sense be "blamed", *why* does he quit? At no point in the novel is his decision directly addressed, an omission that should not produce charges of slack construction or inadequate characterization. The question raises the broader issue of Fitzgerald's narrative technique. Cause passes from persons into objects viewed as metaphors or, more properly, as plot-miniatures and encapsulated narratives. Fitzgerald's nine-year struggle with the construction of *Tender is the Night* reflects his fear that "story" no longer issues from "voice", even as action no longer resides in he who acts. Commodity, perceived as having a particular history, becomes the new narrative centre. Things, and characters as their carriers, "determine" action. Such a view is focussed by Marx in his definition of the commodity form: 'It is nothing but the definite social relation between men themselves which assumes here, for them, the fantastic form of a relation between things.'[47] 'Things' grow positively hydra-headed as they register a marked shift in the system of production and so in relations between men.

At the risk of repetition and in order to re-approach the issue of Dick's "decision": *Tender is the Night* establishes that a beach umbrella casts the 'shadow of the fantastic phallus',[48] which as it falls assumes the restless forms of changing accumulation and modified manners. The umbrella is typical of the Divers' belongings in that it comes to mean through various human processes. If the meaning of an object is not an idea but a 'petrifaction of action',[49] things are always and necessarily human: it follows that action may recognize itself in those objects of which it is a part. I have been reading Fitzgerald's perceptual habits through Sartre's 'practico inert'; further quotation may help: 'The idea of a thing is in the thing, that is to say, it is the thing itself revealing its reality through the practice which constitutes it, and through the instruments and institutions which define it.'[50] The *practico inert* is a large constituent of our subjectivity, since it is that which surrounds us *ad nauseam*, and in whose worked matter we learn, almost without learning, how to work. Things so defined operate as a strict but scarcely felt necessity at the heart of human relations: 'Materialized practices, poured into the exteriority of things, impose a common destiny on men who know nothing of one another.'[51] Sartre would surely concede Marx's point that under capital 'destiny' cannot finally be 'common' because the interests and actions of those who labour and those who invest are not necessarily at one. Within commodity production, matter is not fully coherent, since it bears contradictory inscriptions and contending futures. Fitzgerald knows that 'folding beach cushions' and 'miniatures for a doll's house' are products 'of much ingenuity and toil' (p. 65), not the least of it going on in chicle factories and canneries, and that consequently, if 'toil' changes, the future latent in cushions and dolls must change. Again Sartre clarifies: '[things] possess an inert future within which we have to determine our own future. The future comes to man through things insofar as it previously came to things through man.'[52]

For 'future' it is tempting to say 'futures', particularly of 1929, and still more particularly of 1929 viewed from 1934. It would be gratifying to see the Crash as *annus mirabilis*/the time of changes when 'destiny' shifted from the Manifest to the several. What is striking is that, having timed Dick's dive for the summer of 1929, and having provided a glimpse of flame on Wall Street, Fitzgerald implies calmly that capital survives through structural transformation and that futures, though they should be legion, may not even number two. In a much-quoted passage describing Nicole's shopping, Fitzgerald sets global capital aboard a fast train running anarchically from Chicago to a Parisian shop window; his extended metaphor implies a crash the better to avert it:

> these were some of the people who gave a tithe to Nicole, and as the whole system swayed and thundered onward it lent a feverish bloom to such processes of hers as wholesale buying, like the flush of a fireman's face holding his post before a spreading blaze. She illustrated very simple principles, containing in herself her own doom, but illustrated them so accurately that there was grace in the procedure, and presently Rosemary would try to imitate it.   (p. 65)

Nicole illustrates capital's tendency to recurrent crisis.[53] Her family money 'contains its own doom' because, by investing in the massive expansion of production during the post-war decade, the Warrens promote overproduction and the attendant dramatic fall in their own profit. The plot has a twist (as incest had two faces): Nicole's graceful buying mirrors capital's self-correcting concern for consumers and consumption. So, standing at 'the exact furthermost evolution of [her] class' (p. 30), Accumulation's child may yet give a lesson to the daughter of Reproduction, and eventually find her 'grace' imitated in the movies. By such indirections do the imperatives of accumulation metamorphose into the necessities of reproduction. The moral is as simple as the story: 'The market's narrative is self-healing and absolute.'

What is initially odd about this passage is that it ignores one of its own fiercest insights: that things are the loci of more or less antagonistic connections between classes. At which point Fitzgerald could be charged, as James was charged, with wilful amnesia, except that Fitzgerald's style of omission is not Jamesian. What he leaves out he points to. In *The Bostonians* 'the social dusk' of the 1870s remains 'mysterious' and unthreatening because it gets no further than Charlie, who vanishes. In contrast, Fitzgerald indicates that if 'love-birds' come tagged 'chicle factory' then labour *makes* leisure. There is no need for the critic to slip an unsolicited economic sub-text into *Tender is the Night*, since the novel's dating ensures that 1929 shadows all events; the fact that it has so little final effect is neither ambiguous nor evasive, it is merely decisive. Fitzgerald's muffled Crash implies the continuity of capital. Labour has no 'future', beyond consumerism, because capital ensures its own vitality by switching plots.

Once again I return to my two available master-stories – Accumulation and Reproduction. The one archaic, the other curative; each implies different typicalities of subject and object. Dick's decisive dive, though less dramatic, is rather more telling than suicides from tall corporate premises. His long marination in the realm of carefully considered objects – be they beach cushions or words from a couch – makes him capable of a 'delicate empiricism which so intimately involves itself with the object that it becomes true theory'.[54] His problem in 1929 is that the objects are changing as market 'practice' and 'the instruments and institutions' of capital change. Dick appreciates, but will not make, that particular transition. Instead he disengages himself from his marriage and from the *haute bourgeoisie*, old and new.

Initially the facts of the new life do not support an act of severance; indeed, the final chapter repeats the pattern of the larger narrative. Repatriation and return to Buffalo, the last parish of the good father, suggest a ghostly reversion to 'whole soul[s]', while Dick's choice of subsequent domicile (Geneva), allied to a disruptive association with a 'girl', indicates that disintegral elements persist. However, several details carry hints of Dick's 'interior laughter'. The choice of Lockport, given that Dick viewed himself as both key and janitor, is a striking revision of autobiography: the name splits – Nicole's keeper is now a creature of passage between several ports of call. His unfinished manuscript, whose title 'would look monumental in German' (p. 227) (a taxonomic work, preoccupied with 'Uniform . . . Classification'), is carried with him as a sexual come-on: the proximity between 'much admired by the ladies' and 'the big stack of papers on his desk' (p. 338) is more than suggestive, it is a comic recapitulation of Dick's first love – after all, if his profession got him a wife, why should it not make him a less orderly "ladies' man"? Just as a Shakespearian sub-plot will often re-perform high doings among the lower orders, so the last chapter of *Tender is the Night* repeats the novel from an entirely different perspective. Dick is no longer a psychiatrist but a general practitioner, and his 'girl' is now culled from a 'grocery story' (I am reminded of the 'girls' who 'worked rudely at the Five-and-Tens on Christmas Eve' to pay their 'tithe' (p. 65) to Nicole). Once social/semantic inversion is recognized, other terms become 'loopholes', issuing covert glances towards another class.[55] Dick stops for a time in Geneva, a town which Nicole locates with an atlas as being in 'the Finger Lakes' section of New York: since Dick has quit his adoptive class and wanders from town to smaller town to 'very small town', he doubtless practises or will practise among manual workers. Perhaps her session with the atlas reminded Nicole that she was 'born hating the smell of a nurse's fingers dressing her' (p. 260); maybe the name even triggers Frau Gregorovious's body-odour, 'less a smell than an ammoniacal reminder of the eternity of toil and decay' (p. 260)?

Such speculation has less to do with Nicole's psychology than with the novel's tendency to double articulation. Words like 'Lockport' and 'Finger', once set within their associative networks, tend maliciously to distort themselves, hinting at diversity and implying that their diversity rises from social conflict. Take Nicole's final effort to map Dick – she likens him to Grant: 'Perhaps, so she liked to think, his career was biding its time, again like Grant's in Galena' (p. 338). The simile is an inappropriate Algerism: Dick has gone from high to low and from low to anonymous, but Nicole requires him to be Grant on the brink of a commission and the path to presidential office, because the liberal myth that you can't keep a good hero down comforts her even as her own integrity is dispelled among brand names. But while Fitzgerald's carefully tentative phrasing ('Perhaps, so . . .') invites us to expose exactly why the simile belongs to Nicole, he reminds us that earlier it belonged to the drunken Abe North and to the 'omniscient' voice ('*again* like Grant's . . .'; my italics). His point is that words and figures always belong to someone and that therefore their meaning is partial and open to distrust; in this instance the novelist should distrust his own voice. Commenting, in book II, chapter 1, on a brief résumé of Dick's Zurich period (1917–20), Fitzgerald had noted:

The foregoing has the ring of a biography, without the satisfaction of knowing that the hero, like Grant, lolling in his general store in Galena, is ready to be called to an intricate destiny. Moreover, it is confusing to come across a youthful photograph of someone known in a rounded maturity and gaze with shock upon a fiery, wiry, eagle-eyed stranger. Best to be reassuring – Dick Diver's moment now began.   (p. 132)

His own omniscient usage is the more elaborate of the two: to learn that the Grant/Diver 'destiny' is 'intricate', having just read book i, is to locate intricacy in the vocabulary of aesthetic appreciation. So placed, Grant's career seems to summon the epithets of etiquette: 'complete' (p. 28), complex (p. 30), 'hard, neat' (p. 14), immobile (p. 27); it becomes an object ripe for contemplation, joining the 'exquisite consideration' of Dick's manner (p. 37) or 'the intensely calculated perfection' of the Villa Diana (p. 37) within a particular aura of consumption. As an '*intricate* destiny' (my italics), Dick's story is impelled by Accumulation. By repeating the simile, Fitzgerald allies his voice with Nicole's, only to give both voices the lie. Part of him, like Nicole, wishes to 'reassure', and therefore begins 'Dick Diver's moment' and ends his novel by alluding to an heroic version of the Alger plot – from drunken poverty to 'intricate' wealth. However, Nicole omits the 'general store', and her omission is noisy; the reader can hardly forget Dick's recent sexual entanglement with a 'grocery store'. The facts of Dick's new life may be gathered by Nicole, but their phrasing belongs to Fitzgerald, consequently 'again' is a crucial instruction. The reader compares the similes only to find that she is comparing the final paragraphs of two brief biographical chapters, one of which (book ii, ch. i) purports to be the beginning and the other (book iii, ch. 13) the end of Dick Diver's 'moment' (p. 194). Beginnings and ends are notoriously arbitrary, but these are downright subversive: instead of marking out an area within which causality may be constructed, this beginning and this ending, like a counterplay within a play, erase the marks. Dick's life within the *haute bourgeoisie* shrinks to a 'moment', and as 335 pages give way before five (book ii, ch. i plus book iii, ch. 13), Accumulation and Reproduction no longer seem absolute. Other social formations, other imperatives, other wills and authorities open up. Time, from being circumscribed by the demands of one class, becomes diverse. Dick, after all, started his career without 'feudal' monies and has chosen to go back to the 'general store' – a context in which 'intricate' may simply mean complicated or even 'entangled', and where 'destiny' is liable to sound hyperbolic when applied to a life that seeks anonymity and silence.[56] Here re-reading means learning to unread.

The double articulation which characterizes the last chapter of the novel is different from that into which the reader is elsewhere invited. The conflicting semantic determinants of 'Finger' and 'Lockport' may be traced to a suppressed dispute between voices, each semantic possibility deriving its intention from a markedly different class position; in contradistinction the debate about 'frail' and 'trick' – or even the broader duplicities of the incest story – depend upon and express the changing dynamic of a single class. It is tempting to read book III, chapter 13 as a return of the repressed, and therefore as Fitzgerald's exoneration of Lukács's judgement that the proletariat (though hidden in puns and masked in simile) is the only radical class, because it sees the entirety of the system from the base[57] (and so must murmur threats through the established meaning of dominant groups). Such a reading would carry "reading against the grain" towards a pet pathology. For all his sensitivity to double-directed words and fissured referents, Fitzgerald recognizes that capital – albeit capital in transition – determines semantic collisions. Labour, even in 1934, has to his ear only sufficient voice to whisper from the depths of concluding puns.

It might be objected that my reading of Fitzgerald has made far too much of multivalency, that polysemy has been induced and puns provoked by reference to associative networks that may look all very well on these pages but bear little relation to the pages of *Tender is the Night*. I can only appeal again to Fitzgerald's perception of economic history to explain his proclivity if not for puns then for internally polemic terms. In 1922 Fitzgerald described himself as 'a socialist' nervous about 'the people';[58] in 1932 he described Dick Diver as 'a communist–liberal–idealist, a moralist in revolt', adding, 'the hero . . . is a man like myself brought up in a family sunk from haute burgeoisie to petite burgeoisie'.[59] A reading of the letters suggest that to combine any and all these terms would be to approximate to the vagaries of Fitzgerald's political position(s). What is clear is that he read some Marx, advocated the reading of Marx[60] and by the late thirties believed that 'most questions in life have an economic base (at least according to us Marxians)'.[61] The throw-away parentheses are typical: writing to his cousin Ceci Taylor in 1934 he appends a confidential post-script to a letter preoccupied with the problems of making money from scripts and stories:

> P.S. Apropos of our conversation it will interest you to know that I've given up politics. For two years I've gone half haywire trying to reconcile my double allegiance to the class I am part of, and the Great Change I believe in . . . I have become disgusted with the party leadership and have only health enough for my literary work, so I'm on the sidelines . . . This is confidential, of course.[62]

The two-year period in question (1932–4) spans his most concentrated work on *Tender is the Night*. A *Ledger* note of November 1932 reads,

'Political worries, almost neurosis.'[63] Just as in the last chapter of the novel Fitzgerald alludes to a class dispute that is contained within a semantic dispute, so, in his letters, those aspects of his life that threaten the social fabric to which he is committed, are bracketed or set to one side. Nonetheless, while writing *Tender is the Night*, Fitzgerald experienced 'double allegiance' with troubling intensity; his decision to bracket the political, and to interdict family talk about that decision, suggests that a certain leakage of anxiety into the manuscript was inevitable.[64] In which case, the divided semantics which I have been tracing within the novel's language may be said to arise from Fitzgerald's acute, awkward and partially prohibited sense of the inter-relations of class and change.

Fitzgerald is not a punster in any simple sense of the word: the valency of his language is the product of significant quibbles within capital. Capital changes, particularly during the merger wave of the twenties and the early Depression years, dividing the bourgeoisie: social planes collide within a class, yielding divided objects, subjects and meanings. As capital perfects its translation from the monopoly form to what has variously been designated 'late', 'multinational' or 'post-industrial' capital; as it summons the electronic and eventually nuclear means to realize its evolving structural imperatives; as it creates and colonizes mass desire, so its objects and subjects stabilize, at least for a time. The fissured owning-class heals itself and continues (Nicole is 'cured'). Fitzgerald's quibbling registers a revolution within a class. The instability of his text (also realized in its nine-year multiform gestation, and in its preoccupation with wounds, scars and surface 'completeness') is a response to a revolution within capital. Because, during the twenties, capital contained pronouncedly different kinds of capital, 'emergent' and 'residual' forms necessarily clashed within social and semantic relations. Read historically, Fitzgerald's puns are not playful; behind them lie voices arguing for different ways of life.

To hear the vectors within Fitzgerald's language is eventually to discern two prevalent impulses each directed towards a different mode of cultural production: at the semantic level these might be described as 'dense' (Accumulation) and 'transparent' (Reproduction). Put crudely, one may read the novel as a Jamesian spin-off or as a proto-Harold Robbins; what is particularly troubling is that the options co-exist, and that their co-existence informs the novel's structure from narrative, through character to language. The incest which generates the plot puts good and bad fathers together in Dick. Nicole and Rosemary are not simply anti-types; both are Daddy's girl and each takes on the other's style. The play within 'frail' can be read through its antonym 'hard' (Accumulation) or through its synonym 'quick trick' (Reproduction); once heard, each stays to irritate the other, they become polar similarities. Because we hear both and can suppress neither, at all these levels, the process of reading and re-reading *Tender is the Night* provides what Late Capital must deny: history – a history, from drawing-room to Hollywood, of the very thing that would revoke history – commodity.

5

Iconic narratives: or, how three Southerners fought the second civil war

I

Cotton prices stood at twenty cents a pound in 1927, by 1931 the going rate was five cents. Political leaders realized that in order to raise prices they would have to restrict production, and in 1933 the Agricultural Adjustment Act offered Southern landowners between seven and twenty dollars an acre (depending on estimated yield) to plough their cotton under. Fifty-three per cent of the South's cotton acreage went out of production. Since a share cropper, cropping on a half the crop agreement, would by rights receive half the federal payment for the sacrifice of any of his acres, it paid landowners not to sign share-cropping contracts for the following year. Instead, they might hire the same cropper on a wage, pay him to plough the crop under, and reap the entire subsidy themselves. Between 1935 and 1940 the Southern tenantry declined by more than 25 per cent while the number of hired labourers increased proportionately. Necessarily, land use changed: the fragmented plantation, divided between numerous tenant families, was replaced by the neo-plantation, a single and enlarged unit of production. Enclosure swept the cotton South during the late thirties.

The conversion of share croppers into cash workers sounds like little more than a local disturbance: even re-phrased as the destruction of a peasantry and its replacement by wage labour, the shift remains a piece of agricultural history. Yet the transformation of a labouring class is necessarily the transformation of the class that owns, while a change in the social relations of production signals a change in the regime of accumulation – in which case, Jonathan Wiener's claim, that the thirties saw the South's 'second Civil War', is apt.[1] Arguably, the influx of federal subsidy cheques induced a more thoroughgoing revolution than that achieved by the influx of federal troops. To make the case, it will be necessary to gloss the Southern economy from 1850 to the Depression. In the cause of brevity, and because I am concerned eventually to talk about a literary preoccupation with land ownership, I shall attempt my potted history from a single perspective, that of the owning class.

In the antebellum South the large slaveholder, if he was a capitalist, was a 'human capitalist';[2] that is to say, he held his capital in human form and was indifferent to alternative patterns of accumulation. With cotton a boom crop, the owner sought only to spread his investment across as many acres as possible, thereby generating more cash to invest in more slaves. There seemed little point in raising the value of land through investment in canals, railways or towns, when human capital yielded such a high return. However, the Civil War sought to modify the owner's habit of accumulation. By emancipating the slaves the North destroyed the Southern planter's most valuable body of movable property and his only credit collateral. 'Masters without slaves' could no longer be 'labour lords' and became instead lords of the land, much of it destitute. A post-Reconstruction call for "internal improvements" did draw substantial Northern capital into town development and transport networks: indeed, the 1880s saw a high rate of industrial beginnings as some Southern owners, in an act of 'ideological capitulation'[3] sought to make a capital gain on land itself. Nonetheless, in large part the South remained an agricultural region. The majority of planters did not turn themselves into industrialists; instead they sought to extract profit from freedmen as an available, though initially resistant, workforce. Since the Civil War settlement did not involve the redistribution of plantation lands to ex-slaves, and since most freedmen had acquired no property under slavery, the owners, as landlords, controlled the employment chances of the great proportion of black Southerners. Consequently, Northern hopes for the development of a free market in the South proved fragile; freedmen were sufficiently "free" to resist gang labour and vagrancy acts, but, lacking capital, they were not "free" enough to avoid being bound in yet another "peculiar institution" – the institution of share cropping.

Share wages differ substantially from free wages. The owner contracts to pay his labourer at the close of the growing season; payment takes the form of a pre-determined "share" of the crop. Should the yield be low, or the international price of cotton drop, or the market be glutted, the cropper may not make enough to pay the merchant who has furnished his seed and his sustenance on credit for the year: in which case, the tenant becomes a peon insofar as he is bound to labour to pay the debt.[4] The debt holder, be he the merchant, or the planter, or both as one, exerts an absolute authority over the labourer. As an Arkansas share cropper put it

in 1939: 'De landlord is landlord, de politician is landlord, de shurf is
landlord, ever'body is landlord, en we ain't got nothin.'[5] From the
owner's point of view, being a landlord, operating share wages, was
tantamount to being a 'labour lord' all over again.

Jonathan Wiener argues that, because owners maintained 'involun-
tary servitude' as 'the special Southern form of wage', from Reconstruction to New Deal, they cannot be spoken of as 'classic capitalists'.[6] In the
North, capital developed sequentially: mechanization led to a considerable division of labour and an increased surplus, which in turn prompted
competitive investment in technology. Innovation raised output, and
the threat of overproduction ensured a "high-wage" economy, in which
workers doubled as consumers. Capitalists, too, had to change,
converting their "captaincy" from industry to consciousness, in order to
maintain consumption. Southern owners had little interest in transform-
ing either their workers or their technology or themselves; share
cropping guaranteed a low-cost labour force tied to the land and
delivering a good profit for as long as cotton remained high in
international markets;[7] moreover, mechanization appeared redundant
in the context of a large and "bound" labour force. Indeed, machinery
would only disrupt a social and political order founded on the owner's
capacity to pay low across the board: that order 'constituted a fully
formed system', whose difference from Northern 'classic capitalism'[8]
rested on labour-repressive production enforced by state restrictions on
the mobility of workers.

Whether or not one sets the South on Wiener's 'Prussian road'[9] seems
less important than the recognition that owners – at least in the
agricultural section, and at least until the late thirties – were not a
bourgeoisie in any sense that Fitzgerald would have understood. The
planter's concern with the preservation of repressive social relations, as a
means to a "low-wage" economy, marginalized those props to the
bourgeois world – individual freedom and consumerism. Consequently,
the planter was at best a bourgeois in an impacted state of development.
Harold Woodman argues, of the period from 1870 to 1900, that the new
South experienced the evolution of a bourgeois society rooted in
capitalist relations, but did so with 'the remnants of a society and political
structure and an ideology' antagonistic to the transition.[10] In this the
South differed strikingly from the North, whose modernization, half a
century earlier, had the ideological backing of the dominant institutions.
For some historians of the South 'modernization' is complete by the
thirties. Jack Kirby points out that by 1934 the average income of
planters was on a par with that of white-collar professionals (physicians,
attorneys and dentists). He therefore concludes that 'planters were of the
modern world. Their tenants to varying degrees were not.'[11] His

distinction ignores the degree to which the very process of maintaining a peasantry casts the maintainer in a pre-modern mould. He who preserves long-standing prohibitions – denying access to the debt book or mystifying market procedures – does so to perpetuate a dispensation that has been naturalized by time, in the light of which those who command service are liable to see themselves, aristocratically, as more father than farmer. The planter, equipped with the share-wage agreement, continued to be (in Woodman's terms) an antagonistic remnant, liable to resist his own 'modernization'.

Not until the thirties did the combination of an unreversed downturn in cotton prices and government subsidies break the share-wage system. Under pressure throughout the decade, planters 'altered their mode of production fundamentally',[12] and as a result, between 1933 and 1950, most share croppers and share tenants were evicted or converted into cash labourers. Kirby refers to 'a shocking modernization', in which pre-modern paternalism, laced with capitalist exploitation, was ousted by the impersonal rule of the national labour market, backed up by federal government in its capacity as off-season welfare source.[13] Federal support for the cash nexus completed the work undertaken by the Freedman's Bureau in the 1860s. Not only were the "bound" conclusively "freed", but planters were finally deprived of their status as lords of labour, and were required to farm their fields like factories, or risk incorporation into the nearest successful unit of production. The neo-plantation was an enclosed space of mechanical innovation on which labour was hired and fired in accordance with the rhythms of technical change. 'Most Southerners watched the technological blitz from behind their mules or from the North.'[14] Nonetheless, since 1940 the per capita income of the South has persistently grown at rates well over the national average; economic growth from the forties to the sixties has ensured that 'it is now virtually impossible to find an essentially regional Southern identity in economic life'.[15] As soon as it was no longer necessary for planters to defend a low-wage economy, Northern industrial capital (with its high-wage potential) ceased to be a threat. After 1945 a recruitment drive by Southern states prompted an influx of "outside money", particularly in defence-related activities. The small farmer and the occasional agricultural worker could at last try to come out from behind their debts.

Arguably, the end of the share-wage contract, and of the social relations that preserved it, was the end of the South's singular regime of accumulation, itself the basis of the region's distinctiveness. If so, the owner, who during the thirties might just have thought of himself as a part-time pre-modern patriarch, could, by 1945, do little more than accept his full-time white-collar status with grace.

II

The burden of my earlier chapters suggests that a culture committed to wage labour and its attendant forms of accumulation generates a commodity aesthetics, within which particular narrative options exist for the writer. It should follow that a culture, or a cultural fragment, which resists wage labour and the consequent spread of the shop window, will generate an aesthetics of anti-development. During the thirties the South produced a number of writers for whom the agricultural section of the economy became both a preoccupation and one source of a distinctive poetics (I am thinking particularly of the New Critical interest in the 'verbal icon'). The Agrarian essays collected in *I'll Take My Stand* (1930) share with the New Critical writings of John Crowe Ransom and Allen Tate a concern for images whose iconicity depends overtly upon their capacity to withstand market forces. Let me clarify by reading part of Andrew Lytle's account of a midday meal on a small Tennessean farm, circa 1930, through a critical stencil designed by Ransom in *God Without Thunder* (1931) and *The New Criticism* (1941):

> And they eat with eighteenth-century appetites. There is no puny piddling with the victuals, and fancy tin-can salads do not litter the table. The only salad to be seen on a country table is sallet, or turnip greens . . . It has the appearance of spinach; but, unlike this insipid slime, sallet has character, like the life of the farmer at the head of the table. The most important part of this dish is its juice, the pot licker, a rich green liquid, indescribable except as a pot-liquor green . . . Particularly is it fine for teething babies. If the baby is weaned in the dark of the moon and fed a little pot liquor, he will pass through the second summer without great trouble. This will not relieve the pain of cutting. To do that a young rabbit must be killed, its head skinned, and the raw flesh rubbed on the gums. If this fails, tie a spray of alderberries around its neck, or hang a mole's foot. But sallet will do everything but cut the pain.[16]

To eat here is to consume both medicine and minor miracle; sallet is occult in its baby-raising capacity. The food sustains diversity because the family remembers past usage, indeed, the juice grows encyclopaedic as Lytle catalogues the do's and don'ts surrounding sallet. By shifting the vegetable from cure towards incantation Lytle ensures that sallet cannot be canned: its status as magic defends it from capitalist rationality. The progression from particularity to miracle is entirely in keeping with Ransom's conviction that the poetic word is a house of 'demons'. The word is first and foremost an icon: 'aesthetic signs are "icons" or images. As signs they . . . refer to objects, but as iconic signs they also *resemble* or *imitate* these objects.'[17] He adds that 'the icon is particular. A particular is indefinable; that is, it exceeds definition.'[18] Part of that excess is homeopathic: the verbal icon will restore to wholeness bodies damaged by the language of scientific functionalism;[19] part is religious: Ransom regrets the passing of 'dryads', 'oreads' and 'nymphs', but finds their peers released by the reading of a poem:

> Poetry intends to recover a denser and more refractory original world which we know loosely through our perceptions and memories[20] . . . [insofar as] . . . it gratifies that impulse of the mind, perhaps not so common an impulse with us as the religious impulse, to contemplate for its own sake the object as a concrete object, or as an inexhaustible complex of attributes. Hence the demon or concrete ghost.[21]

New Critical exegesis discovers that the side-dish and the word are a single species of object:

> The object appears to us to be constituted of more qualities than the one carried in its definition, and in fact to be a concrete object or infinite variety of qualities. And this produces for us the infinite series. We look *inward* on the object, undertake the impossible task of finding all its qualities, and presently bring the effort to a conclusion by the bold hypothesis: *This infinite variety is demon.*[22]

The 'infinite series' is neither indeterminate nor free insofar as it goes back somewhere, and takes direction from that source. For Ransom the series leads to a God *with* thunder; for Lytle the series stops 'at the head of the table', though the family's eighteenth-century appetite suggests that the patriarch is linked genealogically to an authoritative point of origin. Whether one consumes the salad or the poem one is granted access to an unchanging authority by means of a pattern of aesthetic response which mirrors, and trains the memory to recall, a preferred set of social relations. The verbal icon and the sallet share a quasi-sacral particularity. Given that an emphasis on the miraculous characterizes both poem and pot liquor, it is perhaps permissible to approach the Southern aesthetic of anti-development by considering miracles.

III

What happens when at certain times and in certain places a particular crucifix is deemed to bleed? If one has small faith in miracles, but allows that investigators found no tube or duct, one is left with the belief of the witness. To speak of auto-suggestion, hallucination or neurosis may be to disguise the point. When an icon so convinces its observer that it is what it designates, it is merely an extreme version of what Frege calls the general tendency in language to shift from 'sense' to 'reference'. In Paul Ricoeur's terms, the bleeding cross exhibits 'ontological vehemence',[23] being so thrown forward into the world that it offers evidence on behalf of its own story. Arguably, blood does not flow from wood, ivory or plaster, but from a narrative told and re-told to the point of materialization. Saint Francis and Saint Teresa were perhaps consummate tellers of one story; such was their preoccupation with the Passion that their chosen text wounded them. The blood in the palms of Saint Francis is so compliant that it forms itself into the shape of nails. Saint Teresa's heart, removed by surgeons at her death, carries a wide horizontal fissure;[24] in her autobiography the saint plainly describes her vision of an angel who thrust with a gold spear into her chest. Even supposing that in her case the surgeon slipped, or more generally that ecclesiastical witnesses blink and that therefore the relic in the shrine at Alba de Tormes is a forgery, nonetheless it and its postcards are iconic images whose essence is textual.

Allen Tate might have been offering a gloss on stigmatics when, in *The Fathers* (1938), he has his narrator, Lacy Buchan, 'passionately desire to hear the night':[25]

> And I think we do hear it: we hear it because our senses, not being mechanisms, actually perform the miracles of imagination that they themselves create; from our senses come the metaphors through which we know the world, and in turn our senses get knowledge of the world by means of figures of their own making . . . To hear the night, and to crave its coming, one must have deep inside one's secret being a vast metaphor controlling all the rest: a belief in the innate evil of man's nature, and the need to face that evil, of which the symbol is the darkness. (pp. 218–19)

Lacy Buchan is arguing by analogy from the source text, *Genesis*. Fallen man sees in the 'darkness' an iconic presentation of his lapsarian condition. So powerful is the ur-story that it shifts Virginia's secession, the event at the centre of the novel, towards a second Fall from grace. Tate, writing in the late thirties, as the South experienced traumatic shifts in land ownership and labour organization, may have found some comfort in the iconic moment of his narrator's 'controlling' metaphor. If so, three discrete falls – Adam's, Secession and the New Deal – condense into one plot, which is then further condensed into a metaphor whose vehicle is 'the night'. The understanding of two or perhaps three events within one perceptual act gives immense persuasive power and intrinsic concreteness to that act. What Lacy Buchan 'hear[s]' is the sound of a repeated narrative as it produces a sensation in his mind's ear.

It may be objected that I have turned 'metaphor' into a synonym for 'icon': I do so because I am persuaded of their affinity by Paul Ricoeur. He argues that metaphor is commonly spoken of in visual terms, as a 'figure of speech' which 'sets before the eyes', because the innovation that results from the interaction of its terms often takes a pictorial form. As the literal collapses under the metaphoric strain, previous categorizations prove unable to explain the compatibility proposed by the analogy:

> In order that metaphor obtain, one must continue to identify the previous
> incompatibility *through* the new compatibility. The predicative assimilation
> involves . . . a specific kind of tension . . . between semantic incongruence and
> congruence . . . To see the *like* is to see the same inspite of and through the
> different.[26]

The conceptual need for a reconciling image produces neither double
vision nor a weakened sensorial impression, but Ricoeur has problems
moving beyond a negative definition of the kind of picture produced.
'Split reference', a 'display [of] relations in a depicting mode', or 'the
iconic as felt . . . [as] density' are less persuasive than his appeal to the
figure-ground. All of us know that two silhouettes in profile pushed
close form a sort of candlestick, but none of us can see both images
simultaneously. The jump from one to the other and back may be
executed with greater and greater speed, but faces and candlestick avoid
one another. The experience of visual tension induced by the figure
conveys something of the iconic moment in metaphor. Lacy hears the
night with such intensity that he paralyses any tension between
'darkness' and 'innate evil'. There can be no 'semantic incongruence'
when both the figure's terms are rendered 'congruent' by a story of such
predicative assimilation that it has no need to appear. The metaphor
rigidifies into its iconic moment, which bodies forth an entire narrative.
As Tate put it, in an essay on Dante (1951), where the analogic forcefully
informs the sensory, a quasi-religious 'proximate incarnation of the
Word' occurs.[27]

The ability to interpenetrate textual and figural is shared by Saint
Catherine of Siena, in Tate's account of her attendance on a young
Sienese noble unjustly condemned for treason. Her instruction on the
meaning of the Cross and the healing powers of the Blood, had such
good effect that the youth was reconciled to his death. The scene is the
subject of a letter to Brother Raimondo of Capua, in which Saint
Catherine likens the condemned man to 'a gentle lamb', blesses him, and
recommends him to the block as to a 'bridal'; once prostrated, she
receives his head in her hands and recalls to him 'the Blood of the Lamb',
adding 'I will' to his 'Jesus! . . . Catherine!': 'When he was at rest my soul
rested in peace and quiet, and in so great a fragrance of blood that I could
not bear to remove the blood which had fallen on me from him.'[28]
Tate's exegesis hints at the perceptual structures latent in iconic
reception:

> When St. Catherine 'rests in so great fragrance of blood', it is no doubt the
> Blood of the Offertory which the celebrant offers to God *cum odore suavitatis*
> but with the literal odor of the species of wine, not of blood. St. Catherine had
> the courage of genius which permitted her to *smell* the Blood of Christ in

> Niccolo Tuldo's blood clotted on her dress: she smelled the two bloods *not alternately but at one instant*, in a single act compounded of spiritual insight and physical perception.[29]

The smell that inter-animates wine, fresh blood, ritual blood, blood from a bridal bed and from Christ's wounds is produced by a singular concentration upon the Passion story, doubtless told and re-told by the saint and her pupil. Consequently, to locate the iconic moment in the pure phenomenological 'genius' of the perceiver is to miss exactly half of the point. The iconic perceiver perceives nothing without a narrative; put another way: there is no such thing as an icon without a narrative blueprint for that icon. Tate's 'spirit'/'body' dualism further obscures the textual process that organizes the saint's olfactory editing. Saint Catherine's letter draws together a diversity of detail, sexual, political and familial. Each element is discretely present at the block, yet none of them is capable of disrupting the saturation of the scene by the language of theology. Saint Catherine smells the Blood of Christ through it *all* because she suffers from what Umberto Eco calls perceptual cramp:

> At a certain point the iconic representation, however stylized it may be, appears to be more true than the real experience, and people begin to look at things through the glasses of iconic convention . . . [in a] sort of perceptual cramp caused by overwhelming cultural habits.[30]

The problem with Eco's cramping is that although it releases iconicity from the limited notion of dependency upon visual relationship, it is unhelpful about exactly how culture causes cramps. Before investigating further, it might be wise briefly to rehearse some elements of the theoretical arguments over the nature of the iconic sign, which have led Eco from "resemblance" to "cultural attribution".

In his original threefold division of the sign into 'symbol', 'index', and 'icon', C.S. Peirce stressed that icons 'stand for something because they resemble it', though he was later to modify his definition by proposing that the icon 'may represent its object mainly by similarity'.[31] The shift from "resemblance" to "similitude" allows for greater flexibility in how one judges the link between the sign and its designation, but that link remains primarily visual. The relationship troubled Peirce, who was also to speak of icons 'exhibit[ing]' and 'exemplify[ing]' their object. Charles Morris tinkered with the problem and produced the broader definition: 'an iconic sign . . . is any sign which is similar in some respects to what it denotes. Iconicity is thus a matter of degree.'[32] Eco remains dissatisfied, arguing that however it is phrased a visual account of iconicity naturalizes the sign along some version of the equation:

$$\text{iconic} = \text{analogic} = \text{motivated} = \text{Natural}$$

He objects that "similitude" is always a learned thing and never a found thing: 'to say that a certain image is similar to something else does not eliminate the fact that similarity is also a matter of cultural convention'.[33]

Where "Nature" stood, "Culture" now largely stands, or more properly "Cultural Education". For example, it is all too easy to assume that the simple outline of a horse drawn in pencil on paper stands for the horse because it 'resembles' it, or is 'similar in some respects' to it. But the black line is precisely what no moving horse possesses; even static against a white barn, light, shade and perspective would render the iconic line decidedly selective. Resemblance has been produced and recognized primarily through a graphic convention which reinforced a perceptual convention (which would have it that all things have "out" "lines" around them). At a more elevated level, it is clear from the work of Gombrich that imitation in art depends upon changing conventions. To the modern eye Constable's 'Wivenhoe Park' may seem decidedly photographic, in its concentration upon the actual effects of light. However, when Constable's works first appeared they were frequently held to be taking strange liberties with reality. By offering such examples Eco does not erase resemblance from the icon; rather, he diminishes its explanatory presence, and substitutes 'the notion of convention'.[34]

Peirce has generally been read as drawing a clear distinction between 'symbol' and 'icon'. 'Symbols' (for example most printed words) are defined as 'arbitrary', in that their link with their referent depends upon 'mental association or habit': the word 'dead' is an arbitrary gathering of phonemes bearing no traceable relation to a corpse. Eco blurs this distinction: to suggest that iconicity is largely learned at least implies that the visual sign ('icon'), like the verbal sign ('symbol'), is made meaningful by 'mental association or habit'. Habit is a great leveller, linking 'symbol' to 'icon' on a scale of motivation whose unit of measure is cultural pressure. The quality of being arbitrary, like the quality of being iconic, is, it would seem, a matter of degree.[35]

One way in which this terminological collapse may be taken is to assume that all signs are potentially iconic. To adapt Strawson: iconicity is not something that a sign does, it is something that a sign can be used to do. Cocks must be tired of crowing in semiotic texts to prove that phonemes too can be iconic (cock-a-doodle-do); not quite so tired as multilingual cocks, who go on to show with their 'cocquerico' and 'chicchiricchi' that onomatopoeic resemblance owes more to habits of transcription than to oral similitude. Nonetheless, whether English, French or Italian, the fowl's phonemes, bearing little or no association to

its sound, are held to it by habit. A happier fate than that of the
nightingale: 'jug jug jug tereu', however lambently apt to Elizabethan
ears, is arbitrary and ugly to ours.

> Above the antique mantel was displayed
> As though a window gave upon the sylvan scene
> The change of Philomel, by the barbarous king
> So rudely forced; yet there the nightingale
> Filled all the desert with inviolable voice
> And still she cried, and still the world pursues,
> 'Jug Jug' to dirty ears.[36]

Eliot may put the dirt down to cultural decay, but in fact it derives from
no more than lack of exposure to the conventions which might
naturalize Lyly's ornithology. The real problem here, as with any iconic
question, is to discern what in a culture at any one time exerts the
pressure that makes the habit that holds the sign iconographically close to
its referent.

Cleaning our ears to receive verbal icons from the South will involve
listening to further economic history – but not yet. Before attempting a
detailed economic archaeology for Southern iconography during the
Depression, I need some account of what Tate, Ransom and Faulkner
(my representative iconographers) understood by verbal icon.

IV

In his essay, 'Literature and knowledge' (1941), Tate asks 'What is the
nature of the object referred to in poetry?' and answers – 'image', as it is
'apprehended' in cognition, stressing 'apprehension', where 'the primary meaning of apprehension is a grasping or taking hold of'.[37]
Apprehension should therefore involve a 'complete' response to
'experience', which in turn depends upon 'mythologies'. Mythology,
for Tate, is a counterpunch prompted by Science:

> Before the development of positivist procedures towards nature . . . the poetic
> subject was the world of ordinary experience; but as soon as the subject –
> Nature – became the field of positivism, the language of poetry ceased to
> represent it; ceased, in fact, to have any validity, or to set forth anything real.[38]

The poem will recover the 'full body of experience' if, and only if, its
'images' can be set within, or subsume, 'mythology'. The inter-
dependence of 'image' and 'myth' is difficult to characterize, but may
provisionally be glossed in the suggestion that 'completeness', 'experience', 'the whole or concrete object', 'the body and solid substance of the
world' (terms and phrases which move almost interchangeably between
the critical essays of Tate and Ransom), exist only where details are

experienced as "having a story to tell", or being "that about which a story could be told", or even "that about which a story *must* or *has* been told, in order to prevent the telling of another and very different story". I am aware that I am eliding 'myth' and 'plot': in temporary self-defence I would add the rider that a myth is a plot which hides itself. Tate quotes I.A. Richards, approvingly:

> [Mythologies] are no amusement or diversion to be sought as a relaxation and an escape from the hard realities of life. They are the hard realities in projection, their symbolic recognition, coordination and acceptance . . . The opposite or discordant qualities in things in them acquire a form . . . Without his mythologies man is only a cruel animal without a soul . . . a congress of possibilities without order or aim.[39]

Stress 'form', 'order' and 'acceptance' and one has a recipe for 'organicism'. 'Myth', and its sub-species, the organic poem, proposes a harmonious and static world whose body is 'full', inert, fantastical, and all the more sweet for that. The dubiety of these delights is well detailed; my point is that whether 'organicism' is used to praise or blame, it must not be allowed to obscure the plot co-ordinates that lie behind and project its images.

In his contribution to *I'll Take My Stand* Tate describes the experience of one such image:

> the horse cropping the blue-grass on the lawn[40]

The equine image is 'immediate' not because the grass is blue but because the animal contains two distinct narratives which Tate specifically discusses in terms of contrasting historiographies. To look with the eye of Science (invariably, in Tate, a synonym for the North) is to see 'half a horse' or 'horsepower' (p. 157), an 'abstraction' which, set in an 'abstract series', typifies the 'Long View of history' (p. 161). Mythology, 'in conviction immediate, direct, overwhelming', (p. 156), produces the spectacles of 'contemplation', through which the 'whole horse' becomes one image in a 'concrete series' which makes up the 'Short View of history' (p. 161). The horse has to carry a considerable historical burden, among whose elements are Thomas Jefferson, the mediaeval Church and the Southern economy. Tate suffers from a compulsive analogism which cannot resist discovering serial similarities. The whole horse, we are told, was widely available prior to the Renaissance, during which period, in a kind of conceptual fall, the supernatural was made plausible. The resultant rational bent, driven by the animus of what's 'workable' (p. 157), produced a preoccupation with quantity, logic and abstraction. The attendant model of history (the Long View) was really a long graph charting the progress of instrumentalism, or perhaps a table of categories within which Christ and Adonis are entered under the same heading ('vegetation rite' (p. 162)) for speed of utilization. In the South whole horses are still occasionally visible because of a preference for the Short View: a decidedly eccentric alliance between Jefferson, soil, the Eastern Church and the cotton trade as a living link with Europe enables Southerners to see the grass as blue. The lawn is just one of a 'vast clutter of particular images' which constitute history in the form of 'a concrete series that has taken place in a very real time' (p. 160).

To be faced with a plethora of 'absolute and inviolate objects' (p. 169) would seem potentially overwhelming (rather like living forever in a poem according to New Criticism) were it not that Southerners – and Tate's essay stands testimony to this assertion – tell stories:

> for the Short View, history is the specific account of the doings of specific men, who acted their roles in a vast and contemporaneous setting which somewhat bewildered them and which prompted them to make up stories with an obvious moral. (p. 161)

Stories enable them to see the 'image' set within the 'series' of which it is part, and from which it derives its 'fullness of body'. In effect, Tate suggests that Southerners make good idolators (p. 172), perhaps because their images issue as icons whose semantic density derives from impacted plots.

The only liberty that I have consciously taken with Tate's argument is to leave out a lot of examples. I have inclined to parody in order to highlight a method. Tate's fondness for the historical detail used to announce something also historical and real – as the correspondence between Jefferson and Adams is used to announce the Civil War (pp. 171–2) – involves a kind of plotting, whereby history rapidly ceases to be what happened, and becomes what can be narrated. One thing after another is transformed into one thing because of another, all of which things back up behind, and are expressed by, the last thing in the explanatory series. The historian proceeds backwards from his own time cancelling contingency by grasping events together in an absorbent configuration: as Louis Mink puts it, 'there are no contingencies going backwards'.[41] His 'synoptic judgements' produce 'retrospective intelli-gibility', which, if challenged, tends to prove itself merely by expanding its series.[42] The methodology is practised by some historians, but more generally by genealogists, etymologists and iconographers. In each case, the discovery that an item may be set in a series makes that item meaningful. As Panofsky has it, 'iconology is a method of interpretation which arises from synthesis rather than analysis'.[43] However, perhaps the purest exponents were the Church Fathers whose figural interpretations linked the Old Testament to the New. Moses and Joshua prefigure Christ, even as Christ *is* the Passover, 'inasmuch as the Passover is a figure of Christ through the likeness of the saving blood and the flock'.[44] No element in any series becomes an allegorical sign in that each is deemed to retain its own historicity. Auerbach's definition catches something of the multivalency of the figural character:

> Figural interpretation establishes a connection between two events or persons, the first of which signifies not only itself but also the second, while the second encompasses or fulfills the first. The two poles of the figure are separate in time, but both, being real events or figures, are within time, within the stream of historical life. Only the understanding of the two persons or events is a spiritual act, but this spiritual act deals with concrete events whether past, present or future, and not with concepts or abstractions.[45]

The historicity of a Moses or a Joshua is at best sketchy: the very 'concrete events' with which we associate them derive less from their actions or from what they themselves might have thought about oceanography or civic collapse, than from a mode of causality that identifies them as one of a class. The explanatory power of Passover blood is relational, to risk a pun (or an epistemological mini-series), that blood's very sanguinity depends upon consanguinity

A species of the figural lies behind the New Critical faith in the verbal icon, itself a Southern product growing out of the Agrarianism of the late twenties and early thirties. In *God Without Thunder* Ransom challenges the thinning of America by an all-pervasive commercial production; his chief weapon is a non-exchangeable 'particularity', whose market resistance lies in a theological story. God plus Thunder is Ransom's means to secede from Northern corporate capital; he gets the thunder back by isolating and correcting a piece of bad figural reasoning on the part of the Church Fathers. In 1054 the Roman Catholic Church sanctioned the doctrine of the Filioque, displacing the Father from his dominance within the Trinity in favour of the Son. The coup proves, for Ransom, 'the most critical moment in our history',[46] enabling the Western Church to become 'a definitive historical polity' (p. 335):

> Since then the world has been for the Occident a rational and possessible world, while the irrational and evil world which the orient contemplates has vanished from our horizon. Western empire has developed out of that choice, and Western science, and Western business. But empire, science and business have been sponsored all along, with a tolerably consistent loyalty, by a Western Church.   (p. 335)

Ransom produces a counterseries from a hybrid of genealogical and etymological reasoning. The Old Testament authors held God to be 'ruah' (wind), which became 'pneuma' in the Greek. As 'ruah' God was pre-paternal, fatherhood being seen as a way of reducing divine demonism. According to Ransom the Trinity was already a form of fall from plenitude, the Holy Ghost being defined as 'the ghost who came to bear witness to God in his fullness' (p. 344). New Testament writers very nearly lost 'ruah' altogether in their affection for the 'logos' or personified Christ. To substitute 'logos' for 'pneuma' involves usurping the Father's rightful place and de-demonizing God.

The resistance of the Oriental Church to the Filioque decision enables Ransom to recover his alternative theodicy and to demonstrate how it issues in alternative objects. The series that runs from the Roman Catholic Church to the Sears Roebuck catalogue is met by a series running from the Eastern Church to the Southern farmer or to the poem. The subsistence farmer and the Vanderbilt student of literature (1930s) both confront different forms of 'inexhaustible fullness' (p. 70). In his economic writings Ransom outlines measures that will reduce dependency on cash crops: fertilizers are to be priced out of reach; bank loans ought to be taxed to restrict borrowing; government subsidies could be high for *small* landowners; and agricultural schools might be required to teach subsistence production. By such means – so the argument goes – the farmer may be encouraged to recognize that an agrarian economy can produce 'aesthetic' as well as economic 'deliverance', in that the production of his hands will prove dense with the particularity of his own non-exchangeable labour.[47] In *God Without Thunder* Ransom insists that those who work the land are the best 'religionists' because 'soil' is infinitely various and can therefore stand in for the 'inscrutable God' (p. 266). The poetry is likewise capaciously synonymous, absorbing Thunder and use value, so that when Ransom calls for an ontological critic (*The New Criticism*), the job description might specify theological and agricultural experience. The verbal icon is a veritable textual demon which the reader uses to recover a 'denser and more refractory original world'.[48] Ransom praises 'that great word ... "embodies"' (p. 291):

> Ontologically, it is a case of bringing into experience both a denser and a more contingent world, and commanding a discourse in more dimensions. (p. 330)

> In brief, under the iconic sign the abstract item is restored to the body from which it was taken. (p. 285)

Ransom's theological, economic and aesthetic writings isolate three historical groupings: twelfth-century Church Fathers, Depression farmers and literature students during the forties and fifties; the three are linked by a figural series that extends from 'ruah' to the USA's second industrial revolution, and each has to hand a variety of icons (demonic particularity, use value, poetic density) that may prove indigestible to the workings of corporate capital.

v

The affinity between figural narrative and the iconic may perhaps best be illustrated by an appeal to an icon *in* a text rather than to critical accounts of textual iconicity. Faulkner's *Go Down, Moses* (1942) contains one explicit icon. In 'Delta autumn', an aging Ike McCaslin contemplates the contraction of the wilderness:

> He had watched it, not being conquered, destroyed, so much as retreating since its purpose was served now and its time an outmoded time, retreating southward through this inverted-apex, this ▽-shaped section of earth between hills and River until what was left of it seemed now to be gathered and for the time arrested in one tremendous destiny of brooding and inscrutable impenetrability at the ultimate funnelling tip.[49]

It is tempting to label the shape 'Virgin' and move on; however, the presence of a geometrical figure on the printed page of a novel resists easy assimilation. Some might object that the shape is no more than a triangle standing for an area of land, but in a Faulkner text ▽ can be neither a triangle nor innocent. As the tree-line and hair-line elide, so, guiltily I draw in the anatomical signature ▽ , only to erase it, recognizing that erasure is stipulated by Faulkner's repeated stories about unrupturable hymens.[50]

The pudenda appear in the text to preserve the impenetrability of the land. However, since the Civil War that land had been systematically despoiled. The undeveloped South stood in a colonial relation to the developed North, providing raw materials and rawer labour in return for industrial goods imported at an unequal rate of exchange. During the thirties its dependent status as an 'internal colony'[51] became more obvious. The 1926 crash in cotton prices initiated a spate of mortgage foreclosures which was to characterize the Depression years, and constituted the start of a structural shift in the patterns of pay and ownership. Banks and insurance companies re-possessed small and "unproductive" units of land in order to centralize production. The dispossessed tenant became a casual wage-labourer or a migrant.

Roosevelt's victory (1932), with its extension of the state into the market via crop restrictions and relief programmes, simply intensified the shrinkage of tenancy. Labour was re-distributed away from the land, and farm operations were increasingly mechanized, with a consequent transformation in the relationship between land and people. Faulkner counters what is in effect both an agricultural revolution and a revolution in social relations with a hymen – an iconic enclosure which isolates the land within a natural female function and then modifies that function. Only the density of narrative concentrated within the hymenal figure allows it to withstand the shock of the economic story. The funnel-tipped triangle is an explicitly female figure; however, because the wilderness is a game reserve reserved for men, it designates an almost exclusively male space. There is one significant breach of the male rule; Roth's octoroon mistress carries her child into the inner sanctum of the hunter's tent, but as though to counter the female principle she must enter dressed as a man, 'in a man's hat and a man's slicker and rubber boots' (p. 252). She and her burden, Roth's child, are expelled North in part to protect the exclusively male-engendering that characterizes the triangle. Ike McCaslin, the last keeper of the figure, experiences a double birth which minimalizes female participation. In 1867 he is born of Sophonsiba Beauchamp and Theophilus McCaslin; however, since Sophonsiba achieves motherhood at an unnaturally late age and immediately vanishes from the text, his conception would seem to devolve onto a male couple whose nicknames, Buck and Buddy, divide gender responsibilities, even as their original names, Theophilus and Amodeus (in translation 'God–Lover') imply a still more immaculate insemination. The second birth is emphatically miraculous. Ike is born again in the wilderness-womb from what looks suspiciously like a liaison between a man and a bear. As he enters the 'impenetrable' woods for the first time, he feels that, aged ten, he is 'witnessing his own birth', and that he has 'experienced it all before . . . not merely in dreams' (p. 138). Quite simply, he knows how the camp is going to look because Sam Fathers has been his 'mentor', the wilderness his 'college' and the bear ('so long unwifed and childless as to have become its own ungendered progenitor') his 'alma mater' (p. 149). His first sight of the male mother is pure *déja vu*. 'Sprawling, he looked up where it [the bear] loomed and towered over him like a thunderclap. It was quite familiar, until he remembered: this was the way he had used to dream about it' (pp. 149–50).

Much of my case for Ike's dream of an alternative parentage is the commonplace of Faulkner scholarship. Critics, however, do not generally pursue the perverse natal logic to its source. As the child of an all-male match (or matches), featuring God and/or a bear, Ike achieves an alternative genealogy and is thereby released from the miscegenated McCaslin line. The original miscegenator, his grandfather Lucius Quintus Carothers McCaslin, is displaced, nominally by Sam Fathers who will effectively die *as* the bear dies and at the hand of the bear's killer, and who is therefore an extension of the bear's spirit. Consequently, Sam Fathers is merely a paternal surrogate who will teach the boy his true father. The task is made easier by Sam's own genealogical experience; Sam's Chickasaw name means Had-Two-Fathers, his biological father (Ikkemotubbe) copulated with a quadroon, and then married the pregnant woman to a slave. Sam is miscegenated three ways, and yet no guilt attends him, perhaps because his proximity to the unworked land (∇) excuses him from the tortured history of racial crossing as it grew from the Southern system of labour. More probably, his innocence is a genealogical and etymological trick which filters the "white" and "black" bloods out of him. Ikkemotubbe was also known as Du Homme/The Man. Given his poisonous behaviour, it is small wonder that he falls from the grace of his Indian title, to be called Doom. The most doomed man has to be Adam, consequently the history of the name suggests that Sam is Adam's son. If so, when Sam addresses buck or bear as 'Oleh' ('Grandfather'), he is speaking directly to God. Where God is a grandfather and His spirit walks the earth in animal forms, the reader may be sure that the Delta contains the possibility of a prehistorical existence.

Ike is reborn, outside history, by means of figural interpretation: that is to say, the synoptic counterseries that I have been tracing results from a particular kind of historiography. Education, according to Sam, involves all manner of woodland skills, but its central lesson is serial perception. Ike is taught to perceive iconically and to recognize through the iconic sign a God-plot that leads straight to the Father. The lesson is well learned; in 'Delta autumn', as he stands inside the ∇, at the grave where Sam and the bear fuse, Ike encounters a snake. He addresses it 'without premeditation' as 'Chief . . . Grandfather'. The snake glides away:

> moving erect yet off the perpendicular as if the head and that elevated third were complete and all: an entity walking on two feet and free of all laws of mass and balance and should have been because even now he could not quite believe that all that shift and flow of shadow behind that walking head could have been one snake. (p. 235)

The movement is described with precision as simultaneously reptilian and upright: one snake contains post- and pre-lapsarian time because Ike's eye makes icons whose immediacy or 'ontological vehemence' stems from deep plots.

The habit makes him hard to argue with, since unconfessed plots produce perceptions that few can follow. When, in 'Delta autumn', Ike likens male orgasm to achieved divinity, only his age protects him from mockery. Yet, coming from Oleh's grandson, who has set his wife aside for an alternative triangle in which even the snake is rehabilitated, the claim has some credence. Ike's phrasing is at once explicit *and* Pauline:

> I think that every man and woman, at the instant, when it dont [*sic*] even
> matter whether they marry or not, I think that whether they marry then or
> afterward or dont never, at that instant the two of them together were God.
>
> (p. 246)

Ike's instant had involved withdrawal on a grand scale, from wife,
parenthood and inheritance – a coitus so interrupted that generation ('If
this dont get you that son you talk about, it wont be mine' (p. 224))
became *de*-generation, flowing back along the genealogical line to the
fount (Oleh). In this instance the fount is an alternative grandfather
incapable of the double offence of incestuous miscegenation. Just as
Faulkner re-structures the hymen, so Ike re-makes male emission; release
becomes regression in a direct mirroring of Ike's final experience of full
sexual congress, detailed at the close of section four of 'The bear'. His
wife offered sex in return for a promise to take up the 'farm'; Ike refused
but climaxed saying 'Yes' (p. 224). Repudiation and orgasm elide in an
absolute contradiction. In his seventies at a male camp in the triangle, Ike
revises the memory so that sex-denied and plantation-denied can be seen
through ∇ – taken but untakable (whether as hymen or as land).
"Married" to the land, Ike *is* God. Orgasm, repudiation and ∇ form a
series in which each retains its historical specificity but reveals and
prophesies Oleh. Again Auerbach best glosses this kind of imagination in
his account of figural interpretation as

> the idea that earthly life is thoroughly real, with the reality of the flesh into
> which the Logos entered, but that with all its reality it is only *umbra* and *figura*
> of the authentic future, ultimate truth, the real reality that will unveil and
> preserve the *figura*. In this way the individual earthly event is not regarded as a
> definitive self-sufficient reality . . . but viewed primarily in immediate vertical
> connection with a divine order which encompasses it, which on some future
> day will itself be concrete reality . . . But this reality is not only future; it is
> always present in the eye of God.[52]

For years Faulknerians have debated the ethics of Ike's decision not to
inherit,[53] but the structure of his imagination has been ignored. Ike's
decision is neither moral nor political, since it is not in any full sense a
decision. As Sam's child, Ike has been raised to live intuitively in a
reversed world and to perceive 'in immediate vertical connection with a
divine order'; to revert to Eco's terminology, his is a state of perpetual
perceptual cramp. In the much-discussed fourth section of 'The bear',
Ike does not argue a case for repudiation, he insists on theodicy. God *is*
John Brown (p. 203) because Southern history, from Ikkemotubbe to
Ike, has been a God-plot.

Ike's views are not Faulkner's, but the author shares his character's
perceptual persuasion. The event that is generally read as exposing to Ike
the irresponsibility of his repudiation, itself makes a figural case. When

Roth's mistress enters Ike's tent with evidence of the continuity of racial crossing, she also evidences the genealogical persistence of the grandfather's seed. In June 1833 Lucius Quintus Carothers McCaslin's son, Turl, was born of his daughter Eunice (*'stars fell'* (p. 191)): in 1940 Roth Edmonds's son is born of a descendant of that match (in Europe an 'Austrian paper-hanger' pulls things down (p. 239)). Lucius Quintus Carothers McCaslin has the last and vaguely apocalyptic laugh on Oleh. However, despite the shock of a repetition of miscegenated incest (albeit at many removes), Ike is not exposed to the reality of racial history; he is simply and devastatingly told that his figural series is inappropriate. The counterseries knocks the ontological stuffing out of him because of the vehemence of its own plot in which the sins of the patriarch recur from the first fall, through Lucius, to Roth. ∇ is ousted by ∇ , where the second icon is black. This is racial nightmare rather than racial history. I am not here concerned to analyse the nightmare,[54] but to indicate that Ike's dream of natal revision and the rude awakening engineered by Faulkner are designed on exactly the same historiographic principle.

The pervasiveness of the figural habit and of its iconic spin-offs may perhaps be conclusively seen in a reading of 'Pantaloon in black'. The story concerns a black family having no genealogical links to the McCaslin lines, indeed reference to things McCaslin is minimal. Rider's wife, Mannie, dies. The husband's grief is overcome through a perverse form of self-extinction. The names are striking: Rider, understood by Faulkner as a synonym for a sexual athlete;[55] Mannie, a woman's name made from a male term and a potential play on 'eye' and the first-person pronoun. Rider's way of dying involves killing a white gambler for cheating, though his crooked dice have been recognized for years. The gambler's name, Birdsong, initially seems innocent, until, and with increasing insistence, the story reveals itself as an anthology of animals. Rider is a 'horse' (p. 104), given to 'wolfing' food (p. 106), who spends time in the 'bull pen' (p. 115), and when drunk claims to be 'snakebit' (p. 112). He is attended by a large hound. Playful possibilities are released from names by the ambivalent tone of the narrative: a lynch story, featuring a giant, named for the disappointed lover in *commedia dell'arte*, whose animalism has less to do with racial typing (Beast) than with the land of faery (when he drinks, whisky springs 'columnar and intact' from his throat; for him the air is 'silver' (p. 109)). Faery story crosses into gothic tale when Mannie's ghost appears, vampirically absorbing Rider's air and convincing him that he must lose his own body: 'he could actually feel between them the insuperable barrier of that very strength which could handle alone a log' (p. 103). Rider's grief is explicitly and repeatedly presented as a compulsion to rejoin his wife. One attempt involves a self-mutilating act of strength: returning to the saw-mill, his place of work, Rider lifts a log:

> It was as if the unrational and inanimate wood had invested, mesmerized the man with some of its own primal inertia. Then a voice said quietly: 'He got hit. Hit's off de truck', and they saw the crack and gap of air, watching the infinitesimal straightening of the braced legs until the knees locked, the movement mounting infinitesimally through the belly's insuck, the arch of the chest, the neck cords, lifting the lip from the white clench of teeth in passing ...
> 'Only he aint gonter turn wid dat un', the same voice said. 'And when he try to put hit back on de truck hit gonter kill him.' But none of them moved. Then – there was no gathering of supreme effort – the log seemed to leap suddenly backward over his head of his own volition, spinning, crashing and thundering down the incline. (p. 116–17)

Attention is so focussed on the log that 'his volition' seems inaccurate; '*its* volition' attends, as an antonym, fusing the impersonal with the personal pronoun and miming Rider's desire to move from the animate to the inanimate (prefaced by his shift from the human to the animal). The means eventually chosen – rendering Birdsong inanimate – involves lynching, a choice which Rider must recognize is liable to lead to dismemberment. Faulkner notes that Rider's body is found 'hanging from the bell-rope in a negro schoolhouse' (p. 112); no mention is made of its state, but its exemplary position at least implies mutilation. The ground is re-entered, possibly sans gender sign: that ground embodies Mannie. Parallels with the plots latent in ∇ are inescapable; just as Sam, and Ike are linked to the bear (and Boon sleeps with Lion), so Rider (half-man/half-animal) recovers his identity (Man→I) via a penetration of what is simultaneously, male and soil. The logic is figural; it appeals because the figural series (impacted in and expressed by the icon) discovered at its head or point of origin a strong patriarch. Rider, dying back into Mannie, re-enters a female earth which resembles Ike's chosen figure (∇). That triangular piece of virgin land contains Oleh or the grandfather as God (who erases memories of a miscegenating patriarch).[56]

I have rehearsed several examples of a narrative logic which pervades *Go Down, Moses* in order to suggest that what looks at best like eccentricity and at worst like nonsense, is in fact the product of a habit of mind which, though I hesitate to describe it as regional, does characterize the work of several Southerners during the second civil war. Ike's intuitively figural perception convinces him that he has 'experienced it all before' (p. 148), a conviction which stems from his configurative training, since in any series each item receives its iconic specificity from the prior items, even as those items deprive it of its singularity. In temporal terms, recollection (often so embedded as to appear "innate") expels anticipation (the future) from perception (the present). The pastness of the present contains the future. My phrasing is as occluded as the structure it describes; however, the temporal distortion latent in *figura* and *icon* is well caught by Tate, who, in 1912, 'felt that I had been shifted into the past and was looking into the future that nobody but myself at the end of the eighteenth century could have seen'.[57] The occasion involved Tate's childhood visit to Aunt Martha, his great-grandmother's maid: the ex-slave is blind, of uncertain age (but apparently over one hundred and twenty), and the miscegenated half-sister of Tate's great-grandfather. As she feels the boy's face she notes, 'He favours his grandpa' (p. 13). Tate, writing in 1972 corrects her – 'she must have meant my great-grandfather' (p. 13) – but he can escape neither her hand nor her foreshortening of time:

> If the sense of a past comes less from parish registers, old houses, family bibles, old letters, county records and tombstones, than from the laying on of hands from one generation to another, then what sense of a living past I may have goes back through the bird-claws of an ancient female slave, my blood cousin who, ironically enough, in family authority seemed to take precedence over my mother.
> (p. 14)

Aunt Martha embodies continuity, her touch so intensifies that primarily genealogical fact that the bloodline contracts, drawing the boy back to a time prior to his own engendering (the father is unmentioned and the mother's priority is cancelled). At the level of temporal experience, the laying on of hands (more accurately, the application of figural logic) cancels the present (the parents) and elides the past (great-grandfather) and the future (the boy's capacity to anticipate alternatives). Continuity becomes prophecy; and, as a genealogical series turns into a quasi-astrological table of prediction, so history stops.

Tate's 'sense of past' is like Panofsky's iconology, synoptic rather than analytic: consequently, shorn of discord and contingency, history becomes an iconic programme in the form of a series of predicative family portraits – 'Great-Grandfather', 'Grandfather', 'Father', 'Son'. The portraits resemble, more *or* less, a notional patriarch whose painting is missing. The Great-Great-Grandfather is named (Dr John Armistead Bogan: 1766–1814) but plays no part in anyone's memory, which is surprising, since he fathered Aunt Martha. The omission seems in this instance less a repression of miscegenation than an intensification of the patriarchal principle – that origins should be generic and continuous rather than particular. The Southern patriarch functions as a diminutive Emperor for whom Kermode claims 'a kind of perpetuity': 'His natural body is subject to time, but his *dignitas* exists perpetually . . . in this sense the emperor or king "never dies"; Rome never dies, but invests Byzantium or Moscow; the *maiestas populi romani* persists in the nations of Europe.'[58]

Once again we find ourselves on the brink of nonsense, or a level of causality that approaches Abracadabra. Under the figural spell, the historian or the iconographer can protest that the series assimilates, that it, not he, is the source of predication. Take Tate's account of memory: 'Memory arrests the flow of inner time, but what we remember is not at the command of our wills; it has its own life and purposes; it gives us what *it* wills' (*Memories and Essays*, p. 13; italics in source). Consequently, Tate can describe the inception of *The Fathers* as a telepathic moment: the occasion – a party in Washington; the medium – a psychometrist; the enabling object – Tate's gold collar-studs (previously the property of the novel's prototype, Major Buchan); the source – Tate is unspecific, but implies a collective memory in which, 'Pleasant Hill had somewhere an objective existence almost a century after it was burnt':

> She clasped [the stud] . . . for a silent minute, then said: 'The original owner was a small man with bushy white hair and a hawk's nose, formal and pompous; he lived in a big frame house on a hilltop, which one reached by a lane bordered on one side by cedar trees.' As I write these words the *frisson* of that moment returns. (p. 9)

The house rises phoenix-like from a collar stud, not because of psychometric 'revelation' (whatever Tate may say), but because the author wills it to. In 1938, as the South loses its second civil war, Tate resurrects a patriarchal mansion from the ashes of the first defeat. Only a conviction of continuity, allied to figural habits, allows him to extract absolute contiguity from pure coincidence. Only an eye for iconic density allows him to infuse an innocent domestic item with enough narrative for a novel, and then to deny his own plotting.

VI

On the face of it ruah, Oleh and Major Buchan share little beyond being patriarchs brought into focus through 'the glasses of iconic convention' (Eco). However, their respective literary datings – ruah (1930), Oleh (1942) and Buchan (1938) – suggest a further affinity: each instances a need to recover or rehabilitate a supreme father at the very moment when paternalism, as a key to Southern social relations, is losing its economic currency. I return to the history of Southern labour because it is my case that out of these relations grew both the agrarian demand for the patriarch and the aesthetic forms used in his defence.

In the antebellum South, paternal ideology negotiated a central contradiction in slavery. The institution is peculiar in part because it implies that the slave is an extension of the master's will, and is therefore will-less or an object. Chattel status is palpably impossible, since no person can be will-less (should he choose to be, his choice indicates will's presence). Naked force necessarily lies at the root of white power over black will, but that enforcement may be disguised or even relaxed by recasting the black as 'child' (Sambo means 'son of'). Granted a limited and provisional will and guaranteed a "family", slaves could expect "responsibility" from their "white folks" in return for filial "duty". Through self-representation as 'father', the master traded limited recognition of blacks for a degree of black tractability; slaves accorded with the trade because the idea of *mutual* obligation tacitly acknowledged the slave's humanity.[59] Stabilized by the ideology, the slave's life – always poised on the underlying fact of 'social death' and 'natal extinction'[60] – might be bearable. As Eugene Genovese emphasizes, most labouring groups, if unsentimentalized, are understandably committed to order, since life is difficult enough without uncertainty and confusion.

The Civil War provided both but insufficiently enough to prompt a sustained re-distribution of land. Consequently, during Reconstruction blacks were freedmen without means, while landowners lacked capital but retained the land which, if worked, might generate surplus. After several stand-offs, centring on the issue of gang labour, "share wages" negotiated the crisis in labour relations. It is important to recognize that the labour crisis also involved a crisis in partriarchal relations. Genovese maintains that the antebellum development of paternalism and its defence of Southern slavery as a positive good was not simply an ideological rationalization or nostalgic fantasy; he stresses that it

> signalled the maturation of the ruling class and its achievement of self-consciousness. Far from being mere apologetics . . . it represented the formulation of a world view that authentically reflected the position, aspirations, and ethos of the slaveholders as a class.[61]

His argument is that through paternalism the planter class articulated a consciousness of its own situation and its position with regard to the capitalist economic relations of the North; the idea of the father was used to define a series of organic relations which were directly opposed to the forms of individualism associated with the capitalist market. Like Marx, the Southern planter-class came to argue that capitalist relations organized all human relations through the cash nexus, and paternalism was therefore a pattern for defining exchanges between the members of society which would counter the forms of acquisitive individualism associated with the market. This can be seen in the way in which Fitzhugh and others discussed the ties between slavery and the family:

> Fitzhugh linked slavery and the family in two ways: by suggesting that the majority even in free society was subject to a despotic power – that is, that it consisted of slaves in all except name – and by showing that despotic power, when conditioned by ties of affection and a sense of rational responsibility, need not be feared.[62]

The share wage preserved, in muted form, the fatherly despotism with which the planter distinguished himself from the Northern employer. Both Harold Woodman and Jonathan Wiener have argued that share cropping allowed blacks limited autonomy, and whites limited paternity. The post-war freedman sought to become free in more than name by claiming "individual" and "autonomous" status as a wage earner in a market that the North was keen to de-restrict. However, owners resented the "free contracts" that would nominally signal such an identity. The compromise was "work on shares", which allowed blacks to believe that they had rights to a say in production, while permitting owners a continuing belief in black dependency. The ease with which "share wages" could be shifted into peonage, if the tenant defaulted on his debt, indicates who best benefited from the compromise.

"Free labour" in the rural South, up to and beyond the First World War, could and did share easily into "bound labour". As the agricultural historian Gilbert Fite puts it, 'Sharecropping and tenancy were more than economic systems. In many areas these economic arrangements were the basis for social control of blacks and poor whites.'[63] However, the 1930s saw the breakdown of the "share-wage" compromise and with it the collapse of the Southern labour system. Desperately low cotton prices from 1929 meant that planters and landlords, fearing that crop values could not meet the value of advances, tended to "furnish" credit for six months instead of a year. Massive tenant displacements resulted, while many independent farmers, equally unable to make profits, found their mortgages foreclosed. The new, and often corporate, owners tended to rent farms only to those who could finance a crop; consequently many former tenants and small owners alike fell into day labour, working only during the busy seasons.

Such structural shifts were the beginning of the centralization, capitalization and eventual mechanization of Southern agriculture. Armed with wage labour, in a market finally responsive to the imperatives of capital, the typical new owner (be he the old owner, a bank, or an insurance company), no longer needed the delusion of parenthood – indeed "children" were proving considerably more expensive than casual labourers.

Even at this level of reduction, my brief history of paternal relations may seem over-extended, particularly as it exists only to bring me back, almost full circle, to Eco's case for the cultural determination of icons. I should substitute 'class' for 'culture', and in this instance, classes in a state of considerable indeterminacy. As I have already argued, the tenant unrest of the early and mid-twenties and the "share-wage" failure during the thirties were the final stages of a protracted process of class formation. Between 1870 and 1930, with painful slowness, "freedmen" learned to be "free workers" and patriarchs learned to be employers. However, both the emergent working class and the new bourgeoisie functioned in a market kept far from "free". Jim Crow, tenancy and the absence of alternative forms of work held labour semi-bound and persuaded owners that they might still be 'Master'. The Depression imposed a free market, and gave Southern authors their infamous cricked necks. Ransom, Tate and Faulkner's backward glance is class-specific. They look to find the Father whose paternalism held in abeyance those economic and social forms associated with full market relations. Consequently, they experience, in singleness of vision, a species of historical insistence that induces a cultural cramp, which in turn produces the perceptual cramp, that enables them to fight a literary war on behalf of an abandoned plantation house. The patriarch having quit, figurae and icons in his name can only, by dissembling that name, call for his re-instatement.

VII

The Fathers exemplifies a narrative principle shared by icon and figura: the telling (by embodiment) of one story in order to block the telling of another. Tate opens his narrative with an iconic odour:

> It was only today as I was walking down Fayette Street towards the river that I got a whiff of salt fish, and I remembered the day that I stood at Pleasant Hill, under the dogwood tree. It was late April and the blossoms shot into the air like spray. My mother was dead.   (p. 3)

Strictly speaking, the smell is indexical: as smoke is to fire, so whiff is to fish; but from Lacy Buchan's perspective the memories latent in the smell 'embody' it with a 'fullness' or 'density' similar to that of Ransom's verbal icon. A whiff moves the narrator through half a century, from 1910 to 1860, because, as he puts it:

> there is not an old man living who can recover the emotions of the past: he can only bring back the objects around which, secretly, the emotions have ordered themselves in memory, and that memory is not what happened in the year 1860 but is rather a few symbols, a voice, a tree, a gun shining on the wall – symbols that will preserve only so much of the old life as they may, in their own mysterious history, consent to bear. (p. 22)

There is nothing mysterious about the history of such objects; they are icons whose figural series can be traced to a long-gone patriarch. To Lacy they are a 'mystery' (and he will add 'chance' and 'trifle' to his lexicon of secrecy) because *as* a 'mystery' they allow him to ignore his own narrative dissembling. Through them he tells one story in order to repress another, and then, via their 'density', he represses the story he told in the first place. Memory, he would have us believe, just happens, intensely, immediately and without a historian or a principle:

> Memory is all chance, and I have learned that you remember things not because they are important; you remember the important things because they help you fix in the mind the trifles of your early life, or the trifles simply drag along with them through many years the incidents that have altered your fortunes. (p. 131)

Lacy and his whiff sounds very much like Tate among the blue horses, those 'immediate, direct, overwhelming' images from 1930, the long 'contemplation' of which 'initiates a habit of imitation' based on and realizing 'absolute standards' that are 'an interior discipline of the mind' (*I'll Take My Stand*, p. 169).

A final exercise in icon exegesis may serve to clarify the 'discipline', by setting it in the historical context that made such 'standards' attractive. The smell of fish contains more than one death. In 1861 Lacy saw the corpses of the first two men to die in the Civil War:

> To this day I can see without effort the dark moustache of dead Mr. Jackson lying in Colonel Ellsworth's blood, the two bloods mingling there at the foot of the stairs; Colonel Ellsworth the first and Mr. Jackson, papa's friend, the second to fall of the many thousands that were soon gone. (p. 118)

The deaths are associated with 'the taste of crawfishy water' (p. 263). Running back across the Northern lines, the narrator will characterize his loss of direction as akin to the death of his grandfather, 'dead as a herring' (p. 269). The series extends to the living: George Posey, the brother-in-law, ambivalent over secession and an early spokesman for agricultural reform, 'does something about fish' (p. 133). We are told that 'George would sell anything for the pleasure of buying something else; he had to keep moving' (p. 135). Oysters are simply one of Posey's commercial ploys. It is Posey's money and his mercantile flair which, from 1860, have maintained the Buchan house. Tate's opening echo of Eliot's opening echo of Chaucer's 'Prologue' is surely intended: Posey is the 'fish man' (p. 135) (almost a king to Lacy) who brings order to Pleasant Hill and causes blossoms to shoot from an estate wasted by debt. 'Shot' (p. 3) rises, muffled, from Lacy's memory, since Posey's potency was indirectly responsible for the death of the father. Prior to Bull Run, Posey had been using his commercial connections to smuggle guns across the lines to the Confederate forces. During the opening engagements of the war he remains suspended between sides, staying at Pleasant Hill, itself caught in the middle ground. A Federal troop visits the house and accuses the anti-secessionist Major Buchan of being a rebel, to which Posey responds by assaulting the officer. Later, in Posey's absence, the troop returns and threatens to burn Pleasant Hill. The patriarch hangs himself in his house, which is subsequently fired.

Initially, it would seem that the smell of fish contains the cancellation of a genealogical series – grandfather, father, mother, each perceived in relation to the deaths that signal the fall of Southern culture. Posey, who survives to become a Northern capitalist, is present in the series as its iconoclast. However, the novel's title pluralizes paternity. Tate allows Lacy to draw Posey (an entirely inapproriate object) into a configuration which will accentuate his restoration of the plantation house, rather than his contribution to its erasure. The strain of contradictory inclusion is caught in the last paragraph of the novel. By the burned house Lacy and Posey part; Posey, taking off his Confederate uniform, replaces it with an apothecary's suit taken from a carpetbag (p. 305), emblem of the post-war Northern Reconstruction. Posey rides North, Lacy turns South:

> He cantered away in the dark. I waited until I heard the change of the hoofbeats on the big road. I kicked the old nag in the sides and headed back into the lane that ran by the South field. I'll go back and finish it. I'll have to finish it because he could not finish it. It won't make any difference if I am killed. If I am killed it will be because I love him more than I love any man.   (p. 306)

The tense-change at the centre of the passage is pivotal. Given that the narrator recalls 1861 from 1910 we might have expected 'I had to go back', with an attendant adjustment of the future in favour of the past throughout the final sentences. The fact that Lacy, aged sixty-five, cannot write, 'It would not have made any difference if I had been killed', indicates the degree to which for him (and for Tate in 1938) the Civil War remains unfinished business. Figural logic allows the present (1910) to hold the future (1938?) hostage to a past prior to defeat (1861). Lacy's substitution of 'love' for 'loved' is still more striking, in that it suggests how he has succeeded in eliding Major Buchan and George Posey – the 'he' who could not 'finish it' applies equally to the major and to his son-in-law (and, by extension, to the son who has still not finished it).

Lacy's 'love' for the 'fathers' fuses antithetical figures, thereby releasing Posey from his post-war history, a history of which Lacy is fully aware, since it is Posey's capital that puts him through medical school. By including the iconoclast within the Buchan genealogy, Lacy neutralizes his impact, cancelling his more obvious filiations with the North and the nominally free market. The suppression involves partial amnesia undertaken to resist a much fuller amnesia. Lacy had heard Posey's small daughter reiterate 'Papa make money' (p. 279); he acknowledges that Posey 'characteristically transposed' most things 'into cash figures' (p. 136). A black half-brother can be sold to realize 'liquid capital' (p. 54), the slave becoming a horse so that his ex-owner may win a wife. Political alliance can wait, throughout the turmoil of secession, until the line of greater profit is clear and followable. Yet Lacy insists 'He cared nothing for money' (p. 279). Posey's 'pleasure' (p. 135) is in the movement that money allows. He is the entrepreneurial principle *par excellence*, always trading and never concerned for the accumulations. A house is gained; a house is burned. One identity gives way to another; Confederate becomes carpetbagger. Death is hated, not, as Lacy suggests, because it involves decay, but because to die means to stop, and worse, to be fixed in memory. There is an intended if anguished irony in Posey's insistence at Mrs Buchan's funeral, 'I want to be thrown to the hogs. I tell you I want to be thrown to the hogs!' (p. 107). The 'fish man' is quite happy to become a pig-man, by means of the gastronomic processes of swine, since hogs go to market and a dead Buchan goes only to a changeless monument.

One result of such metamorphic addiction is that the addict is most alive within the act of exchange. His apparent indifference to wife, child, side and past is part of a wider economic indifference which only a brief excursion into exchange theory can adequately explain. Marx notes the instability of any object as it makes the transition from use to exchange (I have used the quotation before, but perhaps it will bear repeating): 'Not an atom of matter enters into the objectivity of commodities as values; in this it is the direct opposite of the coarsely sensuous objectivity of commodities as physical objectives.'[64] The hand dedicated to such matterless matter must experience a curious frisson, and we are told that 'George was a man who received the shock of the world at the end of his nerves' (p. 185). To deal and to live only for dealing is to experience absolute isolation, since everything, even oneself, is discontinuous, being liable to change in the act of exchange. Lacy registers the 'shock' through George, but seeks to control it by locating it elsewhere in the 'abyss', 'void' or 'chasm' (synonyms for another and Northern country). He comes analytically closer with his judgement, 'He cared nothing for money but was interested in it because he could feel only himself' (p. 279). An accusation of selfishness disguises its own recognition of the appalling freedom latent in the protean principle of exchange. (Slightly re-phrased, and with emphasis added, the sentence might read, 'He cared nothing for money but he was interested in it because he could *only* feel himself *in it*.') Posey's life exemplifies the money form. He is 'a stranger ... everywhere' (p. 161), who is always riding off or 'living somewhere else' (p. 173). So pure is his displacement that he is necessarily 'a man who could take both views of anything' (p. 250), since any *one* view would damage his (dis)integrity. Lacy catches the contradiction exactly when he describes his brother-in-law as 'self-possessed' only 'by virtue of motion' (p. 144). The integral and the disintegral fuse in money and in Posey alike; both become *the* form of sociability by being that which can convert any social form (from a black half-brother to a brother-in-law's mistress) into an 'independent substance' shared by all (exchange value). That 'substance' is notably lacking in 'atom[s] of matter' because merchants who go compulsively to market are required to believe market requirements; the "free", "equal" and "autonomous" wills who engage in exchange with one another are, by self-definition, ideological wraiths who suppress past, future and person to ease the passage of contract. Consequently, confronted with his mother's death, Posey can feel no grief ('She's dead ain't she?' (p. 256)), there being in Posey, the exchange-man, nothing of substance to feel with. Lacy observes, 'I believed [then] that he was imponderable, that I could have put my finger through him' (p. 256).

As money, Posey is a supreme iconoclast; neither image nor series can hold him. It is not that he transgresses limits (though he does), but that he is offended by the very idea of limit. He will shoot his brother-in-law, not for shooting his black half-brother, not even because his wife declared that she would leave him if he allowed Semmes to kill 'for [him]' (p. 253), but because his wife 'threatened him' (p. 269). Constraint elicits a rictus of violent refusal. Posey is as compulsively formless as Tate's notion of exchange. In 1932, answering the question, 'Who owns America?', Tate provided what could be read as an economic gloss on his future character. He described the progressive absorption of 'need' and 'use' into the sphere of exchange, and noted:

> finance capitalism has become so top heavy with a crazy jig-saw network of exchange value that the individual is wholly at the mercy of the shifting pieces of the puzzle at the remote points where he can possibly assert his needs and rights.[65]

On these terms Posey is not an individual. As he criss-crosses the lines of territory and blood generated by secession, so his remoteness grows more apparent. Without 'needs', and having scant respect for the 'rights' of others, it is as difficult to represent him as it might be to give an image to 'the objectivity of commodities as values'. Posey is a problem for anyone believing in 'density' or 'the body and solid substance of the world', but the problem must be overcome, if icons, figurae and patriarchs – along with the economic preferences that lie behind their synoptic processes – are to survive the market transition which he presages. Consequently, Lacy iconicizes Posey, placing him in a figural series where he has no place, which nonetheless throws him forward into the world as that most Southern of icons – the equestrian statue: 'I always come back to the horseman riding off over a precipice. It is as good a figure as any other' (p. 179). And better than most, since, high on Lacy's high-horse, Posey is doubly and inappropriately patriarchal: the father killer becomes one of the Fathers, and, despite being a non-combatant Northerner, joins a long line of Confederate cavalry heroes.

Two civil wars finally opened the South fully for finance capital; where Ransom countered with ruah, and Faulkner with ∇, Tate offers an iconic horseman. Each icon, ontologically vehement through its impacted plots, is made to counter the narratives latent in a different kind of subject – the commodity, as it sits in the ubiquitous shop window of a consumer culture. These three Southerners fought with one species of 'image' (projected by a highly selective way of remembering) against what they saw as an intrusive, Northern amnesia. The Southern icon is "told" to block the telling of another object's story: the results are objects that Hemingway would not have begun to understand.

6

Fordism: from desire to destruction (an historical interlude)

Fordist mass consumption was created in the 1920s and generalized in the 50s: by the 60s, with profits tending to fall, its 'integrative capacities'[1] were at breaking point. The purposes and limitations of Fordism are inherent in its early forms. When, in January 1914, Ford offered the five-dollar day, he did so to counter rumours of unionization and a labour turnover running at 380 per cent for the previous year. His logic was impeccable: profit may be gleaned from mass production only if producers are able to consume *en masse*. A high wage inflated by credit and directed by advertising makes the poor "rich" and the rich stinking – or so the reasoning runs. Of course, in a competitive market beset by overproduction and valorization problems, the best laid logics fail; witness 1929. Yet the Crash is unsurprising, given the strained coalition perpetrated within the Fordist bargain: 'a de facto political alliance between labour, wage-good capitalists, merchants, finance, capital orientated to consumer credit and professional and salariat organiza-tions'.[2] (Some bargains are merely accords papered over discord.)

Fordism aims to stabilize the contract between capital and labour. During the twenties the prevalent means was "welfarism"; life-insurance schemes, company pensions and stock-purchasing drives were variously on offer to promote a consensus within which workers might perceive themselves, if not as capitalists, then at least as capital's ally. "Happy employees", if they ever enjoyed a generic existence, suffered one of two forms of typically rude awakening. The production line is heavily policed by foremen and security departments; "people's capitalism" has a low tolerance for leisurely workers. Alternatively, the corporation might fire its 'capitalists'. In 1927, finding that his market share had fallen from 50 per cent to 17 per cent, Ford shut down the line. Lay-offs were endemic. Eventually, the Model-A replaced the Model-T, and the re-designed lines were re-started and profit levels rose. Under pressure from Chrysler's model range, Ford had revolutionized his first revolution by turning mass production into flexible mass production.[3] By far the most protean element in all this was the work force: hired, fired and re-hired, its flexibility evidenced the degree to which the welfare of labour was secondary to the welfare of its employer, which in turn was subject to the play of the competitive market. If corporate accumulation was to continue with an intensity sufficient to finance incessant product changes, then the market had to be regulated. In other words, unorganized corporate or monopoly capitalism (1900–35/40) had to become organized corporate capitalism or full Fordism (1940–74).[4]

Depression and war made and re-made the organizational point. The Crash presented capital with a difficult choice: popular uprising or drastic state intervention. Throughout the thirties capital responded by prevaricating, a decision eventually emerging from the need for a strong state to militarize the economy. The history of the New Deal can be read as an anthology of re-deals, rigged deals and changing partners in which organized labour, the Democratic Party and corporations form shifting allegiances in the hunt for a workable contract, that is for a consensus under which private profit might still be made.

Roosevelt's inability to arbitrate is perhaps understandable, given that various parties intervened wilfully to change the name of the contractual game, while still others quit to play other games simultaneously. For example, following the decimation of liberal democrats in the Congressional elections of 1938, a resurgent block of Bourbon Southern Democrats allied with Republicans to take control of Congress away from New Dealers. Such circumstances make ameliorative social reformism difficult and strengthen the corporate hand. Indeed, needing to win support for increasingly interventionist foreign policies, Roosevelt cut public relief drastically (1939), sparking widespread riots which in their turn induced renewed state repression of strikes. Any partnership with labour was doubly difficult in that resurgent right-wing trade unionism divided labour against itself: the American Federation of Labour (AFL) proved perfectly capable of colluding with big business to prevent the Committee of Industrial Organization (CIO) radicalism. It was hard for Roosevelt to support, even tacitly, the CIO in the promotion of "responsible" negotiations (1936–7) when at the local level the AFL signed secret 'sweet-heart' contracts with employers and agreed to the chartering of company unions (1937–8). The New Deal is finally a no-deal resolved by the onset of war.

However, read retrospectively from within the rhetoric of Roosevelt's third term (1941–5), the decade can seem like necessary preparation for desirable and inevitable consensus. The plot might go as follows: state, capital and labour combine to create, via the War Labour and War Production Boards, the substantial and institutional order of collective bargaining which was to characterize the industrial peace and progress of the post-war decades. In other words, and at last, class sinks without trace into consensus as organized corporate capital rises from its own disputatious ashes. The New Deal is dealt by an honest broker (the state) who only and ever sought to provide judicial and legislative means towards an equitable contract between labour and employer. It is a tough story to swallow, yet it remains the master narrative. Consensus, the bedrock and horizon of liberal optimism, blankets the fifties. A typical interpretation of the Treaty of Detroit serves to make the point: the 1950 agreement between General Motors and the autoworkers was to 'cast American labour relations in their postwar mould',[5] in that it involved guaranteed wage levels made invulnerable to deflation. The contract struck the editors of *Fortune* as an 'affirmation . . . of the free enterprise system':

> First the autoworkers accepted 'the existing distribution of income between wages and profits as "normal" if not as "fair"'. Second, by explicitly accepting 'objective economic facts – costs of living and productivity – as 'determining wages', the contract threw 'overboard all theories of wages as determined by political power, and of profit "as surplus value"'. Finally, 'it is one of the very few union contracts that expressly recognize[s] both the importance of the management function and the fact that management operates directly in the interest of labour.[6]

So read, the contract looks good and the post-war corporate system seems set fair towards "The Age of Affluence" and "The End of Ideology". The resonance of these generic clichés resides in two subcontracts. The workforce/capital accord, mediated by the unions and founded on a full consumption basket (whose fifties brand-names were "suburb" and "white collar") depended first upon the *Pax Americana* and second upon a citizen – capital agreement. Without Bretton Woods (1944) there could have been no Treaty of Detroit; without government accommodation (or at least gestures of accommodation) towards state welfare provision, workplace grievance (sit-down, wild-cat, walk-out and lock-out) would have been more than single-plant or single-industry issues. Consensus is a contractual balancing act of considerable ingenuity.

For full Fordism to work at home, it must go global. Bretton Woods gave the US effective control over the International Monetary Fund (IMF); with the dollar installed as the key global currency and the IMF headquarters located in Washington, Keynes's vision of an international bank as 'a genuine organ of international government'[7] becomes a licence for neo-imperialism. American aid pumped into the world system returns as requests for American exports. As US corporate leverage increases, giving access to raw materials on cheaper terms, so the value of long-term US investment abroad grows (at 8.8 per cent per annum between 1948 and 1966).[8] Mandel summarizes:

> The growth of the 'permanent arms economy' after the Second World War also performed, among other things, the very concrete function of protecting the 'free world' for 'free capital investments' and 'free repatriation of profits' and of guaranteeing U.S. monopoly capital 'free access' to a series of vital raw materials. In 1957 the chairman of the board of Texaco frankly stated that in his view the primary task of the American government was to create 'a political and financial climate both here and abroad conducive to overseas investment'.[9]

With demand at home underwritten by demand from outside, the tendency of the rate of profit to fall may seem less remorseless. Indeed, profit looks profitable for all. But if what is good for General Motors is genuinely to seem good for the country, the overlap between labour contract and international contract must be further reinforced by a welfare contract. The state must stand where Ford stood at the beginning of the twenties, with the notable difference that the state should not flinch. The New Deal, the Fair Deal and the Great Society are in their very different ways (and flinches) extensions of the Highland Park personnel department, the aim of each being the provision of a welfare safety-net. The net, whether financed by the corporation or the state, ultimately depends upon the legitimacy of private capital whose stability can therefore always be appealed to by any administration seeking "temporarily" to shelve welfare measures (Roosevelt in 1939, Truman in 1948 and Johnson in 1966). Nonetheless, the net seems safer in the hands of the state, since 'capitalists behave like capitalists wherever they are . . . pursu[ing] the expansion of value through exploitation without regard to social consequences'.[10] A government, no matter how corporatist its inclination, must at least claim to have the interests of all in mind. Consequently, the increasing corporatism of post-war American administrations legitimizes the 'expansion of value' while reiterating a nominal 'regard for social consequence'. If the claim sticks (and can be paid for), so will consensus. However, the logic of corporatism and the possibility of consensus are at odds.

Corporatism seeks to renew or sustain the threefold bargain between capital – its labour, its citizens and its world. Priority is given to an increased investment rate achieved through the transfer of income to large corporations: necessarily, the redistribution is regressive, placing in corporate coffers what has been taken from the generic pocket of the worker and the consumer. The corporatist must therefore talk greater labour participation while tightening labour's belt; offer democratic teamwork while centralizing the state; advocate widening trade while re-militarizing the economy. The contradictions creak: the Kennedy/ Johnson administrations – nominally liberal-Keynesian – promoted an investment boom via tax concessions (the drop in taxes on corporate profit was equivalent to the transfer of 1 per cent of the gross national product from government to business).[11] At the same time, Kennedy sought to guarantee labour "peace" by turning the National Labor Relations Board into an active and innovative agency. Except that what looks like fair arbitration on the basis of national wage guidelines supported by the Supreme Court, can be read another way as: '[an attempt] to create an overpowering regulatory and legal framework for forcing union members to accept unlimited grievance arbitration in exchange for abjuration of the right to strike'.[12] Despite their unions, labour sensed the double-talk, with wild-cat strikes reaching a post-war record by 1968. Rank-and-file pressure similarly lay behind the rapid increase in contract rejections, a rarity in 1962, but by 1968 standing at one-eighth of all contracts negotiated. Nonetheless, arbitration, whether called "consensus" or "coercion", worked. The rate of wage increases slowed to stagnation between 1960 and 1965.

Meanwhile, the War on Poverty and the war in Vietnam simultaneously bled and fed the corporate boom. The welfare net, conceived under Kennedy and raised by Johnson, sought to incorporate the "Other America" within the mainstream of the domestic high-wage economy. (Liberalism must watch its margins, since from the excluded will come the evidence that consensus is myth.) It failed: blacks largely stayed outside.[13] The South-east Asian war was neither to succeed nor to fail; it simply went elsewhere. The Green Beret who seeks to make the world safe for the Peace-Corps volunteer does the national economy a double "service": military production booms in the hope that one day, just as in Western Europe so in Asia and South America, mass-consumption economies will proliferate along American lines. Guns mean "democracy" means Pepsi. As the Bay of Pigs becomes Vietnam becomes Chile . . ., so the political legitimation for holding open the door to the American Century thins. Once 'global Fordism' is re-cast as 'bloody Fordism', talk of "ballot boxes" and "stabilized democracy" sounds like so much PR for a permanent-arms economy.[14]

Military promotion was essential during the sixties, contributing to the survival of corporatism and its consensual public face. The social contracts, strained on all fronts, needed Kennedy's military-Keynesianism and Johnson's Asian war to keep the pivotal consumption basket reasonably full. Stated abstractly, faced by the increased uncertainty of consumer-durable mass markets, US corporations re-orientated towards the volatile high-profit sector of military production. What "desire" was to the economy of the twenties, "destruction" is to the economy of the fifties and sixties.

In 1919 the US demobilized, whereas after the Second World War it expanded militarily, with the result that by 1955 10 per cent of the GNP was being spent on 'preparedness'. Percentiles cannot capture the enormity of the investment: between 1945 and 1970 the US government expended $11.1 trillion for military purposes, an amount which exceeds the 1967 valuation of all the nation's business and residential structures.[15] In effect the USA became 'a defence economy' through which the state, as chief purchaser, might regularize and direct accumulation. The USA's levels of military production have been so great and so consistent that Mandel has lengthened Marx's shorthand in order to catch what constitutes a structural shift within late capitalism itself:

> we must convert Marx's reproduction scheme, which operates with two sectors – Department I: means of production; Department II: consumer goods – into a scheme with three sectors, adding to the two Departments a third Department producing means of destruction.[16]

The notion that capital can be stabilized through the manufacture of destruction has its illogicalities, yet to the corporatist it is logic itself. While the liberal (via Keynes and the New Deal) tells the one about the state as an honest broker (mediating between competing interests in the cause of controlled competition and continued accumulation), the corporatist (essentially an efficient liberal) arms Keynes and puts him in charge of Department III. Daniel Bell, writing in 1960, notes the affinity between Keynes and mobilization: he assumes that, 'if the Keynesian formula is workable, then the last of the major reasons for alarm over American capital dissolves', and adds the rider that the Cold War acted as capital's guarantor:

> a defence economy does require a considerable degree of planning and direction – masked as they may be. And the 'readiness economy' which has now become a bedrock feature of the society makes moot the question that agitated liberals for many years: whether the marvellous productivity of the American economy can be utilized to the full without war orders. The fact is, that for the foreseeable future, 'defence' and large budgets will be with us.[17]

'Masked . . . planning' is the crucial notion: when Washington becomes the Pentagon, and the nation fails to notice, then capital will enter its golden age.

For Bell the transition is easy and almost over: the permanent-arms economy is his brief and covert way between the liberalism of *The End of*

Ideology (1960) and the corporatism of *The Coming of Post Industrial Society* (1974). The third technological revolution (cybernetic and nuclear), pump-primed by defence budgets, marks the end of classes and the emergence of non-class formations (technocracy and bureaucracy); with 'the computer [as] the tool' and 'decision theory [as] its master,'[18] government becomes a matter of rational calculus. There is a proviso: 'technological decision making' depends upon intense accumulation

> to the extent that the investment process has been routinized and the 'class conflicts' encapsulated, so the issue of class strife no longer acts to polarize a country around a single issue, those older problems of an industrial society have been muted if not 'solved'.[19]

QED – to the extent that military expenditure works in its 'masked . . . direction' of the economy, consensus will be preserved. 'And without consensus is only conflict, and persistent conflict simply tears a society apart.'[20]

Bell's post-industrial society is to the Pentagon what Huxley's *Brave New World* (1932) was to the Ford plant, with the singular exception that Bell makes claims to fact. His conviction that 'planning' plus 'the centrality of theoretical knowledge' can reduce economic and political indeterminacy, thereby delivering 'the social control of change',[21] is a plea for the perpetuation of Eisenhower's military–industrial complex. The institution and the eulogy alike depend upon appeals to 'technological rationality' in order to disguise the degree to which state science is directed towards destruction, and state funding towards the circulation of capital. Bell talks of computers as *the* tool of 'the new intellectual technology', and nominates IBM as 'the paradigmatic-corporation of the last third of the century'.[22] Few would deny it, but some might remember that the electronic digital computer was developed for ballistic calculations, while miniaturized circuits (the precursor of micro-electronics and so of the micro-computer) were first used in proximity fuses for bombs. For that reason the cost of their development, which stood at $1 billion and involved a third of the electronics industry, was largely paid for by the government.[23] In 1964, two-thirds of the research costs of the entire electronics-equipment industry were state-funded: such levels of 'planning' suggest that there is no technology without wealth and no wealth without technology, while further implying that both are heavily dependent upon government backing.[24] The case for the state as the administrator of the surplus profits of the capitalist class virtually makes itself, and yet the narrowness of the corporatist-state's class interest remains 'masked' for as long as "Science", "Rationality" and "Progress" legitimate the struggle to maintain corporate profitability.

Legitimation is easier within the consensual assumption that political and economic questions are managerial issues to be debated by interested parties in the light of the GNP. Should the nation's productivity be linked to the nation's safety, such hypothetical discussions are liable to seem less notional. War, or its promise, tightens the consensual accords. 'Korea came along and saved us', because it proved 'international Communist conspiracy';[25] Dean Acheson's words echo Charles Wilson's complaint, 'Russia abroad, labour at home',[26] a lament from 1946 that was soon to be re-phrased in celebratory tone as 'With Russian abroad we can control labour at home.' Fear of Russia's European buffer zone and of Chinese intentions prompted the de-radicalization of the CIO. A red scare re-casts the worker as the concerned citizen and anti-union activities as national defence. The colder the war the more likely the populace to win the struggle for the post-war corporate system, while imagining itself engaged in quite another battle.

Where "Science" is tied by the Cold War to "National Interest", its primary bond to profit can be forgotten, and its secondary function as the expression of "Reason" can wear the mask of political enthusiasm ('Democracy"). Given that scarcely existent spies (the Rosenbergs, 1951) and non-existent missile-gaps (Kennedy's 1960) can materialize from this particular conjunction of convictions, it is altogether credible that consensus and its classless cast should exist as a real fantasy ensuring cultural cohesion, rather than as a perceived ploy 'to convince the victims of alienated labour that it is senseless to rebel'.[27]

The resiliency of the integrative capacities of the Fordist consensus (nationalism or no) finally resides in its founding accord – the contract drawn up between labour and capital. Contract is the key to consensus. The post-war USA saw the emergence of institutionalized collective bargaining across the core industries. Contracts were typically produced binding workers in no-strike agreements lasting from two to five years: contracts were detailed in their specifications and localized in application. One result of the creation of a multitude of individual contracts was the recomposition of union officialdom as a vast bureaucracy: 'Nowhere else has there developed such a dense mass of private "common law", nor so extensive a substitution of legal bureaucratization and arbitration for administrative state intervention or public judiciary.'[28] Mike Davis's comment conveys the translation of labour conflict into an issue of legal rather than political (or even economic) dispute. Because the union, armed with procedural legalism, substitutes both for the state and for capital, violation of contract precipitates the violator into a legal wrangle. He is doubly isolated: having in all likelihood broken an agreement negotiated by his own official and collective voice (the union), he finds himself moved from the industrial marketplace into the industrial court. As a legal subject, like his twin the economic subject, he stands alone because 'in the United States, collective bargaining is legally derived from a classically liberal concept of consent to representation . . . Despite the mass struggles of the 1930s, the word "union" does not appear in either the Wagner or the Taft–Hartley Acts.'[29] Given this tradition, when the chips are down, "collective" and "union" are limited terms. As a party to an essentially private contract between specific employers and specific workers, overseen by a union with managerial imperatives, the violator feels that his "rights" are "individual". Davis notes:

> Because [the] legitimacy [of collective bargaining] is . . . based on individual consent, the rights of American unions under law are provisional and revocable; anti union campaigns on the right are thus always waged in a Jeffersonian language of 'the rights of individual workers'.[30]

I would contend that the post–war American worker (particularly when possessed of a white collar and a full consumption basket) contains his own anti–union campaigner who is always liable to wage war against a "collective self" on behalf of an "individual self".

Attrition is encouraged by the influx of law into the workplace. As a legal subject and an economic subject – both cast in a 'classically liberal' mould – the worker, whether he violates the contract or merely signs it, acts as a possessive individual.[31] He is collectivity's antithesis because he has chosen *freely* to alienate his labour (or to withdraw it) in order to take possession of himself as a *will* to *value*. Value, in the form of abstract labour-time, grants him his *autonomy* and makes him everyone's *equal*. I have italicized certain terms in order to indicate how extensively the language of the law and of the liberal market re-echo one another.[32] As the subject stands in relation to contract, so he stands in relation to law. Each institution produces a particular kind of subject and reinforces the subject produced by the other. In both cases a trinity of terms is posited, having limited relevance to a corporatist society – "free", "equal" and "autonomous". The terminology derives from the ideology of just exchange, which in turn depends upon a free market: both sources are called into question by late capitalism, under which increasingly large segments of the market are indirectly administered by the state. The terms are resilient because, although corporatism is the emergent form, a residual "free market" persists, ensuring that "bourgeois individualism" continues to determine, at least in part, the way that labour thinks about itself and acts. For many (particularly women and blacks) the potential and the savagery of the competitive labour-market is the only option. Nineteenth-century wage-relations are alive and well and embrace a sizable segment of the working population. In the USA millions of workers are not unionized, and in addition are excluded from the safety net of basic labour and social legislation. To those outside the core industries, employment involves a contract of "individual sale", "freely" entered by the "autonomous" will: potentially, should the will be wilful enough, the individual will rise (as the story goes).

Since liberal capitalism survives as a very substantial periphery to organized corporate capitalism, its contract, self-images and plots are sedimented in the mind of labour and capital alike. The sediment deepens once it is recognized that the wage in the USA, whether in residual or emergent form, has never been a social wage, whereas in Europe wages (predominantly) through taxes contribute to a "strong" and "universal" state-welfare provision. In the USA that provision, for the most part, derives from bargaining. More than minimal welfare is a matter of commercial agreement and is therefore substantially a deferred wage. Consequently, during the fifties and sixties, what is a citizen's "right" in Europe is a contractual incentive in the USA. For the collective notion of the citizen who contributes is substituted the individualist notion of the consumer who bargains or has his union bargain for him (in which case individual self-interest is simply serviced by institutional self-interest). Since American "citizens" find their collective welfare in a private consumption basket, their "citizenship" and "collectivity" are liable to wither to a defence of personal appetite. I exaggerate in order to underline the reasons for the continuing power of consensual ideas in a society whose system of production is geared to the privatization of need and the fragmentation of sociability. The pervasiveness of "contract" and "exchange", of money and its negotiations, as *the* forms of sociability launders memory, so that the reciprocity of social labour (production) is suppressed for the pleasure of isolated gratification (consumption).

My abstraction from history is undertaken in order to characterize pervasive economic circumstances in which it is difficult for areas of collectivity to resist or emerge. Class issues degenerate to contractual niceties and consensus sounds like a truism. As Daniel Bell puts it in 1960, reviewing the fifties: 'in an open society the political arena . . . is a place where different interests fight it out for advantage. That is why, usually, the prism of "class" is too crude to follow the swift play of diverse political groups.'[33] Bell deems the 'fight' clean because interested parties are held to be self-refereeing – each sees in the other the managerial constraints closest to its own heart:

> the methodological promise of the second half of the twentieth century is the management of organized complexity . . . the identification and implemen-tation of strategies of rational choice in games against nature and games between persons, and the development of a new intellectual technology

which, by the end of the century, may be as salient in human affairs as machine technology has been for the past century and a half. (1974)[34]

The name of the 'game' is corporatism (subtitle post-); all classes learn it and become post-classes as the blue collar is bleached white by the growth of service industry and an attendant decline in the production of goods. Consequently, 'the new "class struggles" of the post industrial society are less a matter of conflict between management and worker in the economic enterprise than the pull and tug of various organized segments to influence the state budget.' (1976)[35]

Bell's case rests on an undoubted class shift. As early as 1951 C. Wright Mills traced the emergence of a 'new middle class': his figures suggest that in 1870 over three-quarters of the total employed were engaged in producing things, as against slightly less than a half in 1940.[36] The post-war years clarified and intensified the shift. Fred Pfeil has followed the careers of the 'baby-boom' generation born between 1945 and 1955; 37.4 million in number, 22.2 million of them had by 1980 gained employment in managerial or professional speciality occupations (ranging from systems analysis to therapy). 'The statistics attest to a striking convergence of middle and working class trajectories in the post-war period.'[37] During the fifties the white collars described themselves as "employees" rather than "workers"; by the sixties they were "professionals"; and in the seventies – as the babies began to boom in earnest – "yuppie" was the chosen term. Whatever the name, the group constitutes a growing professional managerial class (or PMC). B. and J. Ehrenreich define the PMC as mental workers, caught between labour and capital, 'whose major function [is] the reproduction of capitalist culture and capitalist class relations'.[38] These are the 'co-ordinators' of full Fordism; if it is to work, they must make it work. As a sizable 'technological intelligentsia', who do not own the means of production, their principal filiation may not be to class but to specialism – to the professional network of their own technology or bureaucracy. Of course, in the last instance, as 'managerial capitalists', whose expertise perpetuates corporate profitability, they are corporatist by persuasion. Their class allegiance is seemingly clear: yet at the same time they are an 'intellectual proletariat' whose mental labour reproduces a pattern of ownership which excludes them by rewarding them well. The salariat, if it thought about itself, might have a divided consciousness. My point is that it is not encouraged to think as a class. These are Daniel Bell's people, for whom the imperatives of managerial efficiency positively counter social awareness.

White collar and blue collar alike maintain a provisionally classless world through interpretive systems which advocate "individualism" while maximizing the common ground. The key to such systems is their promotion of the singular interest in a way that seems open to generalization, so that "privacy" and "consensus" can sound synonymous. Witness how the blue-collar contract elides contrary forms of individuality: the bourgeois individual, self-regarding and self-reliant (throw-back to the residual wage-relations of liberal capitalism), liaises with the corporate servant (product of Fordist collective bargaining), whose interests accord with the general interests of the corporation. A similar and contradictory elision characterizes white-collar "rationalism", which fosters corporate profit-levels (via competitive *self*-interest between the divisions within a multidivisional corporate entity) and yet insists on truth to the "truth" of de-politicized "Science" ("Progress" as being "in the general interest"). Meanwhile, for both groups, consumerism struggles to maintain generalized access to the terrain of cultural consensus with its emphasis on individualized consumption.

The shop window remains central to the classless bargain, since only if it continues to empty itself into the collective and yet private basket of workers can Fordism remain solvent. By the sixties solvency grows problematic as inflationary difficulties shadow Department II.[39] The fantasy is that capital will respond by flowing into the bottomless opportunity of Department III. At which point the shop window and the military enter into symbiosis, and from guns will come still more butter. However, the expansion of Department III only inhibited the tendency of capitalist production to crisis.[40] Capitalism cannot lastingly be stabilized through its defence budget because arms expenditure is financed through taxes which eventually produce a marked reduction in the consumer wage, at which point Department II suffers. Furthermore, the incidence of constant capital in Department III is higher than the social average: arms research, so much the motor force behind the post-war technological fix, invests enormously in machinery, plant and product on which it is inherently difficult to realize direct profits. Nuclear weaponry is valorized through sale (necessarily limited even in an American century) or war (an unstable market). Since the state is both the provider of the orders and the receiver of the goods, it falls to the state to engineer some sort of solution. In American terms, the Capitol (as capital) must draw closer to the Pentagon, with the attendant risk that Adam Smith's long-gone, but notionally operative, 'invisible hand' will not only prove visible but identifiable as the hand of the state. At which point – should too many people see – the freedom of the free market, from which derive the several contracts that buttress the liberal consensus, might be *openly* at risk. Those capable of sight experience a violent metamorphosis as they are cast from the consensus of their freely competing "individualism" back towards the contending class fragments that they always were.

On 21 October 1967, Norman Mailer undertook the short but

significant walk from the Capitol to the Pentagon. He did not go alone, since with him, among others, was his fragmentary 'self'. The meaning of the walk was quite probably heightened for the novelist in that his novel of the same year, *Why are we in Vietnam?*, is spoken from the centre of the Capitol/Pentagon propinquity; D.J., the narrator, is the precocious child born of capital's new forms. As D.J.'s ventriloquist, Mailer marches possessed of a double knowledge: he knows the voice of the enemy, and he knows it to be a strand of his own voice.

7

Why Are We in Vietnam?: *because the buck mustn't stop*

In 1953 Charles Wilson left the presidency of General Motors to become Eisenhower's Secretary of Defense; in 1944 he had coined the phrase, 'the permanent war economy'. 1960 saw Robert McNamara move from the top post at the Ford Motor Company to Defense. Vietnam was to preoccupy him. Both men were candidates for Big Luke Fellinka's guided hunting trips in the Alaska Brooks Mountain Range. Comparing their relative powers, D.J., the narrator of *Why Are We in Vietnam?* (1967), notes of Big Luke:

> he was a *man*! You could hang him, and he'd weigh just as much as Charley Wilson or Robert Bone-head McNamara, I mean you'd get the same intensity of death ray off his dying as you'd get from some fucking Arab sheik who had ten thousand howlers on horses to whoop and scream for the holy hot hour of his departure to Allah.[1]

D.J. reads Burroughs at fifteen (p. 14) and is a sometime experimenter in funeral parlours; he must therefore know that hanging involves male orgasm even as the sphincter releases. Spending here is a complex: sperm, excrement, corporate capital, state capitalism and the permanent-arms economy exist in uneasy yet unforced relation. Why? I shall propose an answer, but before doing so I need to establish two things: first, Mailer's abiding interest in the related history of corporations and military expansion; second, an economic context to which that interest can in the last instance be tied.

In *Barbary Shore* (1951), Mailer's second novel, McLeod, the carrier of 'the remnants of a socialist culture'[2] bases his 'political formulations' on 'the thesis that war is inevitable' (p. 228). Lovett, the obscurely wounded amnesiac who takes up 'the heritage' in order that he can 'elect to have a future' (p. 250) can do no more than duplicate McLeod's analysis while listening to the military closure of that future: 'From out the unyielding contradictions of labour stolen from men, the march to the endless war forces its pace' (p. 256). For a condensed, if eccentric, survey of Marx's 'law of value' (p. 182), one could do far worse than read chapters 24 and 25 of *Barbary Shore*. It is unlikely that Mailer made his narrator's voyage 'of two thousand pages and . . . other endless books' (p. 181), but what he has read is made to work.[3]

Lovett and McLeod between them offer notes towards a structural reading of the history of American capital. The nineteenth-century captain of industry (chief product, his own accumulations) becomes the twentieth-century captain of consciousness (chief product, the consumer) before graduating of necessity as captain of the state (with special responsibility for defence). Wilson and McNamara are testimony to a pattern whose necessity stems from continuing problems over the realization of profit. For McLeod 'monopoly capitalism' has entered 'permanent crisis' (p. 231):

> the productive capacity of monopoly had become so tremendous, its investment in machinery so great in comparison to the labour that it could exploit, that only the opening of the entire world market could solve its search for investment and profit even temporarily.   (p. 228)

In other words, investment in constant capital (machinery, buildings, etc.), with its slow yield, far outweighs the surplus that can be extracted from variable capital (the labour force). Accumulation must involve an increase in the proletariat since, for a Marxist like McLeod, the worker is the sole source from which surplus is drawn. Monopolies that automate in order to reduce their labour-bill, while increasing the output that labour must buy, are eventually engaged in 'an unyielding contradiction'. To kill the goose that lays the golden egg is one thing; to require then that it stuff itself is quite another. The technological fix must therefore fail; expensive innovation may reduce the cost of variable capital but with iron logic it will promote over-accumulation in the form of unsold inventories and under-used capacity. Cold comfort – and McLeod is killed by an agent of the state for dispensing it. Lovett is left with no options: without past or long-term future, class or party, he leaves the novel through a back window, a 'traveller' (p. 256) without fellows, whose only available role is that of Jeremiah.

Mailer perfects the jeremiad with *Cannibals and Christians* (1966): the essays run from 1960 to 1966, but McLeod's voice persists in Mailer's analytic despair:

a world whose ultimate logic is war, because in a world of war all overproduction and
overpopulation is possible since peoples and commodities may be destroyed wholesale
– in a breath, a world of such hypercivilization is a world not of adventures,
entrepreneurs, settlers, social arbiters, proletarians, agriculturalists, and other
egocentric types of a dynamic society, but is instead a world of whirlpools and
formlessness where two huge types begin to re-emerge, types there at the beginning of
it all: Cannibals and Christians.[4]

'War', 'overproduction' and 'hypercivilization', three linked terms which need economic glossing before the cannibal in the whirlpool can be named. The prime economic grievance of the late sixties was inflation. In the autumn of 1967 Gallup asked the old one about 'the most urgent problem facing you and your family', and received a 60 per cent response for 'the high cost of living'.[5] In 1960 Eisenhower had returned a balanced budget; with the exception of 1969, there had not been another. However, deficit spending by governments is simply a symptom of the more general problem of 'overproduction'. Kennedy, an eventual Keynesian, sought to increase demand by federal spending, particularly in the spheres of space and defence; Johnson 'upped the ante' with Vietnam and The Great Society; yet both were failed supermen in a sluggish supermarket. The USA, even with state supervision, could not buy a way out of its problems. Government debt reflected corporate debt reflected consumer debt. The figures for business indebtedness are particularly striking: in 1959 debt servicing represented 9 per cent of the gross receipts of American companies; by 1973 the cost ran at 33 per cent.[6] Only a comparison between state debt and private debt reveals the full extent of the problem: between 1950 and 1980 US government debt grew by 340 per cent; in the same period private debt rose by 1,624 per cent.[7] The sixties, like the twenties, was a decade of accelerated credit.

Credit is essential to the capitalist because he is too good at 'progress'. Having innovated, and deepened his investment in highly productive and highly expensive machinery that he is still paying for, he finds himself in a crowded market. Glut intensifies competition – more machinery, faster turnover, more unsold lines, much of it to be financed with profits from as yet unrealized sales. Finance capital is keen to bail industry out in just these circumstances because the interest-bearing monies of the money capitalist are most lubricant and profitable while they remain flexible. Ideally, the investor in bonds and shares wants to lend capital for as brief a period as possible; to have his money tied to a specific use means that he cannot move it when better speculative opportunities occur. Consequently, to invest in future appropriation rather than in actual production maximizes his freedom. Marx has a phrase for it – 'fictitious capital', in which everything is 'doubled and trebled and transformed into a mere phantom of the imagination', because, 'all connection with the actual expansion process of capital is . . . completely lost, and the conception of capital as something with automatic self-expansion properties is thereby strengthened'.[8] The arena of fictitious capital is the stock market, where investors trade titles or 'paper duplicates' in companies whose value is fixed by present and anticipated revenues. Anticipation approaches fantasy in a market characterized by over-accumulation and dawning inflation; over-accumulation produces 'overproduction', produces 'fictitious capital', which produces over-accumulation and so on *ad infinitum* or until the crisis comes.

Crisis management falls to the state. As the institutions of a credit economy emerge and proliferate, so the state becomes capital's administrator, arbitrating the through-flow of the savings of a class (surplus). Late capital's valorization problems increasingly recompose the state as a Strong State in the image of capital, with overall duties to act as an "accelerator". State monies cover research and development costs in aerospace and nuclear power, support ailing industries, underpin essential infrastructural work, pay police and army, etc., all to implement the interests of capital. As Mandel puts its: 'A State apparatus that did not preserve the social and political order would be as unthinkable as a fire extinguisher that spread flames.'[9]

II

By setting 'overproduction' in an economic and political context it may be possible to understand the historical force of Mailer's linked terms, 'hypercivilization' and 'war', terms which are central to a reading of *Why Are We in Vietnam?* 'Hypercivilization' crosses 'hype' with 'hyper' to catch the ever-changing sheen which characterizes Mailer's sense of America's last days. Credit is a multiplier prompting the diversification of commodities. In the hunt to realize surplus, commodities must go where commodities have never gone before – space is the new frontier of a market in need. D.J.'s father, Rusty Jethroe, takes his son to Alaska only to replace Al Percy Cunningham, managing director of Tendonex, who at the last minute is tied up in a struggle for the contract 'to put a plastic Univar valve and plug into the bottom of the collapsible built-in space suit chemical toilet in the Gemini (Roman Numeral Unstated)' (p. 47). While the commodity travels to new markets it must take new forms in order to elicit and assuage new needs: 'Difficulties in the realization of surplus value induce a growing trend for the monopolies to alter the form of commodities perpetually, often in a senseless way from the piont of view of rational consumption.'[10] The race for product differentiation (cooker *and* micro-wave; black and white *and* colour television) is eventually counterproductive, since it puts great strain on industrial capital. New products mean spiralling research costs, expensive re-tooling and a heavy outlay on new production. With each capital unit seeking to fix the new commodity as a new need, 'fictitious capital' expands. The post-war paper economy grows, bringing with it permanent debt, fiscal and liquidity crises and eventually high inflation.

Mailer's fictional corporation, CCCCP (Central Consolidated Combined Chemical and Plastic) mirrors the market leaders. Rusty heads a subsidiary whose main product is a plastic cigarette filter: the only problem is that the filter (Pure Pores) cause lip cancer. The problem is an opportunity according to D.J., for whom the interior space of the body, as 'America's last frontier' (p. 30), is ripe for exploitation. Recognizing that corporations may hesitate 'to get in on the bright new fortunes being made along the rim-scab of Carcinoma Cruds' (p. 30), D.J. projects more plausible market possibilities. Since the filter is 'the most absorbative substance devised' (p. 31) it might be taped on as an underarm deodorant or inserted as a vaginal contraceptive. 'The filter with the purest purosity of purpose' (p. 31) is potentially an internalized bathroom. Given that large masses of capital are no longer achieving valorization in the post-war USA, non-capitalized parts of social life and of the human body are perversely interesting to industry. Any gap or hole that yields no profit must be commodified. Consequently, during the fifties and sixties there is a large increase in service-sector investment. The aim is to transform collective, familial or private services into separate industries, and so into separate chances for corporate surplus. Just as at the turn of the century the tailor became the ready-made garment industry, the cobbler became the shoe department and the cook became the mass-produced-food chain, so in the 1950s the theatre and cinema became television, and the family meal (already de-socialized by tins) was further atomized as the TV dinner.[11] D.J.'s plans for Pure Pores are a quantum leap for the concept of services. In the twenties capital shrank the kitchen (the housewife as a consumer of electrical goods, precooked food and store-bought clothes needed less space in which to offer her diminished services). D.J. projects the entire abandonment of bathrooms, in their place consumers will carry individualized sanitary amenities close to their skin.

D.J., who defines his own 'genius' as 'pure American entrepreneur' (p. 194), has an eye for orifices and inner skins. Other notional product lines are a plastic sphincter and an electric come machine (p. 9): both evidence the extent of commodification, since with overproduction elsewhere D.J. turns inwards for his surpluses. The anus and the vagina represent the furthest recesses of the biological realm, the former as yet largely untapped by capital. Anality links to inertia and to death, D.J. will contemplate marketing the odour of death (p. 194). There is, however, a catch in the Pure Pores project: anally inserted, the filter renders female users unable 'to tinkle' and they 'will die *emmerdé*!! Whang! Whang!' (p. 31). If I may translate: the uses of perpetual porosity do not include retention as an interior lavatory. This is not, however, a health warning: those addicted to the logic of commodity might be intrigued by the ultimate in consumer testing, 'Are you consumer enough to be absorbed totally by the product?' *'Emmerdé'*, to foul oneself; 'Whang', slang for phallus. In its exclamatory form, a masturbatory injunction, implying that the image of insertion and subsequent female absorption and evacuation should accelerate male ejaculation. The old alimentary joke, about the body under consumer capital being no more than a conduit for commodity, is told from the particular perspective of the finance capitalist. Pure Pores unites the consumer and the commodity in an impure flux. Industrial capital as it overproduces has problems with through-put. Finance capital offers relief. For the financier, 'capital is value only when it is in motion'.[12] However, any process of economic circulation involves blocks:

> As long as [capital] remains in the productive process it is not capable of circulating; and it is virtually devalued . . . As long as it cannot be brought to market, it is fixed as a product. As long as it remains on the market, it is fixated as a commodity.[13]

The commodity and the consumer are therefore 'fixations' or potential barriers. Remedies are available, producers may spend on marketing, information gathering or advertising to speed their capital's transition towards surplus. Finance capital offers to clear the blockage by promoting credit-based expansion. Marx has words of warning: 'As long as [capital] remains in circulation, it is not capable of producing . . . As long as it cannot be exchanged for conditions of production, it is fixated as money.'[14]

The financier would comply with the charge of money fixation, since for him money is self-expansive. By shifting his entire attention from problems of production to problems of exchange, he reduces all terms to credit flow, in whose fantastical motions machines, products, workers and purchasers are no more than temporary impediments to the highest truth of motion. To borrow from the Marxist alphabet, the financier's logos is M–M–M^1.[15]

Unsurprisingly, economies which choose to sail to prosperity on a sea of debt divide their own capitalist class into finance capitalists, who make money from money, and industrial capitalists, who make money from production. Lenin comments: 'The twentieth century marks the turning point from the old capitalism to the new, from the domination of capital in general to the domination of finance capital.'[16] Pure Pores is an enema fit for a financier's heart. Clearly, I am reading excremental flow as an analogy for motion which in its turn is the quintessence of money. *Why Are We in Vietnam?* is riddled with streams: a stream of consciousness, in the form of a stream of radio waves, serves to spread much talk of piss, shit, jism, blood and above all electricity, the entirety of which is just possibly being recorded on an endless tape-circuit in the anus of the narrator. D.J. is rather more than an entrepreneur; he is the embodiment of flow, and in his mastery of its logistics exemplifies financial 'genius'. Through him Mailer cartoons the perverse tactics of late capital, under which financier and state liaise to counter and disguise the tendency of the rate of profit to fall.

D.J. refines perversity, witness his prototype for the electric come machine. *En route* to the Brooks Range, Edison is reproached for omitting to make the gadget: I am reminded that as a boy Gatsby vowed to 'study electricity etc.' and 'other needed inventions'.[17] Gatsby engineers profit from forms of liquidity (liquor and bonds). D.J. is a speculator designed for more fluid times: using the knowledge that certain metals are superconductive at low temperatures, he reasons that a vagina lined with a rim of thalium and cooled to absolute zero would require a single stroke (or minimum male expenditure) to be converted into a perpetual source of current:

> why you just take a run and plunge your dick through the near absolute zero
> ring, zing into that gone ice snatch, whoo-ee! whoo-ee! pull it out before you
> rock stone ice pinnacle prick. You just set up a current, man, is going to keep
> that cunt in charge for months.   (p.174)

The mechanism is a desire machine that gratifies its own desire without ever producing satisfaction. Where current is money and desire is a means to profit, D.J. has made a device capable of multiplying M to infinity (M^1–M^2–M^3 . . .). In a market which promotes isolated consumption in order to maximize yield, the design looks to be a winner. Except that it is useless. Given that D.J. shows no interest in female pleasure, what he has built is a fake vagina which excludes the phallus, and which is simultaneously a metaphor for the workings of money capital. Marx observes of the financier, 'Interest bearing capital . . . is the consummate *automatic fetish* . . . money making money, and in this form it no longer bears any trace of its origin.'[18] The fantasy of the financier is that his money earns its slice of the surplus (interest) in a sealed system via relations with itself ('fictitious capital'). Likewise, the sexual fetishist suppresses the real workings of the female body – in all its ambivalence – the better to concentrate on a single part which is, of necessity, a closed object, lacking all extension to a social or moral world.

In *Advertisements for Myself* (1959), Mailer notes that 'sex has become the center of our economy'.[19] If so, that economy is conspicuously without a centre, since commodified sexuality involves segmentation of the body and isolation of the consumer – aims which are a small part of a larger de-centring latent in 'fictitious capital.' As we've seen, the introduction to *Cannibals and Christians* anthologizes 'egocentric types' rendered archaic in the 'whirlpools and formlessness' (p. 3) of the sixties. Credit and the ego are antithetical because credit carries the principle of diffusion into all substantial forms, be they factories or persons. Capital's lateral shift from problems of production to problems of exchange produces the requirement that persons and things should have less centre. Capitalist preocupation with just how to reproduce accumulations casts all forms of the constant and the fixed as risks. Capital embodied in machinery may de-value before that machinery has covered its cost; shift work is one way in which owners seek to get their money back before engineering advances outflank them. Equally, capital locked into commodities will de-value if the product does not sell fast enough; in order to cover themselves, producers increasingly sell not objects but 'temporary collections of imputed characteristics'. For example, an item of food is a focal point for a number of messages about nutrients, convenience, appearance and texture, implied environment of consumption; ditto clothes, cars and even bodies. If objects in shop windows are in a constant state of dispersal, so too are their purchasers, as William Leiss has it: 'In a high intensity market setting commodities . . . become fragmented . . . and lose their independent identity so to speak; this process stands in reciprocal relation to the fragmentation of needs.'[20] When desire is fixed, capitalists will lose out; they must diversify the subject's needs, finding in the consumer-as-legion a legion of markets. The de-centring of minds, persons and things is an imperative of capital in its current phase: put another way, capital is increasingly at war with any barrier to its own expansion. Inflation intensifies the war for at least the average rate of profit, fixed forms are subject to mutation, and, as Mailer puts it, 'the country [is] in disease' (*C & C*, p. 42). Mailer means cancer, his favourite economic metaphor. Cancer catches exactly how proliferation and dispersal have become imperative for all units of late capital, right down to the individual cell in the single body of the consumer. Entering a bathroom in the San Francisco Hilton in 1964, Mailer (the Egon Ronay of plastic) smells 'burning insecticide' – the odour of the plastic cement used to finish the tiling which is still not dry; he comments, 'molecules were being tortured everywhere', and adds,

'Well, that was American capitalism gainfully employed' (*C & C*, p. 7).

'Overproduction', 'hypercivilization', 'war' and 'cancer' form a close-knit lexicon whose generic term is 'cannibalism'. In an overproduced world, capital is constantly employed consuming its own forms. Over-accumulation yields an excess of surplus relative to opportunities to deploy it. Surplus can escape its own glut along two linked paths: owners can export profits in search of lower labour costs (multinationals), or they can invest in the production of the means of destruction (the permanent-arms economy). After 1945, with considerable money-flight into arms and the related technology of aerospace, the USA's spatial-fix has improved its teeth. For a time the teeth seemed unnecessary. The USA fought the Second World War in part for an open door through which to trade on a global scale. It worked, temporarily. With the post-war world reeling from one of the most savage bouts of de-valuation ever recorded, and with that destruction unevenly distributed, the USA could afford to be the world's banker, financing the spatial expansion of its own market. However, during the late fifties and the sixties the door looked less open. As independent centres of accumulation reformed (Germany, Japan) and as regional alliances began to resist American commercial penetration (witness Kennedy's arguments with the Common Market and Johnson's with South-east Asia), so the spatial-fix and the arms-fix seemed fixated on war as the ultimate form of de-valuation. Indeed, some would argue that only through the reduction of the total quantity of capital (de-valuation) can capital hope to survive the crisis of 'overproduction'. Mailer, surveying the American economy from the thirties to the sixties, echoes McLeod: he argues that the USA solved the Depression by going to war, and subsequently substituted a cold war for a hot one, a cold war that developed not from a real communist threat, but because 'capitalism would never survive without an economy geared to war' (*C & C*, p. 42).

III

In order to offer respite from an argument which seems to dither densely between theoretical terms, global prognostication and dirty talk, I shall try to answer a simple question via conventional literary methods of close reading. 'Where is the narrative voice coming from?' D.J. is nominally the son of a corporate executive. While at a dinner in celebration of his eighteenth birthday and imminent departure for Vietnam, he recalls an Alaskan hunting trip two years before. However, his initials read as 'Dr Jek' (p. 9) imply a hidden Hyde. Ever eager to proliferate explanation, D.J. suggests that he, the trip and the party are projected by 'a crippled Harlem genius' (p. 57), in which case the novel is perhaps a fantasy produced by a 'Disc Jockey to the world?' (p. 24) loose on the airwaves. White or black, Texas or New York, bourgeois or proletarian – the possibilities proliferate. Let us assume that the question is not which but why. Why should D.J. assume a black voice? Mailer has always ghosted himself with gangs of doubles, but here the doubling has a traceable plot. Intro Beep Four encourages the reader (otherwise known as 'Sherlock Onanist Holmes' (p. 50)) to read the novel as a sustained vocal who–dunnit. Remember, D.J. warns 'there is no security in this consciousness' (p. 133):

> am [I] in fact a figment of a Spade gone ape in the mind from outrageous frustrates wasting him and so now living in an imaginary white brain, or is that ether-load man? is not D.J. really white, really walking at sixteen into the vale where the death of breath crosses all external wires, and D.J. is merely tapped in for touches of intellectual luxury to some fucked-up little bedridden Spade, or is that the abortive consciousness of a tumor beginning right under the medulla oblongata of his white brain a knot of psychic hatreds congregated in molecule dance to design a new kind of flesh, sarcoma, melanoma, carcinom' and Nome and Barrow, Alaska, Fairbanks – late afternoon?   (p. 58)

'Medulla', inner portion of an organ, marrow or essence; 'sarcoma', tumour of fleshy consistency; 'melanoma', morbid deposit of black matter usually malignant in the organs of the body (often a skin cancer). The black-up hides clues under various jargons: the vocabulary of 'carcinom[a]' or cancer is less interesting than the motives that form beneath it. 'Oblongata', coupled with a double iteration of flesh, elongates the essence of the white brain into a phallic shape. Since D.J. will later define 'the first seed of tumor' as the incest trauma (p. 137), the phallus at the root of cognition carries two embattled names – father and son (Rusty and D.J.). The introduction of the notion of abortion is therefore complex, D.J. suppresses or aborts his hatred for the father, a father who has already tried to murder his five-year-old son. Add to this 'knot of . . . hatreds' two more associative skeins and one has something akin to a gordian problem. Cancer has already been read as a synonym for 'overproduction', but in this case the cancer is specifically malignant and black. Mailer wrote the novel in the summer of 1966; summers were very soon to be associated with burning cities, and the New Left was already talking of student radicals as 'internal guerillas'. Fanon (1965)[21] had argued that the violence of colonial rule made counterviolence inevitable. It was therefore a small step for the Left from riot to colonial struggle and from ghetto to inner colony. Prior to the fires, in 1963, Mailer was proposing aesthetic arson with the suggestion that a black and white cast, playing Genet's *The Blacks* in Birmingham, Alabama, might 'put some grey in Bobby Kennedy's hairy Irish head'.[22] The metaphor of the irritant within the imperial beast proved popular: Jerry Rubin recalled Guevara when telling a group of young Americans illegally visiting Cuba in 1964: 'You North Amerikans are very lucky. You live in the middle of the beast. You are fighting the most important fight of all, in the center of the battle'[23] – a sentiment echoed by Rap Brown one month after Detroit had burned (1967): 'We live in the belly of the monster. So it's up to us to destroy its brain. When we do this, not only will Africa be free but all people oppressed by "the man".'[24] D.J.'s brain, so close to the corporate "man", contains its own 'Spade gone ape . . . from outrageous frustrates.' For 'ape' read 'gorilla', and add that the guerilla most in question in 1966 is Kong, whether in Harlem or Vietnam. The novel abounds in apes; Alaska's bears are driven 'ape' by hunting technology (most significantly by helicopters referred to as 'cop turds', a phrasing that elides military and civic usage); Medium Asshole Pete dreams of a grizzer like 'a Nigger woman gone ape with a butcher knife' (p. 88), while *the* bear in dying has 'wise old gorilla eyes' which carry 'message[s]' about 'D.J.'s future' in a look that he will see nowhere else 'in any Texan's eyes . . . (or overseas around the world)' (p. 146). Tracing ape pedigrees to their inception point is all very well, except that the original metaphor encysted in 'ape' belongs firmly to the Left, while D.J. is filiated to the corporate right and furthermore is keen to kill Kong in Vietnam. Why then should he adopt a voice from the social and political tradition of his enemy?

Once again *Cannibals and Christians* offers insights. Mailer visits the Republican Convention in 1964 on a vocal expedition, to find the voice of the newly emergent Right. Sensing the bankruptcy of Kennedy and Johnson's liberalism and the break-up of the perceived consensus upon which Keynesian policies depend, Mailer listens for the backlash and experiences 'a moment of rage at the swindle' (p. 44). Not for the first time he arrives politically early and is forced to offer an afterword – apology for 'the extraordinary error' of assuming that Goldwater would do well; he adds, '*the real possibility of what he* [Goldwater] *had to offer American would not appear until Vietnam*' (p. 46; italics in source), not, that is, until the war had irritated the liberal Left, exacerbated American inflation[25] and stockpiled right-wing resentment. Nonetheless, lessons were learned in 1964; if Goldwater's voice was finally 'not a great voice' (p. 40), his supporters offered pointers to elocution; the thin men among the California delegation 'looked like they were sitting on a body – the corpse of Jew, Eastern, Negritudes – and when the show was over, they were gonna eat it' (p. 36). Outside demonstrations from CORE march and chant, 'white girls and Negro boys walking side by side': 'Yes, kill us, says the expression on the face of the nunlike girl with no lipstick, you will kill us but you will never digest us' (p. 45). Mailer's money is on the digestive tract of the Right; D.J. has eaten a black and retained his virtue, 'a great voice'. Mailer notes of cannibals:

> *the pure cannibal has only one taboo on food – he will not eat the meat of his own family. Other men he will of course consume. Their virtues he will conserve in his own flesh, their vices he will excrete, but to kill and to eliminate is his sense of human continuation.* (*C & C*, p. 4; italics in source)

The construction of D.J.'s voice involves a political reconstruction and critique of the rhetoric of the New Left – the belly of the state, as it moves right, is capacious and will consume what it contains. 'A shit storm' is indeed 'coming' (*C & C*, p. 41) but one that Baldwin will not recognize and Mailer fears, during which the Right-white will eat blacks on the street. To the objection that D.J.'s diet is unhealthy (it gives him melanoma), the victim might object that every cancer is potential profit for Rusty's corporation as CCCCP expands into chemotherapy.

The white ventriloquist with a black doll was first projected in 'The white negro'; however, the essay of 1957 based the trick on psychopathology rather than on politics. The white hipster mimes the black, or more specifically the black criminal, in order 'to change his nature': to do so, he must 'go back to the source of [his] creation', a regression that involves a potential passage through orgy, rape, homosexuality, drugs and violent crime to the 'hopeless contradiction[s]' of the child. To express 'the buried infant' is to lessen tension and perhaps 'to remake a bit of the nervous system'. Once the contradiction at the source has been encountered, analogous adult contradictions may he handled with grace:

> For if he has the courage to meet the parallel situation at the moment when he is ready, then he has a chance to act as he has never acted before, and in satisfying the frustration if he can succeed – he may then pass by symbolic substitute through the locks of incest. (*AFM*, p. 278)

Read from this perspective, D.J.'s gambit contracts to oedipal dimensions: the family rather than the state becomes the locus of ventriloquism.

Why Are We in Vietnam? features much tampering with the incest-lock. The narrative voice is directed first and foremost to the ear of God the Father: we are told that 'the good Lord', having transitorized every bowel in creation, is 'getting a total tape record of each last one of us' (p. 24). But the biological father has the Lord's ear; D.J. assures us that Rusty is 'up tight with G.O.D. – Grand Old Divinity (biggest corporation of them all?)' (p. 111). As an 'intimate to the Lord' (p. 111) Rusty bugs his son. The father hears it all, conscious and unconscious: 'Unless you can put false material into the tape recorder. Think of that' (p. 26). So D.J.

assumes a black voice with which to trouble the father; from behind it he issues oedipal threats, insisting that 'there is no logic to projects but incest family bugger' (p. 150).

To talk incest is also to talk economics, albeit in code. An author who insists, 'sex has become the center of our economy' (*AFM*, p. 351) expects to be read as though the economy were central to his exploration of sexual pathology. Mailer spots phalli in the supermarket. Mailer readers must look for commercial potential in the oedipal imbroglio. Like Fitzgerald before him, Mailer treats incest as an economic metaphor. In *Tender is the Night* (*TITN*; 1934), the story of a paternal incest became a means to explore a shift in the nature of capital from problems of accumulation to problems of reproduction. It is clear from the work of Alfred Chandler on changes in the managerial structure of American capital that the economic problems of the late twenties remained unresolved. Chandler argues that during the 1920s pioneer capitals recognized that expansion into new markets and lines was imperative if 'overproduction' and the attendant under-utilization of plant and labour was to be countered. Crash, depression and war impeded the experiment. Consequently, not until the forties and fifties did US capital *in general* face the problems of reproducing itself efficiently.[26]

Mailer, who is forever re-writing Fitzgerald,[27] borrows the central metaphor of *Tender is the Night* but alters its dynamic in order to achieve a different economic emphasis. Incest in which the father is the instigator involves considerable multiplication of roles (*TITN*), but where the child is the aggressor roles are further proliferated: the son in penetrating his mother becomes son and lover and father, even as he makes his parents over into mother, mistress *and* adultress, father, rival *and* cuckold. Role proliferation implies a disintegral selfhood, in which self-diffusion mirrors accumulation's continuing post-war problematic of self-transgression (whereby capital must seek unrealized relations and forms). Mandel offers figures that indicate the recurrent nature of accumulation's tendency to inertia: he notes that between 1966 and 1974 there was a steady fall in the utilization of productive apparatus:

> The long term deterioration becomes especially pronounced when account is taken of the enormous amount of American production wasted on military or paramilitary products. If we take this factor into consideration, we arrive at a virtually permanent non-utilization of nearly one-third of existing productive capacity in the United States.[28]

D.J., of a paramilitary bent, yet equipped with Pure Pores and an electric come machine, has a foot in capital's two major markets, arms and desire. He is the designer/entrepreneur that late capital deserves. Moreover, his incestuous desires push innovation to a point which threatens the familial boundaries of the self.

In arguing that forms of capital determine forms of subjectivity, I am simply following Mailer, for whom *Das Kapital* is the 'first of the major psychologies' (*AFM*, p. 289). Complaining that radicals were 'in danger of abdicating from all imagination', in 1957 he outlined a project that reads like a plot survey and critique of *Why Are We in Vietnam?*: by hypothesizing a 'revolutionary time', he advocates the delineation of a 'neo-Marxian calculus', whose function would be to translate all social processes ('from ukase to kiss') into flows of human energy. Given such a system of quantification, economic and psychological events would be set on a single scale, and relations of production could be recognized as part and parcel of sexual relations: 'until the crisis of capitalism in the twentieth century would yet be understood as the unconscious adaptations of a society to solve its economic imbalance at the expense of new mass psychological imbalance' (*AFM*, p. 289). To return to the novel, and specifically to incest and to 'energy': D.J. proposes, on tape and in the ear of his father, to corner the market in electricity by breaking the incest taboo. Once electricity is understood as the flow of capital, and the incest ban as a form which impedes that flow in the name of the father, then economic relations can be approached through sexual relations, and *Why Are We in Vietnam?* may be read as a parable of psychological and economic imbalances.

Rusty claimed D.J.'s bear. More than that, he killed the animal even as D.J., doing a passable imitation of Ike McCaslin, sought truth in the 'wise old gorilla eyes' (p. 146). An ursine Kong epitomizes anti-American 'virtues', containing not only South-east Asian communists and the USA's urban blacks but also the Russian people. Although Alaska was purchased from Russia in 1867, the territory did not enter the Union as a state until 1958. Since the deep memory of the place is Russian, it stands as an apt location for the pursuit of the Soviet national beast. D.J. eye-wrestles with a summation of the USA's enemies. The corporate son, proud digester of 'a Spade gone ape' (p. 58), locks gazes for global prizes. Consequently, the presumption of the corporate father, in stealing the prize, kindles murderous longings in the son; however, D.J., rather than kill, goes north towards the pole with Tex, there to encounter, in ascending order of intensity, the Aurora Borealis, the Beast and a homosexual stand-off which redesigns the oedipal triangle. Each encounter shares a common denominator, each is a treatise on electricity. From the outset the family is located as prime electric generator 'in old electric land' (p. 24). The aphorism, 'incest is electric man' (p. 125) derives from two oedipal traumas. Aged five, D.J. was beaten by Rusty, the mother intervened: 'little man saved by cunt, virility grew with a taint in the armature of the phallic catapult; call it tumor if that's what D.J.'s got in his brain, cause brilliance is next to murder man' (p. 138). The beating is recalled at the very moment when father and son first find bear tracks, at which point, 'while . . . thinking of murdering his father' (p. 138), D.J. is transformed into a receiver; 'monomaniacal electric yodelling' (p. 138) reaches him from virtually all Alaskan surfaces. When the son is thirteen, paternal punishment is repeated: in a less than playful football practice father bites son 'in the ass . . . and man he hung on he nearly lifted D.J. up in the air with his deathly teeth' (p. 40). Filial vengeance is taken with a pick-axe handle to the paternal head: Rusty does not fall; instead he generates electricity: 'an electric shock travelled from his head down the pick-axe handle into D.J.'s overheated heart' (p. 41). Again maternal intervention reconstitutes the family. Prior to reconciliation Halleloo 'stashed' her son in a 'hideout in Mineral Wells' (p. 31): since Rusty is an oilman described as a 'geyser of love' (p. 13), the 'hideout' hides little of its anatomical proclivities. As an infant and as an adolescent D.J.'s proximity to the maternal vessel generates electric flows. Hidden in the mother's 'well', the boy is oil; as a 'stash' he is a financial hoard – on two counts he steals from the father. 'Incest is electric' has a double articulation: it implies that the taboo generates current, yet simultaneously suggests that violation might yield greater charge. Certainly, as the son outdared the father by approaching the dying grizzer, 'he got psychic transistors in his ear'; who knows what other 'gift[s]' of electronic hardware might have been forthcoming from those 'gorilla' eyes had not Rusty intervened and claimed the bear for his own.

D.J. walks north, away from father killing: his walk becomes a purification rite. Given Mailer's frequent and overt references to *Go Down, Moses*, Faulkner's 'The bear' offers itself as an interpretive stencil.[29] Ike McCaslin reneges on land as an economic form (the plantation) and takes up instead land outside production (the big woods). In 1942 in the South it may just have been possible to fantasize with some conviction about non-capitalized land (witness the efforts of the Agrarians during the thirties), but in 1966 there is nothing organic left in Mailer's USA, even towards the pole. Electricity is everywhere, and everywhere mimes in its flow the imperatives of capital. Where Ike regresses to a pre-capitalist past, D.J. approaches the logic of a capitalist future. For D.J. any space is a 'fix' whereby surplus may yet be realized; by moving towards the ultimate space (the pole as a hole) he is likely to gain knowledge of capital's emergent forms, and so prove better than the father at the father's game. The pole is an 'orifice' into which flow the dreams of the nation; the pattern of their flow is initially cryptic:

> where you going when you sleep? Well, hole, there's only one place you go, and that's into the undiscovered magnetic-electro fief of the dream, which is opposed to the electromagnetic field of the earth . . . that mind of yours leaps, stirs and sifts itself into the Magnetic-Electro fief of the dream, hereafter known as M.E. or M.E.F., you are part of the spook flux of the night like an iron filing in the E.M. field . . . and it all flows, mind and asshole, anode and cathode, you sending messages and receiving all through the night. (p. 170)

'Fief' is a key term; as a 'fief' the dream is an estate held from a superior on condition of military service. The electricity generated by dreams, that is by the desires of isolated consumers as they sleep (ME), is 'opposed' to the land. D.J. writes electronic equations based on what he has learned from hunting: i.e. nature is a 'field' of materials whose resistance to appropriation simply stimulates that appropriation. Among the several American dreams witnessed – 'let me make it', 'Oh God let me hump the boss' daughter' (p. 206) – executive dreams are singled out for attention:

> and if you clean as milk and had your nose all day up the antiseptic asshole of Big H the Corporate Hospital Corporation, why then your dreams got to go through the incinerator where they pile all the old hospital bandages, all that dried blood puss shit green gangrene bladder gut mess – that's a battery – from all the surgery of the day which surgery had duly excised and thereby assassinated one hundred plus organs from seventy-eight patients, a confusion in the Divine Economy, as all those organs taking millions of years to make (think of the evolution of the cells) are now being flushed in a gush into the incinerator while the surgeons get their clean whiskey-free libidinal juice –
>
> (p. 171)

The characterization of the corporation as a hospital whose generator runs on disused organs involves a recognition that capital cannibalizes itself: fixed capitals that no longer produce at the average rate of profit are de-valued; re-purchased at far below value, they become the base for new and innovative formations. The logic of the extended metaphor has it that amputated parts, re-cycled, produce energy, allowing surplus value to flow again. In this instance, the parts are those ever-malleable consumer dreams.

D.J. takes a crash course in electrical theory, which is also (as Samuel Insull might have told him) a course in 'engineering . . . the dollar'.[30] Lesson learned, he attempts to alter the circuitry of the Northern Lights. Camped with Tex in a hidden valley, he listens to the lights:

> the lights were saying that there was something up here, and it was really here, yeah God was here, and He was real and no man was He, but a beast, some beast of a giant jaw and cavernous mouth with a full cave's breath and fangs, and secret call: come to me . . . In the field of all such desire D.J. raised his hand

to put it square on Tex's cock and squeeze and just before he did the Northern lights shifted on that moment and a coil of sound went off in the night like a blowout in some circuit fuse of the structure of the dark.   (p. 202)

D.J.'s homoerotic advance recomposes the incest configuration: we are repeatedly told that D.J. has his mother's 'ass' and that Tex, his 'blood brother' (p. 204), has designs on the original of that ass. Consequently, for D.J. to touch Tex is to risk anal rape. The permutations grow off-putting: if Tex buggers D.J., Tex becomes simultaneously the father (who has been bugging the son throughout the novel) *and* the son, since D.J. has often used Tex as a surrogate 'mother fucker' in his own imagination. The three oedipally charged roles – vengeful father, compliant mother and penetrative son – are recomposed within a single male coupling. All the limits set by the ban are transgressed. The transgressive intention is sufficient to blow the electric circuitry, presumably due to overload. However, rape does not occur and the promised new distributions remain unrealized. Just as D.J. almost killed the father, so in perverse surrogateship he almost penetrates the mother, with the net result that the circuits re-form and issue a communication. Since the structures of electricity are so consistently capitalized and oedipalized, the voice that speaks can only be that of the corporate father: 'for God was a beast, not a man, and God said, "Go out and kill – fulfill my will, go and kill"' (p. 203). Instructions could not be clearer: having mastered the technology of desire, the corporate son is to learn late capital's last fix, the spatial-fix in Vietnam. The 'fief' of the US corporate state is safe for as long as its ingenious children are dedicated to re-working the fixes that sustain its over-accumulation.

8

Fordism, voiced and unvoiced: Mailer's *vocalism and* Armies of the Night

I

The Committee behind the National Mobilization to End the War in Vietnam chose the Pentagon because it, and not Congress, is the 'source ... of real power in America'.[1] For Mailer the Pentagon is quite literally the embodiment of the state:

> American Civilization had moved from the existential sanction of the frontier to the abstract ubiquitous sanction of the dollar bill. Nowhere had so much of the dollar bill collected as at the Pentagon, giant mudpie on the banks of America's Nile, our Potomac! (p. 158)

As a corporatist entity, oriented to private profit, the Pentagon needs only one orifice, the anus; it is therefore spoken of as 'the sphincter' (p. 38). It follows that 'the anus of corporation land' is also its 'eye' (p. 113), because it oversees capital's flow; necessarily, that eye is 'morally blind', even as the Pentagon is mute – 'a dumb valve' (p. 114) imposing silence on its 'masked' economic directives (Bell). The valve can be specified: 'the Pentagon looked like the five-sided tip on the spout of a spray can to be used under the arm, yes, the Pentagon was spraying the deodorant of its presence all over the fields of Virginia' (p. 117). (Within Mailer's wider metaphoric networks 'cancer' and 'plastic' are the anti-commodities that emerge from the can.) The state as deodorized anus may truly be said to have no spine (p. 228) or loin (p. 229); indeed the building is designed specifically to lack a centre. Nearly twenty miles of 'passageway' (one is reminded of the large-gut of the nation) are laid out in the form of a five-sided 'spider-web' (p. 228) without a traceable spider. Since the next best thing to a centre is the cafeteria and shopping mall (p. 230), the spider is present but in transparent disguise: at the nub of the corporatist state is the permanent-arms economy, at whose architectural core lies private profit in the palatable form of mass consumption. For the Mobilization Committee to contemplate entering the Pentagon by force in order to take and hold its centre, is to contemplate absurdity (p. 230). The liberal army that captures the source of the 'ubiquitous . . . dollar bill' will have overthrown that which 'sanctions' its own class security. As Mailer notes, the middle class is a 'collective dead ass' (p. 37), probably because its bureaucratic and technological ministrations have kept 'the government's ass' (p. 38) 'masked'.

To pursue Mailer's metaphoric account of the body politic, circa 1967, is to recover an impacted political plot. However, in order to understand how he explores what is essentially the story of an impasse for the bourgeois self, and for himself as bourgeois, it is necessary to consider those vocal selves who ghost Mailer's progress. The attendant fragments are legion: Proust's 'equal' (p. 17); 'a poor man's version of Orson Welles' (p. 32); Behan (p. 37); Cassius Clay's 'shade' (p. 49); Lyndon Johnson's '*dwarf* alter-ego' (p. 49; italics in source); Churchill. The list is far from complete and stands merely as a sub-section in a more extensive collection of generic terms: 'Beast' (p. 13); 'émigré prince' (p. 18); MC (p. 36); 'arriviste baron' (p. 41); 'comic hero' (p. 53); 'Mailer'. Perhaps Mailer is his own best bestiary and anthologizer:

> Watching himself talk on camera for an earlier documentary, he was not pleased with himself as a subject. For a warrior, presumptive general, ex-political candidate, embattled aging enfant terrible of the literary world, wise father of six children, radical intellectual, existential philosopher, hard-working author, champion of obscenity, husband of four battling sweet wives, amiable bar drinker, and much exaggerated street fighter, party giver, hostess insulter – he had on screen in his first documentary a fatal taint, a last remaining speck of the one personality he found absolutely insupportable – the nice Jewish boy from Brooklyn. Something in his adenoids gave it away.
>
> (p. 134)

His adenoids are generally more flexible, ranging from bad-mouth to 'country squire' (p. 196), from 'righteous old toot' (p. 9) to Black Power (p. 38), often with an attendant commentary on speech production: a larynx with gears characterizes the polemicist (p. 85), while the 'spooks' in the circuitry of the Ambassador's public address system are carefully articulated as 'hawking and squabbling and hum' (p. 35). Mailer has a 'scrupulously phenomenological' ear (p. 119) for speech acts and consequently for their reception. He spends much of *Armies of the Night* listening to or making or preparing to make public utterances. Audiences are numbered, speakers are contrasted and put into the order of their likely appeal. Indeed, oral opportunities are so abundant that speech sub-genres emerge: literary reading, private phone call in public, comment to the press, court plea, prayer; and in all the forms Mailer ponders some version of 'wild yells and chills of silence from different reaches of the crowd' (p. 38). To read is to be made aware that 'the novelist' is a talker who 'loved to speak, he loved in fact to holler, and liked to hear a crowd holler back' (p. 36).

The pleasure of the hollered word is that it is 'directed toward an answer' and exists under 'the profound influence of the answering word it anticipates'.[2] Immediately there is a problem, the speaker who self-consciously directs his word towards two speech centres divides himself quite possibly against himself. The split, once recognized, extends to encompass that to which the speaker refers because the referent will be traduced and fissured by the different 'dialogic threads',[3] which define its materiality through their disputation. Addressees must split themselves at least two ways – into speakers of the mother tongue and translators: on receipt of a word belonging to two speech centres (and potentially to two belief systems) they translate by offering '*counter words*'[4] that accommodate the word to their own, now markedly singular, mother tongue.

Bakhtin's work on polyphony can be used to chart Mailer's vocal symptoms:

> The direct word, as traditional stylistics understands it, encounters in its orientation towards its object only the resistance of the object itself . . . but it does not encounter in its path towards the object the fundamental and richly varied opposition of another's word . . .
>
> But no living word relates to its object in a singular way: between the word and its object, between the word and the speaking subject, there exists an elastic environment of other, alien words about the same object, the same theme, and this is an environment it is often difficult to penetrate.[5]

Mailer explores the ontology latent in the difficult environment of polyphony; if words are overpopulated, living always between the quotation marks that result from someone else's use of them, then their speaker is hybrid rather than singular. To adapt a Bakhtinian aphorism: where 'meaning belongs to word in its position between speakers',[6] speakers will become meaningful via their position between words, which words are always already occupied. What is proposed is that the self can no more coincide with itself than it can with others. Stated as a cartoon, the self is a multitude camped in a bad acoustic. Bakhtin catches the problematic when he insists: 'It is just as impossible to forge an identity between myself, my own "I", and that "I" that is the subject of my stories, as it is to lift myself up by my own hair.'[7] Mailer stresses the distance between himself and his fictional selves by constructing a generic term, 'Mailer', and setting it between quotation marks. Already my distinction between a self who writes and those selves of whom he writes simplifies the non-tology of *Armies of the Night*. Mailer 'the novelist' and Mailer 'the historian' cannot rest easy in the integrity of their tasks, since both write to contractual deadlines. As parts in a spectacle whose "life" is the shop window from which his (or better, their) books will be sold, all the Mailers must sustain 'a most developed sense of image' (p. 5). Having posited *Advertisements for Myself* (1959) and subsequently turned self-quotation into a literary form,[8] Mailer is necessarily ready to stand his writing self between speech marks. In part 1, chapter 2, entitled 'In the den', we are assured that even this authorial sanctuary is no longer safe because 'Pen Pals' and telephones are always 'driving some psychic equivalent of static into the privacies of [its owner's] brain' (p. 4). It should be clear from *Why Are We in Vietnam?* that 'electricity', in all its forms, is Mailer's shorthand for the motions of capital: in which case, any 'static' self embattled at the writer's desk, is provisional – a nostalgic 'image' momentarily generated as relief from the need to make money in an intensely public marketplace. Mailer is at some pains to emphasize that 'the real Norman Mailer' cannot 'stand up' (p. 127) or speak a single word, because, as someone always liable to be made 'news' by *Time* (p. 3), he is in essence a diverse punster.

Polyphonic disciples of Bakhtin are all too easily read as semantic existentialists. Poirier's version of Mailer, for all its lucidities, is just such a reduction. According to *The Performing Self*, Mailer is an existential hero balanced rebarbatively out on the ledge of his own last cliché (generally some version of 'to become in order not to be').[9] What saves Bakhtin and Mailer from semantic brinkmanship is their mutual recognition that vocal and ontological flux is determined by capital, to a degree that is determinable. Bakhtin argues that the polyphonic novel is necessarily a child of capital, and more particularly of its Russian form, since in Russia capitalism's sudden and 'catastrophic arrival' caused 'an untouched variety of social worlds' to clash. Where the gradual advent of capitalism in Europe fostered vocal confidence among capitalists (based on a 'calmly reflective monological consciousness'), in Russia, individual worlds, off-balance and colliding, ensured that 'the objective conditions for the essential multileveledness of the polyphonic novel were met'.[10] But pre-revolutionary Russia is hardly Fordist America, and no matter how coherently Bakhtin insists that capital throws things about, corporatists could object that their contracts deliver an environment where everything stays firmly in its place. On the surface integrative mass–consumption looks like an ideal way to promote vocal equanimity, with its beguilingly "calm . . . monologue" suppressing production. To the Fordist the voice of labour is revocable in that it can be called back into the single and yet general voice of the consumer, at least for as long as desire calms the under-class. The crossing of collars inside the big consumption basket underpins 'individualism', which, as the right to consume privately, ratifies the productive logic of corporate capital. Corporations, Desire, the State and Destruction gather under the Logos of Liberal Individualism to speak in many voices as one.

It would seem that Bakhtin's claim does not travel well. However, the work of Richard Lichtman on the relation between individual motivation and economic facts can be used to show that sub- and multi-vocalizations are an inevitable feature of the mass market. Lichtman argues that production continues to be a linguistic presence for all of us. His central premise is that the production and exchange of commodities involves crucial suppressions of reciprocity and social labour, suppressions which are the source of deep yet partial forgetfulness which, in turn, is the origin of a 'structural unconscious'.[11] Like Freud's unconscious, capital works "behind one's back" and "in one's depths" in ways which seem quite beyond representation. However, Lichtman emphasizes that, although social structure is not visible (else why "mystification" and "alienation"?), neither is it "invisible" or "beyond" lived experience. Only through lived experience can the forms of capital have their being and take on their "real appearances". Lichtman avoids the dichotomy between structure and individual, since such division verifies the extant social structure by presenting it as a platonic form. He emphasizes that structures do not act, that only human beings act. Consequently, though we may misconstrue our social existence (whose real structures lie deep within our ordinary awareness), yet there cannot be such a thing as a separate social institution. Our consciousness, under capital, is therefore generated by our own self-deception (they did it to us even as we go on doing it to ourselves). Lichtman's 'structural unconscious' is the forgotten social complexity, 'the repository of irreconcilable conflicts between capitalist reality and bourgeois appearance'.[12] Inevitably, therefore, it swells, because 'the ubiquitous, over reaching contradiction in capitalism between apparent independence and actual dependence . . . [is] too excruciating to be continually recognized and consciously confronted'.[13]

The pain of conscious recognition is more likely during those periods when the consensual balm of consumerism fails. Witness the career of Fitzgerald: prior to the Crash, in *The Great Gatsby*, 'social complexity' is contained within a single and essentially bourgeois voice – Nick Carraway's narrative subordinates its own disruptive class sub-text. After the Crash, sub-vocalization moves, at least in part, out from the novel's semantic unconsciousness into the plot: with *Tender is the Night*, Fitzgerald realizes a shift in the imperatives of endangered capital through contrasted heroines and the adultery of the hero. (Put crudely,

Dick Diver tries and abdicates from changing forms of consumption. His return to production remains, however, obscure.)

Mailer's work in the sixties is not so readily divisible into 'before' and 'after', perhaps because the decade's turbulence issued in inflation rather than Crash. Nonetheless, *Why Are We in Vietnam?* (1967) and *Armies of the Night* (1968) can be counterpoised as semantically antithetical texts, the one a monologue, the other a polyphony. D.J. assumes a black voice primarily to taunt his corporate father, whose competitive logic he explores and espouses. The crippled Harlem Disc Jockey is not, therefore, in contention with his ventriloquist: both voices serve the same speech centre, which is firmly oriented towards private profit. Having explored what is basic to the maintenance of corporate profitability, Mailer, as the historian of the march on the Pentagon, elicits the voices that traduce the liberal consensus upon which that profitability depends. Both texts, despite their different vocalities, 'consciously confront' the 'over reaching contradictions in capitalism' between 'capitalist reality and bourgeois appearance'. They, respectively, anatomize 'individualism' and expose 'consensus', before, together and in grief, charting the protean victory of 'bourgeois appearance'.

Prior to an attempt to demonstrate this conclusion, I must intrude yet another methodological interlude. My elision of the work of Lichtman, Bakhtin and Mailer aims simply to underline the profound illiberality of the linguistic model that these works together outline. Bakhtin could be detailing the experiential and semantic substance of Lichtman's 'structural unconscious' when he describes, from a linguist's point of view, 'the lowest, most fluid, and quickly changing stratum of behavioural ideology':

> The world of an experience may be narrow and dim; its social orientation may be haphazard and ephemeral and characteristic only for some adventitious and loose coalition of a small number of persons. Of course, even these erratic experiences are ideological and sociological, but their position lies on the borders of the normal and the pathological. Such an experience will remain an isolated fact in the psychological life of the person exposed to it. It will not take firm root and will not receive differentiated and full-fledged expression; indeed, if it lacks a socially grounded and stable audience, where could it possibly find bases for its differentiation and finalization? . . .
>
> To this stratum, consequently, belong all those vague and underdeveloped experiences, thoughts, and idle, accidental words that flash across our minds. They are all of them cases of miscarriages of social orientations, novels without heroes, performances without audiences. They lack any sort of logic or unity. The sociological regulatedness of these ideological scraps is extremely difficult to detect. In this lowest stratum . . . only statistical regularity is detectable; given a huge quantity of products of this sort, the outlines of socio-economic

regulatedness could be revealed. Needless to say, it would be a practical impossibility to descry in any one such accidental experience or expression its socio-economic premises.[14]

I quote at length because, as an account of semantic amnesia, this could scarcely be bettered. Lichtman adds that capital's plots are detectable within forgetfulness. 'Psychological life', in a successful consumer society, such as that enjoyed by the USA during the explosive growth of privatized consumption in the sixties, may be partially generalized. Each person takes, or aspires to take, a crash course in amnesia at the pervasive shop window. As corporations locate cheap labour abroad, and as technocracy, bureaucracy and services expand at home, so it becomes increasingly difficult to remember the reciprocities of production that give rise to the consumer's daily cake.

For the USA's post-war professional classes (at the very least), a social orientation away from the world of production turns labour into 'a performance without an audience', and renders the working class 'haphazard and ephemeral', lost in a third-world-elsewhere which 'lacks any sort of logic or unity'. Fordist integration represses its own 'socio-economic premises', thereby creating two languages – a consumer language of "individualism", "consensus" and "reason", and a subconscious language in which an occasionally remembered and putative under-class feature as "demons". Any ebb in the Fordist success rips the veil of consumerism and allows the other USA of blacks and agricultural labour to be glimpsed. By confining between a third and a quarter of the population to 'the border of the normal and the pathological', the middle classes ensure that the language and substance of their capitalist-realism will be hedged with anxiety.

The way of confidence for the professional and managerial classes is to insist that their speech of reason is culturally general. Bell's writings again prove instructive: between 1960 and 1976 his political arena is ideally occupied by a sequence of model planners – corporate managers (1960) give way to technocrats (1974) who, after two years, are replaced by members of the Supreme Court (1976). Judges enter because by the seventies Bell is belatedly prepared to admit that 'the unspoken consensus',[15] having long gone, 'rational calculus'[16] might need legal back-up. Although confident that 'the US Supreme Court is unique in [its] acceptance by the entire polity . . . as the normative arbiter',[17] he advises judges to read Kant. For Kant the law was a matter of formal decisions rather than substantive adjudication: a Kantian judiciary would therefore be doubly protected against partiality. The notion that either managers or judges are disinterested stems from amnesia on a scale that would grace a yuppie.

Like a begowned version of Bell's Scientist, Bell's Judge sits reading

Bell's Kant inside an already decided axiomatic system – one of a group of interlocuters who, as experts, declare their conversation to be universal reason. They would do better to read Habermas, or at least his *Legitimation Crisis* (1976), in which he too seeks to challenge 'the impenetrable pluralism of . . . value orientations'[18] by locating 'justifiable norms' based in 'rational consensus' and distinguishable from standards that are no more than 'stabilized relations of force'.[19] Unlike Bell, he will not select the jargon of one profession as a common tongue, or declare the interest of a class fragment to be the best interest of the nation. Rather, he discovers collectivity latent in everyday speech: 'To the highest stage of moral consciousness there corresponds a universal morality, which can be traced back to fundamental norms of rational speech.'[20] The home of the 'rational' or 'discursively formed will'[21] is the 'public sphere':

> By the public sphere we mean first of all a realm of our social life in which something approaching public opinion can be formed. Access is guaranteed to all citizens. A portion of the public sphere comes into being in every conversation in which private individuals assemble to form a public body. They then behave neither like business or professional people transacting private affairs, nor like members of a constitutional order subject to the legal constraints of a state democracy. Citizens behave as a public body when they confer in an unrestricted fashion – that is, with the guarantee of freedom of assembly and association and the freedom to express and publish their opinion – about matters of general interest.[22]

The faith that communicative reason is latent in ordinary speech situations, no matter how coercive or distorted, is an act of redemptive will not unlike Marcuse's final insistence to Habermas that he knew 'wherein our most basic value judgements are rooted – in compassion, in our sense for the suffering of others'.[23] Faced with the collapse of 'world maintaining interpretive systems',[24] Habermas argues that 'normative validity claims' remain possible for so long as they 'can be discursively redeemed – that is grounded in the consensus of the participants through argument'.[25] Speech takes on great social urgency: as participants argue, so they realize, within their language, a tendency to 'rational will'. Private individuals by dint of vocal labour become citizens whose 'discursively formed will' issues in a collective subject. Consensus is redeemed by talking. Bell and Habermas might stand, respectively, as publicist and philosopher to the PMC; together they constitute the linguistic antithesis of Bakhtin.

I have simplified Habermas (though not Bell) in order to characterize what a thinking liberal might expect of his speech in the USA in the sixties. Mailer is perfectly capable of this voice but expects and experiences more. During *Armies of the Night* he will stand corporatist-vocalism on its head, speaking in one voice but as many; among the many will be several that deeply embarrass the liberal inflexion. Take Mailer's behaviour as MC at the Ambassador: superficially, his task is simple, he has to introduce speakers on the eve of a Vietnam War rally and to encourage the donation of monies towards a legal fund for those arrested during the demonstration. Appeals to buggery and excrement can hardly have been calculated to prompt consensus or underline legality. Mailer charts his path to vocal effrontery with considerable care, using chapter headings as signals. He leaves 'The Liberal Party' (ch. 4) and moves 'Toward a theater of ideas' (ch. 5), in which the Beast released by the Prince of Bourbon (p. 33) will attempt 'A transfer of power' (ch. 6). There is every indication that when the sartorial 'gent' (p. 13) starts talking dirty he may be attempting to become 'Ambassador' to a consciousness quite other than that notionally shared by 'the dark middle class depths of [his] audience' (p. 41). The 'real' Norman Mailer comes apart before their very ears in order to let them know that their every word is or ought to be disputed territory, and that their unanimity is a front. Questions on whether there are any blacks or reporters in the house or as to the unamplified audibility of his voice dramatize the degree to which utterance is shaped by its audience, which should not settle back into a fantasy of univocality. Consequently, as Mailer says 'piss', he hears within it a babble of quotation and misquotation, of prior and post-usage: reporters will report 'shit' (p. 50), as certainly as students 'wail [with] delight' and the professionals 'chill' (p. 38). Mailer 'the orator' (p. 38) proliferates obscenity, while Mailer 'the novelist' (p. 11) imposes asterisks ('p*ss'). The writer's asterisk-impulse alludes to the translation of the Texan 'fuck' into 'fug' by publisher's fief in 1948 (p. 59). The diminution of the expletives in *The Naked and the Dead* proved counter-effective, since by 1967 'fug' had entered the language of the counter-culture; on 21 October the Fugs were to act as a 'theatrical medium' (p. 120) for an attempt to levitate and exorcise the Pentagon. Given the sedition built into its sub-plot, the asterisk must appeal to the full weight of High Culture if it is to keep its vowel down. As the compromised creator of the double-voiced 'Fug', Mailer has stood in both cultural camps at once; he does so again, duly noting that *The New Yorker* has 'strictures against the use of sh*t' (p. 38), but adding that '*' may be likened to 'rocket-bursts and the orbs of roman candles' (p. 50). 'I' and 'u' are at once erased and restored, plus velocity. In effect, Mailer has set a political transcription test. He gives the reader an opportunity for vocal omission and asks for an oral report. Confronted with, 'F*ck you he said to the heckler but with such gusto that the vowel was doubled. "F*-*ck you" was more like it' (p. 50), readers are liable to polarize, as did the audience at the Ambassador. However, the provision of editorial commentary alongside vocal content ensures that the vowel has a class root: to object to the vowel is to take a decision about value. Two initially contradictory voices speak from under the asterisk, which, in the force of its own unvoicing, reveals itself as a class inflexion. Mailer's chosen idiom for profanity is Black Power (p. 38), yet his memory of the word 'shit' carries him 'on a river of obscenity from small-town storyteller . . . below the banker and the books and the educators and the legislators' to 'a skinny Southern cracker with a beatific smile on his face saying in the dawn in a Filipino rice paddy, "Man, I just managed to take me a noble shit". Yeah that was Mailer's America' (p. 48). Of course, neither the black radical nor the 'cracker' *is* Mailer's America, he wears too good a suit. His vocal enrolment in groups having little that is pleasant to say to each other, in front of an audience that doesn't want to listen, is undertaken explicitly to articulate the class repressions from which the liberal middle class have forged their limited integrity.

Mailer challenges the political credibility of his audience by invoking two voices that the PMC have no wish to hear. Those who march on the Pentagon have distanced themselves historically from blacks and from labour. Black peace-protestors will eventually quit the demonstration, leaving the middle-class army limping on its 'Achilles' heel black as tar' (p. 101) towards troops gathered from the working class and deployed to defend corporate interests at the Pentagon. Betrayals will proliferate as, come 'the night', the professional parents desert their student children, leaving them to suffer cruel defeat at the hands of the sons of labour. Mailer is unequivocal as to the class make-up of the contending forces. He takes his title from 'Dover beach':

> Ah, Love, let us be true
> To one another! for the world, which seems
> To lie before us like a land of dreams,
> So various, so beautiful, so new,
> Hath really neither joy, nor love, nor light,
> Nor certitude, nor peace, nor help for pain;
> And we are here as on a darkling plain
> Swept with confused alarms of struggle and flight,
> Where ignorant armies clash by night.[26]

Arnold's armies may 'clash' obscurely, but Mailer's can be identified in the light cast by Fitzgerald's 'The crack-up'. After his arrest and on the way to prison Mailer recalls:

> 'That long dark night of the soul when it is always three o'clock in the morning.'
>
> Ah, yes, thought Mailer, as the shopping street flickered past the bus window at a rate not faster than a good horse's trot, yes, bless Fitzgerald for his

clear line . . . Yes, how much of Fitzgerald's long dark night may have come
from that fine winnowing sense in the very fine hair of his nose that the two
halves of America were not coming together, and when they failed to touch,
all of history might be lost.   (pp. 157–8)

'The six inches of no-man's land' (p. 255) between the US army and the
demonstrators is 'the gulf of the classes' (p. 270), across which the small
town confronts the city and the South faces the North again; all of which
makes 'the night' identifiable. Mailer misquotes Fitzgerald, granting 'a
real dark night'[27] specificity as 'the long Capitalist night', through
which 'blindfold' armies march (p. 267). Mailer's armies are self-deluded
rather than 'ignorant'. The PMC (an army of the day), those 'mediocre
middle-class middle-aged masses of the left' (p. 96), march against their
own best interest and cannot be expected to deliver, since they are 'the
first real champions of technology land' (p. 96). Their children (an army
of the night) are by and large enrolled in higher education (p. 246) and
will eventually service the very corridors that briefly they attack.
Working-class delusions stem from a more complex disorientation.
Mailer stresses that to march from the Lincoln Memorial to the Pentagon
is to cross into Virginia and to meet a Southern army. During the sixties
capital passed that way, from the North-east to the Sunbelt, and from
unionized to non-unionized labour, underlining the South's continuing
status as an internal colony. By recruiting workforces (farmers and
housewives) without previous union experience, corporations were able
to reduce labour costs in the new military–scientific complex, while
'implanting, from the beginning, the manipulative structures of the
"communications" model of personnel management geared toward
worker individualism'.[28] Southern troops, defenders of capital's new
route to cheaper labour, fight for what exploits them: their 'blindfold' is
of a corporate issue.

Mailer, who has been doing Southern voices since *The Naked and the
Dead*, would not have it so. Faced with 'the unspeakable barbarities [his
country] invented with every corporation day' (p. 171), he can out-
mystify Ike McCaslin in his search for a Southern working class whose
collar has not turned. Instead, he finds a region 'caught between the old
frontier and the new ranch house' (p. 144), where penetration by
corporate capital has fossilized a form of life associated with poverty yet
considered "individualistic". The emergent form offers 'the bypasses
and the supermarkets and the shopping centers' (p. 152), the whole
infrastructure of "autonomous individualism". Two portraits, both
semi-generic, encapsulate possible responses to loss – the Marshal and the
prison guard.

The Marshal with 'stone larynx, leather testicles [and] ice cubes for eyes' (p. 155) has bought the state's line: he poises on the brink of a third civil war in which the South, as the final bastion of American values, must fight in Washington and Vietnam on behalf of the corporation against Reds (p. 144). For Mailer, the Marshal is 'any upstanding demonstrator's nightmare'. Full of 'American rectitude', he loves action in defence of what he knows to be right (ranging from the right to carry guns to the right to hate urban Jews and to drink clean water), and yet he is himself a pollutant, caught 'in that no man's land between the old frontier and the new ranch home'. Fearlessly to defend a pure anachronism that your mortgage despoils is to experience an intense contradiction; the Marshal resolves his difficulty by enrolling as 'the Knight of God' and blaming someone else, 'the evil was without, America was threatened by a foreign disease'.

The Knight's pedigree runs back to Croft (*The Naked and the Dead*) and forward to Gilmore (*The Executioner's Song*) but casting for the seventies and eighties would surely involve Eastwood in the dirtiest and most saintly of his Harry moods.[29] Mailer's Marshal is an Avenger with a star whose 'no-man's land' stretches westward from the South; his helmet fools no one. The musculature derives from a nineteenth-century elision of Civil and range wars, as they are re-fought in the movies. Mailer puts the face 'somewhere . . . between Steve McQueen and Robert Mitchum' (p. 144), but adds that lunar acne and blowtorch eyes would prevent a career in Hollywood. The point remains that the Marshal is designed by mass culture (for corporate profit), hardened in Vietnam (for corporate profit) and ready to fight communists (for corporate profit), and yet considers himself opposed to 'despoliation' and 'city ways'. The corporate 'blindfold' is effective.

Alternatively, the Southerner can take the ranch-house in the suburbs and make his own modifications (pp. 197–8): where the mortgage-holder is a guard with a 'poverty-ridden rural childhood', he may dig the psychic equivalent of a cellar beneath 'the hierarchies of schizophrenic ranch-house life'. His implement, and revisionist way back to the 'stingy gruel' of his parents, will be the small act of kindness ministered alike to the 'poor Negroes and the poor whites'. By such means he will undo the 'stinginess' of his own childhood and so 'remake [his] nervous system'. The cure, it seems, is to become a hipster in your own basement.[30] The guards daily quit their residences in 'corporation land' to recover their past in prison. Their chosen 'route back' involves self-'reconstruction' through a re-working of the master–slave relationship in the form of the warder–prisoner dependency: supremacy is retained, but sweetened by 'kindness'. The antebellum South is recovered and re-cast in a Second Reconstruction which, unlike Kennedy's, allows Southerners an Old, 'secret' and patriarchal South, beneath the New. Both solutions involve real fantasies whereby working-class Southerners live their lives on active service to a corporatist state, as though this were not the case. Mailer fantasizes for them because he too needs a 'cellar' and an 'old frontier' down South as routes to the right, away from his liberal, middle-class allegiances.

II

While summoning Fitzgerald to draw class lines in the night, Mailer refers to 'a good essay' he once wrote on the failure of 'any major American novelist' to write a novel for the non-reading public, for 'that American audience brainwashed by Hollywood, and *Time*' (p. 157). The essay appears in *Cannibals and Christians*. Since Mailer is a fine literary critic who happens also to be Fitzgerald's disciple, his comments may be taken as comments on himself:

> Some upper class writers like Fitzgerald turned delicately upon the suppositions of their class, lost all borrowed strategy and were rudderless, were forced therefore to become superb in tactics, but for this reason perhaps a kind of hysteria lived at the center of their work.[31]

There is nothing delicate about the way in which Mailer turns on his audience at the Ambassador; though as a vocal and political tactic it is superb, nonetheless he shares with Fitzgerald an abiding suspicion of his class. Both writers carry an eye for wealth away from more or less secure middle-class childhoods. Fanny Mailer describes the Mailers as living among 'middle class people making their way up – merchants, professionals, office workers', and she might be paraphrasing Fitzgerald as she counts dollars and berates her children, 'What do you mean, money doesn't matter? Where'd you get that idea? Money always comes out on top. You have money, everybody looks at you different.'[32] Having got the money, Mailer, like Fitzgerald, turns on the suppositions that attend it and is left 'rudderless'. His social disorientation can be articulated politically by asking why so much of his work investigates liberal principles in order to murder or malign those who hold them? The question is doubly problematic in that, during the fifties and sixties at least, liberalism and the Democratic Party proved the traditional and only home for most of the best and brightest of Mailer's kind. Paul Buhle notes, in a recent study of American Marxism:

> the overwhelming majority of the 1930s–40s political survivors and their young counterparts had come to accept the welfare state led by a liberalized Democratic Party as the inevitable starting point of future change. Rejection-ism they viewed as a replay of their own youthful folly.[33]

Mailer's links to *Dissent*, however strained, are links to the last major journal of the Old Left – a journal whose editors supported the Cold War and Democratic Party openings towards wider welfarism; they were equally consistent in their hostility to changing political tastes.[34] For Mailer, a contributing editor to *Dissent* during the fifties, any hunting of the middle-class liberal necessarily involved self-betrayal or self-division. Two examples should serve to make the point.

The *Naked and the Dead* (1948) could be read under the sub-title *The Education of a Body Servant*. General Cummings ('reactionary'[35]) takes Lieutenant Hearn (disaffected son of capital (p. 72) and 'liberal' (p. 84)) as his aide; on offer is an illiberal education in which a 'bourgeois liberal' (p. 586), via services to the master's body, will become an extension of the masterful mind and ripe candidate for a 'reactionary century' (p. 85). Hegel's 'Lordship and bondage' is the best gloss, with the singular difference that when Cummings senses that his integrity derives from the labour of the servant (in the matter of the cigarette-butt, pp. 317–27) he executes the servant, rather than recognize that 'something has come about quite different from an independent consciousness. It is not an independent, but rather a dependent consciousness that he has achieved.'[36] The general's only signal of body-loss, at the loss of that which constitutes his body, is diarrhoea (evacuation of the minimal gratifications provided by the servant). No Hegelian self-consciousness for Cummings: instead he sends Hearn on what is in effect a suicide mission, whose very geography reiterates the futility of the servant's assault on the body of the lord. Hearn must scale Mount Anaka if he is to get behind enemy lines – Anaka is for Cummings the island's 'axis' and 'keystone', and he and it 'understood each other' (p. 563). Identification grows anatomically specific as Hearn's patrol advances; rock becomes 'fleshlike', 'slimy' and capable of 'rous[ing] panic' in the men (p. 663). With Hearn dead, the platoon leader, Croft, is 'inflamed' by the 'sheer mass' of the mountain (p. 638). The shadow of the authoritarian phallus falls so heavily across the work that when Anaka's tip is approached by Croft, he and the survivors are driven back by disturbed hornets: the orgasm is poisonous and effective (p. 700). The schematic moral would seem to be that liberal (Hearn) and working class (Croft) must finally die or ally under the shadow of a power as natural as the land itself. Hearn, reflecting on his own politics (p. 169), notes that 'self-interest' would eventually move him away from his isolated position of the left, back 'towards the ideas of his father'; the force of the General's influence can only hasten that process. However, his reactionary drift stems primarily from the absence of a convincing socialist option in America (pp. 585–6). During a time likely to see the elevation of Cummings, terrorism or anarchy or quietude or empty gestures seem the only available moves for those who have 'to keep resisting'. So, 'when he got back he would do [the] little thing' in the hope that 'when things got really bad' the Left would shelve its differences. For Cummings, harmed in his political ambition by the ineffectiveness of the Anopopei campaign, disguise may yet be the route to the Pentagon (p. 718). Convinced of the inevitability of war with Russia, and equally sure that 'few Americans . . . would understand the contradictions' of the period leading up to that conflict, he intends to approach 'control' at the Pentagon indirectly via the State Department, where he will masquerade 'under a conservative liberalism'. Neither Hearn nor Cummings can achieve his preferred political destiny directly.

Mailer's day at the Pentagon repeats the same imponderables: he too cannot sit back and wait, yet called to the front rank to do 'a little thing' for an essentially liberal alliance, he pronounces himself a 'Left Conservative' (p. 185) and moves off in three directions at once: left, towards gentle anarchy laced with terror (the revolutionary anarchy of the Fugs (Hearn's anarchists) crossed with the National Liberation Front (Hearn's terrorists)); right, towards Southern blue-collar corporatists (latter-day Crofts), and straight on into the lenses of the media – destination, the cultural consensus that sustains the Pentagon (Cummings at the State Department). In 1967, as in 1948, the liberal centre cannot hold or be held to, but neither can it be deserted.

For all its schematic faults *The Naked and the Dead* lays down a political paradigm for Mailer's literary career; at the heart of the diagram lies one 'Mailer', the inadequate and dead liberal. The problem remains, in the absence of anything coherent to the left of the Democratic centre, to kill the liberal is to empower the Right. For a moment in 1960 it seemed that liberal politics might find an adequate national voice in Kennedy: 'Superman [had come] to the Supermarket.' However, *The Presidential Papers* (1962) are finally a study in disillusion, so that when Kennedy comes again with his brother inside *Marilyn* (1973) – the nation's sexual supermarket – their coming is poisonous. I indulge innuendo to catch the bitterness of Mailer's political disappointment. In 1967 he struggled on a 'collective journey through the dark' (p. 185) to write a 'précis' or 'condensation of a collective novel' (pp. 216 and 255): eventually, "collectivity" was to prove a politically impossible term.

Faced with 'the long night of capital' and the poverty of the liberal consensus, he turns in his isolation back to the family and to what he considers to be its teleological source, the male sperm. Privacy compounds privacy and emerges, via an obsession with Egyptology, as a metaphysics for an alternative collectivity. *Ancient Evenings* appeared in 1983, but since it was written between 1973 and 1982 it is effectively

Mailer's ur-text for the seventies. The novel covers the nineteenth and twentieth dynasties, or the one hundred and eighty years between 1300BC and 1121BC, and yet issues almost entirely from a single orgasm. Very early in the novel the Ka of the dead Meni, who considers himself one of the reincarnations of Menenhetet (the book's narrator) fellates the Khaibit of Menenhetet. 'Ka' means 'double'; 'Khaibit' may be translated as 'memory'. Role diffusion seems considerable, but is in fact minimal. During congress the couple(?) visualize the Night of the Pig in the Palace of Rameses IX; the occasion is dedicated to fictional licence in that any and all stories are permitted: what the narrator(s) see(s) and hear(s) is the substance of the novel. If Meni *is* Menenhetet, then he sucks himself, albeit in another incarnation, and the jism drawn from this one act of necrophiliac onanism carries a cast list and plot beyond the ambition of the bulkiest soap or saga. Read against the grain of its obvious scholarship, *Ancient Evenings* is an extended parody, its subject being not Egypt but liberal creativity; the pivotal question becomes, 'Just how much can the isolate author jerk out of himself?'

In *The Naked and the Dead* (1948) Mailer made a mountain out of a phallus, but gave to the ejaculation a clear political plot. In *Cannibals and Christians* (1966) masturbation was used as a cultural metaphor for the privatization of consumption. 1971 saw Mailer discoursing on the structure of the sperm as part of a debate with feminism (*The Prisoner of Sex*), and in *Marilyn* (1973) the sperm of the liberal heroes turned rancid in a quasi-political accusation. In contradistinction, with *Ancient Evenings* the male seed has become the vehicle of much repetition but very little history and absolutely no politics. The choice of epigraph is revealing:

> I believe . . . that the borders of our mind are ever shifting, and that many minds can flow into one another, as it were, and create and reveal a single mind, a single energy . . . and that our memories are part of one great memory.
>
> (W.B. Yeats, *Ideas of Good and Evil*)

Poirier is probably right to discover in the novel's final chapter a genealogical condensation that calls on 'the assembled strengths of Menenhetet, Meni, all the characters they have loved, the Egyptian gods, along with their latest manifestations in Christian mythology'.[37] However, by extending the series to include in 'a composite "I"'[38] all Mailer's earlier literary selves, Poirier underlines his own missing historical sense. Mailer's wandering doubles have often previously found political roles that will not reduce to mythological mulch. Mailer's appeal to a 'great memory' does scant justice to his best recollections, and may be reproved by Adorno's judgement that, 'the notion of collective consciousness was invented only to divert attention from true objectivity and its correlate, alienated subjectivity'. Adorno adds, 'it should be clear and sufficient warning that in a dreaming collective no differences remain between classes'.[39] Memory, in this instance, is a bolt hole down which, with much erudition, Mailer has bolted. Writing in 1955, Philip Rahv understood the impulse to myth as an escape from temporality via an appeal to 'the ever-recurrent':

> Myth is reassuring in its stability, whereas history is the powerhouse of change which destroys custom and tradition in producing the future . . . In our time the movement of history has been so rapid that the mind longs for nothing so much as something permanent to steady it. Hence what the craze for myth represents most of all is the fear of history.[40]

Mailer engages history for as long as he pursues the disappointed liberal (in the USA and himself) down class lines. The only problem is that the pursuit leads him, like Fitzgerald before him, 'to turn upon the suppositions of [his] class', so that he is left 'rudderless', in 'a kind of hysteria'.

From the 'hysteria', at least during the late fifties and the sixties, comes the 'tactic' of polyphony. During the seventies American hegemony declined, and with it the holding power of Fordism. Without a *Pax Americana*, liberal corporatism looks shaky; as soon as the international liberalism of Bretton Woods stops delivering the goods for a growth economy at home, Keynes (no longer protected by his uniform – military Keynesianism) dies yet again, welfarism fails and the liberal centre moves to the right. Mailer's voice, ever a political register, can no longer find or perhaps believe in its favoured irritant.

One might have expected that the failure of Fordist accords would release conflict from the consensus. That expectation ignores the strength of an insurgent but narrowing middle class, and the depth of 'the ever fattening military pork-barrel'.[41] Mailer's 'army of the day' push through a revolution of self-interest during the seventies, as a result of which the many and repressed articulations previously audible within the consensual "one" are muted. Mailer no longer hears politically convincing voices at the margins of the conscience of his class. *Ancient Evenings*, for all its vocal pyrotechnics, is a monologue. But my concern is with the forms of successful mass consumption: in 1967 Fordism, bloody, global and nominally Keynesian, stands at its climacteric.

9

Armies of the Night: *a familiar romance?*

In 1967 Mailer's 'hysteria' was purposive, his goal – the Pentagon as an image of full and troubled Fordism. Between 1929 and 1934 partial Fordism too had its troubles. Capital invariably cures itself by wounding the selves of one of its primary sources of profit, the American consumer; it follows that for the novelist of American manners, be he Mailer or Fitzgerald, *the* locus of attention is the middle-class interior (preferably in crisis) as its furnishings and psyches shift and re-form. To discover, while reading *Tender is the Night*, that any referent can fissure (the beach at Cap D'Antibes) and that the most literal-seeming word ('hard') may be a metaphor whose network extends, via synonym and antonym, through four decades of capital's human history, is indeed to experience mild 'hysteria'. Turning on while turning within the middle class is presumably a less than comfortable 'tactic', especially when one's own 'den', library, child (children), wife (wives) are situated therein. Mailer is consequently uneasy at a pre-march party in the home of 'an attractive liberal couple' (p. 13); 'his deepest detestation was often reserved for the nicest of liberal academics, as if their lives were his own life but a step escaped' (p. 15). Immediately, 'as if' summons a further simile; the home's smell depresses him 'like the scent of the void which comes off the pages of a Xerox copy'. Since liberal academics are also referred to as 'liberal technologues' (p. 15) whose living rooms 'looked like offices' (p. 16), the logic of the Xerox analogy is impeccable: academics are bureaucrats servicing the corporate state, and, quite properly, as teachers of Mandel's 'intellectual proletariat', their quarters smell of the master. During the sixties Xerox would feature on any earnings list of representative corporations. However, the smell is 'but a step' from

217

home; *Armies of the Night* was written to a tight contract for *Harper's*, doubtless Xerox was part of the writing process, perhaps a computer graces the 'den'?

The shade of the unwanted double is escaped via an attack on the hosts' design sense from the point of view of a Victorian interior decorator: there is much talk of 'cornerstones', 'family furnishings' and even of 'the gold standard of the psyche' (p. 16). To invoke a specie pervasive enough to spread its golden mean from the IMF to the minds of the middle classes is to summon a fabulous archaism, particularly in a year during which the USA in practice abandoned its Bretton Woods promises to back each overseas dollar with gold on demand.[1] Mailer knows that times are inflationary, he notes of his hosts:

> just as money was a concept . . . to the liberal academic, and needed no ballast of gold to be considered real . . . so position or power in society was also a concept, desirable, but always to be relinquished for a better concept. They were servants of the social machine of the future in which all irrational human conflict would be resolved, all conflict of interest negotiated.   (p. 16)

The Coming of Post Industrial Society may yet be read as an etiquette primer, a new, if far less abrasive, *Theory of the Leisure Class*. Where gold and green-back give way to 'concept' as currency, the unit of exchange is the financier's computer print-out. In which case, manners (ever the index of capital's prevalent form) will no longer embody a secure property base; instead, social grace shall reflect the fictitious but credit-worthy 'concepts' of finance capital (where we are led to believe there is 'conspicuous[ly]' little time to 'waste' on Veblenite graces). Mailer knows his Fitzgerald well enough to appreciate the change in his hosts:

> [they are] brusque to the world of manners, they had built their hope of heaven on the binary system of the computer, 1 and 0, Yes and No – they had little therefore to do with the spectrum of grace in acceptance and refusal. (p. 17)

The notion that their furnishings should bear a traceable relation to accumulations held as bullion in the family vault is as inappropriate as the idea of Edith Wharton behind a reception desk in the foyer of an IBM building, or of Mailer playing Proust:

> If he was on many an occasion brusque, he was also to himself at least so supersensitive to nuances of manner he sometimes suspected when in no modest mood that Proust had lost a cell mate the day they were born in different bags.   (p. 17)

At other moments during the Washington weekend he will contemplate alternative nineteenth-century literary costumes, casting himself as an unspecified 'character in a novel by Balzac' (p. 8), as a Jamesian amanuensis (p. 118), and as Huysmans' Des Esseintes (p. 160). In each case the emphasis is on the aesthetics of accumulation – Proust for 'nuance', James for 'cumulative rising memories' and Huysmans for 'cumulative memories' made 'precious': 'Like an emotional connoisseur . . . he wished now to steep essences of this experience at his leisure . . . savoring, installing, banking the value of the experience, by way of some enjoyable reverie' (p. 160). All this is a city whose architecture 'spoke of a time when men and events were solid, comprehensible, often obedient to a code of values, and resolutely non electric' (p. 54). Despite his best efforts, Mailer cannot re-enter that time (particularly since he has a 'thunderous electronic headache'); the cultural and financial solidities of the Jamesian bourgeoisie are extinct. Yet as he marches on the Pentagon he will persist in exhibiting the 'courtly sentiments' of a Victorian or perhaps Edwardian gentleman (p. 119); he will discuss his servant's genealogy with an arresting officer (p. 147), and worry about the condition of the windsor knot in his regimental tie after a night in prison. His sartorial struggle is made no easier by the approach of his lawyer wearing a moss green jacket, compatible lemon pants, a red shirt and sneakers (pp. 201–2). The meeting between Gatsby's pink suit and Buchanan's crimson carpet is hardly less shocking: both encounters are calculated to reach beyond colour clash – in 1922 liquid assets confronted inherited accumulations, in 1967 the 'gold standard of one century' (wearing filthy cuffs) *liaises* with the 'concepts' of the next.

Similar reverberations modify the semantics of Mailer's initial attempt to redecorate an academic living room; musing on Proust and manners, Mailer adds a parenthesis which turns 'bag' into a pun: 'Proust had lost a cell mate the day they were born in different bags. (Bag is of course used here to specify milieu and not the exceptional character of the mothers, Mme Proust and Mrs I.B. Mailer)' (p. 17). To activate 'bag' is to transform 'cell mate' into a semantic echo-chamber. One might have expected 'soul mate' given Mailer's fondness for Black Power idiom; however, Proust's preferences suggest that 'mate' carries sexual latencies, while 'cell', in the context of Mailer's subsequent arrest, casts shades of the prison house across the biochemistry of conception. Since at the Ambassador Mailer will declare in a black voice that he intends 'to stick it up the government's ass . . . right into the sphincter of the Pentagon' (p. 38), there is some justification for assuming that he and Proust are detained for anal rape on the nation's military–industrial complex, or indeed for joint buggery of L.B.J. If this is the case, a secondary charge emerges: again on stage, Mailer confessed to being 'Lyndon Johnson's little old *dwarf* alter ego' (p. 49), consequently to interfere with the president is to interfere with himself. Sub-plots within a pun push scatological humour towards a class plot which is at once political and linguistic. Since Mailer (the author) knows that hippies plan to kidnap the president as a prelude to removing his trousers (p. 244), he also knows that Mailer's (the orator's) declaration of anal intent constitutes a political alliance with the more anarchic elements of the New Left, an affiliation of which Mailer's Proustian incarnation (even in black-face) could only despair. Proust and Mailer need a continuing entrée into the bourgeois living room, their writing depends on it; such rooms in the 1960s rest on a firm foundation provided by the permanent-arms economy. Assault on the Pentagon is therefore assault on fictional currency, a point well understood by literary mothers. To return briefly to the maternal source of this particular political story, to 'Mme Proust and Mrs I.B. Mailer', the manner of address highlights initials which yield MP and an anagram of IBM[2]. Perhaps literary mothers have always feared that their sons may betray their class, so that military police and leading corporations lurk defensively behind the formalities of the maternal name. Mailer can hear the institutions in his mother's tongue because he knows the depth of his offence: 'bag' moves via male 'mate' towards 'sh*t', a word whose class conflicts prove to be the thinly veiled substance of the son's positively anti-ambassadorial address.

The hermeneutics of 'bag' are almost as deep as they are deeply unreasonable. Mailer uses the word while claiming supersensitivity to manners, thereby producing an idiomatic slip that grows more offensive in direct proportion to its capacity to prompt rumours of insurrection and self-division borne on the implied vocabulary of anal obscenity. The capacity of 'bag' to encourage inferences that are socially antagonistic to one another is a measure of Mailer's conviction that alternative meanings form within unacknowledged collectivities beneath his most Mailer-esque assertions. If 'individualism' is necessarily coterminous with social fragmentation, Mailer, against the interests of his class (the class most committed to the ideology of self-creation), hears class fragments collude to produce a subversive sub-text from what he says.

I have traced a pun as it draws a plot out of the network of its associative logic. The plot could not have hatched at a worse time; Mailer opens the semantics of 'bag' to an 'impenetrable pluralism' of unaligned voices, even as he attends a party to launch the 'rational consensus' of a class. My phrasing derives from Habermas,[2] who along with Bell, could only be disappointed. You may object that a questionable kind of critical adroitness did it, that Mailer didn't. If so, perhaps his version of 'white bread' will confirm that the 'tactic' of semantic 'hysteria' is both conscious and politically calculated. Hung-over and over-dressed at a meeting of draft-card burners on the lawn of a Congregational church, Mailer responds positively to an orientation given by Dickie Harris, leader of representatives from Resistance. Food has been passed around – a few loaves, a jar of peanut butter, some milk – general abstemiousness indicates a 'collective philosophy' easily worn:

> The neat remains came back eventually to Harris' feet. Since he had just finished asking if everything was clear about the action at the Department of Justice in the afternoon and the meeting to discuss further action at night, he now stared out at the listening onlookers, picked up the bread and said, 'Anyone like some food? It's . . . uh . . .' he pretended to look at it, 'it's . . . uh . . . *white* bread.' The sliced loaf half-collapsed in its wax wrapper was the comic embodiment now of a dozen little ideas, of corporation-land which took the taste and crust out of bread and wrapped the remains in wax paper, and was, at the far extension of this same process, the same mentality which was out in Asia escalating, defoliating, orientating; yeah; and the white bread was also television, the fun of situation comedy shows with commercials, the humor they had shared as adolescents when pop art was being birthed; the white bread was the infiltrated enemy who had a grip on them everywhere, forced them to collaborate if only by imbibing the bread (and substance) of that enemy with his food processing, enriched flours, vitamin supplements, added nutrients; finally, and this probably was why Harris chuckled when he said it, the bread was *white* bread, not black bread – a way to remind them all that he was one of the very few Negroes here. Who knew what it might have cost him in wonder about his own allegiances not to be out there somewhere now agitating for Black Power. Here he was instead with White bread – White money, White methods, even White illegalities. It was exorbitant, Mailer decided glumly, to watch such virtuosity with a hangover. (pp. 62–3)

Mailer senses the dullness of his brief essay beside Harris's idiomatic timing, exposition being no substitute for the ability so to inflect a word that it calls into itself 'a dozen little ideas' as it moves between speakers. Thanks to Harris's 'virtuosity', 'white bread' becomes a 'theme'[3] within which racial, corporatist and student filiations may debate alliance and betrayal. Despite his hangover, Mailer tries the trick and leaves exposition to his reader. Clue: Black Power is to white bread as Harris is to English tailoring? Answer: tweed. The association is not "free": Mailer wears an 'English vest and suit' (p. 62), while Harris's sartorial style warrants the epithet 'panache (as an English journalist once described it)' (p. 61). Traces are laid. Exposition: if the word 'tweed' flashes across your mind creating an improbable sympathy between a 'Left Conservative' (p. 185) and a black student radical, on the morning of the Pentagon march, then I would suggest that you have learned the verbal trick and can practise what Mailer speaks. Supplementary Exposition, Theoretical (apply to 'bag' and 'white bread' and 'Harris'): such alliances are not the stuff of marches, at best they are momentary ensembles hanging by a thread on the brink of betrayal, existing perhaps only in the disputed semantics of a turn of phrase. Vološinov is the theorist of such events, underwriting Mailer's ear for sub-texts. The work of both is attuned to 'the lowest most fluid and quickly changing stratum of . . . ideology'. Down there 'accidental words flash across the mind', the 'social orientation' of speech miscarries; 'erratic' associations imply 'loose coalitions of a small number of persons'; puns tug everyday terms towards 'the borders of the pathological'; 'underdeveloped experiences' prove central; 'isolated facts in the social life' strive for full expression on some as yet unrealized 'social ground'; novels are 'without heroes', and 'performances' never quite find their audience. Not surprisingly, down there, "reason", "consensus" and "individualism", the key-words of the liberal polity, break up.

Earlier I quoted an extended passage from *Marxism and the Philosophy of Language*,[4] which has been my resource in a re-write that seeks to approximate to the experience of reading the dispersive prose of *Armies of the Night*. The question remains, even if his prose works in the ways that I suggest, why is it that for Mailer so few meanings can be received meanings? Or, in its extreme form, why is the literal so often unacceptable? I have tried, through close readings, to characterize a political and semantic habit of mind which might be called "metaphoricity". For the Mailer of 1967 everything is liable to stand for something else, and to do so without the reassuring signal of 'like' or 'as'. Fitzgerald shares the habit (circa 1934). In both instances the reasons are cultural. As I have already argued of the twenties, deepening markets lead to double bodies because the body of the consumer, along with the thing consumed, tends to turn into a dependent variable of the process of capital valorization. What was true of partial Fordism is necessarily more true of Fordism at full stretch.

To live under Fordism is therefore potentially to live as a double surrounded by doubles: in one sense, the other who walks always beside you is your better self, re-made through advert, shop window and PR; in another you are merely the transitory phase or shadow cast by the value that you realize as both consumer and producer. In both senses you add up to a metaphor – in you two terms meet, price and person. The market would have it that in this instance tenor (price) should swallow vehicle (person) in an act of profitable catachresis. However, depending on its cultural moment, the meeting will throw up a number of possibilities ranging from mere substitution to full catachresis. For some, price is no more than a person's decoration (a substitution to be paraphrased away by wealth-tax or revolution); for others, the two terms constitute a trope of such amity that only one idea is presented (in catachresis who can recover calf and thigh from 'table leg' or 'wealth' from a rich man?).[5] Of course it has long been a commonplace that for every person there is a price; my point is simply that in a Fordist context people are under pressure so to conform to that commonplace that they partake of the world through it. In Gramsci's terms 'price' becomes the 'spontaneous philosophy' proper to every person. Gramsci questions that conformism through which we '"think" without having a critical awareness'. His account of the origins of such "common sense" is useful:

> [we] take part in a conception of the world mechanically imposed by the external environment, i.e. by one of the many social groups in which everyone is automatically involved from the moment of his entry into the conscious world (and this can be one's village or province; it can have its origins in the parish and the 'intellectual activity' of the local priest or aging patriarch whose wisdom is law, or in the little old woman who has inherited the law of the witches, or the minor intellectual soured by his own stupidity and inability to act.[6]

Despite the incongruity of an analogy between pre-Fordist Sardinia and Fordist USA, I quote at length to prompt the recognition that shopping malls too have their priests, patriarchs, witches and soured intellectuals. To walk among shop windows (particularly during the twenties and sixties) is to receive philosophical instruction. The mall is filled with 'amorous glances' promoting Progress and Classlessness; fashion instructs in metamorphic Individualism, with a "new look" latent in its every accessory; stores fitted out as conceptual theatres promise that with each item an "image" will pass to the purchaser (Mass Culture); all items propose the ready availability of the "bourgeois" style of life (American-ism). The mall is filled with opinion, the greatest body of which would cast persons as personifications of capital's imperatives. The lesson is of course reductive, the mall is one conditioning environment among several; the workplace and the home will offer contending philosophies. However, one of the imperatives of Fordism is to extend capital's range so that white collars may be worn on the shop floor, and a TV-set sell in every room. In 1955 the AFL and CIO merged, securing the expulsion of communists from the American labour movement; the merger affirmed that business and labour contracts in the USA should in future be drawn up only on anti-political terms, in ways that would privilege the white male labour force as it climbed towards the middle class.

Even so, it is possible to present the sixties as a period of disruption for capital conceived globally. De-colonization produced third-world revolutionary movements whose 'liberation' claims were echoed by blacks and students at home. Yet as peasants proved intransigent in Vietnam, as sit-ins sat in the South, and as Northern cities burned, it would perhaps be wise to remember Marx's stricture, that 'a crisis always forms the starting point of large new investments'.[7] De-colonization gave rapid rise to neo-colonialism as capitalization of third-world agriculture (the Green Revolution) pushed the logic of capital into pre-capitalist areas. Expansion abroad, the spatial fix in agricultural form, was paralleled by a domestic credit explosion, resulting in 'a tremendous expansion of the media apparatus and the culture of consumerism'.[8]

As the point of view of exchange broadens, so the pressure of price on person intensifies to catachretic proportion; indeed, Jean Baudrillard argues that the price fits and that the person has vanished (with a consequent cessation of tension between the terms). He reads consumer capitalism as 'the age of simulation' which begins with 'a liquidation of all referentials' and the 'substituting [of] signs of the real for the real itself'.[9] The motive is simple: signs are almost infinitely ductile and therefore lend themselves to the needs of a troubled surplus value. In Baudrillard's conceptual world "the real" may be constructed and torn down wherever the price is right; 'it is always a question of proving the real by the imaginary, proving truth by scandal'. The scandalous device is the 'precessive' 'simulacrum', a model or image which, set within the system of signs that is the spectacle of consumerism, constitutes an original referent from the energy of its own 'magnetic field'. 'Facts', he insists, 'no longer have a trajectory of their own, they arise at the intersection of models.'[10] As a result, California doesn't fool Baudrillard, he knows that Los Angeles is merely Pirate Land and Fantasy World *en masse*. Indeed, Disneyland provides a national scenario, being there

> to conceal the fact that it is the 'real' country which is Disneyland . . . Disneyland is presented as imaginary in order to make us believe that the rest is real . . . Moreover, Disneyland is not the only one. Enchanted Village, Magic Mountain, Marine World: Los Angeles is encircled by these 'imaginary stations' which feed reality, reality-energy, to a town whose mystery is precisely that it is nothing more than a network of endless, unreal circulation.[11]

The sentiments resemble those of Oedipa Mass; as (*c.* 1965) she first glimpses San Narciso, 'less an identifiable city than a growth of concepts' developed around the aerospace industry, 'she thought of the time she'd opened a transistor radio to replace a battery and seen her first printed circuit'.[12] It is reassuring to learn that, when Doctorow's Daniel made the trip in 1967, he took Baudrillard's point, but only up to a point, noting: 'The ideal Disneyland patron may be said to be one who responds to a process of symbolic manipulation that offers him his culminating and quintessential sentiment at the moment of a purchase.'[13] A list of corporations offering exhibits is appended. Nonetheless, Daniel can still tell the simulacra from the trees, largely because 'people are all over the place in Disneyland':

Thus the customers on the Mark Twain Mississippi steamboat look into the hills and see the customers on the mule pack train looking down at them. There is a constant feedback of human multiplicity, one's own efforts of vicarious participation constantly thwarted by the mirror of other's eyes.[14]

Baudrillard generalizes the 'vicarious . . . moment of purchase', turning a pressure-sold cultural option into a cultural totality. *Simulations* gives us consumerism from the perspective of an ad-man's wildest dream. As an analysis of the fetishized click of consumer desire, the essay is central, but as cultural history it can make its point only by standardizing 'human multiplicity'.

Baudrillard's error is both culpable and understandable; Fordism sells hard, but sales pressure is directly proportional to the degree to which overproduction is a perceived problem. To express capital's conundrum gnomically: price into person must go at the very moment when it is least likely to do so – consequently, crisis shadows catachresis. Indeed, James O'Connor argues that capital is not simply crisis ridden but crisis dependent. Crises enforce new production methods, re-locations of capital, mergers and re-organizations of labour markets, all of which necessarily require upsets in social relations. An economic crisis is therefore a potential political crisis during which 'the hegemonic ideology of capitalist society, namely "commodity" and "capitalist fetishism"'[15] may be strained to breaking point. At the very least 1967 (and 1929) are unpredictable historical moments during which the 'spontaneous philosophy' of price can be doubted. Liberal re-deals may deflect some questions, but oppositional voices will persist in the public sphere. To summarize: even as crises provoke the restructuring of capital, so they give rise to extreme social and political revisions – ranging potentially from reformism through revolution to counter-revolution. O'Connor persuasively calls capitalist crisis a 'cauldron', in which classes and nations are recomposed, and 'new political formations are born'.[16]

Full Fordism offers 'new formations' a clearer target than its partial predecessor, in that "invisible" market forces become visible as soon as they don the garments of the state. As has been seen, a permanent-arms economy involves a substantial deepening of the state's role as an economic regulator; the resultant system has variously been called, 'state capitalism', 'the mixed economy', 'the administered society'; however, 'political capitalism' comes closest, in that the more an economy requires political regulation, the more the economic system is politicized. 'Increasingly . . . the state apparatus is seen as an area of struggle to impose (and resist) capitalist forms of activity.'[17] In cartoon form: Vietnam finds the state standing in a shop window dedicated simultaneously to destruction and desire, the shop is called *Pentagon*. Mailer knows it and is not alone in his knowledge. The rise of the anti-war movement indicates that by the mid-sixties large sections of the middle class recognized that for as long as 'the marvellous productivity of the American economy' (Bell) remained geared to Bloody Fordism, their consumption basket would feature embarrassing stains. The consensual conviction that everyone has the right to individualized consumption becomes awkward in such circumstances, particularly if your children re-discover poverty, by reading Harrington's *The Other America* (1962), and propose that US democracy is synonymous with profiteering in its support for murderous foreign dictators. Suddenly, in boom times, successful accumulation threatens itself by threatening the 'consensus' and 'individualism' through which it legitimates its own market practices. Perhaps this is what Habermas means when he argues that 'the extension of the administrative–instrumental control [by the state] may lead to its own process of demystification'.[18]

The consumption basket remains central to Fordist legitimacy, and the commodities that fill it are the pivot of the 'spontaneous philosophy' upon which Fordism rests: around commodity, and its practices, other terms cluster: "consensus", "individualism" and "reason". As long as price and person meet in commodity to commit catachresis, the corporatist (along with his philosopher, Baudrillard) is happy. However, once commodity is problematized, price and person will remain at odds, and all capital's technological and spatial "fixes" are liable only to make the "fit" seem worse; at which point, the unnoticed everyday metaphoricity of consumer culture may strike some as an economic and political impertinence. One kind of metaphor (catachresis) will give way to another (tensional), particularly among middle-class liberals who know something of Marx.

II

In order to stop talking in riddles, let me return to Mailer in the mid-sixties: a cursory reading of *Armies of the Night* reveals that the normative power of 'individualism' has lost its authority for Mailer, who experiences dramatic problems holding himself together. His most typical symptom involves sub-vocalization, taking the form of a hysterical surfacing of under-articulated elements at the edges of his confidence about himself and his class. Effectively, 'Mailer' becomes a metaphor for the seemingly imminent collapse of his culture's central metaphor – commodity. Homeopathy is undertaken via a crash-course in historical writing, during which he regards his several selves as a documentary resource for the composition of what amounts to a history of Fordism in its final days.

Mailer is well placed both to suffer sub-vocalizations and to analyse them. His biography is a classic of class ascent – from the most petty of the petty-bourgeoisie to the highest of the *haute*. During the thirties young Mailer asked his father 'Did you get a job today?', while his mother supported the family by working in 'Uncle Dave's company';[19] the scenario scarcely requires Malaquais's caption nominating young Norman as 'the Horatio Alger of the time' (circa 1949).[20] As though to confirm the plot, he married Lady Jeanne Campbell, daughter of the Duke of Argyll: the marriage lasted a year (1962–3), time enough for Mailer to become more 'ducal', since by proxy he was 'nobility'.[21] The Alger model has to be modified in that this hero goes in for descents. In August 1960, as laureate to Kennedy, he walked the Hyannis Port lawns; in November 1960 he spent time in the cells of West 100th Street Police Station, New York. Having cast an aristocratic presidential candidate as a hipster, he created himself (mayoral candidate for New York on an Existential Party ticket) as his own white negro. The stabbing of his second wife, Adele Morales, is interestingly glossed by the victim, 'Things like this don't happen to people like us. They happen to black people in Harlem and Puerto Ricans but not to us.'[22] 'People like us', when applied to Mailer, encompasses an anthology of social selves, whose existential edginess during the sixties remains informed by their grounding in a clear 'class apprenticeship'.[23] Jewish Algers don't forget class lines, particularly when their memory is sustained by extensive reading within a socialist tradition.

One upshot of the Malaquais grounding in politics and political economy between 1949 and 1952 is *Barbary Shore* (1951), in part a premature epitaph for the American Communist Party, extinct circa 1956. At the novel's close, Lovett is left 'the remnants of [a] socialist culture' by McLeod, the instructor who scrawls at the foot of his will, 'may he be alive to see the rising of the phoenix'.[24] During the sixties the phoenix had its moments; at the time, the ashes of the urban ghettos and of South Vietnam's forests must have struck some as promisingly warm. However, positive sightings were rare and required new habits of seeing. Jameson characterizes the period as a moment when a global enlargement of capital produced a great outpouring of social energy; among the forces released he lists ethnic movements, regionalisms and the student and women's movements as bearers of 'surplus consciousness'. Such was the energy flow that it challenged the class model of traditional Marxism, and implied 'a realm of freedom and voluntarist possibility'.[25] It follows that the expulsion of the communists from the American labour movement may be read as one aspect of 'a crisis in the institutions through which real class politics had however imperfectly been able to express itself'.[26] The triumph of McCarthyism and the attendant consolidation of the anti-political social contract between business and labour ensured that blacks, women workers and other minorities were further marginalized. Displaced from the institutions of an older working-class politics, they were in a sense 'liberated' from social class and forced to find new collective identities in the politics of race and gender. The emergence of new 'subjects of history' in the USA can only be understood as part of a far wider pattern running from Krushchev's de-stalinization to the third-world independence movements. In each instance, social resistance transcends traditional class-categories, or at least breaks with those institutions through which social classes have previously realized themselves. The argument is Jameson's: he notes that three events signalled 'the unleashing of the new social and political dynamic of the sixties' in the USA.[27] Mailer attends to each of them. The disappearance of the national Communist Party (CP) marked the closing of a classical conceptual scheme along with the groups that propounded it (witness Lovett's impasse). Castro's Cuban success (1959) proved that revolutions could work outside Leninist or Marxist models (witness the letter to Fidel Castro[28]). The assassination of Kennedy de-legitimized the state for many students, fostering the emergence of the New Left (witness Mailer's brief, disappointed and misguided belief that Kennedy's life as an existential Democrat might change the nature of the state. See particularly, 'A last open letter to John Fitzgerald Kennedy'[29]). Mailer's reaction to Cuba's revolution best catches his eagerness for possibilities without paradigms, within which (given a hero) movements might form. Castro is that hero, Mailer casts him as 'the ghost of Cortes . . . riding Zapatas' white horse'[30] down from a third-world mountain top into the streets of New York. The image is situated by the preface to the letter in which it occurs. The letter was written to be read at a press conference announcing the author's candidacy for Mayor of New York, but went undelivered because Mailer was in the cells for assaulting his wife. A supporter of third-world revolution prevents himself from entering the American democratic process by an act of criminal hipsterism – an act which his victim considers socially beneath him. Alger, existentialist and Marxist collude and collide in the event and in the letter, all three speaking at once with an offer to ghost-write a dialogue between third and first worlds, in which a proletarian and an aristocrat might mutually address the relationship between revolution and corporation.[31] The letter is of course 'open'.[32]

Jameson writes of the 'surplus consciousness' of a decade; Mailer inflicts, interrogates and suffers that consciousness. In 1957 it leads him,

via the publication of 'The white negro', to embarrass the liberal
Democrats at *Dissent* by re-writing the nascent Civil Rights Movement
as a terrorist charter for criminal consumption in Northern cities. Mailer
eyes the phoenix again in 1967 when he endorses a fund-raising appeal
for Students for a Democratic Society (SDS). Irving Howe remembers
that Mailer justified himself by insisting that the opinions of the SDS
were irrelevant: what mattered was their 'energy' and their position 'at
the forefront of history' during a time of 'upheaval'. He thought of it as
'a goad to the historical process'.[33] The upheaval is intense where history
is experienced as an undefined energy patterned by contradictions which
reach towards a family past. Existentialists who remember their 'class
apprenticeship' and have read 'political economy' will speak with
polyphonic tongues. The immediacy of the very objects to which they
give existential primacy prompts them to address the historical process in
its totality, even as it reminds them that particular objects, though
particular, are generally owned. My point is that 'surplus consciousness',
realized as sub-vocalization and semantic pluralism, makes Mailer
politically acute about the sixties; it does not make him comfortable with
himself or easy on us.

Dressing up as someone else can be a comfort; Marx notes:

> just when [men] appear to be engaged in the revolutionary transformation of
> themselves and their material surroundings, in the creation of something
> which does not yet exist, precisely in such epochs of revolutionary crisis they
> conjure up the spirits of the past to help them; they borrow their names,
> slogans and costumes so as to stage the new world-historical scene in this
> venerable disguise and borrowed language.[34]

So Luther got himself up as Paul, the French Revolution draped itself in
togas and Mailer comes on as Henry James. For all his marching, Mailer
is never far from the nineteenth-century drawing-room. More than
nocturnal forces are borrowed from Matthew Arnold; 'Dover beach'
implicitly invokes a silent or absent wife:

> Ah, Love, let us be true
> To one another![35]

Armies of the Night is dedicated 'To Beverly' Mailer, whose absence
shadows the entire novel. It is as if a ghostly separate sphere, properly
equipped with nurturing mother and nurtured offspring, haunts the
novelist. As a result, the family, with its central rites of property
dramatized through marriage, adultery and inheritance, provides a
stencil through which Mailer reads the politics of protest.

The American Left in the fifties is cast as a middle-class family, split by
'rifts' that are organized 'with all the scheming that goes into the writing
of a will' (p. 222). During the sixties political re-alliance occurs in the

form of adulteries: the 'virile' Old Left, free of its 'punch drunk' mother-in-law (the CP (p. 16)), 'invest[s] itself deep in the liberal purlieus of mass peace', the purlieus in question belonging to the 'not un-sexy' middle-class disguised as a 'wealthy heiress' (p. 223). 'Orchard' is offered as a synonym for 'purlieu' ('deodorized orchards' (p. 223)); a purlieu is a 'suburb', or, more traditionally, a tract of land on the border of a forest, hence 'outskirt', but the word can also refer to streets. The anatomical specificity of depth ('deep in') activates the etymology of 'purlieu', to suggest that the propertied parts of the middle-class female solicit a range of attentions; her real estate is scented, care of corporatism (the Pentagon was likened to 'the spout of a spray can' (p. 117)), but is fêted by suitors from forest ways and disreputable quarters (ghettos?). While "invest-ment" proceeds in the vaginal suburbs, the liberal children go off with the hippies (themselves 'middle-class runaways' (p. 104)) to consummate the New Left (p. 222). Pre-marital experience among the young does little to reduce parental worries about their bad language (p. 248); indeed, bourgeois parents are loath to let their children go to the Pentagon at all unless the walk is properly supervised (Dr Spock 'must be induced to join in' (p. 236)).

The family plot is not always so comic. Throughout book 1 a single inflexion struggles, if not for authority, at least for substantial recognition. The voice of the father is frequently heard lamenting, instructing, worrying and generally seeking the last word. We learn early that Mailer 'has six children of his own' (p. 11). Coercions and homilies follow on a fairly regular basis, ranging from drugs and dress through junior-league football to absentee parenting. The point would seem to be that despite, or perhaps because of, his 'odyssey . . . through three divorces and four wives' (p. 123), Mailer is an informed recruit to the leadership of what is essentially a child's crusade: at the Ambassador, attempting an oratorical breech-birth (p. 37), Mailer observes that his 'troops' are primarily 'mad middle-class children' (p. 34). Since the state has misappropriated the minds of the young through the 'fix' (p. 47), "poke", "probe" (p. 87) or 'whip' (p. 252) of television, an alternative authority must emerge. The march is headed by academics, ministers, writers and Dr Spock: the University, the Church, Literature and Baby Care have turned on the state and will no longer legitimize its processes. The question facing any father with a daughter in her freshman year (p. 5) and two young sons suffering from 'fragile . . . ego[s]' (p. 168) must be 'Who will now educate the bourgeois child, and to what?' The 'night', we are warned, is as long as capitalism is 'dark'.

One of Mailer's answers involves the return to family values: gone is the decade's potential for loose coalitions – it is a 'wise father' (p. 134) who gathers his extended family about him on weekends (p. 167). Such

patriarchs, when imprisoned, will miss their wives (p. 182), will recall
sons with 'painful . . . clarity' (p. 167), and at the imposition of a five-day
custodial sentence will suffer the feelings of a 'doomed *pater familias*' (p.
206). More striking than the length of Mailer's *curriculum vitae* for the
post of Good Father is a single omission – the father's phallus. Elsewhere
in his writing the paternal member casts a long shadow; here that
extension is virtually missing, or perhaps better, is significantly re-
designed and re-located.

Oedipus is absent from *Armies of the Night*. Indeed, offered the role of
father as rival to the son, Mailer turns away; half the 'kids' admitted to
the Occoquan prison on the second night 'expected him to serve as the
poor man's Papa'. But only through a 'real fight' could they test their
'admiration' (p. 200); and Mailer will not be drawn: 'visions of his wife
and family kept him on his bunk' (p. 200). Despite just a hint of Achilles
in his tent, Mailer has reneged on the role of phallic father: the man who
sinks his differences with Dr Spock (p. 99) is hardly likely to stand up for
Hemingway.

The patriarch, though de-oedipalized, remains possessive about the
body of the wife. The centre of the novel shifts accordingly from incest
(*Why Are We in Vietnam?*) to adultery. Mailer, claiming 'one
appropriated a culture with a wife' (p. 170), conflates the bodies of his
wives and presents them as a national monument called Beverly. The
appropriation is gargantuan in extent and detail (pp. 170–2). To
paraphrase: wife one brings 'Jewish genius' and a 'love for the oppressed'
from the urban North-east; wife two supplies dramatic culture laced
with 'Latin desperation', by implication her purlieu is Hispanic; the third
is English and satisfies an Anglophile instinct for 'manners and the mode
of social murder in well established places' (her territorial dowry is the
fashionable city, a movable feast); the fourth is Southern and has both
Nordic and Indian blood – her work for TV commercials ensures that
she contributes the ubiquitous sensuality of commodity to the marriage.
Beverly is 'an American girl'; the definite article would seem more
appropriate, given that 'sunlight advertise[s] her' (p. 194) and that she
stimulates 'sentiment[s]' involving 'healthy families and sunlight on
water' (p. 171). Promotional writing indicates a recognition that
candidates for the national body must possess a second skin.

The composite Mrs Mailer is a melting pot whose essence is Beverly:

> Mailer finally came to decide that his love for his wife while not at all equal or
> congruent to his love for America was damnably parallel . . . We will
> remember that Mailer had a complex mind of sorts. He would have considered
> it irretrievably heavy-handed to have made any direct correspondence
> between his feelings for his wife, and the change in his feelings towards
> America . . . but he would also have thought it cowardly to ignore the relation,

> and dishonest to assume that none of his wife's attractiveness (and unattractiveness) came from her presence so quintessentially American.
>
> (p. 171)

Denials of heavy-handedness prompt consideration of just what is being palmed. Mailer may feel damned by a parallel that he senses to be simplistic; nonetheless, that parallel persists, becoming an 'occult theme' about which a 'medley of whispers'[36] begin to add up to an adultery plot. If Mrs Mailer *is* the USA, and the USA *is* 'corporation land' (p. 117), who owns Mrs Mailer? The question implies that Mr Mailer's march is motivated by rivalry, or perhaps by suspicion of infidelity. At issue is the possession or re-possession of a wife. Accusations must remain veiled because the rival is present only in his absence. If a whisper is not to attenuate to a sigh, I had best excavate the intimations.

The separate sphere is arguably a space in which the fruits of the father's combative authority are realized in tranquillity. This father is positively 'neo-Victorian' (p. 24) in his desire to recover that space. Since he goes to considerable lengths to conflate the right wife and to put on appropriate costume, he is not a little troubled by the indifference of the children. Their failure to respond to repro-nuances in the furniture and to the vocal gold-standard implies that the drawing-room is already occupied by a second father, whose very lack of paternity claims, far from indicating lack of interest, may signal all-pervasive influence. My sub-plot résumé hardens conjugal anxiety into a divorce brief, but overstatement may be justified if it supplies a context for Mailer's comments on "the youth of today".[37] Witness his views on the young who break into the Pentagon only to sit down:

> The brain is washed deep, there are reflexes: white shirts, Star-Spangled Banner, saluting the flag. At home is corporation land's whip – the television set. Who would argue that there are no idea-sets of brave soldiers, courageous cops, great strength and brutal patriotic skill in the land of authority? Obvious remarks, but it is precisely the huge and much convinced unconscious part of oneself which a demonstrator has to move against when he charges.
>
> (pp. 252–3)

The verbal sleight of symmetry which moves 'set' from 'television' to 'idea' submits the juvenile unconscious too readily to the hegemonic influence of 'corporation land'. Mailer sounds like Baudrillard, assuring us that children commit catachresis with TV. If so, the unconscious will be post-Freudian. Fitzgerald followed Freud in discovering the oedipal father latent in the cumulative energy of key-words and images. Mailer seems content to find television under 'reflex' (a term short on the layers implied by 'condensation', 'displacement' and 'slip'). Presumably, 'white shirts' head the list of reflexes because the brain, 'washed deep' in television, is in its depths stain-free. Indeed, without an oedipal plot to secrete, the very notion of "depth" or "stain" grows redundant. Mailer came early to the fashionable territory of "the dead subject"; Jameson, addressing the corpse of 'the autonomous bourgeois monad or ego or individual', conducts a historical autopsy, concluding, 'that a once existing centred subject, in the period of classical capitalism and the nuclear family, has today, in the world of organizational bureaucracy, dissolved'.[38] Faced with the all-American child in front of the all-American TV, Mailer recognizes that the corporate father sits where the nuclear/oedipal father sat, and that the resulting children have 'reflexes' where they once had traumas, and that shallows lie in their depths. juvenile dissolution induces adult disillusion.

Yet elsewhere, faced with things both American and corporate, Mailer resists, insisting on libidinous depths. A hamburger has 'libido' because it 'taste[s] better if pictured [with] billboards and drive-in waitresses with tight silk pants and cowboy boots' (p. 172). The mind that tastes these pictures eats the air promise crammed with television signals that have been doctored. Appreciating that the USA's second skin comes sexually powdered, Mailer parodies the deodorized commodity aesthetic by adding gender and orifice to much that is not even animate. The key to official commodity fetishism is that it is clean: as Baudrillard notes, the fetish fascinates because it 'radically excludes in the name of . . . perfection . . . [becoming] a smooth body, without orifices, doubled and redoubled by a mirror'.[39] Being 'neo-Victorian', Mailer feels that sex is 'better off dirty than clean' (p. 24); readers of the anal penetration of Ruta by Rojak (*An American Dream*) will recognize hard-pornography as one of the author's middens: his reasoning would seem to be that dirt puts the genitalia back on the 'body without orifices'. To trace the logic: vagina, anus and phallus, as sites of blood, excrement and semen, restore temporal and biological processes to the body; they therefore wound desire's second and 'smooth' skin (that imaginary and textual emptiness in which phallic-props rub against ancillary objects marked "she"). I remain unpersuaded that this *is* the way back to the "whole body", since social and not biological process would seem the crucial access point for the recovery of body from "parts".

Despite the dubiety of Mailer's position, what *is* clear is that the television room, unlike the hamburger bar, is a site in which his ingenious libido fails him. Yet he acknowledges TV as a key to corporate authority. The metaphors used are significant: the 'set' is a 'whip' and elsewhere a 'fix', instruments whose phallic tenor is cruel but remote and fairly diminutive, perhaps because the ultimate source of the set's influence is in its 'embodiment' squat (p. 113). The corporate crux looks like the spout of spray can (p. 117) and is given to deodorizing the national body.

Cultural reasons for the de-oedipalization of corporatist authority are available: Fred Pfeil argues that during the forties and fifties suburbanization severed the nuclear family from networks of neighbourhood and kin (with their clear patterns of male dominance). As these cultures died, and a new and enlarged middle class emerged (the PMC), 'the attenuated family "unit" stayed home in its own private living room and watched T.V.'.[40] The socially backed authority of the father shrank accordingly, since not only did increased public schooling (equipped with television) extend the state's responsibility for socialization, but mothers (re-made as "experts" in home-care by the small screen) simultaneously entered the previously male sphere of the paid workplace in ever larger numbers. It follows that 'the Father [became] an increasingly diminished and abstract principle'.[41] The corporation, having replaced the father, can afford to be seminal without assuming a male identity.

Corporatism's phallic refusal is bad news for the would-be Victorian father. A memberless rival can perform neither as an adulterer nor as a replacement in the traditional family romance, whose structures Mailer is tacitly renovating as a mainstay to his own "self"-recovery. Without a threatening patriarch against whom to define his properly patriarchal tone the incumbent may lose heart. Indeed, when Mailer marches on the Pentagon to recover his wife and to redeem his children, he quite simply gets lost. Lengthy quotation is necessary in order to identify his disorientation:

> a great happiness came back into the day as if finally one stood under some mythical arch in the great vault of history, helicopters buzzing about, chop-chop, and the sense of America divided on this day now liberated some undiscovered patriotism in Mailer so that he felt a sharp searing love for his country in this moment and on this day, crossing some divide in his own mind wider than the Potomac, a love so lacerated he felt as if a marriage were being torn and children lost – never does one love so much as then, obviously then – and an odor of wood smoke, from where you knew not, was also in the air, a smoke of dignity and some calm heroism, not unlike the sense of freedom which also comes from when a marriage is burst . . . here, walking with Lowell and Macdonald, he felt as if he stepped through some crossing in the reaches of space between this moment, the French Revolution, and the Civil War, as if the ghosts of the Union Dead accompanied them now to the Bastille, he was not drunk at all, merely illumined by hunger, the sense of danger to the front, sense of danger to the rear – he was in fact in love with himself for having less fear than he had thought he might have . . . they were going to face the symbol, the embodiment, no, call it the true and high church of the military-industrial complex, the Pentagon, blind five-sided eye of a subtle oppression which had

come to America out of the very air of the century . . . yes, Mailer felt a
confirmation of the contests of his own life on this March to the eye of the
oppressor, greedy stingy dumb valve of the worst of the Wasp heart, chalice
and anus of corporation land, smug, enclosed, morally blind Pentagon,
destroying the future of its own nation with each day it augmented in strength,
and the Novelist induced on the consequence some dim unawakened
knowledge of the mysteries of America buried in these liberties to dissent –
What a mysterious country it was. The older he became, the more interesting
he found her. Awful deadening programmatic inhuman dowager of a nation,
corporation, and press – tender mysterious bitch whom no one would ever
know, not even her future unfeeling Communist doctors if she died of the
disease of her dowager, deadly pompous dowager who had trapped the sweet
bitch.   (pp. 113–14)

What is odd here is not the hyperbole; after all, marching South under
'the great vault of history', half a mile from Virginia, and accompanied
by the author of 'For the Union dead', any author might be forgiven
precedents. No, in this context, what is eccentric is his bracketing of
marital struggle with the French Revolution and the Civil War. While it
may be allowed that the Bastille fell to forces lead by Marianne, whose
torso has entered revolutionary iconography, the presence of the generic
Mrs Mailer remains difficult to place. Her husband's 'searing love for his
country' is premised on a 'division' which elides marriage and nation: as
he crosses the Potomac at the head of a nineteenth-century force (the
Union dead) to engage in an amalgam of nineteenth- and eighteenth-
century conflicts, he scents that nadir of nostalgia for a pre-industrial and
post-marital time, 'wood smoke'; the experience involves both 'great
happiness' and lacerating division. The 'divide in his own mind' has a
double characteristic, being at once temporal and marital. To walk from
1967 to 1861 and back to 1789 is to experience divorce on a grand scale
('he felt as if a marriage were being torn and children lost'). The gain is a
'sense of freedom' dependent upon domestic isolation: the 'burst'
marriage allows him to be 'in love with himself'. *Sans* wife, *sans*
children, he is a soldier from utterly the wrong century marching against
'the military–industrial complex'. To achieve a clean and inappropriate
revolutionary costume, he has sacrificed what he went to fight for, the
body of the USA realized through the bodies of his wives and children.
The contradiction stems from Mailer's recognition that he, his wives and
children – like the PMC to which they are inescapably allied – are snug in
the 'anus of corporation land'. D.J., oedipal habits aside, is the
representative child of Fordist times. Mailer, like Carraway before him,
must 'beat [his] boats against the current' if 'for a transitory and
enchanted moment' he is to find a 'continent . . . commensurate to his
capacity for wonder',[42] a continent that is without marriages. Unlike

Carraway, he understands that his own 'desire' is inappropriate: the body of *his* USA is a wife, not a mother, and comes equipped with a second skin; the outer skin of a 'dowager' – turned iron-maiden – just possibly contains trapped within it the inner skin of a 'tender mysterious bitch'. Since the book is dedicated to a synonym for the 'American girl', one might believe that Mailer, setting his divorces behind him, will yet redeem her innocent skin in the separate sphere. However, Beverly is no Marianne; her links are to the Fordist future: two brothers fight in Vietnam, a step-father organizes back-up troops for the Pentagon (p. 167), and her own advertising images decorate the dowager.

Mailer too has made his contribution; he spends much of the march being filmed by a BBC documentary crew, apt practice for one who lives in the 'sarcophagus of [a public] image' to which he claims marriage (p. 5). The 'dowager' is copious. However, Mailer's commercial "self" is consistently interrupted by an ur-Mailer. To crib from *Tender is the Night*: it is as if the Reverend Diver rather than Devereux Warren has refused to die. Released from prison into the microphones of the media, and 'required to deliver the best of himself' (p. 213), Mailer all but quotes Matthew Arnold. Just as 'Dover beach' involves a silent and perhaps absent wife ('Come to the window, sweet is the night-air!'), so he, on breathing the 'sweet air' of freedom invokes the 'shining conception of his wife' (p. 212). 'Deliver' and 'conception' signal the seminal nature of the family plot. The 'best' that Mailer has to offer is the image of Beverly as a God-fearing, wifely vessel; his essence (sons) is preserved in her sphere. The 'mother of his two – would they be mighty? – boys' (p. 213) ensures his continuity, and incidentally the continuity of the literary genre he is trying to re-conceive. The interpolated question as to the might of Mailer's inheritors remains no more than a hesitation: at this stage the patriarch is in good voice, perhaps because of the proximity of his precedents; whispering Matthew Arnold is latent in his public announcement. It is apt that an eminent Victorian (albeit disguised) should officiate at a ceremony that closes book 1 on a celebration marking the "delivery" of the 'wise father' as minister to the nation. Mailer's prayer is traceably neo-Arnoldian: both men are prompted to essay the failure of faith while fixed in trans-oceanic reverie:

> The sea of faith
> Was once, too, at the full, and round earth's shore
> Lay like the folds of a bright girdle furl'd.
> But now I only hear
> Its melancholy, long, withdrawing roar,
> Retreating, to the breath
> Of the night-wind, down the vast edges drear
> And naked shingles of the world. ('Dover beach')[43]

Or, as Mailer puts it:

> 'You see, dear fellow Americans, it is Sunday, and we are burning the body
> and blood of Christ in Vietnam. Yes we are burning him there, and as we do,
> we destroy the foundation of this Republic, which is love and trust in Christ.'
> He was silent.   (p. 214)

Arnold enters Mailer via Lowell: any source hunt would have to include
the closing verses of 'Waking early Sunday morning':

> Only man thinning out his kind
> sounds through the Sabbath noon, the blind
> swipe of the pruner and his knife
> busy about the tree of life . . .
>
> Pity the planet, all joy gone
> from this sweet volcanic cone;
> peace to our children when they fall
> in small war on the heels of small
> war – until the end of time
> to police the earth, a ghost
> orbiting forever lost
> in our monotonous sublime.[44]

However, the best-laid combinations fail. Lowell, Boston 'patrician',
translator of verses on imperial decline, and sometime 'personification of
ivy climbing a column', (p. 44) ventriloquized through Arnold's 'eternal
note of sadness', with its penchant for 'Wandering between two worlds,
one dead/The other powerless to be born',[45] cannot sustain Mailer's
tonal affectation of the weary but still willing patriarch. 'He was silent.
Wow', the exhalation sits ill with archaism. Having turned the vocal
trick, Mailer immediately recants; we are told that the keeper of his
felicities is less than pleased to see him:

> Mailer met his wife at D.J. Clarke's for dinner, but their luck was poor: an old
> girlfriend of the novelist passed by, tapped him possessively on the hair, and so
> he spent the evening in a muted quarrel with his wife, the actress Beverly
> Bentley.   (p. 214)

'Mailer' and 'Bentley' are at odds: Mailer's first and only use of his wife's
maiden-name suggests that her capacity as a vessel is being re-assessed; a
body capacious enough to contain first the USA and then the novelist's
'best', if not dispossessed, is re-addressed as a professional artificer who
might make her own way outside the separate sphere. The family plot is
in danger of aborting on "delivery".

"Plot" is probably the wrong word. I have been tracing a 'potential
story' or 'virtual significance' that could be considered as a pattern of
'pre-understanding' through which experience is 'figured'. Every story

told is antedated by an '(as yet) untold story', since action itself (the pre-history of the story) is experienced as tending to have a story to tell, insofar as the imminent cultural norms, within which it happens, require that it takes on 'latent readability'. The language derives from Ricoeur, who offers two common situations as evidence for the existence of prefiguring plots,[46] otherwise known as the text in the texture. During psychoanalytic sessions the analyst draws from the analysand various bits and pieces having the form of lived stories; the fragments are re-plotted as a case history. Over the period of the analysis, untold and repressed stories are moved towards a full narrative, through which the analysand may reconstitute a personal identity. The 'inchoate story', set within a symbolic framework (perhaps the 'Oedipal dragnet'), realizes itself as an actual story insofar as the analysand (first teller of the '(as yet) untold story') regains contact with the conventions, institutions and beliefs which make up his or her culture.

Ricoeur's second situation involves a judge attempting to understand a character and a course of action by unravelling the tangled plots in which the character is ensnared:

> The accent here is on 'being entangled' . . . The entanglement seems more like the 'prehistory' of the told story . . . and gives it a 'background'. This background is made up of the 'living imbrication' of every lived story with every other such story. Told stories therefore have to 'emerge' . . . from this background. With this emergence also emerges the implied subject. We may say thus, 'the story stands for the person' . . . Telling, following, understanding stories is simply the 'continuation' of these untold stories.[47]

Feeling like neither an analyst nor a judge, I have isolated an untold story whose consistency raises it above several of the sub-articulations and dialogic conflicts that traduce the novel. Perhaps my role has been that of a lip reader, amplifying one of Mailer's most regular doubles as it materializes on his inner ear and solidifies as a sub-vocalization. The double in question, patriarch to a de-oedipalizing family, spends much time entangled in a legal background from which, crucially at the end of book I, emerges a second and supportive "implied person". The father is joined by the legal subject. Mailer ministers to the press immediately after he has stood before an altogether higher court of appeal.

In order to understand how one particular Mailer rises from the 'tangle of plots' voiced in Commissioner Scaife's tribunal, it is necessary to go back to the moment of arrest. A reporter was present:

> 'Why were you arrested Mr. Mailer?' . . .
> 'I was arrested for transgressing a police line' . . .
> 'I am guilty', Mailer went on. 'It was done as an act of protest to the war in Vietnam.'

'Are you hurt in any way?' asked the reporter.
'No. The arrest was correct.'   (pp. 138–9)

Mailer's sister cannot hear her brother in the word 'transgress', and will later insist that he was misquoted (p. 137). His voice is unrecognizable because it is full of law. Indeed, it is debatable whether the crime or the procedural niceties of apprehension are responsible for his 'feel[ing] important in a new way . . . as if this picayune arrest had been his Rubicon' (p. 138). Maturation descends: the 'real Norman Mailer' seems 'ready to stand up', but on all the wrong terms. He is solid ('[he] felt as if he were a solid embodiment of bone, muscle, flesh and vested substance'); he is re-integrated ('he . . . felt as if he were finally one age, not seven'); he is monologic, having a singularly proprietorial attitude to his own voice (the reporter is rebuked for misquotation, as a prelude to a self-rebuke, issued for inaccuracy, 'it was a *Military* Police line he had crossed' (p. 138; italics in source)). Mailer, at last, is *one* man, because, presumably, he is a guilty party who has been taken to law.

The double need for guilt and due legal process might pass as a momentary aberration were it not repeated before the commissioner. "Guilt" is not at issue in Scaife's court; unofficial negotiations between the movement's lawyers and the administration's representatives have resulted in a contract: in return for a waiver on rights to jury trial, all prisoners will plead *Nolo Contendere* and accept a US commissioner's verdict involving a universal five-day suspended sentence. Mailer's wish to plead guilty violates this 'tacit agreement' (p. 204). However, much more is involved, since *Nolo Contendere* is simply the last in a long line of contracts through which the Mobilization Committee and the state's agencies have turned revolt into civil disobedience, and have further constrained that disobedience by limiting it to particular times and sites. Book II details 'the pattern of meetings' (p. 249) through which protest is legalized so that the army of the night may occupy the enemy heartland on a 'two-day permit' (p. 281). The purpose of 'adjudication' is to maximize the 'common ground' between forces having 'incompatible ends' (p. 239); the rise of Boulwarism during the early sixties proves that contracts have been forged from less.[48] As with the labour–capital conflict, so with conflicts between citizen and state, legalization and bureaucratization transform collective activity into 'a galaxy of individual contracts' (Mike Davis). Tough bargaining ensures that the interests of demonstrators and the interests of that against which they demonstrate are co-ordinated, while a network of 'permits', 'regulations' and 'agreements' recompose a mass movement as a gathering of individual citizens having individual rights and obligations. Since contract implies that the contractors speak the same language, conflict is muted and discord is re-voiced as consensus.

Nolo Contendere is an exact summation of what the state wants from citizens whose compliance is likely because the state is asking for nothing new: under full Fordism the USA's citizens are already passively entangled in a background of imbricated contractual stories (of which the workplace–capital accord and the international accord are simply two). The contractual plot sends them out into the world as persons pleading *Nolo Contendere*, insofar as consensus rather than contention governs their sense of an ending, even when the story stops at the Pentagon. A plea of guilty won't do, because guilt is not something one feels over an error; as a plea out of all proportion to the offence, 'guilty' re-establishes the possibility of dimensions commensurate with political protest, whereas the powers-that-be would prefer to establish a contract violation.

By pleading guilty Mailer appears to bring the entire weight of a contractual culture to bear on his case: the underpinning and threefold bargain of corporatism (with its citizens, its labour and its world) leans on him – but tacitly. Triggered by the word 'guilty', Commissioner Scaife's court echoes with 'whisper', 'mutter' (p. 204), and 'murmur' (p. 209): ellipsis and exhalation multiply and brim with 'unspoken dialogue' (p. 209) as de Grazia reads Mailer an equally 'unspoken exposition' on the workings of the law (pp. 203–4). 'Without saying a definite word' the lawyer hints at chambers behind chambers and courts behind courts; 'a subtle clearing of the throat' suggests 'massive legal operations'; 'a nod of the head' implies "word passed down from high office"; 'a light in the eye' intimates covert actions by agents of the state; and 'hesitation' infers violence against political prisoners. Mailer changes his plea, complying with the state's wish to present dissent as assent (he notes in book II that 'even a revolution can be negotiated' (p. 239)).

In effect, Mailer reverts to the consensual/contractual deep-plot of corporate liberalism. As his words pass through that pre-history they stabilize, and in turn stabilize the person whom they push forward into the world. The untold story subverts Mailer's semantic self-dispersal by offering him plot typologies which, in turn, derive from a class desire. Mailer wants to go home to bourgeois appearances (the separate sphere); before doing so he will address the nation (the word of the Father as authoritative word) in a single voice that will do justice to all (the public sphere). Habermas and Bell may theorize consensual speech, but Commissioner Scaife practises it. Mailer finds in his judge a comfortable double, whose voice, though 'bottomless' (p. 205), is 'neutral as a spirit level' (p. 206) – vocal capacity and equanimity, it seems, are not mutually exclusive. Eye contact establishes the secret sharers as 'equals'

(p. 206), though perhaps Mailer's need to discover vocal authority overcomes his focal length when he awards the commissioner a regimental tie 'almost indistinguishable from his own' (p. 205). A ringer for 'a well-made son of Virginia gentry' (p. 209) is hardly likely to have graced a Texan infantry regiment.

Mailer's proclivities are all the more surprising given that his official spokesman – Hirschkop, 'a tough Jew' (p. 209) – is more obviously symbiotic. Hirschkop's credentials as alternative double extend to his obtaining bail for H. Rap Brown in circumstances that 'precisely parallel Mailer's' (p. 210). Since Mailer's Black Power idiom at the Ambassador struck Macdonald as 'white H. Rap Brown' (p. 64), Hirschkop would seem the ideal advocate. Yet at the end of the case, 'prompted by some shade in the late afternoon air of lost Civil War protocols in Virginia' (p. 211), it is to Scaife that Mailer turns: '"Some day in quieter times I hope we have the opportunity to meet and discuss some of these matters." "Yes, Mr Mailer", said Scaife, "so do I."' (p. 211). It was a near thing: 'shade', in a context that contains Civil War and H. Rap Brown, retains a black inflexion, but Mailer suppresses his sub-vocal habits – the 'shade' is kept down. Perhaps it is truer to say that for one sub-vocalization he substitutes another: having listened to a Jew and a Virginian celebrate procedural legalism through judicial conflict, and having admired his own consequent translation into a non-contentious legal subject, he alludes to a discursive space in which fundamentally rational men may yet discuss the future of civic duty. Mailer, in part un-Mailered, discovers himself as an agent for the redemption of consensus through speech: he is doing Habermas.

Vocally re-designed, he moves from the Court to join with the Church in speaking to the Nation about the Family in a chapter called 'The communication of Christ'. The semantic conversion appears positively Pauline; the Reverend Boyle 'looked pleased'; Leiterman 'looked ecstatic' (p. 214), he has 'the end to [his] movie', but we have only the virtual end to book 1. Almost as an afterword to a book entitled 'History as a novel', Mailer appends a single-page chapter, 'Skins and hides'. The title is gnomic, but may allude to the author's fondness for stalking-horses: he notes that on TV, discussing his contract to write an account of the march, 'he was half as militant . . . as H. Rap Brown', whereas in prison 'he had been half as conservative as Russell Kirk' (p. 215). It appears that 'skins' can be costumes and costumes can be 'hides', which are thick skins, particularly if one is writing 'history in the costume of a novel' (p. 215). (Mailer has not given up on Proteus or puns.) The phrase refers only to book 1, which 'insisted on becoming a history of himself over four days and therefore was' a costume novel, or, as he later puts it, 'history in the guise or dress or manifest of a novel' (p.

255). Conflated, Mailer's titular phrasings add up to a new genre 'History as a novel in the costume of the novel as history'. Translation finds trickery alongside innovation. To write history in the form of a novel, and to do so from within the acknowledged tradition of the nineteenth-century fiction of bourgeois manners, is to write a family romance. Tony Tanner's hyperbole serves my polemical purposes:

> Marriage . . . is a meaning by which society attempts to bring into harmonious alignment patterns of passion and patterns of property; in bourgeois society it is not only a matter of putting God where your treasure is (as Ruskin accused his age of doing) but also of putting your libido, loyalty and all other possessions and products, including children, there as well. For bourgeois society marriage is the all-subsuming, all-organizing, all-containing contract. It is the structure that maintains the Structure, or System . . . The bourgeois novelist has no choice but to engage the subject of marriage in one way or another . . . What he discovers, I will suggest, is that the bourgeois novel is coeval and coterminous with the power concentrated in the central structure of marriage.[49]

Tanner might be glossing book I, with its under-articulations and semantic collisions quashed by the configuration of the 'wise father'. However, take the same book and open it out; re-articulate it, stressing the pattern of its dispersed and conflicting sub-vocalizations; hear in the word of the Father 'the richly varied opposition to another's word',[50] and an entirely different book results. Effectively, book I, 'History as a novel', read from the bottom up rather than the top down – that is to say, inverted – becomes 'The novel as history'. Tracing Mailer's inflexions to their political sources can be as tricky as stabilizing his titles, since self-polemicized terms are liable to leave some betrayals half-heard. Alternatively, the habit of eavesdropping on oneself can yield revelations, in disguise. For example, read through his own account of Fitzgerald, the prayer on release from the Occoquan jail is a 'superb' and tactical verbal 'costume'; having 'turned upon the suppositions of [his] class', by transgressing against one of the central institutions of liberal corporatism, he invokes another – the Family – so that by looking at himself with the eyes of the nineteenth century he may become a responsible citizen. Hysteria still 'live[s] at the centre', but it is masked.

III

Having masked at the close of book I, Mailer unmasks at the close of book II to reveal a specific kind of hysteria – hysterical pregnancy on a national scale. Such swellings are endemic to a culture of consumption. If 'the phallus has to come to the supermarket' and 'the vagina leaves . . . her spiral in every third or fourth commercial',[51] impregnation is a matter of time, and those who walk in the ways of Safeways are not so, since what they consume may consume them, converting purchasers (gender irrelevant) into mothers of considerable invention, surrogates to inanimate progeny. The fantasy has its illuminations, allowing an exploration of the implications of the commodity aesthetic as it overwrites 'use' with 'promise', and thereby sexualizes most surfaces. Surfaces so induced will swell; Haug argues that as commodities become emptier in terms of 'use' and fuller in terms of 'promise', they exist as a solicitous 'space' — a 'vacancy' of 'electrifying emptiness' which, if successful, is filled with 'inner movies' inscribing 'contours of acts' and 'inklings of identity' on the longings of those who pay the price.[52] Plainly, punters will only populate these imaginary spaces in their own desires with real persons and real practices should their imaginary world prove total. Since one of the functions of "individualism" is to promote singular achievement while delivering isolated ineffectuality, the capacity of the space to be full should not be under-rated.

As early as 1959, back from the supermarket, Mailer notes a growing desire 'to put one's dream of love into the deadness of an object'. 'The heart . . . lives in the wish to move away from the life outside oneself, grow God-like in the vault of the brain, and then move to give . . . the gift of life to what does not have life.'[53] This particular heart's desire is judged 'insane', 'psychotic', 'schizophrenic' and common; just how common being caught in Mailer's account of a car as an object pregnant with inner movies of impregnation:

> A car is sold not because it will help one to get a girl, but because it already is a girl. The leather of its seats is worked to a near skin, the color is lipstick-pink, or a blonde's pale-green, the tail-lights are cloacal, the rear is split like the cheeks of a drum majorette.[54]

It might be objected that 'lip', 'tail', 'rear' and 'cloacal' indicate that the thrust of the imagery is to oral or anal penetration, and that, consequently, impregnation is not the point; my claim is only that under full Fordism, and for Mailer, things are promiscuous voids whose generic image-*in-extremis* is that of an inexplicable tumescence. In order to clean up my act, it might be helpful to allude to an earlier argument about Hemingway, for whom metaphoricity is also a constant, albeit an unseen one. Speaking impressionistically, his objects (under partial Fordism) are lean rather than swollen. Nonetheless, with every turn of phrase Hemingway would have them become their own more perfect form; in effect, they are metaphors for themselves reproduced as abstract value. Not wishing to rehearse the case, I would simply indicate that by the twenties tumescent surfaces are part of the landscape, because the USA's landscape is increasingly read for its economic immanences. Since full Fordism would read every surface from the viewpoint of exchange, its environment is ideal for hysterical inflations.

Armies of the Night closes with the discovery that the USA is about to give birth. Retrospectively, the knowledge comes as no surprise, once it is recognized that the second half of the novel is designed to chart the history of alternative pregnancies. Book I, part IV has eleven chapters, and starts on a climax to which I shall return. Book II also has eleven chapters: that some sort of homologue is intended grows clearer as schematic nuances deepen. A parallel structure details parallel births. Book I, part IV, chapter I – Mailer is arrested and taken into the belly of the state. Erection prefaces ingestion:

> One of the oldest devices of the novelist – some would call it a vice – is to bring his narrative (after many an excursion) to a pitch of excitement where the reader no matter how cultivated is reduced to a beast who can pant no faster than to ask, 'And then what? Then what happens?' At which point the novelist, consummate cruel lover, introduces a digression, aware that delay at this point helps to deepen the addiction of his audience.
> This, of course, was Victorian practice.   (p. 133)

The use of a 'Victorian practice' on a twentieth-century reader is, we are told, tantamount to 'employing a device' (p. 133): the phrasing plays with connotations of foreplay; remembering the penchant for 'dirty' sex, and the earlier anally couched threat against the Pentagon, reader arousal in this instance may be mere flirtation, prelude to orgasm elsewhere. The coupling is a matter of latencies; Mailer is eventually taken to the 'rear' of the Pentagon (p. 146); the Pentagon is a 'sphincter'; the arm of the arresting marshal 'trembled' in what might be 'an onrush . . . of "unruly latent homosexuality"' (p. 137). Innuendo is drawn towards sub-plot by the nine-chapter "gestation" which details the author's enclosure. Like Carraway's Gatsby, it would seem that Mailer springs from the 'Platonic conception of himself',[55] but only after doing time in the state's belly.

That the 'anus' of 'corporation land' might be the route to its womb should surprise no one. The de-oedipalization of the corporate Father involves the failure of his phallus: compensation takes the form of an erogenized anus. Readers of *Why Are We in Vietnam?* will recognize that the orifice most associated with substantial flows is necessarily sexualized. Economic surgery achieves cosmetic heights when it enables the corporate body (male) to conceive and carry a child. Yet all that Mailer has done in his revision of the body politic is to push the nation's commodity aesthetic to its logical, if extreme, conclusion – auto-eroticism as competent androgyny. Ever innovative in matters of self-generation, the logician is on hand to lend a hand at his own birth: the title of chapter 9, 'Mailer, De Grazia, Hirschkop, and Scaife', lists the obstetricians who induce Mailer to give birth to himself as a single-voiced bourgeois subject.

The first birth-chart is contradicted by a second, noting an altogether more elusive pregnancy, indeed one that can only be made out by working back from the onset of labour. Book II, chapter 11, 'The metaphor delivered' alludes to the first chapter of its book, 'A novel metaphor', whose initial statement has 'The Novelist . . . passing his baton to the Historian [with] a happy smile' (p. 219). The Historian is a man up a tower, grinding a lens and using a telescope to spy out the land: within the linked purviews of pregnancy and Beverly, he is well equipped as an impregnator of the body of the USA. But the 'happy smile' of phallic fancy is insubstantial ground from which to explain a "delivery" that happens in the eleventh rather than the ninth chapter. Chapter 9 does, however, feature an expulsion – that of the last occupiers of the Pentagon. Since the Pentagon has already proved to be the orifice through which Mailer gained access to the corporate womb, readers with an eye to homology will recognize that a discharge repeatedly described as a 'rite of passage' is some sort of birth:

> one has voyaged through a channel of shipwreck and temptation, and some of the vices carried from another nether world into life itself (on the day of one's birth) may have departed, or fled, or quit; some part of the man has been born again, and is better.   (p. 281)

Yet all is not well; a chapter entitled 'The aesthetic forged' can be unmade by the second meaning of 'forged' as it implies that *a* birth is not *the* birth. To reach its authentic conclusion, the passage must end in prison, 'probably . . . in Occoquan and the jail in Washington D.C.' (p. 286). One thousand arrests produced six hundred charges of which two were taken to to trial, where both resulted in acquittal; however, several groups of prisoners remained in jail, refusing to accept the terms of their suspended sentences. Held over in the body of the state, these prisoners constitute the collective subject whose birth is immanent at the novel's close. The end of book II is difficult on several counts, but some light is cast by reading it through its structural analogue. Book I closes with release, birth, prayer and a re-conception (in 'Skins and hides', Mailer re-conceives 'Mailer' as a nineteenth-century 'character', in whose 'skin' he will 'hide', prior to delivery by contractual agreement with a publisher). Book II closes with a 'false labour' (p. 288), entry into labour proper, a prayer and a disputed conception. Whereas the "child" who emerges from book I is a citizen, a father and a commodity, his analogue in book II has no name.

Before pursuing the question of paternity, it might be wise to consider the plight of the mother:

> Brood on that country who expresses our will. She is America, once a beauty
> of magnificence unparalleled, now a beauty with a leprous skin. She is heavy
> with child – no one knows if legitimate – and languishes in a dungeon whose
> walls are never seen. Now the first contractions of her fearsome labor begin – it
> will go on: no doctor exists to tell the hour. It is only known that false labor is
> not likely on her now, no, she will probably give birth, and to what? – the most
> fearsome totalitarianism the world has ever known? or can she, poor giant,
> tormented lovely girl, deliver a babe of a new world brave and tender, artful
> and wild? Rush to the locks. God writhes in his bonds. Rush to the locks.
> Deliver us from our curse. For we must end on the road to that mystery where
> courage, death, and the dream of love give promise of sleep.   (p. 288)

The prognostication is apocalyptic and consequently a tissue of riddles:
'Name the lock that holds good for God'; 'When doctors can't tell the
time, who can?'; 'What is the dungeon whose walls are never seen?' The
answers are available, if formulaic. The name of the lock is Paradise,
securing the USA as a paradisal space, apt site for a re-run of the War in
Heaven (circa 1640–1967). Just as Carraway envisaged a 'fresh, green
breast of the new world'[56] flowering before Dutch Puritans, so Mailer
recalls the 'unnamed saints' (p. 288) who in the seventeenth century held
America to be an expression of God's will. God still willing, the body of
the nation may yet be divinely pregnant. The birth is problematic
because the early saints have been joined by nineteenth-century 'military
heroes' (p. 288), and the paradisal plot has been secularized as Manifest
Destiny[57] – a story that updates the celestial city for the 1840s and runs it
through the Open Door policy straight to the portals of the Pentagon.
The child's identity will be known only with the "unlocking" of the
nation's birth canal. On hand at the locks will be saints and military
personnel, closely attended by Mailer's readers: prompt in that they,
unlike the doctors, have been supplied with the necessary charts. The
dungeon without walls is the body according to the commodity
aesthetic, whose walls are invisible because they are the skin within
which the consumer lives. The temporal distinction between 'once a
beauty . . . now . . . with leprous skin' suggests that consumerism, by
progressively re-casting the woman as fetish (circa 1880–1967), has
imprisoned her in her own body. Since she (the USA) is also a mother-
to-be, her body further imprisons its embryo (the national future).

Readers may wonder just how many rabbits one hat can hold.
Puritan, Imperialist, Fordist – each quasi-allegorical figure rises from a
multilayered prose to indicate another plot: those plots must be
generically tagged, since they give rise to persons who may have
fathered the Future, or at least be prepared to claim paternity. Since 1967
is for Mailer 'the Historian' a moment of historical crisis (a crisis that
extends through Fordism to its liberal plots), his writing is necessarily

diversely stranded and at the last impacted. Where for Mailer, 'the Novelist' and author of book I, history proved plottable within the configuration of the bourgeois family, for Mailer 'the Historian' and author of book II, the question of configurative authority within history, once posed, proves intractable. Book I asks, 'Who did it?' and finally answers ' "Mailer . . . the character" did', as a representative of the liberal bourgeoisie. Book II asks again, but only to cite multiple insemination on the basis of which paternity has to be disputed. Nonetheless, inseminators are nominated and, upon occasion, their acts are located. Certain candidates are self-evident favourites – Mailer (as proposed by book I) and corporatism (which overcomes its anatomy to have conspicuous dealings with the national body).

Book II adds a double entry from below: both entrants are outsiders, though the first has clear affiliations to the state. Chapters 7 and 8 detail The Battle of the Wedge and its causes: 'the wedge' is a group of soldiers who drive into and divide the mass of protestors gathered on the steps of the Pentagon. The description is anatomically and socially precise: wedge (working-class phallus) splits the feminized body of the generic bourgeois child. I shall do no more than sketch how Mailer achieves his rapacious incarnation of social conflict. The wedge rises from an earlier defeat: on first reaching the Pentagon steps and facing a working-class army, 'the sons of the urban middle class' (p. 258) feel empowered by the seeming inertia of their enemy. Mailer is explicit: the middle-class army of the night steals the 'balls' and 'meat' of the state's Southern working-class troops (p. 259). Semen is metaphorically spread all over the place. For example, the burning of draft cards on the steps is sexualized (p. 270): 'a flutter of anxiety' is followed by 'a release of fire', which prompts the burner to 'look for a girl to kiss in reward'. This 'glut of elation' from the 'stomach' focusses a network of references to "seed" and "light". Rubin and the New Left seek, on the same steps, to 'put a radiance in the seed of their oncoming night' (p. 267): one of their 'visionary' means is marijuana; pot is smoked, turning the dark Mall into 'a field of fires' (p. 270). Radiances elide: draft card, pot and seed illuminate the environs so that 'In the gathering dark it looked like a dusting of fireflies over the great shrub of the Mall' (p. 262).

'It', in this instance, refers to 'the light of the burning card[s]'; however, given that 'burning' is several, the dust of fireflies spells out phallic defeat, if viewed from 'the dark bulk of the Pentagon' (p. 268). The wedge, sexually taunted (p. 271), counter-attacks; it is stressed that 'the marshals aimed particularly at women' (p. 262), and that with the onset of battle the first victims are 'the girls in the front line' (p. 272). The assault is littered with sexual accessories: 'bull horns', 'clubs', 'a spill in the dark', 'Jew female stew'. Perhaps one incident will serve to demonstrate that for Mailer the wedge exists to 'drive something into the flesh' (p. 276). He quotes Harvey Mayes's account of a single beating (mine is an edited version):

> One soldier spilled the water from his canteen on the ground in order to add to the discomfort of the female demonstrator at his feet . . . The girl tried to move back . . . At least four times that soldier hit her with all his force, then as she lay covering her head with her arms, thrust his club swordlike between her hands into her face . . . She twisted her body so we could see her face. But there was no face there: all we saw were some raw skin and blood. We couldn't see even if she was crying – her eyes had filled with the blood pouring down her head. She vomited, and that too was blood. Then they rushed her away.   (p. 276)

In context, the spillage of water and blood, accompanying the thrusting of a club into a barely protected face, is sexualized, converting the mouth and its emission into a flooded vaginal aperture. The only question is whether the assault is an act of rape or an appalling birth-sequence. We are told (within a page) that the wedge allowed the working class to 'pluck all the stolen balls back' (p. 277). However, in the larger structural context of gestation, the assault taking place in chapter 8 could be read as an induction of premature labour, during which the child of the middle class is expelled from the Pentagon's entry. Denied full 'rite of passage' and violently chastised, that child may yet become an apt member of the PMC. In which case, penetration is obstetric as much as phallic. Whatever the preferred reading, and both are invited, the body of the middle-class protestor is appropriated for the state by the repressive apparatus of the state (the working class).

In *The Naked and the Dead*, Cummings effectively murdered his insubordinate liberal body-servant, and in so doing elevated the working class (Croft). Croft, it will be remembered, lead the assault on Anaka which resulted in the release of hornets. If Anaka is to be taken as Cummings's member, then the general is serviced. Between 1948 and 1967 it would seem that neither the problem nor the plot has much changed: with the nascent liberal impulse dead and the working class bound to the state, what, apart from corporatism, can form the national future? In answer, book II ghosts a second, quasi-seminal entry undertaken by those protestors retained within (rather than expelled from) the body of the state. The plight of the Quaker contingent is exemplary: refusing to eat or drink, they are fed intravenously, stripped naked and the males among them are 'thrown in the Hole' – 'cells so small that not all could lie down at once to sleep' (p. 287):

> Here was the last of the rite of passage, 'the chinook salmon . . . nosing up the impossible stone', here was the thin source of the stream – these naked Quakers on the cold floor of a dark isolation cell in D.C. jail, wandering down the hours

in the fever of dehydration, the cells of the brain contracting to the crystals of their thought, essence of one thought so close to the essence of another – all separations of water gone – that madness is near, madness can now be no more than the acceleration of the thought.

Did they pray, these Quakers, for forgiveness of the nation?   (p. 287)

The Quakers elide the Puritan 'saints' and the exhausted salmon of Lowell's much quoted 'Waking early Sunday morning'. As a result, two forms of archaism meet redemptively within them, one paradisal and one a 'green breast'. Just as the salmon 'beat on . . . against the current',[58] 'alive enough to spawn and die',[59] and the 'unparalleled . . . beauty' of the USA fades, so these prisoners, 'naked' and lying quite literally in a 'hole' on the body of the USA, are a 'thin source', becoming thinner. Perhaps only the analogic prayer – albeit reduced to a hypothesis – signals their seminal claim to paternity and to a collective voice:

> The prayers are as Catholic as they are Quaker, and no one will know if they were ever made . . . [but] who is to say they are not saints? And who is to say that the sins of America were not by their witness a tithe remitted? (p. 287)

Whether the Quakers themselves are inseminators, or whether they are an essence deposited by the army of the night as it broke into the Pentagon, is a nice question – too nice, in that at the last the Quakers are an irrelevance. Themselves a displacement of the political into the spiritual, they are re-cast as an ecumenical body capable of paternity, dressed as Puritans and set at the 'locks' to dispute the claims of the 'military heroes'. Mailer's footwork is adroit but unpersuasive. Attempting to name the future, he can do so only from a site in the past whose resistance to the incipient forms of that future has long since failed. Seeking to write 'a collective novel' (p. 216) that will protest the crime of Bloody Fordism, he discovers no group from within which to articulate that protest. As a result, his voice fails him. He has spent the entire novel listening to himself, sifting his speech for evidence of its socio-economic inflexions, testing the varied strata of his own meanings for patterns of allegiance; he has found no sign in himself of sustainable opposition.

In order to summarize Mailer's historical disappointment at the political poverty of his own depths, I shall turn back to Vološinov's account of 'unsystematized and unfixed inner and outer speech' as it strains through conflict towards meaning:[60] since I have already quoted the account at length, I shall simply use it as a stencil through which to characterize Mailer's position. Having taken part in an 'adventitious and loose coalition' of groups, he has encountered in his voice an 'adventitious and loose coalition' of meanings; his skill has been to trace the history of these 'haphazard and ephemeral' allegiances to their social and political sources. But knowledge has not altered the historical case: Fordism, despite its crisis, will still call the future. Mailer, by entering 'the lowest, most fluid, and quickly changing stratum' of his own speech, has turned himself into a novel fit for a prodigiously unstable decade; in so doing, he has become a novel without an adequately political hero, a performance longing for an audience which neither it, he, nor the USA deserves.

Or, as Mailer put it at the close of his first political novel about corporatism and the permanent-arms economy:

> for the present the storm approaches its thunderhead, and it is apparent that the boat drifts ever closer to shore. So the blind will lead the blind, and the deaf shout warnings to one another until their voices are lost.[61]

Conclusion

I am aware that much of my discussion in this book borders on economism. The essays seek to relate two kinds of history, economic and personal, apparently emphasizing the former. However, by discussing such issues as privacy and desire as overlaps between etiquette, gender, labour and sales, I hope to imply that economic forms are necessarily lived forms. As such any system of production, despite its saturation of all social levels, is never simply determining. Poulantzas argues:

> The type of unity which characterizes a mode of production is that of a *complex whole*, dominated, in the last instance by the economic . . . what distinguishes one mode of production from another and consequently specifies a mode of production is the particular form of articulation maintained by its levels.[1]

All social formations are necessarily heterogeneous: a particular crossing of differing forces achieves a form that determines a pattern for their own inter-relation. This form may be said to "overdetermine" several separate determinisms, which, because they retain their own energies of plot, assumption, metaphor and social role, can never wholly fit in with the system which together they temporarily promote. So, for example, in reading *The Fathers* I concluded that Lacy Buchan could 'hear the night' because a triple violation of Southern integrity, involving the Fall, Secession and federal funding, made the onset of darkness palpable. Only the last violation is overtly economic, yet Roosevelt's monies take on theological colours in that for Tate they represent the South's last lapse back into the Union. Deciding which semantic strand should have primacy is difficult. My point is simply that the critical task is to delineate the determinants and to assign them a place in what is a complex articulation of historical meaning.

251

Brecht expresses the indeterminancy of determinism with playful clarity:

> Me-ti said: physics has just declared that the fundamental particles are unpredictable; their movements cannot be foreseen. They seem to be individuals endowed with free wills. But individuals are not endowed with free will. Their movements are difficult to predict, or cannot be predicted, only because there are too many determinations, not because there are none.[2]

Fitzgerald senses the plethora of 'determinations': in *Tender is the Night* he treats particular events and artifacts as metaphors; that is to say, he shows them by showing the activities that went into them, almost by going on a long detour through their surfaces. The reader is encouraged to read objects and actions as provisional networks of determinants rather than as given entities. By these means Fitzgerald's mimesis mimes the complex articulations which comply in that singular social formation described elsewhere as the second industrial revolution. A left-wing reviewer objected to *Tender is the Night*, insisting, 'Dear Mr. Fitzgerald, you can't hide from a hurricane under a beach umbrella.'[3] The review misses the point: Fitzgerald understood, as the reviewer did not, that hurricanes are of limited duration – and that the Crash, and the continuity of capital despite the Crash, can best be understood by recognizing the nature of the beach umbrella as the site of determining conflicts within capital.

Whether one watches a Southern night (circa pre-history, 1861, 1938), or studies beach furniture (circa 'feudal' monies, 1929, 1934), one is potentially looking at a realization of 'a social whole, in the widest sense, at a given moment in its historical existence'.[4] Any such moment is riddled with 'determinations', containing vestiges and survivals from older social forms and perhaps intuitions of forms to come. In Boston, according to James, the emergence of a single national market and the insecurities of old money within that market impact on one character: Olive Chancellor cannot be allowed to talk at the Music Hall because opposed impulses in a 'mode of production' have James by the throat. In Hemingway's Paris dismemberment occurs when the body according to consumption meets the memory of a vestigial body of social needs. In both my examples, here crudely reiterated, I seek to show an economy at work as a political fact within fictional events. The phrase 'mode of production', like 'in the last instance', is a signal of intent rather than a formula for reading. At the worst, it is an abstraction that serves to remind me that economic relations are there, quite literally, being produced inside the social relations, from within whose contradictions the fictions are forced. Again Poulantzas's perspective is helpful:

> The mode of production constitutes an abstract-formal object which does not exist in the strong sense of reality. Capitalist, feudal and slave modes of

production, which equally lack existence in the strong sense, also constitute abstract-formal objects. The only thing which really exists is a historically determined *social formation* . . . which is a real-concrete object and so always original because singular . . . a specific overlapping of several 'pure' modes of production.[5]

My preoccupation has been with a considerably cluttered 'mode of production' (Fordism) during the period running from the 1920s to the end of the 1960s. Just as it is historically permissible to speak of 'France under Louis Bonaparte' or 'England during the Industrial Revolution', so I have addressed Fordist USA as an 'historically determined . . . social whole',[6] in which the economics of consumption operate as the 'absent cause' giving an 'inexorable *form* [to] . . . events':[7]

From the 1920s through to the 1960s, commerce, influenced by factors such as economies of scale, attempted to construct a highly predictable, homogenized and consistent market, which would allow for longer factory runs and high profitability . . . Commerce was thereby attempting to create a world mirrored in modernist imagery of science-fiction, a future in which all forms of ethnic or regional particularity have been suppressed and replaced by a homogeneous, 'designed' population. Observers who lived through the fifties may have seen it as representing the triumph of the logic of technocracy.[8]

Clearly, the homogeneous ambition of the market is unrealized; yet what Marchand calls 'capitalist realism'[9] remains a useful stencil through which to read the works of the period. Marchand's conviction that ad-men, as 'missionar[ies] of modernity',[10] invented a reality based on purchase and its promises, identifies the work-face of Fordism as a 'cultural dominant'.[11]

My essays, in different ways, have dealt with how a prevalent form of capital produces types of individuality, promotes preferred narratives and gives texture to events. Inevitably, since the necessity inherent in designing the consumer curtails desire, limits the real and perfects amnesia, I have also and simultaneously been interested in how life under Fordism is premised on suppressions. The identity of 'Mailer's' voice, like the integrity of Jake Barnes's body, is posited on the non-identity through which it has passed to find itself. To read either invention is to be continuously aware of how each is constituted on anxiety. For as long as the promise of the broadening consumption basket holds good, worries about its underside remain a variously corrosive, though pervasive, sub-plot. Jake's body and 'Mailer's' speech join Olive Chancellor's silence, Lacy Buchan's 'night' and Dick Diver's 'umbrella', as sites at which determinants meet, determinants that constitute the conflicted stuff of reality: they are therefore 'in the last instance' exemplars of an economic period, and I have tried to read them as such.

Notes

INTRODUCTION

1 Nathaniel Hawthorne, *The American Claimant Manuscripts* (Columbus, OH: Ohio State University Press, 1977), p. 287.

2 Frederick Olmsted, *Civilizing American Cities: A Selection of Frederick Olmsted's Writings on City Landscapes*, ed. S.B. Sutton (Cambridge, MA: MIT Press, 1971), p. 79.

3 *Ibid.*, p. 78.

4 *Ibid.*, p. 96.

5 *Ibid.*, p. 70.

6 *Ibid.*, p. 96.

7 Henry James, *The Bostonians* (London: John Lehmann, 1952), p. 293.

8 Olmsted, *Civilizing American Cities*, p. 78.

9 See Thorstein Veblen, *The Theory of the Leisure Class* (London: Unwin, 1970). Writing in 1899, Veblen described 'conspicuous leisure' and 'conspicuous consumption' as keys to understanding leisured existence.

10 Olmsted, *Civilizing American Cities*, p. 96.

11 Veblen, *The Theory of the Leisure Class*, p. 107.

12 *Ibid.*, p. 121.

13 *Ibid.*, p. 103.

14 *Ibid.*, p. 103.

15 *Ibid.*

16 James, *The Bostonians*, p. 281.

17 Edith Wharton, *The Age of Innocence* (London: Constable, 1966), p. 220.

18 *Ibid.*

19 Veblen, *The Theory of the Leisure Class*, p. 164.

20 F. Scott Fitzgerald, *The Great Gatsby* (New York: Scribners, n.d.), p. 23.

21 Veblen, *The Theory of the Leisure Class*, p. 46.

22 James O'Connor, *Accumulation Crisis* (New York: Blackwell, 1984), p. 29.

23 James, *The Bostonians*, p. 26.

24 *Ibid.*, p. 158.

25 Theodor Adorno and Max Horkheimer, *Dialectic of Enlightenment* (London: Verso, 1979), p. 149.

26 Quoted by Stuart Ewen, *Captains of Consciousness: Advertising and the Social Roots of the Consumer* (New York: McGraw-Hill, 1976), p. 80.

27 I am thinking particularly of the work of Baudrillard, Bowlby and Michaels. See Jean Baudrillard, *For a Critique of the Political Economy of the Sign* (St Louis: Telos Press, 1981), particularly pp. 130–42; Rachel Bowlby, *Just Looking: Consumer Culture in Dreiser, Gissing and Zola* (New York: Methuen, 1985); Walter Benn Michaels, *The Gold Standard and the Logic of Naturalism* (Berkeley: University of California Press, 1987), particularly pp. 3–28. It should be added that Michaels's exploration of capital as a system of representation within which naturalist texts are formed is of great subtlety, yet he remains convinced that the culture of consumption is both infinitely various and singularly absolute: so that when he asks himself whether or not Dreiser disapproves of consumer culture, he can only dismiss the question of resistance as inappropriate: 'Although transcending your origins in order to evaluate them has been the opening move in cultural criticism at least since Jeremiah, it is surely a mistake to take this move at face value: not so much because you can't really transcend your culture but because, if you could, you wouldn't have any terms of evaluation left – except, perhaps, theological ones. It thus seems wrong to think of the culture you live in as the object of your affections: you don't like or dislike it, you exist in it, and the things you like and dislike exist in it too. Even Bartelby-like refusals of the world remain inextricably linked to it – what could count as a more powerful exercise in the right to freedom of contract than Bartleby's successful refusal to enter into any contracts? Preferring not to, he embodies . . . the purest of commitments to laissez-faire, the freedom of contract to do as one likes' (pp. 18–19).

28 Baudrillard, *Critique*, pp. 92–3.

29 At times through the book I have used double inverted commas to enclose particular words or phrases; these are not to be understood as quotations drawn from the work of others, they are simply a device whereby I seek to stand at a distance from a term or habit of expression. My reasons vary: sometimes I wish only to stress a word, elsewhere I signal a common usage and ask that the habit be inspected.

30 Michaels, *The Gold Standard*, p. 20.

31 Bowlby, *Just Looking*, p. 2.

32 Jean Baudrillard, *Simulations* (New York: Semiotext(e), 1983), p. 36.

33 Bowlby, *Just Looking*, p. 34.

34 Alfred D. Chandler, Jr, *The Visible Hand: The Managerial Revolution in American Business* (Cambridge, MA: Harvard University Press, 1977), p. 232.

35 Karl Marx, *Capital*, vol. 1 (Harmondsworth: Penguin, 1976), p. 165.

36 V.N. Vološinov, *Marxism and the Philosophy of Language* (New York: Seminar Press, 1973), pp. 19–21 (Vološinov's italics).

37 *Ibid.*, p. 21.

38 M.A.K. Halliday, *Language as Social Semiotic* (London: Arnold, 1978), p. 77.

39 Paul Ricoeur, *The Rule of Metaphor* (London: Routledge and Kegan Paul, 1978), p. 74.

40 Roland Marchand, *Advertising the American Dream: Making Way for Modernity, 1920–1940* (Los Angeles: University of California Press, 1985), p. xviii.

41 Paul Ricoeur, 'The metaphoric process as cognition, imagination and feeling', collected in *On Metaphor*, ed. Sheldon Sacks (Chicago: University of Chicago Press, 1979), pp. 146–7.

42 *Ibid.*, p. 149.

43 Ricoeur, *The Rule of Metaphor*, pp. 77–8.

44 Ernst Mandel, *Late Capitalism* (London: Verso, 1980), pp. 245–7. See also Alfred Chandler, Jr, *Strategy and Structure* (Cambridge, MA: MIT Press, 1962), pp. 386–90.

1. SOME SLIGHT SHIFTS IN THE MANNER OF THE NOVEL OF MANNERS

1 Thorstein Veblen, *The Theory of the Leisure Class* (London: Unwin, 1970), p. 51.

2 Edith Wharton, *The Age of Innocence* (London: Constable, 1966), p. 48.

3 Veblen, *The Theory of the Leisure Class*, p. 47.

4 *Ibid.*

5 *Ibid.*, p. 164.

6 Mary Douglas and Baron Isherwood, *The World of Goods* (Harmondsworth: Penguin Books, 1978), p. 148.

7 Henry James, *The Golden Bowl* (London: Methuen, 1956), pp. 7–8.

8 Henry James, *The Art of the Novel* (London: Scribners, 1948), p. 120 (italics in source).

9 Henry James, *The Bostonians* (London: John Lehmann, 1952), p. 38. Subsequent references will be to this edition and will be included in the text.

10 Henry James, *The Portrait of a Lady* (London: Oxford University Press, 1962), p. 270.

11 See Jean Baudrillard, *For a Critique of the Political Economy of the Sign* (St Louis: Telos Press, 1981), particularly the essay 'Sign function and class logic', pp. 29–62.

12 Eric Hobsbawm, *The Age of Capital 1848–1875* (New York: New American Library, 1975), pp. 254–5.

13 *Ibid*, p. 254.

14 Wharton, *The Age of Innocence*, p. 190.

15 See Anne Douglas, *The Feminization of American Culture* (New York: Knopf, 1979), particularly ch. 2, 'Feminine disestablishment', pp. 44–79; also Elizabeth Fox-Genovese, 'Placing women's history in history', *New Left Review*, no. 133 (May–June, 1982), pp. 5–29.

16 Veblen, *The Theory of the Leisure Class*, p. 107.

17 Fox-Genovese, 'Placing women's history', p. 24.

18 Julia Matthaei argues that the emergence of separate sexual spheres worked to the benefit of women: 'The new relationship between man and woman was one of equality and difference, not superior and inferior. Woman, acquiring for the first time a clearly distinct and social sphere, acquired a distinct and different existence from man, and from her husband . . . Hence woman was no longer considered to be inferior to her male partner, but rather different and equal.' See, *An Economic History of Women in America* (Brighton: Harvester, 1982), p. 116. I am unpersuaded that 'different' means 'equal', particularly when unsupported by earning power.

19 If such a role was palpable fantasy, the work of Anne Douglas and Alfred Habegger reveals how far that fantasy was both real and collective. From the 1840s to the 1880s popular fiction meant fiction for women, by women – a sentimental literature that idealized marriage. As Habegger has it, 'A great deal of nineteenth century women's fiction was a brew laced with opium, alcohol, a pinch of wormwood and buckets of molasses. It was the moral equivalent of soothing syrup (the male drug being alcohol).' *Gender, Fantasy and Realism in American Literature* (New York: Columbia University Press, 1982), p. 31.

20 James, *The Portrait of a Lady*, p. 401.

21 F. Scott Fitzgerald, *The Great Gatsby* (New York: Scribners, n.d.), p 120.

22 Lionel Trilling, 'Manners, morals and the novel', collected in *The Liberal Imagination* (Harmondsworth: Penguin Books, 1970), p. 209.

23 See William Leech, *True Love and Perfect Union: The Feminist Reform of Sex and Society* (London: Routledge, 1981), p. 239.

24 Frederick Olmsted, *Civilizing American Cities: A Selection of Frederic Law Olmsted's*

Writings on City Landscapes, ed. S.B. Sutton (Cambridge, MA: MIT Press, 1971), pp. 78–9.

25 Between 1902 and 1909 electrical output increased nineteenfold, while 3,700 utility companies vanished. On mergers and their statistics more generally, see William Leuchtenburg, *The Perils of Prosperity* (Chicago: University of Chicago Press, 1958), pp. 178–203; Douglas Dowd, *The Twisted Dream* (Cambridge, MA: Winthrop, 1974), pp. 53–77; and Alfred Chandler, Jr, *Strategy and Structure* (Cambridge, MA: MIT Press, 1962), pp. 1–42 and pp. 383–96.

26 Leuchtenburg, *The Perils of Prosperity*, p. 192.

27 Copy from a New York agency (1893), quoted in Frank Presbrey, *The History and Development of Advertising* (New York: Doubleday, 1929), p. 341.

28 Stuart Ewen, *Captains of Consciousness: Advertising and the Social Roots of the Consumer* (New York: McGraw-Hill, 1976), p. 54. Ewen draws the distinction between 'captain of industry' and 'captain of consciousness'.

29 Robert Lynd and Helen Lynd, *Middletown* (New York: Harcourt and Brace, 1929), p. 491.

30 Christine Frederick, *Selling Mrs. Consumer* (1929) quoted by Ewen, *Captains of Consciousness*, p. 22 (italics in source).

31 Paula Fass, *The Damned and the Beautiful* (Oxford: Oxford University Press, 1977), p. 257.

32 *Ibid.*, p. 226.

33 *Ibid.*, p. 257 (italics in source).

34 Detailed accounts of specific advertising trends during the twenties may be found in Roland Marchand. *Advertising the American Dream* (Los Angeles: University of California Press, 1985). My distinction between 'integral' and 'disintegral' selves owes much to the work of Warren Susman on 'character' as opposed to 'personality'. More recently Michael Spindler has used Riesman's categories of 'inner directed' and 'other directed' in a study of American literary change. In both cases (though more particularly with Spindler) the links between the history of the "self" and economic history are insufficiently pursued. See Warren Susman, *Culture As History: The Transformation of American Society in the Twentieth Century* (New York: Pantheon Books, 1984); and Michael Spindler, *American Literature and Social Change: William Dean Howells to Arthur Miller* (London: Macmillan, 1983).

35 Ernst Mandel, *Late Capitalism* (London: Verso, 1980), p. 245.

36 Fitzgerald, *The Great Gatsby*, p. 6.

37 *Ibid.*, p. 67.

38 *Ibid.*, p. 119.

39 *Ibid.*, p. 121.

40 Thomas Cochran, quoted by Alan Trachtenberg, *The Incorporation of America: Culture and Society in the Gilded Age* (New York: Hill and Wang, 1982), p. 7.

41 Chandler, *Strategy and Structure*, pp. 386–90.

42 *Ibid.*, p. 387.

43 Presbrey, *History of Advertising*, p. 266.

44 David Howard, 'The Bostonians', in John Goode (ed.), *The Air of Reality*, (London: Methuen, 1972), pp. 60–80.

45 Theodor Adorno, *Minima Moralia* (London: New Left Books, 1974), p. 235.

46 Leon Edel (ed.), *The Complete Tales of Henry James*, vol. XII (London: Rupert Hart-Davis, 1964), p. 14. The judgement is addressed to the popular journalists Maud Blandy and Howard Blight in 'The papers', however, its application is plainly more general. See Peter Conn, *The Divided Mind* (Cambridge: Cambridge University Press, 1983), pp. 21–2.

47 For a discussion of this phrase within the context of feminist accounts of 'love' during the latter half of the nineteenth century, see Leech, *True Love and Perfect Union*, particularly ch. 5, 'The vindication of love', pp. 99–129.

48 Quoted in Anne Douglas, *The Feminization of American Culture*, p. 66.

49 Guy Debord, *Society of the Spectacle* (Detroit: Black and Red, 1973), section 34 (italics in source).

50 John Goode, 'Character and Henry James', *New Left Review* no. 40 (Nov./Dec. 1966), pp. 55–75. My argument does scant justice to Goode's subtlety. His preoccupation remains the ways and means by which character for James preserves its identity through strategies of possession. The strategies are delightfully various, but possession is paramount. To sum up, 'the intrinsic self can only exist in the condition in which others are contextual . . . In order not to be owned [a character] has to be an owner . . . in the same sense that the author owns his characters in a well made little drama' (p. 72).

51 *Ibid.*, p. 62.

52 René Girard, *Deceit, Desire and the Novel* (London: Johns Hopkins Press, 1965), p. 12. To facilitate application of the quote to *The Bostonians* I have feminized and italicized some of Girard's pronouns.

53 Henry Pelling, *American Labor* (Chicago: University of Chicago Press, 1965), p. 61.

54 Employee pressure did exist, though it is difficult to date its emergence. Susan Porter Benson notes, 'In many early stores, the contrast between the luxurious public areas of the stores and the behind-the-scenes areas reserved for the use of the employees was dramatic.' See her 'Palace of consumption and machine for selling', *Radical History Review*, no. 21 (Fall 1979), pp. 207–8.

55 *The Letters of Henry James*, ed. Percy Lubbock, vol. 1 (London: Macmillan, 1920), p. 101 (italics in source).

56 See Gaines M. Foster, *Ghosts of the Confederacy: Defeat, the Lost Cause and the Emergence of the New South, 1865 to 1913* (New York: Oxford University Press, 1987), particularly ch. 5, pp. 63–75.

57 Charles R. Anderson sets the novel after the end of Reconstruction, and is unusual in offering specific dates (1879–81); however, his account of Ransom as deriving from 'legend' and characterized by 'nostalgia for a vanished past', misses the point of his own specificity. See Anderson's edition of *The Bostonians* (Harmondsworth: Penguin, 1987), pp. 21 and 436.

58 C. Vann Woodward discusses the Compromise in his *Reunion and Reaction: The Compromise of 1877 and the End of Reconstruction* (New York: Doubleday, 1956), and in his *Origins of the New South, 1877–1913* (Baton Rouge: Louisiana State University Press, 1971), pp. 1–106.

59 Vann Woodward, *Reunion and Reaction*, p. 37.

60 Barrington Moore Jr, *Social Origins of Dictatorship and Democracy* (Harmondsworth: Penguin, 1974), p. 141.

61 Quoted in George Monteiro, *Henry James and John Hay: The Record of a Friendship* (Providence, RI: Brown University Press, 1965), p. 97.

62 Quotations are taken from two editorials, 'The Texas–Pacific job' and 'The South and the Texas–Pacific job'; these appeared on 11 January 1877 and on 8 February 1877, respectively, in *Nation*, vol. 24 (January–June 1877), nos. 602 and 606, pp. 23–5 and 82–3.

63 Leon Edel, *Henry James: The Untried Years, 1843–1870* (London: Rupert Hart-Davis, 1953), p. 224.

64 James B. Murphy, *L.Q.C. Lamar: Pragmatic Patriot* (Baton Rouge, LA: Louisiana State University Press, 1973), p. 240.

65 Charles R. Anderson's classification is typical (*The Bostonians*, p. 7). For variously weighted accounts of Ransom's archaic Southernness see Theodore C. Miller, 'The muddled politics of Henry James's *The Bostonians*', *Georgia Review*, vol. 24, no. 3 (Fall, 1972), pp. 336–46; Catherine H. Zuckert, 'American women and democratic morals: *The Bostonians*', *Feminist Studies*, vol. 3 (Spring/Summer, 1976), pp. 30–50; Ruth Quebe, '*The Bostonians*: some historical sources and their implications', *Centennial Review*, vol. 25 (Winter, 1981), pp. 80–100.

66 Susan L. Mizruchi, 'The politics of temporality in *The Bostonians*', *Nineteenth Century Fiction*, vol. 40, no. 2 (September 1985), p. 205. It is only fair to say that Mizruchi reads Ransom's immersion in Scott as representative of a 'stereotyped South'.

67 Vann Woodward, *Reunion and Reaction*, p. 43.

68 Vann Woodward, *Origins of the New South*, p. 157.

69 I am grateful to Alfred Habegger for permission to quote from his as yet unpublished essay, 'The return of the father in *The Bostonians*'. Miller sees Ransom's 'uncertain identity' as 'chaotic' ('Muddled politics', pp. 343–5): Habegger plots the chaos, arguing that Ransom is deeply troublesome to James insofar as the character articulates Henry James Sr's views on marriage as redemptive slavery. The voice of the recently deceased father elicits the son's occasional judgements, but exorcism by sarcasm is incomplete. While disagreeing over the source of Ransom's contrary character, I found Habegger's essay constantly helpful.

70 Ransom notes that the editor's letter, 'makes an era in [his] life' and 'change[s] the whole way [he] looks at [his] future' (p. 316). More to the point, the money finances a month's holiday and the proposal to Verena. David Howard argues that 'it is Ransom's dedication to a cause, his forlorn but powerful hope of public success, that is part of his persuasion of her' (Howard, 'The Bostonians', p. 72).

71 Michael Aglietta, *A Theory of Capitalist Regulation: The U.S. Experience* (London: Verso, 1987), p. 77.

72 Trachtenberg, *The Incorporation of America*, p, 82.

73 Henry James, *The Notebooks of Henry James*, ed. F.O. Mattheissen and Kenneth B. Murdock (New York: Oxford University Press, 1961), p. 47 (italics in source).

2. 'YOU'VE GOT TO SEE IT, FEEL IT, SMELL IT, HEAR IT' BUY IT: HEMINGWAY'S COMMERCIAL FORMS

1 F. Scott Fitzgerald, 'Echoes of the Jazz Age', collected in *The Bodley Head Scott Fitzgerald*, vol. 2 (London: Bodley Head, 1961), p. 16.

2 John Dos Passos, *U.S.A.: The Big Money* (New York: Constable, 1937), p. 562.

3 Malcolm Cowley, *Exile's Return* (New York: Viking Press, 1974), p. 83.

4 Theodore Dreiser, *An American Tragedy* (London: Constable, 1926), p. 51.

5 F. Scott Fitzgerald, 'Echoes of the Jazz Age', p. 13.

6 Robert Lynd and Helen Lynd, *Middletown* (New York: Harcourt and Brace, 1929), pp. 80–1.

7 William Leuchtenburg, *The Perils of Prosperity* (Chicago: University of Chicago Press, 1958), p. 200.

8 C. Frederick, *Selling Mrs. Consumer* (1929), quoted by Stuart Ewen, *Captains of Consciousness: Advertising and the Social Roots of the Consumer* (New York: McGraw-Hill, 1976), p. 22.

9 F.W. Taylor, quoted by D. Montgomery, *Workers' Control in America: Studies in the History of Work, Technology and Labor Struggles* (Cambridge: Cambridge University Press, 1979), p. 114 (italics in source).

10 Elizabeth Fox-Genovese and Eugene Genovese, 'The political crisis of social

history', collected in *Fruits of Merchant Capital* (London: Oxford University Press, 1983), p. 212.

11 James O'Connor, *Accumulation Crisis* (New York: Blackwell, 1984), p. 29. O'Connor's work was generally helpful in the writing of this chapter. His account of how capital counters crisis through recomposition which, in turn, induces class resistance, if read alongside the labour history of David Noble, David Montgomery and Stanley Aronowitz, counters Ernst Mandel's tendency to present economic change as a self-determining function of capital's objective laws of motion.

12 *Ibid*, p. 212.

13 Lynd, *Middletown*, p. 40.

14 *Ibid.*, p. 81.

15 *Ibid.*, pp. 88–9.

16 *Ibid.*, p. 274.

17 The Lynds are particularly good on washing machines as 'an example of the way in which a useful new invention vigorously pushed on the market by effective advertising may serve to slow up a secular trend [i.e. the use of public laundries]. The heavy investment by the individual family in an electric washing machine costing from $60 to $200 tends to perpetuate a questionable institutional set-up – whereby many individual homes repeat common tasks day after day in isolated units – by forcing back into the individual home a process that was following belatedly the trend in industry towards centralized operation. The whole procedure follows the customary, haphazard practice of social change: the issue is not settled on its merits; each Middletown household stands an isolated unit in the midst of a baffling battery of diffusion from personally interested agencies: the manufacturers of laundry machinery spray the thinking of the housewife through her magazines with a shower of "educational" copy about the mistake of a woman's neglecting her children for mere laundry work, and she lays down her magazine to answer the door-bell and finds there the suave installment payment salesman ready to install a $155 washer on trial, to be paid for in weekly installments if satisfactory. The whole question has to be settled in terms of such immediate and often incidental considerations by each isolated family unit' (*Middletown*, pp. 174–5).

18 Ernest Hemingway, *A Farewell to Arms* (London: Cape, 1929), p. 157.

19 Tony Tanner, *The Reign of Wonder* (Cambridge: Cambridge University Press, 1977), pp. 241 and 247. I shall refer frequently to Tanner's work on Hemingway; ch. 13 of *The Reign of Wonder*, pp. 228–57, contains a detailed reading of 'Big Two-Hearted River,' pp. 252–7. All quotations, unless otherwise stated, are from this chapter.

20 Ernest Hemingway, 'Big Two-Hearted River: part I', collected in *The First Forty-Nine Stories* (London: Cape, 1954), p. 187. Subsequent references will be to this edition and will be included in the text.

21 Ernest Hemingway, *Death in the Afternoon* (London: Cape, 1955), p. 10

22 Lynd, *Middletown*, p. 225.

23 Theodor Adorno and Max Horkheimer, *Dialectic of Enlightenment* (London: Verso, 1979), p. 149.

24 Sinclair Lewis, *Babbitt* (London: Cape, 1965), p. 14.

25 Alfred Sohn-Rethel, *Intellectual and Manual Labour: A Critique of Epistemology* (London: Macmillan, 1978), p. 25.

26 W.F. Haug, *Critique of Commodity Aesthetics* (Oxford: Polity Press, 1986), p. 17.

27 Frederic Jameson, *Marxism and Form* (Princeton: Princeton University Press, 1974), p. 412.

28 The phrase derives from the work of Emily S. Rosenberg, *Spreading the American*

Dream: American Economic and Cultural Expansion, 1890–1945 (New York: Hill and Wang, 1982), see particularly ch. 4, 'World War I and the triumph of the promotional state', pp. 63–86.

29 *Ibid.*, p. 122.

30 *Ibid.*, p. 123.

31 *Ibid.*, p. 132.

32 Emily S. Rosenberg and Norman L. Rosenberg, 'From colonialism to professionalism: the public–private dynamic in United States foreign financial advising, 1898–1928', *The Journal of American History*, vol. 74, no. 1, June 1987, p. 65.

33 Quoted by Emily Rosenberg, *Spreading the American Dream*, pp. 46–7.

34 *Ibid.*, p. 135.

35 Gilbert Feis, *The Diplomacy of the Dollar* (Baltimore: Johns Hopkins Press, 1950), p. 48.

36 James W. Cortada, *Two Nations Over Time: Spain and the United States, 1776–1977* (Westport: Greenwood Press, 1978), p. 170.

37 Emily Rosenberg, *Spreading the American Dream*, p. 157.

38 As Marx would have it: 'Within the relationship between value and the expression of value contained therein, the abstract universal (value) does not count as the property of the concrete in its sense-reality, but on the contrary the concrete-sensate counts merely as the phenomenal or sensate form of the abstract universal's realisation.' (Quoted by Lucio Colletti, *Marxism and Hegel* (London: Verso, 1979), pp. 281–2.)

Rather than footnote every paraphrase, phrase or parallel in the discussion of 'value' and 'exchange abstraction', I list those works or sections of works which have been most helpful: K. Marx, *Capital*, vol. 1, part 1 (Harmondsworth: Penguin, 1976), and 'Economic and philosophical manuscripts', collected in *Early Writings* (Harmondsworth: Penguin, 1977); A. Sohn-Rethel, *Intellectual and Manual Labour*, particularly part 1: Colletti, *Marxism and Hegel*, particularly chs. 11 and 12, and *From Rousseau to Lenin* (London: New Left Books, 1972), pp. 71–99; W.F. Haug, *Critique of Commodity Aesthetics*. I am also grateful to Pamela Rhodes for her extensive help in the shaping of this chapter.

39 The phrases "capitalist reality" and "capitalist realist" derive from Roland Marchand's argument that during the twenties advertising agencies created 'capitalist realism'. See Roland Marchand, *Advertising the American Dream: Making Way for Modernity, 1920–1940* (Los Angeles: University of California Press, 1985), pp. xviii–xxi.

40 Ferdinand Léger, 'The machine aesthetic: the manufactured object, the artisan and the artist', collected in, *The Documents of Twentieth Century Art*, ed. Edward F. Fry (London: Thames and Hudson, 1973), p. 56 (italics in source).

41 *Ibid.*, p. 56. See also Walter Benjamin, *Charles Baudelaire: A Lyric Poet in the Era of High Capitalism* (London: Verso, 1983), particularly pp. 158–76.

42 Ernest Hemingway, *Fiesta* (London: Cape, 1954), p. 253. Subsequent references will be to this edition, although I have used the American title (*The Sun Also Rises*) when referring to the novel. Pagination will be included in the text.

43 The quotation is taken from Hemingway's definition of 'temple', *Death in the Afternoon*, p. 331.

44 I have drawn from a number of essays on Hemingway's style: most usefully, Hugh Kenner, *A Homemade World* (New York: Knopf, 1975), ch. 5; Harry Levin, 'Observations on the style of Ernest Hemingway', collected in *Hemingway and his Critics*, ed. Colin Baker (New York: Hill and Wang, 1961), pp. 93–115; Tony Tanner, *The Reign of Wonder*, ch. 13; Larzner Ziff, 'The social basis of Hemingway's

style', *Poetics*, 7 (1978), pp. 417–23. Less determinedly stylistic but at least as useful were Paul Goodman, *Speaking and Language* (London: Wildwood House, 1971), ch. 10; and F. Jameson, *Marxism and Form*, pp. 409–13.

45 Karl Marx, *Grundrisse* (Harmondsworth: Penguin Books, 1974), p. 218. A theological vocabulary was used by Marx to describe what he called 'the mystical character' of the obfuscations enacted within the production, sale and consumption of commodities. 'Exchange abstraction' is simply a generic term for these processes.

46 Cowley, *Exile's Return*, pp. 81–2.

47 Ernest Hemingway, *Death in the Afternoon*, pp. 13–14.

48 E. Hemingway, *A Moveable Feast* (London: Cape, 1964), pp. 16–17.

49 Ernest Hemingway, *Green Hills of Africa* (London: Cape, 1954), p. 33. Subsequent references will be to this edition and will be included in the text.

50 Léger, 'The machine aesthetic', p. 65 (italics in source).

51 F.S. Flint, 'Imagisme', collected in *Imagist Poetry*, ed. Peter Jones (Harmondsworth: Penguin, 1972), p. 129.

52 William Carlos Williams, 'A sort of song', collected in *William Carlos Williams: Selected Poems*, ed. Charles Tomlinson (Harmondsworth: Penguin, 1983), p. 133.

53 W.F. Haug, *Critique of Commodity Asthetics*, p. 114.

54 *Ibid.*, p. 115.

55 Karl Marx, *Capital*, vol. 1, p. 13.

56 *Ibid.*, p. 256. I prefer, and have therefore quoted, the translation offered by K. Heinzelman, *The Economics of Imagination* (Amherst: University of Massachusetts Press, 1980), p. 177. Heinzelman's 'The Psychomachia of Labor', ch. 6, was helpful in the issue of 'price'.

57 Raymond Williams, *The Long Revolution* (Harmondsworth: Penguin, 1965), pp. 64–5.

58 Paula Fass, *The Damned and the Beautiful* (Oxford: Oxford University Press, 1977), p. 257.

59 Lynd, *Middletown*, p. 52.

60 Quoted by Emily Stipes-Watts, *Ernest Hemingway and the Arts* (London: University of Illinois Press, 1971), p. 19.

61 Ernest Hemingway, *Death in the Afternoon*, p. 10.

62 Gestures are made towards icebergs and wounds, but an aesthetics of 'omission' and two hundred and twenty-seven pieces of shell fragment (even where removed from the author's right leg) are scant explanation to place against such conspicuous stylistic self-attrition.

63 T.S. Eliot, 'Hamlet' collected in *Selected Essays* (London: Faber, 1966), p. 145 (italics in source).

64 T.S. Eliot, 'The Love Song of J. Alfred Prufrock', collected in *Collected Poems: 1909–1962* (London: Faber, 1968), p. 15.

65 Philip Young, *Ernest Hemingway: A Reconsideration* (London: Pennsylvania State University Press, 1966), particularly ch. 1, 'Adventures of Nick Adams'.

66 Richard Lichtman, *The Production of Desire: The Integration of Psychoanalysis into Marxist Theory* (New York: Free Press, 1982), p. 77.

67 Any diagram is replete with omissions. Neither capital nor labour is "one", each is plural and diverse. As James O'Connor puts it, 'in historical fact, labour-power is never purely a form of capital; consumption never merely reproduces alienation alone' (*Accumulation Crisis*, p. 180). Consequently, despite having argued that around 1922 the American workforce suppressed itself, becoming 'a form of capital', i.e. the consumer, I would not wish to imply that the pursuit of improved salary and work conditions equals only 'alienation', since it is also a continuing and active form of conflict.

68 Karl Marx, *Grundrisse*, p. 241.
69 Scott Donaldson, *By Force of Will: The Life and Art of Ernest Hemingway* (New York: Viking Press, 1977), p. 23.
70 *Ibid.*, p. 26. See also Nancy Comly, 'Hemingway: the economics of survival', *Novel*, vol. 12, no. 3 (Spring 1979), pp. 244–53.
71 Cowley, *Exile's Return*, p. 82.
72 Emily Rosenberg, *Spreading the American Dream*, p. 152. See also, ch. 8, 'The cooperative state of the 1920s'.
73 Cowley, *Exile's Return*, p. 82.
74 *Ibid.*, p. 223.
75 Edmund Wilson, 'Hemingway: gauge of morale', collected in *The Wound and the Bow* (London: Methuen, 1961), p. 204. Wilson's essay concentrates on the issue of the 'stifled pangs' (p. 192). A later example of the type is Tony Tanner's review of Hemingway's journalism for *London Magazine*, collected in *Hemingway: The Critical Heritage*, ed. Jeffrey Meyers (London: Routledge, 1982), pp. 526–30.
76 Hemingway, *A Farewell to Arms*, pp. 244–5.
77 *Ibid.*, pp. 245–6.
78 *Ibid.*, p. 245.
79 *Ibid.*
80 Alain Robbe-Grillet, *Snapshots and Towards a New Novel* (London: Calder and Boyars, 1965), p. 78.
81 Jameson, *Marxism and Form*, p. 78.
82 Hemingway, *Death in the Afternoon*, p. 11.
83 Paul Baran, 'Crisis of Marxism', quoted by Lichtman, *The Production of Desire*, p. 5.
84 Hemingway, *The First Forty-Nine Stories*, p. 324.
85 *Ibid.*, p. 328.
86 *Ibid.*, p. 326.
87 Hemingway, *Fiesta*, p. 274.
88 See Joseph Flora, *Hemingway's Nick Adams* (London: Louisiana State University Press, 1982), ch. 5, 'Father and son', for discussion of Nick as parent and husband. Flora's case rests rather heavily on his naming of the unnamed narrator of 'A day's wait' and 'Wine of Wyoming' as Nick.
89 Ernest Hemingway, *A Farewell to Arms*, p. 149.
90 The typical Hemingway hero is given to compulsive *ostranenie*: by making strange through making plain, he who perceives is freed from ideological conditioning, only to be left with an object which is substantially ideological – "a fact" according to the dictates of empiricism.
91 The adverb belongs to Nick Adams: as he sits wounded against the wall of a church, he looks, 'straight ahead brilliantly', *The First Forty-Nine Stories*, p. 133.
92 I offer the phrase in the spirit, though not the letter, of Richard Lichtman's work on the relation between individual motivation and economic facts (read by Marx primarily at a structural level). See Richard Lichtman, *The Production of Desire*.
93 Ernest Hemingway, 'Hills like white elephants', collected in *The First Forty-Nine Stories*, p. 249.
94 Peter Munz, *When the Golden Bough Breaks* (London: Routledge, 1973), p. 56 (italics in source). See also Christine Brooke Rose, *A Grammar of Metaphor* (London: Secker and Warburg, 1958), p. 14. Charles Swann uses both words in an intriguing account of the simile/metaphor distinction as it applies to Stephen Crane: see 'Stephen Crane and a problem of interpretation', *Literature and History*, vol. 7 (Spring 1981), pp. 91–123.
95 Theodor Adorno, *Minima Moralia* (London: New Left Books, 1974), p. 235.
96 Ernest Hemingway, *The First Forty-Nine Stories*, p. 186 (italics in source). The

vignette is one of eighteen sketches written in 1922–3, and collected in the 1924 edition of *In Our Time*; it is based on conversations with Mike Strater and Gertrude Stein. See Michael Reynolds, *Hemingway's First War* (Princeton: Princeton University Press, 1976), p. 11.

97 Ernest Hemingway, *The First Forty-Nine Stories*, p. 333 (italics in source).

98 Carlos Baker, *Ernest Hemingway* (Harmondsworth: Penguin, 1972), pp. 440–1.

99 Ernest Hemingway, 'The snows of Kilimanjaro', collected in *The First Forty-Nine Stories*, p. 68.

100 Baker, *Ernest Hemingway*, p. 441. If Harry is deluded, so then is Hemingway. 'It was his later boast that he had used up in this one story enough material to fill four novels. "I put all the true stuff in"', said he, "and with all the load, the most load any short story ever carried", the story was still able to take off like a powerful aeroplane' (p. 44). See Baker for the specifically biographical content of the story; also R.W. Lewis and M. Westbrook, 'The Texas manuscript of "The snows of Kilimanjaro"', *The Texas Quarterly*, vol. 9, no. 4 (Winter, 1966), pp. 66–8.

101 Adorno, *Minima Moralia*, p. 166.

102 This section of the argument relies heavily upon Theodor Adorno's 'Fetish character in music and regression of listening', collected in *The Essential Frankfurt School Reader*, eds. Andrau Arato and Eike Gebhart (Oxford: Blackwell, 1978), pp. 270–90.

103 For Baker, the leopard is 'metaphysical', ('The snows of Kilimanjaro', collected in *Hemingway's African Stories*, ed. John Howell (New York: Scribners, 1969), pp. 55–9). I drew these oppositions from a range of essays collected in Howell's volume.

3. *THE GREAT GATSBY:* GLAMOUR ON THE TURN

1 Quoted by Roland Marchand, *Advertising the American Dream: Making Way for Modernity* (Los Angeles: University of California Press, 1985), p. 6.

2 *Ibid.*, pp. 124–32.

3 *Ibid.*, p. xviii.

4 Haug, *Critique of Commodity Aesthetics* (Oxford: Polity Press, 1986), p. 50.

5 Marchand, *Advertising the American Dream*, p. 7. By 1926 the *Saturday Evening Post* exceeded two hundred pages and carried two indices, one for editorial copy and another for advertisers: the latter may have been of more interest to Fitzgerald than the former. In 1919 he published his first *Post* story; his price peaked at $4,000 in 1931. To call the *Post* 'The grave-yard of the genius of F. Scott Fitzgerald' (Charles G. Norris, quoted by Andrew Turnbull, *Scott Fitzgerald* (Harmondsworth: Penguin, 1970), p. 339) is to miss the point. Zelda Fitzgerald comes nearer when she has Alabama Knight observe, 'We grew up founding our dreams on the infinite promise of American advertizing' (*Save Me the Waltz* (Harmondsworth: Penguin, 1982), p. 228). Arguably, writing for the *Post* helped Fitzgerald to understand the advertising trick even as he turned it. Retrospectively, in 1939, he could see himself as the creator of a 'product', 'stories about young love' for a generation 'that has been told the price of everything' (letter to Kenneth Littauer, *The Letters of F. Scott Fitzgerald*, ed. Andrew Turnbull (Harmondsworth: Penguin, 1968), p. 609). Fitzgerald was very much aware that his writing was a commodity which had to go to market. To read the letters is to follow discussions on the advertising space allocated to *This Side of Paradise* (*Letters*, p. 165), on the price and dust jacket of *The Great Gatsby* (*Letters*, pp. 187 and 171), on shop window displays for *Tender is the Night* (*Letters*, p. 267), and on blurbs for projected short-story projects (*Letters*, p. 208). Fitzgerald liked to keep

records of the sales of his various works in different cities (*Letters*, p. 195). His life-long attention to commercial detail suggests that the notion of Fitzgerald as a 'genius', in the consumptive Keatsian mould, is less than helpful. The *Post*, and not Keats, is the primary point of influence. See Geoff Cox, 'Literary pragmatics – a new discipline. The example of Fitzgerald's *Great Gatsby*', *Literture and History*, vol. 12, no. 1 (Spring, 1986), pp. 79–96.

6 F. Scott Fitzgerald, *The Great Gatsby* (New York: Scribners, n.d.), p. 119. Subsequent references will be to this edition, the 182 pp. Scribners' paperback reprint. Where I have inserted ellipsis during extended quotation, I have noted that usage.

7 Ernst Bloch, Georg Lukács, Bertolt Brecht, Walter Benjamin, Theodor Adorno, *Aesthetics and Politics* (London: Verso, 1980), p. 82.

8 Bertolt Brecht, 'Alienation effects in Chinese acting', in *Brecht on Theatre* ed. John Willett (London: Methuen, 1974), pp. 92–3.

9 *Ibid.*, p. 95.

10 The timing of Nick's writing is problematic. It is certain that he began work between leaving New York (autumn 1922) and autumn 1923 (see p. 2). However, it is equally clear from his opening to chapter 10 that the work engaged him until at least the start of 1924 ('After two years I remember', p. 164). Fitzgerald pinpoints the time span of composition in order to indicate that the book is no memoir, composed easily after the manner of diaries, but a hybrid (somewhere between autobiography and biography) that troubles its author. For an alternative account of the dating as a probable error see Matthew J. Bruccoli, *Apparatus for F. Scott Fitzgerald's The Great Gatsby* (Columbia, SC: University of South Carolina Press, 1974), pp. 118–19.

11 John S. Whitley's reading makes a comprehensive case for Gatsby as a Keatsian Romancer: *F. Scott Fitzgerald: The Great Gatsby* (London: Arnold, 1976). Few interpretations are as thoroughly interesting (though misguided). See also Dan H. McCall, '"The self same song that found a path": Keats and *The Great Gatsby*', *American Literature*, 42 (1970–1), pp. 530–42. More typical of the bland 'dream' school is William A. Fahey, *Scott Fitzgerald and the American Dream* (New York: Thomas Y. Crowell, 1973). For useful and unusually historical readings, see John F. Callahan, *The Illusions of a Nation: Myth and History in the Novels of F. Scott Fitzgerald* (London: University of Illinois Press, 1972); and Brian Way, *F. Scott Fitzgerald and the Art of Social Fiction* (London: Arnold, 1980). Callahan recognizes that 'experience has horrified Carraway into myth' (p. 29) but is imprecise as to the class content of that experience. Though Way offers a declaredly social interpretation, he does so from an essentially static account of Fitzgerald's own class position (see p. 137).

12 Brecht, 'Alienation effects in Chinese acting', p. 97.

13 Thorstein Veblen, *The Theory of the Leisure Class* (London: Unwin, 1970), p. 164.

14 Mikhail Bakhtin, *Problems of Dostoevsky's Poetics* (Ann Arbor: Ardis, 1973), p. 163.

15 With the formation of The Commonwealth Edison Company in 1907 Samuel Insull established a unified power-supply for all Chicago. The monopoly took fifteen years to build, and though Forrest McDonald locates 'the moment of corruption' in 1912 when Gladys Insull 'close[d] her bedroom door' (an intriguing notion of economic motive), chapters 3 and 4 of his biography suggest how fine were the lines walked by Insull between business innovation and financial malpractice, between political influence and the corruption of politicians (MacDonald, *Insull* (Chicago: University of Chicago Press, 1962), pp. 55–101, 147). Whatever 'the moment', when Jimmy Gatz instructed himself to 'Study electricity, etc.', his 'etc.' may well have sought to embrace the energies alluded to in MacDonald's summary of Insull's Chicago career: 'If Samuel Insull had not existed, it would have been necessary for Chicago to invent

him: he became the last and fiercest of the long succession of restless giants who ruled the city and its surrounding prairie countryside. Chicago had men who built and dared on a colossal scale' (p. 55).

16 Terry Eagleton, *Walter Benjamin or, Towards a Revolutionary Criticism* (London: New Left Books, 1981), p. 157.
17 Way, *F. Scott Fitzgerald and the Art of Social Fiction*, p. 115.
18 Bakhtin, *Problems of Dostoevsky's Poetics*, ch. 4 on Carnival. Carnival, like Gatsby and capital, jars together eccentrically different histories and words. Gatsby's laughter remains for the most part silent, since his intent is serious, but as Bakhtin notes of the carnival mode, 'we see laughter's footprints in the structure of reality, but we do not hear the laughter itself' (p. 137).
19 Brecht, 'Aliention effects in Chinese acting', p. 93.
20 Bertolt Brecht, 'Indirect impact of the epic theatre', in *Brecht on Theatre*, ed. John Willett (London: Methuen, 1974), p. 60.
21 Bruccoli, *Apparatus for the Great Gatsby*, p. 134.
22 By the close of the nineteenth century Germans had settled in considerable numbers throughout the Midwest. During the last decades of the nineteenth century the Dutch, expanding from their earliest centres of settlement in Michigan and Wisconsin, spilled over into southwestern Minnesota. By the first decade of the twentieth century Dutch farming communities were well established in Gatz's home state (and in the region of Fitzgerald's birthplace, St Paul).
23 Georg Lukács, *History and Class Consciousness* (London: Merlin Press, 1971), p. 208.
24 *Ibid.*, p. 208.
25 William L. Stidger, *Henry Ford: The Man and his Motives* (London: Hodder, 1923), p. 219. Subsequent page references will be to this edition.
26 *Ibid.*, p. 218.
27 If, as Adorno insists, 'reification is always a form of forgetting', it may also be said to be a way of remembering badly. For discussion of the relation between commodity production and time see Theodor Adorno and Max Horkheimer, *Dialectic of Enlightenment*, (London: Verso, 1979) pp. 120–67; and Eagleton, *Walter Benjamin*, pp. 25–9.
28 Alfred Sohn-Rethel, *Intellectual and Manual Labour* (London: Macmillan, 1978), p. 25.
29 Lucio Colletti, *From Rousseau to Lenin* (London: New Left Books, 1972), pp. 86–7 (italics in source)
30 Lukács, *History and Class Consciousness*, p. 186 (italics in source).
31 *Ibid.*, p. 66.
32 Hugh Kenner, *A Homemade World* (New York: Knopf, 1975), ch. 2.
33 Alger wrote about Edison, stressing that one of his first major successes was the Universal Stock Ticker. Samuel Insull, as Edison's personal secretary, was in charge of his financial dealing; as he once put it, 'My engineering has been largely concerned with engineering all I could out of the dollar.'
34 Raymond Williams, *Modern Tragedy* (London: Verso, 1979), p. 71. Subsequent page references will be to this edition, and will be included in the text.
35 Bertolt Brecht, 'From a letter to an actor', *Brecht on Theatre*, ed. John Willett (London: Methuen, 1974), p. 234.
36 Cited by Giles Deleuze and Félix Guattari in *Anti-Oedipus: Capitalism and Schizophrenia* (New York: Viking Press, 1982), p. 26.
37 Bruccoli notes of the use of 'orgiastic' in the Scribners' edition: 'Fitzgerald clearly intended *orgastic* – not *orgiastic* – and explained to Perkins that "it expresses exactly the intended ecstasy" (January 24, 1925). In Fitzgerald's marked copy an *i* is inserted

in *orgastic*, but it is impossible to identify the hand that wrote this single letter as Fitzgerald's. Beginning with the second edition . . . all subsequent Scribners editions print *orgiastic*' (Bruccoli, *Apparatus for The Great Gatsby*, p. 50). Though quoting from the Scribners' edition, I have restored 'orgastic' to the passage.

38 *Culpeper's Complete Herbal* (London: W. Forulsham, 1653). Fitzgerald may have known of the medicinal use of caraway seed. He describes New York, seen from the Queensboro Bridge, in terms that suggest he might have been familiar with the habit of taking caraway oil on sugar lumps after meals, to ease digestion: 'Over the great bridge, with the sunlight through the girders making a constant flicker upon the moving cars, with the city rising up across the river in white heaps and sugar lumps all built with a wish out of nonolfactory money' (p. 69).

39 Bakhtin, *Problems of Dostoevsky's Poetics*, p. 163.

40 *Ibid.*, p. 27.

4. MONEY MAKES MANNERS MAKE MAN MAKE WOMAN: *TENDER IS THE NIGHT*, A FAMILIAR ROMANCE?

1 Henry James, *The Bostonians* (London: John Lehmann, 1952), p. 27.

2 Mark Poster's account of the emergence of Oedipus as *the* bourgeois family narrative catches something of what I mean. Poster argues that the family, according to Freud, has no history because Freud's family deep-plot (Oedipus) is transhistorical and eternal. An adequate history of the family would serve to show that Oedipus was tailor-made for one kind of home – only in the bourgeois interior is the child likely to experience such aggression and threat (papa), intensive love (mama), lack of alternative persons, and imploded relationships. Further, the oedipalized super-ego is an ideal mechanism for turning out class clones; it requires that the boy be his father; find one, single, life-long mate; and achieve success through deferred gratification (work). Poster summarizes: 'Oedipus reproduces the . . . main conditions of the bourgeois family. It reproduces the social insecurity of the bourgeoisie, since it creates a deep emotional need to become like the father, to be "successful", and it marshals the child's emotional energy through the guardian super-ego toward achievement in work, toward deferred gratification. Oedipus instills a sexual displacement, an economics of the libido that can only find satisfaction in the economics of capital accumulation, at the direct expense of bodily gratification. After all, far from being natural man, *homo economicus* is a rare and strange species' (Poster, *Critical Theory of the Family* (London: Pluto Press, 1978), p. 23).

3 In 1932 Zelda wrote, from Phipps clinic in Baltimore, assuring him, 'Freud is the only living human outside the Baptist church who continues to take man seriously.' (*Correspondence with F. Scott Fitzgerald*, ed. Matthew J. Bruccoli and Margaret M. Duggan (New York: Random House, 1980), p. 284). Fitzgerald's biographers are less sure and eschew any detailed reference to Freud.

4 F. Scott Fitzgerald, *Tender is the Night* (Harmondsworth: Penguin, 1982), p. 41. I am using the Penguin edition (ed. Arnold Goldman) as the best available text.

5 For a crucial history of the revision of managerial structures in American industry during the 1880s see Craig R. Littler, *The Development of the Labour Process in Capitalist Societies* (London: Heinemann, 1982), particularly ch. 11, 'The development of work organization in the U.S.A.', pp. 161–83.

6 Richard Lichtman, *The Production of Desire: The Integration of Psychoanalysis into Marxist Theory* (New York: Free Press, 1982), p. 272. See also Donald M. Lowe, *History of Bourgeois Perception* (Chicago: University of Chicago Press, 1982), particularly ch. 5, 'Embodiment', pp. 85–108.

7 Theodor Adorno and Max Horkheimer, *Dialectic of Enlightenment* (London: Verso, 1979), p. 140.
8 Sigmund Freud, 'The interpretation of dreams', in *The Standard Edition of the Complete Psychological Works*, ed. J. Strachey (London: The Hogarth Press, 1971), vol. 5, p. 577.
9 Sebastiano Timpanaro, *The Freudian Slip: Psychoanalysis and Textual Criticism* (London: New Left Books, 1976), p. 60.
10 'There, in the market place and in shop windows, things stand still. They are under the spell of one activity only; to change owners. They stand there waiting to be sold. While they are there for exchange they are not there for use. A commodity marked out at a definite price, for instance, is looked upon as being frozen to absolute immutability throughout the time during which its price remains unaltered. And the spell does not only bind the doings of man. Even nature herself is supposed to abstain from any ravages in the body of this commodity and to hold her breath, as it were, for the sake of this social business of man' (Alfred Sohn-Rethel, *Intellectual and Manual Labour: A Critique of Epistemology* (London: Macmillan, 1978), p. 25.
11 Giles Deleuze and Félix Guattari, *Anti–Oedipus: Capitalism and Schizophrenia* (New York: Viking Press, 1982), p. 81.
12 *Ibid.*, particularly ch. 2, 'Psychoanalysis and familialism: the holy family', pp. 51–137.
13 Ernest Groves, *The American Family* (Chicago: J.P. Lippincott Comp., 1934), p. 139.
14 Robert Lynd and Helen Lynd, *Middletown* (New York: Harcourt and Brace, 1929), p. 31.
15 Max Horkheimer, 'The end of reason', *Studies in Philosophy and Social Science*, 9 (1941), p. 381.
16 Quoted by Malcolm Cowley in his 'Introduction' to *Tender is the Night* (Harmondsworth: Penguin, 1966), p. 13.
17 Fitzgerald planned that the time span of *Tender is the Night* should run from June 1925 to July 1929. Rosemary first visits the Riviera in the summer of 1925. For a useful discussion of chronological errors, see Matthew J. Bruccoli, *The Composition of 'Tender is the Night': A Study of the Manuscripts* (Pittsburgh: University of Pittsburgh Press, 1963), pp. 214–15.
18 See Alan Trachtenburg, *The Incorporation of America* (New York: Hill and Wang, 1982) particularly ch.1, 'The westward route', pp. 11–37. Trachtenburg discusses the frontier thesis as a form of historiography eminently suited to corporate interests in the 1890s.
19 Given his penchant for toys, it is surprising that Dick declines a ride on a lorry-load of carrots through early-morning Paris with 'a manufacturer of dolls' voices' from Newark (p. 153).
20 The term is used in the novel by Franz Gregorovious (p. 197). For psychoanalysis, 'transference' involves 'a process of actualization of unconscious wishes. Transference uses specific objects and operates in the framework of a specific relationship, established with these objects . . . In the transference, infantile prototypes re-emerge and are experienced with a strong sensation of immediacy . . . As a rule what psycho-analysts mean by the unqualified use of the term "transference" is *transference during treatment*' (J. Laplanche and J.B. Pontalis. *The Language of Psycho-Analysis* (London: Hogarth Press, 1980), p. 455, and pp. 456–60).
21 Bruccoli, *The Composition of 'Tender is the Night'*, p. 157.
22 In the first chapter of *A Farewell to Arms* Hemingway's troops are metaphorically and famously pregnant: 'their rifles were wet and under their capes the two leather cartridge-boxes on the front of the belts, grey leather boxes heavy with the packs of clips of thin, long 6.5mm cartridges, bulged forward under the capes so that the men,

passing on the road, marched as though they were six months gone with child' (Ernest Hemingway, *A Farewell to Arms* (London: Cape, 1929), p. 12).

23 See Claude Lévi-Strauss, *The Elementary Structures of Kinship* (London: Eyre and Spottiswoode, 1969), pp. 12–25; *The Scope of Anthropology* (London: Cape, 1971), pp. 34–37; and Deleuze and Guattari, *Anti-Oedipus*, pp. 160–3.

24 The Parisian hotelier is called McBeth, a name that further ensnares dubious patriarchs in bloody sheets.

25 Deleuze and Guattari, *Anti-Oedipus*, p. 97.

26 The introduction of sound in 1927 also introduced increased costs and a need for higher capitalization. The film industry centralized and by the end of the twenties was a mature oligopoly, attractive to financiers and bankers. 'In summary, then, integration, stability and expansion (especially theater expansion and construction) finally legitimized the film industry and attracted bankers; the conversion to sound and the depression-proof industry myth intensified banker participation; the overextension and the depression, which finally hit the industry in 1931, solidified financial control and further concentrated capital and power within the industry' (Janet Wasko, *Movies and Money: Financing the American Film Industry* (Norwood: Ablex, 1982), p. 52).

27 Fiedler's 'Portrait of the artist as a young girl' is collected under the heading 'Some notes on F. Scott Fitzgerald' in Arthur Mizener (ed.), *F. Scott Fitzgerald: A Collection of Critical Essays* (Englewood Cliffs: Prentice Hall, 1963), pp. 70–6.

28 'The personal pronouns are the last elements to be acquired in the child's speech and the first to be lost in aphasia; they are terms of transference which are difficult to handle. *The shifter* theory seems as yet to have been little explained; yet it is, *a priori*, very fruitful to observe the code struggling with the message', Roland Barthes, *Elements of Semiology* (London: Cape, 1967), p. 23; (italics in source).

29 See Ferrucio Rossi-Landi, *Linguistics and Economics* (The Hague: Mouton, 1975), pp. 124–25.

30 Mandel catches something of this trauma: 'The reduced turnover-time of fixed capital and the acceleration of technological innovation determines a pursuit for new products and new productive processes, which involve inherent risks to capital expansion because of the enormous outlays necessary on research and development, and demand maximum output and sales for the newly manufactured commodities. A spokesman of the American chemical industry has stated unambiguously: "In order to obtain above average profit margins, new products and new specialities must be discovered continually which can give high profit margins, while the older products in the same category drop to being chemical goods with lower profit margins."' Ernst Mandel, *Late Capitalism*, (London: Verso, 1980), p. 318.

31 Guy Debord, *Society of the Spectacle* (Detroit: Black and Red, 1973) section 60.

32 Walter Benjamin, 'The work of art in the age of mechanical reproduction', collected in his *Illuminations* (London: Cape, 1970), p. 233. The essay runs from p. 219 to p. 253.

33 *Ibid.*

34 Quoted in Stuart Ewen, *Captains of Consciousness: Advertising and the Social Roots of the Consumer* (New York: McGraw-Hill, 1976) p. 48. Ewen notes that, 'throughout the twenties, a noticeable proportion of magazine ads. directed at women depicted them looking into mirrors' (p. 177). Arguably, the reflective surfaces in Rosemary's Parisian hotel room are the equivalent of male eyes: Marchand reads the mirrors featured in advertisements as 'surrogates and symbols of these judgemental gazes of the world outside the boudoir'; he assumes, therefore, that 'the formulaic scene of the woman seated before her dressing-table mirror captures the "essence" of woman'. Camay's campaign, during the twenties, is taken as typical: 'Someone's eyes forever

reaching your face, comparing you with other women', or 'The eyes of men . . . the eyes of women judge your loveliness everyday.' See Roland Marchand, *Advertising the American Dream: Making Way for Modernity* (Los Angeles: University of California Press, 1985), pp. 175–6.

35 Jean Baudrillard, *For a Critique of the Political Economy of the Sign* (St Louis: Telos Press, 1981), p. 96.

36 Debord, *Society of the Spectacle*, section 60 (italics mine).

37 *Tender is the Night*, pp. 118–23.

38 See Theodor Adorno, 'On the dialectic of tact', in *Minima Moralia* (London: New Left Books, 1974), pp. 35–7. 'For tact . . . has its precise historical hour. It was the hour when the bourgeois individual rid himself of absolutist compulsion. Free and solitary, he answers for himself, while the forms of hierarchical respect and consideration developed by absolutism, divested of their economic basis and their menacing power, are still just sufficiently present to make living together within privileged groups bearable . . . The precondition of tact is a convention no longer intact yet still present. Now fallen into irreparable ruin, it lives on only in the parody of forms, an arbitrarily devised or recollected etiquette for the ignorant, of the kind preached by unsolicited advisers in newspapers, while the basis of agreement that carried those conventions in their human hour has given way to the blind conformity of car-owners and radio-listeners' (p. 36).

39 Fairly representative are William Troy, 'Scott Fitzgerald – the authority of failure', in *F. Scott Fitztgerald: The Man and His Work*, ed. Alfred Kazin (Cleveland: World Publications, 1951), p. 190; Matthew J. Bruccoli, *Scott and Ernest: The Authority of Failure and the Aurhority of Success* (London: Bodley Head, 1978), p. 112; and Milton R. Stern, *The Golden Moment: The Novels of F. Scott Fitzgerald* (London: University of Illinois Press, 1970), pp. 309–11.

40 I have borrowed the idea of 'split reference' from Paul Ricoeur 'The metaphoric process as cognition, imagination and feeling', in *On Metaphor*, ed. Sheldon Sacks (Chicago: University of Chicago Press, 1979), pp. 141–57. Mikhail Bakhtin's work established the 'dialogic' nature of semantics, from which much of my discussion of puns derives; see particularly his 'Discourse in the novel', in *The Dialogic Imagination* (Austin: University of Texas Press, 1981), pp. 258–422; and *Problems of Dostoevsky's Poetics* (Ann Arbor: Ardis, 1973), ch. 5, 'The word in Dostoevesky', pp. 150–227.

41 Bertolt Brecht, 'Alienation effects in Chinese acting', in *Brecht on Theatre*, ed. John Willett (London: Methuen, 1974), p. 93.

42 Matthew J. Bruccoli, '*The Last of the Novelists': F. Scott Fitzgerald and the Last Tycoon* (Carbondale: Southern Illinois University Press, 1977), pp. 9–10.

43 F. Scott Fitzgerald, 'The crack-up' in *The Bodley Head Scott Fitzgerald*, vol. 1 (London: Bodley Head, 1958), p. 283.

44 For the turning of the trick, see particularly D.S. Savage, 'The significance of F. Scott Fitzgerald', in Arthur Mizener (ed.), *F. Scott Fitzgerald: A Collection of Critical Essays* (Englewood Cliffs: Prentice Hall, 1963), pp. 146–57.

45 Louis Althusser, 'Ideology and ideological state apparatuses', in *Essays on Ideology* (London: New Left Books, 1976), pp. 1–60.

46 *Ibid.*, p. 54.

47 Karl Marx, *Capital*, vol. 1 (Harmondsworth: Penguin, 1976), p. 165.

48 Deleuze and Guattari, *Anti-Oedipus*, p. 97.

49 Jean-Paul Sartre, *Critique of Dialectical Reason* (London: Verso, 1982), p. 171.

50 *Ibid.*, p. 170.

51 *Ibid.*, p. 179.

52 *Ibid.*, p. 178.

53 Mandel makes her 'simple' point somewhat abstractly, 'All the inherent contradictions of the capitalist mode of production periodically blow up in a crisis of overproduction. The tendency to periodic crises of overproduction, to a cyclical motion in production which successively goes through stages of economic recovery, upturn, "boom", crisis and depression, is inherent to this mode of production, and to it alone' (*Introduction to Marxism* (London: Pluto Press, 1982), p. 54).

54 Goethe's remark is quoted in Walter Benjamin, *One-Way Street and Other Writings* (London: New Left Books, 1979), p. 252.

55 Bakhtin speaks of 'the word with a loophole' or 'the word with a sideward glance' when referring to 'double directed words . . . which contain as an integral part of themselves a relationship towards another person's utterance'. He argues for an almost inevitable 'plurality' of meaning, in that 'the word does not forget where it has been', consequently its user, using an entity that arrives from other contexts, 'finds the word already inhabited'. While this may be a semantic fact, it may usefully be applied only to the fictions of those who have ears to hear. See *Problems of Dostoevsky's Poetics*, particularly pp. 150–4, 163–7, 195.

56 To pursue the simile: it might be remembered that Grant died in genteel poverty, largely unsung, with a barely finished manuscript on his desk.

57 Georg Lukács, 'Reification and the consciousness of the proletariat', in *History and Class Consciousness* (London: Merlin Press, 1971), particularly pp. 204–9.

58 Fitzgerald to Maxwell Perkins, *The Letters of F. Scott Fitzgerald*, ed. Andrew Turnbull (Harmondsworth: Penguin, 1968), p. 173.

59 Quoted by Matthew J. Bruccoli, *Some Sort of Epic Grandeur* (London: Hodder and Stoughton, 1981), pp. 335–6.

60 See Sheila Graham, *College of One* (London: Weidenfeld and Nicolson, 1967), pp. 123–6.

61 Fitzgerald to Frances Scott Fitzgerald, *The Letters*, p. 347.

62 *Ibid.*, p. 437.

63 Quoted by Bruccoli, *Some Sort of Epic Grandeur*, p. 347.

64 A general plan for the novel, completed in August 1932, catches how Fitzgerald works out his own 'double allegiance' through projections about Dick: 'He has cured her [Nicole] by pretending to a stability + belief in the current order which he does not have . . . But the years of living under patronage etc. + among the burgeoise [sic] have seriously spoiled him and he takes up the marriage as a man divided in himself . . . He sends his neglected son into Soviet Russia to educate him and comes back to American to be a quack thus having accomplished both his burgeoise sentimental ideal in the case of his wife and his ideals in the case of his son.' For the general plan see Bruccoli, *Some Sort of Epic Grandeur*, pp. 335–40.

5. ICONIC NARRATIVES: OR, HOW THREE SOUTHERNERS FOUGHT THE SECOND CIVIL WAR

1 Jonathan Wiener, 'Class structure and economic development in the American South, 1865–1955', *American Historical Review*, vol. 84, part 2 (1979), pp. 970–1006.

2 Gavin Wright, *Old South: New South: Revolution in the Southern Economy Since the Civil War* (New York: Basic Books, 1986), p. 20.

3 *Ibid.*, p. 49.

4 *Ibid.*, ch. 4 'Plantation, farm and farm labour in the South', pp. 81–123.

5 Quoted by Jack Temple Kirby, *Rural Worlds Lost: The American South 1920–1960* (Baton Rouge, LA: Louisiana State University Press, 1987), p. 239.

6 Wiener, 'Class structure', p. 992.

7 For a correlation between the international cotton price and the pattern of spurt and lapse in the Southern economy, see Wright, *Old South: New South*, pp. 51–60.

8 Wiener, 'Class structure', p. 992.

9 *Ibid.*

10 Harold Woodman, 'Sequel to slavery: the new history views the post bellum South', *Journal of Southern History*, vol. 43, no. 4 (November 1977), p. 554.

11 Kirby, *Rural Worlds Lost*, p. 140.

12 *Ibid.*, p. 51.

13 *Ibid.*, p. 133.

14 *Ibid.*, p. 338.

15 Wright, *Old South: New South*, p. 247.

16 Andrew Lytle, 'The hind tit', pp. 226–7, collected in *I'll Take My Stand*, Twelve Southerners (New York: Harper and Row, 1962), pp. 201–45.

17 John Crowe Ransom, *The New Criticism* (Norfolk, CT: New Directions, 1941), p. 282.

18 *Ibid.*, p. 291.

19 *Ibid.* 'In brief, under the iconic sign, the abstract item is restored to the body from which it was taken.'

20 *Ibid.*, p. 281.

21 John Crowe Ransom, *God Without Thunder* (London: Gerald Howe, 1931), p. 331.

22 *Ibid.*, p. 323.

23 Paul Ricoeur, *Time and Narrative*: vol. 1 (London: University of Chicago Press, 1984), p. 48.

24 For evidence on stigmatics see Herbert Thurston, *The Physical Phenomena of Mysticism* (London: Burns Oates, 1952); Saint Francis, pp. 42–57; Saint Teresa, p. 68.

25 Allen Tate, *The Fathers* (Chicago: Swallow Press, 1974), p. 218. Subsequent references will be to this edition and will be included in the text.

26 Paul Ricoeur, 'The metaphoric process as cognition, imagination, feeling', *On Metaphor*, ed. Sheldon Sacks (Chicago: University of Chicago Press, 1979), p. 146 (italics in source).

27 Allen Tate, 'The symbolic imagination: the mirrors of Dante', *Essays of Four Decades* (London: Oxford University Press, 1970), p. 431.

28 *Ibid.*

29 *Ibid.*

30 Umberto Eco, *A Theory of Semiotics* (London: Macmillan, 1977), p. 205.

31 In defining icon, index and symbol, I have adopted the triadic account of signs offered by Charles Saunders Peirce. My quotations are drawn from *The Collected Papers of Charles Saunders Peirce*, ed. Charles Hartshorne, Paul Weiss and Arthur Burks, 8 vols. (Cambridge, MA: Harvard University Press, 1931–58). The general definitions refer to vol. 3, p. 365. Peirce developed his language theories throughout his career. I found two commentaries particularly helpful: John Fitzgerald, *Peirce's Theory of Signs as a Foundation for Pragmatism* (The Hague: Mouton, 1966); and Douglas Greenlee, *Peirce's Concept of Sign* (The Hague: Mouton, 1973).

32 Quoted in Eco, *A Theory of Semiotics*, p. 192.

33 *Ibid.*, p. 204.

34 *Ibid.*, p. 191.

35 Peirce at times weakened his own symbol/icon distinction: 'Charles Saunders Peirce came to the conclusion that in the end the interpretant of a symbol must reside in a habit and not in the immediate physiological reaction which the sign vehicle evoked, or in the attendant images or emotions – a doctrine which prepared the way for the

contemporary emphasis on rules of usage' (Charles Morris, *Writings on the General Theory of Signs* (The Hague: Mouton, 1971), p. 44).

36 T.S. Eliot, 'The waste land: 1. The burial of the dead', collected in, *Collected Poems: 1909–1962* (London: Faber, 1968), p. 64.

37 Tate, 'Literature and knowledge', in *Essays of Four Decades*, p. 87.

38 *Ibid.*, p. 103.

39 *Ibid.*, p. 104.

40 Allen Tate, 'Remarks on the Southern religion', collected in *I'll Take My Stand*, Twelve Southerners (New York: Harper and Row, 1962), p. 156. Subsequent references will be to this edition and will be included in the text.

41 Louis Mink, 'Philosophical analysis and historical understanding', *Review of Metaphysics*, vol. 20 (1968), p. 686.

42 See Ricoeur, *Time and Narrative*, pp. 155–61.

43 Edwin Panofsky, 'Iconography and iconology: an introduction to the study of Renaissance art', collected in, *Meaning in the Visual Arts* (Harmondsworth: Penguin, 1970), p. 58. It is perhaps symptomatic of the serial method that Panovsky justifies his shift from 'iconography' (the common term) to 'iconology' by means of an etymological series: 'For the suffix "graphy" denotes something descriptive, so does the suffix "logy" – derived from *logos*, which means "thought" or "reason" – denote something interpretative. "Ethnology", for instance, is defined as a "science of human races" by the same *Oxford Dictionary* that defines "ethnography" as a "description of human races', and Webster explicitly warns against . . .' (pp. 57–8).

44 Tertullian, quoted by Erich Auerbach, 'Figura', collected in his *Scenes from the Drama of European Literature* (Manchester: Manchester University Press, 1984), p. 29.

45 *Ibid.*, p. 53.

46 John Crowe Ransom, *God Without Thunder* (London: Gerald Howe, 1931), p. 335. Subsequent references will be to this edition and will be included in the text.

47 John Crowe Ransom, 'Land!', *Harpers*, 145 (July 1932), p. 222. See also Ransom, 'The aesthetic of regionalism', *American Review*, vol. 2 (January 1934), pp. 290–310; Alexander Karinikas, *Tillers of Myth* (Madison: University of Wisconsin Press, 1966), ch. 3; John Fekete, *The Critical Twilight* (London: Routledge, 1977), part 2, ch. 6. Fekete reads Ransom's career largely through a perspective offered by Lukács in *History and Class Consciousness*. The case is persuasive, and many of Fekete's assumptions lie behind my own claims.

48 John Crowe Ransom, *The New Criticism* (Norfolk CT: New Directions, 1941), p. 281. Subsequent references will be to this edition and will be included in the text.

49 William Faulkner, *Go Down, Moses* (London: Chatto and Windus, 1960), p. 242. Subsequent references will be to this edition and will be included in the text.

50 Arguably the iconic and resilient hymen lies at the narrative centre of both *The Sound and the Fury* and *As I Lay Dying*. See my 'William Faulkner and Benjamin Compson: the voices that keep silence', *Essays in Poetics*, vol. 4, no. 1 (April 1979), pp. 1–19; and, 'William Faulkner, Addie Bundren, and language', *University of Mississippi Studies in English*, vol. 15 (1978), pp. 100–23.

51 Ernst Mandel, *Late Capitalism* (London: Verso, 1980), p. 90. See also Susan Willis, 'Aesthetics of the rural slum: contradictions and dependency in "The Bear"', *Social Text*, vol. 2 (Summer 1979), pp. 82–103.

52 Auerbach, 'Figura', p. 72.

53 Among recent expressions of this debate are the opposed essays of Louis Rubin and Richard King, collected by Doreen Fowler and Ann Abadie in *Faulkner and the Southern Renaissance* (Jackson: University Press of Mississippi, 1982). See particularly,

Rubin, 'The Dixie special', pp. 63–92; and King. 'Memory and tradition', pp. 138–57. Richard King's work has been generally useful, though his model of the Southern family is rooted in an at times eccentrically ahistorical psycho-history. See his *A Southern Renaissance: The Cultural Awakening of the American South, 1930–1955* (London: Oxford University Press, 1980), particularly ch. 2.

54 See Eric Sundquist, *Faulkner: The House Divided* (Baltimore, MD: Johns Hopkins Press, 1983), pp. 131–59.

55 In *The Wild Palms* Faulkner has Charlotte say to her unwilling abortionist and "husband", 'What was it you told me nigger women say? Ride me down, Harry.' See *The Wild Palms* (London: Chatto and Windus, 1962), p. 203.

56 I suspect that Faulkner borrowed the idea for his pivotal pun (Mannie) from Poe's 'The tell-tale heart', Patrick Quinn notes a continuing play on 'eye' in the tale, whereby an apparently motiveless-murder story is switched into the story of a suicide. Poe's narrator kills a man whose eye is vulturous and thus rids himself of the eye/I forever. See Patrick Quinn, *The French Face of Edgar Allan Poe* (Carbondale, IL: Southern Illinois University Press, 1957), pp. 233–6.

57 Allen Tate, 'A lost traveller's dream', in *Memories and Essays* (Manchester: Carcanet, 1976), p. 12. Subsequent references will be to this edition and will be included in the text.

58 Frank Kermode, *The Sense of an Ending* (New York: Oxford University Press, 1967), p. 73.

59 See Eugene Genovese, *Roll Jordan Roll* (New York: Random House, 1974), particularly, pp. 3–112.

60 The phrases are derived from Orlando Paterson, *Slavery and Social Death* (Cambridge, MA: Harvard University Press, 1982), particularly part I, ch. 2.

61 Eugene Genovese, *The World the Slaveholders Made* (New York: Vintage Books, 1971), p. 99.

62 *Ibid.*, p. 196. I am indebted to Mark Jancovich for opening up the ways in which the New Critical critique of Northern relations self-consciously extends the paternalist critique developed within the peculiar institution. His unpublished thesis, 'The New Criticism and its critics' (University of Kent) makes the case that modern literary theorists have failed to register that it was from a continuing Southern critique of Northern relations that the New Critics developed many of their positions, and that this failure has limited our understanding of those positions.

63 Gilbert Fite, *Cotton Fields No More* (Lexington: University Press of Kentucky, 1984), p. 5, and ch. 7. See also Peter Daniel, *The Shadow of Slavery: Peonage in the South (1901–1969)* (London: University of Illinois Press, 1972), chs. 7 and 8.

64 Marx, *Capital*, vol. I (Harmondsworth: Penguin, 1976), p. 13.

65 Allen Tate, 'Notes on liberty and property', collected by Herbert Agar and Allen Tate in, *Who Owns America* (Boston: Houghton Mifflin, 1936), p. 84.

6. FORDISM: FROM DESIRE TO DESTRUCTION (AN HISTORICAL INTERLUDE)

1 Mike Davis, *Prisoners of the American Dream: Politics and Economy in the History of the U.S. Working Class* (London: New Left Books, 1986), p. 310. Davis's arguments had a formative influence on the claims of this chapter.

2 James O'Connor, *Accumulation Crisis* (New York: Blackwell, 1984), p. 205.

3 See David A. Hounsell, *From the American System to Mass Production 1800–1932* (London: Johns Hopkins University Press, 1984), particularly ch. 7, 'Cul-de-sac: the limits of Fordism and the coming of "flexible mass production"', 263–301.

4 The periodization derives from Davis, *Prisoners of the American Dream*, see ch. 3, 'The fall of the house of labour', pp. 102–53.

5 *Ibid.*, p. 111.

6 Quoted by Davis, *Prisoners of the American Dream*, p. 112.

7 Quoted in Samuel Bowles, David Gordon and Thomas Weisskopf, *Beyond the Wasteland* (London: New Left Books, 1985), p. 65.

8 *Ibid.*, p. 68.

9 Ernst Mandel, *Late Capitalism* (London: Verso, 1980), p. 308.

10 O'Connor, *Accumulation Crisis*, p. 422.

11 Bowles, Gordon and Weisskopf, *Beyond the Wasteland* p. 79.

12 Davis, *Prisoners of the American Dream*, p. 123.

13 *Ibid.*, pp. 207–8.

14 Alan Lipietz, 'Towards global Fordism', *New Left Review*, no. 132, March–April 1982, pp. 46–7.

15 David Noble, *Forces of Production: A Social History of Industrial Automation* (New York: Alfred Knopf, 1984), p. 5. See also Mandel, *Late Capitalism*, pp. 274–309.

16 Mandel, *Late Capitalism*, p. 277.

17 Daniel Bell, *The End of Ideology* (Glencoe, IL: The Free Press, 1960), p. 83.

18 Daniel Bell, *The Coming of Post Industrial Society* (London: Heinemann, 1974), p. 33.

19 *Ibid.*, p. 116.

20 *Ibid.*, p. 120.

21 *Ibid.*, pp. 115 and 20.

22 *Ibid.*, p. 26.

23 Noble, *Forces of Production*, pp. 3–20.

24 Stanley Aronowitz has gone so far as to say, 'the defence business . . . has to a large extent eliminated the market place as the regulator of economic activity'. See his *False Promises: The Shaping of American Working Class Consciousness* (New York: McGraw-Hill, 1973), p. 269.

25 Quoted by Noble, *Forces of Production*, p. 4.

26 *Ibid.*, p. 3.

27 Mandel, *Late Capitalism*, p. 503.

28 Davis, *Prisoners of the American Dream*, pp. 116–17.

29 *Ibid.*, p. 113.

30 *Ibid.*

31 The phrase derives from the work of C.B. Macpherson; he argues that since 'capitalism produces inequality and consumer consciousness, and must do so to go on operating', it is likely that the USA will remain 'an unequal society, most of whose members think of themselves as maximising consumers' (*The Life and Times of Liberal Democracy* (London: Oxford University Press, 1977), pp. 105 and 92). The assumption that each individual has a natural right to gratify self-interest through the maximization of pleasure ('possessive individualism') is a continuing strand linking seventeenth- to twentieth-century liberal theory.

32 See Eugene Pashukanis, *Law and Marxism* (London: Ink Links, 1978), particularly ch. 4, 'Commodity and subject', pp. 109–33.

33 Bell, *The End of Ideology*, p. 61.

34 Bell, *The Coming of Post Industrial Society*, p. 28.

35 Daniel Bell, *The Cultural Contradictions of Capitalism* (London: Heinemann, 1979), p. 24.

36 C. Wright Mills, *White Collar* (New York: Oxford University Press, 1951), p. 55.

37 Fred Pfeil, 'Makin' flippy-floppy: postmodernism and the baby-boom P.M.C.', collected in, *The Year Left: An American Socialist Year Book*, eds. Mike Davis, Fred Pfeil and Michael Sprinker (London: New Left Books, 1985), p. 265.

38 Barbara Ehrenreich and John Ehrenreich, 'The professional and managerial class', collected in *Between Labour and Capital*, ed. Pat Walker (Boston: South End Press, 1979), p. 12. The PMC has been variously referred to as the 'technical intelligensia' (Aronowitz) and the 'coordinators' (Albert and Hanel). See Stanley Aronowitz, 'Cracks in the historic bloc: American labor's historic compromise in the present crisis', *Social Text*, no. 5, Spring 1982, pp. 22–52.

39 The economic expansion induced by the two-front war and the Kennedy/Johnson business-tax reductions resulted in an extraordinary increase in demand (real output grew by 30 per cent between 1961 and 1966). The go-go economy needed a go-go fiscal policy (with easy borrowing increasing dependency on fictional capital), so that by 1966 corporatism *needed* a recession to stabilize the market. Johnson refined and persisted with an investment boom stimulated by high employment, budget deficits and an expansionist monetary policy. All of which resulted in an exhaustion of surplus labour with an attendant cancelling of the unemployment threat. At the same time, booming American markets experienced massive import penetration, so that corporations could neither bring pressure to bear on labour nor pass on their own rising production costs. Prices rose by an average of 4 per cent per annum between 1966 and 1973, but the parallel rise in average unit labour costs stood at 4.5 per cent. See Bowles, Gordon and Weisskopf, *Beyond the Wasteland*, ch. 5, 'The Missed recession, the great repression and spiralling stagflation', pp. 62–97; also Joel Krieger, *Reagan, Thatcher, and the Politics of Decline* (Cambridge: Polity Press, 1986), pp. 109–29.

40 See Mandel, *Late Capitalism*, pp. 300–1.

7. *WHY ARE WE IN VIETNAM?*: BECAUSE THE BUCK MUSTN'T STOP

1 Norman Mailer, *Why Are We in Vietnam?* (London: Weidenfeld and Nicolson, 1969), p. 47 (italics in source). Subsequent references will be to this edition and will be included in the text.

2 Norman Mailer, *Barbary Shore* (St Albans: Panther, 1971), p. 256. Subsequent references will be to this edition and will be included in the text.

3 Hilary Mills, in her *Mailer: A Biography* (Sevenoaks: New English Library, 1983), traces Mailer's friendship with the Marxist philosopher, Jean Malaquais (to whom *Barbary Shore* is dedicated), but remains less than precise about what Marx Mailer did or did not read. Peter Manso's *Mailer: His Life and Times* (Harmondsworth: Penguin, 1986) reports that while in Paris in 1947 Mailer and Malaquais discussed 'politics and political economy' (p. 113), presumably reading-lists were exchanged. The enthusiasm stuck: a letter of August 1949 has Mailer volunteering to post the three volumes of *Capital* to his friend, the novelist Fig Gwaltney, in Fayetteville, Arkansas (p. 137).

4 Norman Mailer, *Cannibals and Christians* (London: André Deutsch, 1967), p. 3 (italics in source). Subsequent references will be to this edition and will be included in the text. *Cannibals and Christians* will be abbreviated as *C & C*.

5 For useful discussions of American inflation in the sixties see Allen Matusow, *The Unravelling of America* (New York: Harper and Row, 1984), particularly ch. 6; and David P. Calleo, 'American power in a new world economy', collected in *Economics and World Power*, ed. William Becker and Samuel Wells Jr (New York: Columbia University Press, 1984), pp. 391–457.

6 Ernst Mandel, *The Second Slump* (London: Verso, 1980), p. 81.

7 James O'Connor, *Accumulation Crisis* (New York: Blackwell, 1984), p. 89.

8 Karl Marx, *Capital*, vol. 3 (New York: International Publishers, 1967), pp. 464–72.

9 Ernst Mandel, *Late Capital* (London: Verso, 1980), p. 496.

10 *Ibid.*, p. 394.

11 Mandel notes, 'If the availability of large quantities of capital which can no longer be valorized in industry proper is a precondition for the extension of the so-called service sector, an advanced differentiation of consumption, and especially of the consumption of wage earners and the working class, is a complementary precondition for those new forms and domains of capital accumulation' (*Late Capitalism*, p. 389). See also David Harvey, *The Limits of Capital* (Oxford: Blackwell, 1982), particularly ch. 4.

12 David Harvey, *The Limits of Capital*, p. 132, note.

13 Karl Marx, *Grundrisse* (Harmondsworth: Penguin, 1974), p. 621.

14 *Ibid.*

15 A Marxist equation abbreviating the making of money from money without passage through commodity production. The equation M–C–M^1 would represent money made through the sale of commodities.

16 Quoted by Harvey, *The Limits of Capital*, p. 288.

17 F. Scott Fitzgerald, *The Great Gatsby*, (New York: Scribners, n.d), p. 174.

18 Karl Marx, *Theories of Surplus Value*, pt 3 (London: Lawrence and Wishart, 1972), p. 455.

19 Norman Mailer, *Advertisements for Myself* (London: Panther, 1972), p. 351. Subsequent references will be to this edition and will be included in the text. *Advertisements for Myself* will be abbreviated as *AFM*.

20 William Leiss, *The Limits to Satisfaction* (Toronto: University of Toronto Press, 1976), p. 82. The phrasing, 'temporary collections of imputed characteristics', also belongs to Leiss (p. 82). Under the heading, 'From surplus value to the mass media', Mailer sets the fragmentation of need within an historical perspective: 'It is likely that the survival of capitalism is no longer possible without the creation in the consumer of a series of psychically disruptive needs which circle about such wants and emotions as the desire for excessive security, the alleviation of guilt, the lust for comfort and new commodity, and a consequent allegiance to the vast lie about the essential health of the State and the economy ... Nineteenth-century capitalism exhausted the life of millions of workers; twentieth-century capitalism can well end by destroying the mind of civilized man' (*AFM*, pp. 355–6).

21 Frantz Fanon's *The Wretched of the Earth* was published in Paris (1961). A translation appeared in the USA in 1965.

22 Norman Mailer, *The Presidential Papers* (London: André Deutsch, 1964), p. 212.

23 Quoted in Matusow, *The Unravelling of America*, p. 326.

24 Quoted in Matusow, *ibid.*, p. 366.

25 Initially the war struck Keynesians (quietly) as a good thing for the economy. In year one the expenditure on Vietnam ($6 billion) approximated to the fiscal stimulus recommended by the president's Council of Economic Advisors. In 1965 and 1966 war was primarily an economic stimulus; however, by year three (1967) the US economy began to overheat, and fearing galloping inflation, Johnson requested what was in effect a war tax (summer 1967).

26 Alfred Chandler Jr, *Strategy and Structure*, (Cambridge, MA: MIT Press, 1962), pp. 383–96. Mailer offers a broadly similar, though skeletal, account of economic development between 1920 and 1960: for him, as for Chandler, the fifties are a commercial re-run of the twenties, with the attendant threat of collapse and war. See *C & C*, pp. 41–2.

27 Joan Didion comments, 'it is Fitzgerald whom Mailer most resembles' (quoted in

Manso, *Mailer*, p. 403). Those wishing to pursue her intimation might consider *Barbary Shore* as Mailer's re-write of *The Great Gatsby*, and read *An American Dream* as his revision of *Tender is the Night*. See also Richard Foster, 'Mailer and the Fitzgerald tradition', *Novel*, vol. 1, no. 3 (Spring, 1968), pp. 219–30.

28 Mandel, *The Second Slump*, p. 26.

29 Paul Ricoeur summarizes the consequences of systematic intertextuality in terms that apply both to 'the ideology of the absolute text' and to the ideology of commodity as 'the universal category of society as a whole' (Lukács):

> The suspense which defers the reference merely leaves the text, as it were, 'in the air', outside or without a world. In virtue of this obliteration of the relation to the world, each text is free to enter into relation with all other texts which come to take the place of circumstantial reality referred to by living speech. This relation of text to text, within the effacement of the world about which we speak, engenders the quasi-world of texts or *literature*.
>
> (*Hermeneutics and the Human Sciences* (Cambridge University Press, 1981), pp. 148–49;
> (italics in source)

In *The Pleasure of the Text* Roland Barthes celebrates the effacement of reference. Reading Flaubert 'according to Proust',

> I savor the sway of formulas, the reversal of origins, the ease which brings the anterior text out of the subsequent one . . . Proust is what comes to me, not what I summon; not an 'authority' simply a *circular memory*. Which is what inter-text is: the impossibility of living outside the infinite text – whether this be Proust or the daily newspaper or the television screen: the book creates the meaning, the meaning creates life.
>
> (*The Pleasure of the Text* (London: Cape, 1976), p. 36; italics in source)

Intertextuality with its systematic suspension of reference and its appeal to 'the infinite text', might well be the literary form for a mode of production that atomizes objects and alienates persons, only to re-integrate its particles through the promise of 'abstract value' as a universal equivalent. 'Abstract value', realized through money, is effectively the means to social synthesis under capital. For 'abstract value' read Kristeva's 'geno-text'. Just as each worker in the marketplace may 'freely' and 'equally' exchange his or her labour – or so the story runs – each text is 'free' to engage in 'equal' exchange with any other text; their is no hint of discrimination in Barthean openness. 'From each according to his ability, to each according to his needs', would be anathema to Kristeva's 'mémoire infinie de la signifiance':

> the geno-text can be thought of as a device containing the whole historical evolution of language and the various signifying practices it can bear. The possibilities of all language of the past, present and future are given there, before being masked or repressed in the pheno-text.
>
> (Quoted by Jonathan Culler, *Structural Poetics* (London: Routledge, 1975), pp. 246–7)

Like the 'infinite' or 'geno' text, 'value' acts as a missing promise of re-integration: in both the literary and the economic case, a notional measure provides a real fantasy of cohesion. Like Barthes's 'infinite text', 'value' acts as a missing promise of re-integration: both provide a measure of cohesion at the cost of particularity of reference – either by the text to its world, or by men to their immediate needs. Nonetheless, intertextuality is divisive (Barthes cuts 'Sarrasine' into five hundred and sixty-one 'lexia'); it appears most frequently under the banner of subversion:

> Let us first posit the image of triumphant plural, unimpoverished by any constraint of representation (or imitation). In this ideal text, the networks are many and interact, without any one of them being able to surpass the rest; this text is a galaxy of signifiers, not a structure of signifieds; it has no beginning; it is reversible; we gain access to it by

several entrances, none of which can be authoritatively declared to be the main one; the codes it mobilizes extend as far *as the eye can read*, they are interminable.

(*S/Z* (London: Cape, 1975), pp. 5–6)

The 'triumph' is in reality modest, since it most resembles the triumphant workings of the money form. Witness Barthes's reading of 'Sarrasine'. Balzac's story is to the lexia of *S/Z* as 'abstract value' is to money and to its exchange – just as fiction is the entity that guarantees the worth of Barthes's many sub-divisions, so 'value' is the

> integral whole in every single incident of exchange, and in order to be able to serve all incidents in this capacity it must, on the contrary, allow for any degree of divisibility or as the corresponding philosophical term has it, for sheer atomicity.
>
> (Alfred Sohn-Rethel, *Intellectual and Manual Labour*, (London: Macmillan, 1978), p. 21)

Put more generally, 'value' is a non-descriptive substance, which, materialized in money, provides for the inter-relation of an endless number of entities. Likewise, intertextuality (and its parental Derridean 'differance') is a contentless principle of structure which allows all literature, indeed all discourse, to intersect. Intertextuality could be read as the literary mode for advanced capitalism. See also, Pamela Rhodes and Richard Godden, '*The Wild Palms*: degraded culture, devalued texts', collected in *Intertextuality in Faulkner*, ed. Michel Gresset and Noel Polk (Jackson, MS: University of Mississippi Press, 1985), pp. 87–113.

30 Samuel Insull, as Edison's personal secretary, was in charge of his financial dealing; as he once put it, 'My engineering has been largely concerned with engineering all I could out of the dollar' (quoted by John Dos Passos, *U.S.A* (Harmondsworth: Penguin, 1973), p. 1156.

8. FORDISM, VOICED AND UNVOICED: MAILER'S VOCALISM AND *ARMIES OF THE NIGHT*

1 Norman Mailer, *Armies of the Night* (London: Weidenfeld and Nicolson, 1968), p. 226. Subsequent references will be to this edition and will be included in the text.

2 Mikhail Bakhtin, *The Dialogic Imagination* (Austin: University of Texas Press, 1983), p. 280.

3 *Ibid.*, p. 263.

4 V.N. Vološinov, *Marxism and the Philosophy of Language* (New York: Seminar Press, 1973), p. 102.

5 Bakhtin, *The Dialogic Imagination*, p. 276.

6 Vološinov, *Marxism*, p. 102. I am working under the assumption that Bakhtin and Vološinov are one and the same person.

7 Quoted by Gary Morson, 'Who speaks for Bakhtin? A dialogic introduction', *Critical Inquiry*, vol. 10, no. 2, December 1983, p. 241.

8 Mailer exhibits the wares of his writing life, plus commentary, in such collections as *The Presidential Papers* (1963) and *Cannibals and Christians* (1966). Elsewhere, journalistic contracts will be written into the structure of the books that they elicit, as in *A Fire on the Moon* (1970), *Marilyn* (1973) or *The Executioner's Song* (1979). At times it seems that the social relevance of Mailer's life is to provide the gossip that will become the PR through which the writing is sold. See Peter U. Hohendahl, *The Institution of Criticism* (London: Cornell University Press, 1982), particularly ch. 5, 'Promoters, consumers and critics: on the reception of the best seller'.

9 Richard Poirier, *The Performing Self* (London: Chatto and Windus, 1971), pp. 103–11.

10 Mikhail Bakhtin, *Problems of Dostoevsky's Poetics* (Ann Arbor: Ardis, 1973), p. 16. In

this passage Bakhtin is evaluating the critical position of Otto Kraus; while agreeing with Kraus on the historical specificity of the polyphonic, he adds that 'the new structural principle of polyphony . . . retains and will continue to retain its artistic significance under the totally different conditions of subsequent epochs' (p. 30) – an observation that calls into question the seriousness of his homology between the economic and the semantic. Why should polyphony bear a trans-historical relation to capital's various forms? I can only surmise that for Bakhtin the capacity of the capitalist to disguise what he is doing, though various, remains founded on an initial suppression of labour. Semantic clashes under nascent capitalism may have been overtly class based as a market ideology struggled to establish its voice: under Fordism, with the hegemonic voice of a liberal consensus apparently in place, clashes remain but are relocated. It is here that I feel justified in reading Bakhtin's 'multileveledness' through the focus of Lichtman's 'suppressions of reciprocity'.

11 Richard Lichtman, *The Production of Desire: The Integration of Psychoanalysis into Marxist Theory* (New York: Free Press, 1982), p. 252.
12 *Ibid.*
13 *Ibid.*, p. 254.
14 Vološinov, *Marxism*, p. 92.
15 Daniel Bell, *The Cultural Contradictions of Capitalism* (London: Heinemann, 1979), p. 250.
16 Daniel Bell, *The Coming of Post Industrial Society* (London: Heinemann, 1974), p. 28.
17 Bell, *The Cultural Contradictions of Capitalism*, p. 280.
18 Jurgen Habermas, *Legitimation Crisis* (London: Heinemann, 1976), p. 108.
19 *Ibid.*, p. 111.
20 *Ibid.*, p. 95.
21 *Ibid.*, p. 108.
22 Jurgen Habermas, 'The public sphere: an encyclopedia article', *New German Critique*, no. 3 (Fall 1974), p. 49.
23 Quoted by Jurgen Habermas in *Habermas and Modernity*, ed. Richard J. Bernstein (Cambridge: Polity Press, 1985), p. 77.
24 Habermas, *Legitimation Crisis*, p. 123.
25 *Ibid.*, p. 105.
26 Matthew Arnold, *The Poems of Matthew Arnold*, ed. C.B. Tinker and H.F. Lowry (London: Oxford University Press, 1966), pp. 210–12.
27 F. Scott Fitzgerald, *The Crack-Up with Other Pieces and Stories* (Harmondsworth: Penguin, 1965), p. 46.
28 See Mike Davis, *Prisoners of the American Dream* (London: New Left Books, 1986), pp. 129–30. Between 1962 and 1978 nearly 90 per cent of the new manufacturing jobs were created outside the old unionized heartland, 86 per cent of them in the sunbelt. See also David Clark, *Post-Industrial America* (London: Methuen, 1984), pp. 100–7.
29 Mailer first saw Eastwood in a TV re-run of 'Rawhide' in 1967 and wanted to cast him in an off-Broadway production of *The Deer Park*. He wanted him again to play Gary Gilmore in *The Executioner's Song*. At the time of the making of *Sudden Impact* (1983), Mailer notes, 'What an American was Clint Eastwood. Maybe there was no one more American then he! What an interesting artist. He portrayed psychopaths who acted with all the silence, certainty and gravity of saints. Or would it be closer to say that he played saints who killed like psychopaths?' ('Mailer meets his macho', the *Observer*, 29 January 1984, pp. 8–12).
30 Mailer's hipster 'is looking for the opportunity to grow up a second time' by 'remak[ing] a bit of his nervous system'. See *Advertisements for Myself* (London: Panther, 1972), p. 278.

31 Norman Mailer, *Cannibals and Christians* (London: Andre Deutsch, 1967), p. 83 (italics in source).
32 Peter Manso, *Mailer: his Life and Times* (Harmondsworth: Penguin, 1986), pp. 16 and 44.
33 Paul Buhle, *Marxism in the USA: Remapping the History of the American Left* (London: Verso, 1987), p. 225.
34 *Ibid.*, pp. 210–13. Predictably, Mailer's contributory editorship with *Dissent* lapsed, but seems to have run at least from 1952 to 1957 (when *Dissent* published 'The white negro'). See Manso, *Mailer*, particularly contributions by William Phillips (p. 182), Ned Polsky (p. 255), Irving Howe (pp. 184, 253–4, 268, 467–8) and Mailer (p. 184).
35 Norman Mailer, *The Naked and the Dead* (London: Alan Wingate, 1949), p. 84. Subsequent references will be to this edition and will be included in the text.
36 G.W.F. Hegel, *The Phenomenology of Mind*: Vol. 1 (London: Macmillan, 1910), p. 184.
37 Richard Poirier, 'In pyramid and palace', *TLS*, 10 June 1983, p. 592. Poirier's extended review of *Ancient Evenings* is extremely helpful in sorting out the who does what to whom of the novel.
38 *Ibid.*
39 Theodor Adorno, 'Letters to Walter Benjamin', collected in *Aesthetics and Politics*, ed. Frederic Jameson (London: Verso, 1980), p. 113.
40 Philip Rahv, 'Myth and the powerhouse', collected in his *Literature and the Sixth Sense* (London: Faber, 1970), pp. 204–5.
41 Davis, *Prisoners of the American Dream*, p. 229. See also Samuel Bowles, David Gordon and Thomas Weisskopf, *Beyond the Wasteland* (London: New Left Books, 1985), ch. 5.

9. *ARMIES OF THE NIGHT*: A FAMILIAR ROMANCE?

1 Joel Krieger, *Reagan, Thatcher and the Politics of Decline* (Cambridge: Polity Press, 1986), p. 128.
2 Jurgen Habermas, *Legitimation Crisis* (London: Heinemann, 1976), pp. 108 and 111.
3 V.N. Vološinov, *Marxism and the Philosophy of Language* (New York: Seminar Press, 1973), pp. 22–3. 'Let us agree to call the entity which becomes the object of the sign the *theme* of the sign . . . An ideological theme is always socially accentuated. Of course, all the social accents of ideological themes make their way also into the individual consciousness . . . and there take on the semblance of individual accents . . . However, the source of these accents is not the individual consciousness. Accent, as such, is interindividual' (italics in source).
4 *Ibid.*, p. 92.
5 If I may persist with my metaphor of metaphor: metaphor is rarely mere decoration, but involves an act of persuasion in which literal meaning stands under threat of abolition. It is therefore possible to argue, thanks to Paul Ricoeur, that the interaction between "price" and "person" predicates new possibilities for both within one another. 'Metaphorical meaning does not merely consist of semantic clash but of the *new* predicative meaning which emerges from the collapse of the literal meaning, that is, from the collapse of the meaning which obtains if we rely on the common or usual lexical value of our words. The metaphor is not the enigma but the solution of the enigma' (Ricoeur, 'The metaphoric process as cognition, imagination, and feeling', in his *On Metaphor*, ed. Sheldon Sacks (Chicago: University of Chicago Press, 1979), p. 144 (italics in source).
6 Antonio Gramsci, *Selections from the Prison Notebooks*, ed. Quintin Hoare and Geoffrey Noel Smith (London: Lawrence and Wishart, 1971), p. 323.

7   Quoted by James O'Connor, *The Meaning of Crisis* (Oxford: Blackwell, 1987), p. 93.

8   Frederic Jameson, 'Periodizing the 60s', collected in *The 60s Without Apology* (Minneapolis: University of Minnesota Press, 1984), p. 190.

9   Jean Baudrillard, *Simulations* (New York: Semiotext(e), 1983), p. 4. For a study of literature and consumerism heavily influenced by Baudrillard, see Rachel Bowlby, *Just Looking: Consumer Culture in Dreiser, Gissing and Zola* (London: Methuen, 1985).

10 Baudrillard, *Simulations*, p. 32.

11 *Ibid.*, p. 23.

12 Thomas Pynchon, *The Crying of Lot 49* (London: Pan Books, 1979), p. 14.

13 E.L. Doctorow, *The Book of Daniel* (London: Pan Books, 1982), p. 295.

14 *Ibid.*, p. 293.

15 O'Connor, *The Meaning of Crisis*, p. 113.

16 *Ibid.*

17 *Ibid.*, p. 128.

18 Seyla Benhabib, 'Modernity and the aporias of critical theory', *Telos*, 49 (Fall 1981), p. 50. Benhabib is summarizing a key argument in Habermas's *Legitimation Crisis*.

19 Peter Manso, *Mailer: His Life and Times* (Harmondsworth: Penguin, 1986), p. 24.

20 *Ibid.*, p. 132.

21 Bowden Broadwater and Edith Begner, quoted in Manso, *Mailer*, pp. 345 and 346.

22 Quoted in Hilary Mills, *Mailer: A Biography* (Sevenoaks: New English Library, 1983), p. 223.

23 Jean-Paul Sartre, *Search For a Method* (New York: Random House, 1968), p. 58. Sartre notes that 'the person lives and knows his position more or less clearly through the groups he belongs to' (p. 66); as a founding group the family is that which may 'set up unsurpassable prejudices' (p. 60) and provide, within parental functions, plots for social conflicts that are realized through the family, but extend far beyond the family.

24 Norman Mailer, *Barbary Shore* (St Albans: Panther, 1971), p. 256.

25 Jameson adds that 'this sense of freedom and possibility', although 'for the course of the 60s a momentarily objective reality', is with the hindsight of the eighties an historical illusion. See 'Periodizing the 60s', p. 208.

26 *Ibid.*, p. 181.

27 *Ibid.*

28 Norman Mailer, *The Presidential Papers* (London: André Deutsch, 1964), pp. 67–75.

29 *Ibid.*, pp. 269–71.

30 *Ibid.*, p. 68.

31 *Ibid.*, pp. 63–7 and 74–5.

32 Any "openness" which includes a murderous assault on a woman is questionable. Much of Mailer's ability to read between the signs of his times stems from the enthusiasm with which he becomes those signs (or as many of them as possible). An intelligence which stems from its own status as symptom will also know stupidity, intensely.

33 Quoted in Manso, *Mailer*, p. 468.

34 Karl Marx, 'The eighteenth brumaire of Louis Bonaparte', in *Surveys from Exile* (Harmondsworth: Penguin, 1981), pp. 146–7.

35 Matthew Arnold, *The Poems of Matthew Arnold*, ed. C.B. Tinker and H.F. Lowry (London: Oxford University Press, 1966), p. 211.

36 The phrases belong to Frank Kermode, who in 'Recognition and deception' and 'Secrets and narrative sequence' discusses how texts can operate as rhythms or occult, non-referential patterns. See his *Essays on Fiction: 1971–1982* (London: Routledge and Kegan Paul, 1982), pp. 92–133 and 113–55.

37 Part of that context consists of implied narratives often growing from as little as a verbal play; for example, Mailer selects two volumes from the prison "library", *A Primer on Money, Banking and Gold* and a *Life of Saint John Bosco – Friend of Youth*. The titles inter-animate intriguingly. I had to check several dictionaries of saints before unearthing Bosco, sanctified, among other things, for creating hostels for young men and women. 'Youth' can be made consonant with 'Gold', which in turn invites 'home' into its ambience. Earlier, Mailer took the 'home' of a liberal academic to exemplify the failure of 'the gold standard of the psyche' (p. 15): it would seem that adequate child care depends on setting gold in a traceable relation to both money and banking, prior to designing (as a consequence) a different kind of Youth Hostel. The books go unread: their titular network of hints remains, accumulating as part of a pattern of references to the Victorian family.

38 Frederic Jameson, 'Postmodernism, or The cultural logic of late capitalism', *New Left Review*, no. 146 (July–August 1984), p. 63.

39 Jean Baudrillard, *For a Critique of the Political Economy of the Sign* (St Louis: Telos Press, 1981), p. 96.

40 Fred Pfeil, 'Makin' flippy-floppy: postmodernism and the baby-boom P.M.C.', collected in *The Year Left: an American Socialist Yearbook*, ed. Mike Davis, Fred Pfeil and Michael Sprinker (London: New Left Books, 1985), p. 267.

41 *Ibid.*, p. 268.

42 F. Scott Fitzgerald, *The Great Gatsby* (New York: Scribners, n.d.), p. 182.

43 Arnold, *The Poems*, p. 211.

44 Robert Lowell, *Near the Ocean* (London: Faber, 1967), p. 16.

45 Matthew Arnold, 'Stanzas from the Grande Chartreuse', in *The Poems*, p. 302.

46 Paul Ricoeur, *Time and Narrative*: Vol. 1 (London: University of Chicago Press, 1984), pp. 52–76.

47 *Ibid.*, pp. 74–5.

48 Lemuel Boulware was a pioneer in market research and founder of the Marketing Executives Society. He advocated marketing jobs as though they were products: workers should be looked upon as purchasers of employment, individualized and open to the hard-sell. Boulwarism undercut union power: as adopted by General Electric in the late fifties and early sixties, it aided their de-centralization from the North-east to the South and West, via the opening of new, largely non-unionized plants. See Mike Davis, *Prisoners of the American Dream* (London: New Left Books, 1986), pp. 120 and 132.

49 Tony Tanner, *Adultery in the Novel: Contract and Transgression* (London: Johns Hopkins University Press, 1979), p. 15.

50 Mikhail Bakhtin, *The Dialogic Imagination* (Austin: University of Texas Press, 1983), p. 276.

51 Norman Mailer, *Advertisements for Myself* (London: Panther, 1972), p. 351.

52 W.F. Haug, *Commodity Aesthetics, Ideology and Culture* (New York: International General, 1987), pp. 152–3. See particularly, 'Ideological values and commodity aesthetics: the example of "Jeans Culture"', pp. 144–63.

53 Mailer, *Advertisements for Myself*, p. 351.

54 *Ibid.*

55 Fitzgerald, *The Great Gatsby*, p. 99.

56 *Ibid.*, p. 182.

57 For shifts in the style of "Mission" from "New Heaven" to "More Earth", see Frederick Merk, *Manifest Destiny and Mission in American History* (New York: Random House, 1966), pp. 1–23, and Albert K. Weinberg, *Manifest Destiny* (Chicago: Quadrangle Books, 1963).

58 Fitzgerald, *The Great Gatsby*, p. 182.
59 Lowell, 'Waking early Sunday morning', in *Near the Ocean*, p. 13.
60 Vološinov, *Marxism and the Philosophy of Language*, pp. 91–2.
61 Mailer, *Barbary Shore*, p. 256.

CONCLUSION

1 Nicos Poulantzas, *Political Power and Social Class* (London: Verso, 1982), pp. 13–15 (italics in source).
2 Quoted in Sebastiano Timpanaro, *On Materialism* (London: Verso, 1980), p. 40.
3 Quoted in Andrew Turnbull, *Scott Fitzgerald* (Harmondsworth: Penguin, 1970), p. 250.
4 Poulantzas, *Political Power and Social Class*, p. 15.
5 *Ibid.* (italics in source).
6 *Ibid.*
7 Frederic Jameson, *The Political Unconscious* (London: Methuen, 1983), p. 102.
8 Daniel Miller, *Material Culture and Mass Consumption* (Oxford: Blackwell, 1987), p. 10.
9 Roland Marchand, *Advertising the American Dream* (Los Angeles: University of California Press, 1985), p. xviii.
10 *Ibid.*, p. xxi.
11 Frederic Jameson, 'Postmodernism, or The cultural logic of late capitalism', *New Left Review*, no. 146 (July–August 1984), p. 55.

Index